Distinguished Professor Yusufu Turaki is one of Africa's finest Christian minds! This book is one of his tremendous contributions to African theological, social and ethical reflections. Its interdisciplinary and multidimensional approach and perspective makes it a very critical theological handbook. It is technically and theologically comprehensive in nature, and yet very sensible and accessible to a non-technical or specialized audience. It is a must read!

Rev Sunday Bobai Agang, PhD
Professor of Christian Theology, Ethics and Public Policy,
Provost, ECWA Theological Seminary (JETS), Jos, Nigeria
Director, Overseas Council's African Research Consultancy Centre, Nigeria

Professor Yusufu Turaki offers the reader much-needed thought leadership at the crossroads of African Traditional Religion and worldview, approaches to biblical theologizing, and the practice of missions. Turaki, educator and church leader for decades, proposes a way forward that rescues African theology from irrelevance on the one hand, and superficiality on the other – a way that ultimately has the power to bring transformation to African challenges today.

This book is timely for those who have felt unease when applying theology that is generated entirely outside of Africa, and equal unease about some African-born theologies that are not faithful to the essentials of Scripture. On a continent where theological approaches are abundant and diverse, Turaki's book offers guidance from a man who has spent his life dedicated to being profoundly Christian and authentically African.

This book is timely for both African and non-African thinkers. It not only guides the African scholar and pastor, it also models a method of theologizing that can be used by faithful theologians in any culture where a traditional worldview needs to be renewed by the gospel of Jesus Christ. I highly recommend this for any serious cross-cultural worker today.

Dr Joshua Bogunjoko, MD
SIM International Director

Professor Yusufu Turaki has been a trusted and steadfast voice for bibliocentricism among multitudes of scholars with an Afrocentric cultural agenda for doing theology, especially in the African context. He pitches his strong voice a notch higher in this book, suggesting a new methodology in the search for genuine Christian understanding that takes into consideration spiritual and social needs of African Traditional Religions. He helpfully relates biblical

Christianity to pervasive realities of the African traditional religious and cultural worldview.

The tension between academic theology, that is either focused on African culture or foreign Western worldview, is reconciled by focusing on theology that is biblical and Christian, and understandable and applicable in the African context. This is also a recipe for maturing the African church; deepening the "mile long" to approaching the perfect square or cube.

I heartily commend this work, which is worthy of consideration in the church and seminary.

Rev Aiah Foday-Khabenje, PhD
General Secretary,
Association of Evangelicals in Africa

Very few books are written on theological method. It is thus a welcome sight to see one on this subject from an African perspective. If anyone should write such a book, Professor Yusufu Turaki is the right person with over four decades of experience in the academy. This book is not written by an academic who is aloof but by one who is engaged and comfortable in the academy, church, and society. He is recognized as an authority in all of these fields. A rare fit!

Characteristic of Turaki, his treatment is encyclopedic, addressing the issue from every possible angle demonstrating its significance and complexity. As a seasoned theologian in Africa, Turaki understands and explains African realities in the light of the teachings of Scripture. He advocates a way of studying Christianity in Africa that takes African Traditional Religions and culture and the authority of the Scriptures seriously instead of settling for comparative studies.

The outcome of this endeavor is a volume that is not simplistic but yet accessible to serious students in this field and filled with nuggets that scholars can further explore. Though this book is written about the method of doing theology in Africa, non-African scholars will benefit from it.

Bulus Galadima, PhD
Dean, Cook School of Intercultural Studies,
Biola University, Pasadena, California, USA

This is a compendium of robust theological engagement with African culture and religion in society, written for discerning professionals and scholars in that field. It is the summation of the author's lifetime of scholarly work and Christian social engagements globally.

There is plenty of grist for the mill in this work! The book succeeds in moving discourse on religion and culture in traditional Africa into the public domain. In that contested sphere, the Christian stakes in shaping human identity, religious identification, national formation and African's democratic progress, are indeed high, and the leader and follower today, in any capacity, only ignore them to their peril.

This classic from Turaki is a theological road-map for constructing an African Christian theology for public engagement!

Randee Ijatuyi-Morphe, PhD
Director, Hokma House, Nigeria

Engaging Religions and Worldviews in Africa: A Christian Theological Method by Professor Yusufu Turaki is, to all intents and purposes, a definitive text on the methodology for a sound Christian understanding of African Traditional Religion and its pervasive influence on the mindset of Africans that is both biblically rooted and theologically responsible.

Turaki has become somewhat of an oracle on the subject of Christian theology from an African perspective. He has painstakingly shown in this book a practical approach on how Christianity can reasonably and scholarly address African Traditional Religion and the belief system it has on people with informed realism, biblical faithfulness and integrity. Extricating itself from the stranglehold of primitive beliefs emanating from the foundations of ATR and the cultures it spawned has been the debilitating problem confronting Christianity in Africa.

This is a very useful text both for academic purposes and for practical ministry. I strongly recommend it to you.

Pastor Cosmas Ilechukwu, DMin
General Overseer, Charismatic Renewal Ministries, Inc.

Professor Yusufu Turaki states that the use of proof texting in doctrinal formulation from a Western framework on the one hand, and the use of traditional religion on the other hand, as the starting point of doing theology, have proved inadequate. In this book, the author carefully uses a third method that penetrates and engages African Traditional Religion from a biblical, Christocentric and ecclesiastical perspective.

The genius of the book is found in the extraordinary use of a method that reflects on the inner logic and workings of the traditional religious mind and thought in order to formulate an African theology that is relevant and biblical. In this regard, it is a double-edged sword that cuts deeply into African Traditional Religion and presents a truly biblical African Christianity.

Evidently, it is a book that is a result of many years of rigorous research, teaching and writing. I enthusiastically recommend this profoundly important book as a must-read for all students of theology, Christianity and African Traditional Religion, and worldview. It is thorough, fresh, innovative, exciting, practical and engaging.

Samuel Waje Kunhiyop, PhD
Professor of Systematic Theology and Ethics,
ECWA Theological Seminary, Kagoro, Nigeria
Executive General Secretary, Evangel Fellowship International

The relationship between Christianity and African Traditional Religion, worldview and culture, is complex and infinitely varied, requiring careful and sensitive study by wise and knowledgeable theologians. This is a task which Professor Turaki is particularly well equipped to undertake, thanks to his years of teaching and interacting with students on this and other related subjects. There was formerly a dearth of good textbooks covering this important area of theology, but Turaki's work now provides a thorough and detailed study of traditional religion together with the many factors and influences (both ancient and modern) which surround it. The author's focus is not to understand Christianity from the perspective of African traditional culture and religion, but to understand African traditional culture and religion from the perspective of a Christian and biblical worldview.

Turaki has provided a masterly and comprehensive work which will remain a reference point and guide for students and pastors for many years to come. It will surely go a long way to fulfil the author's hope that it will help to strengthen the faith and commitment of African Christians, and that African peoples, societies and nation-states will thereby be renewed and transformed.

The Most Rev Dr Benjamin A. Kwashi
Bishop of Jos, Nigeria
General Secretary, Global Anglican Future Conference (GAFCON)

For many years I have been among the grateful beneficiaries of Professor Yusufu Turaki's theological teaching and writing. I have come to regard him as Africa's leading evangelical theologian. The welcome production of this volume represents the culmination of several decades of meticulous interaction with the Scriptures, as well as with a multitude of other African theologians. Turaki takes his stand as a thorough-going evangelical, with his feet firmly planted on the inerrancy and authority of the Bible. With that as his foundation, he then skilfully demonstrates that we cannot develop a Christian theology for Africa without a thorough understanding of the African traditional religious mindset. In the end we see clearly how the Bible addresses African culture and worldview. I believe this volume will stand for decades to come not only as Professor Turaki's *magnum opus*, but as a cherished guide to serious African Christians and scholars.

Pastor Gary S. Maxey, PhD
New Beginnings International Church
Founder, West Africa Theological Seminary
Ipaja, Lagos, Nigeria

In this fresh dialogue between African Traditional Religion, culture and worldviews, and Christianity, Professor Turaki provides a fascinating, in-depth and practical approach to genuine Christianity within an African context. He rightly recognizes that Western theological methods are inadequate in answering questions raised from this context. His theological method emphasizes that dialogue between the biblical and the African traditional religious worldviews must be initiated from the perspective of a Christian and biblical reflection if it is to be viable. Given the challenges facing the church in Africa (including global worldviews and cultures that shape theological reflection and life), this book is a valuable and timely contribution to the ongoing conversation on the nature and expression of modern African Christianity.

Elizabeth Mburu, PhD
Associate Professor, New Testament and Greek,
Pan-Africa Christian University, Nairobi, Kenya

When I first went through this book, three verbs immediately came to mind: foundational, comprehensive, and relevant. Professor Yusufu Turaki's latest book, *Engaging Religions and Worldviews in Africa: A Christian Theological Method*, is foundational in that it describes the many sources of influence that have shaped contemporary African Christian thought and practice. These have included African Traditional Religions, traditional African cultures (if they can be separated), Missionary Christianity, historic and emerging African theology, Western philosophy and even African leadership and governance styles. The book is comprehensive in that it utilizes many academic disciplines. Sometimes it reads like history, sometimes like anthropology, sociology and psychology, sometimes like hermeneutics and theology, sometimes like philosophy and ethics, and sometimes like missiology. I am personally not aware of any other work that has tied the multiple streams of African Christian development to the African church's structures, values, and practices like this book has. Turaki has also created a book that is relevant to modern Christianity in Africa. Everyone who serves the church in Africa, whether foreigner or indigene, will minister more effectively by reading and understanding the diverse facts and interpretations found in this book. I have often told my students and friends that Yusufu Turaki is Africa's most thoughtful and prolific theologian. This book confirms that conviction by showcasing his vast knowledge, experience, wisdom and hard work.

Danny McCain, PhD
Professor of Biblical Theology, University of Jos, Nigeria
Founder, Global Scholars

Professor Yusufu Turaki's written and spoken words are as powerful as his presence. If you want to know what's happening with the Christian gospel, as presented and received by Africans, this book is a definitive account. *Engaging Religions and Worldviews in Africa: A Christian Theological Method* is an insightful new guide that simplifies and demystifies theological engagement and interaction. Read this book! It will surely help you understand better the African traditional worldviews in the light of the Christian message.

In my over forty years as a pastor and teacher, I have never run across a book that made such profound analysis of the engagement and interaction of religions and worldviews. If I knew then what I know now about a theological method of engagement and interaction between Christianity and African Traditional Religions and their worldviews, I would have become a better leader and teacher than I am now.

I am recommending this book because there isn't another on the shelf that captures this attempt to transform the African worldview with the gospel of Christ.

Rev Bauta D. Motty, PhD
Lecturer/Director, Leadership Centre of Excellence,
ECWA Theological Seminary (JETS), Jos, Nigeria

I first met Professor Yusufu Turaki when he joined the Africa Inland Church Milimani in Nairobi, Kenya, where I served as senior pastor. Coming to know his dear wife and family added much flavour to our relationship. Prof Yusufu

Turaki is an African Christian who in his own right is scholarly, well researched, and deeply rooted spiritually. My interaction with Prof Turaki, firstly as his pastor, but secondly as a close friend and elder of the congregation we both cherished, led me to an understanding of the passion that drives him for the Christian African theological perspective.

Engaging Religions and Worldviews in Africa: A Christian Theological Method is both timely and focussed. The emerging young African Christian is in dire need for an understanding of himself, his environment and his religious challenges within his worldview. The topics addressed in this book vividly display many areas of human life – intellectual, political, social-cultural, spiritual and physical.

The development of the African Christian mind is coming of age; the environment being within multiple facets of surrounding worldviews that threaten the process. Thus this book stands as a firm foundation upon which the building blocks must be laid and the entire process brought to its sure completion.

Whereas there are a few approaches by some African writers on the matter of African Traditional Religion and the Christian faith in Africa, Yusufu Turaki has rightly moved the bar to point the African Christian to the foundation, namely, first let Christianity and the Bible take root. This base forms the sphere of operation for all else.

Rev Dr Matthews K. Mwalw'a
Africa Inland Church, Karen Chapel, Nairobi, Kenya

African theologians for a long time have been concerned about theological method. Because of this concern, different theological methodologies from different Christian traditions have been developed to address issues on Christianity, African Traditional Religions and worldviews. Most of these methods have been "descriptive" or "comparative" in nature. These theological approaches to engage and interact with African worldviews have been described by theologians as doing "theology from below." These methods often lacked theoretical and conceptual methodological framework, except that they tended to promote African concepts, cultures and its religious heritages without critically evaluating them from biblical and theological perspectives.

Engaging Religions and Worldviews in Africa by Yusufu Turaki is an important evangelical contribution to theological methodology in Africa, which is long overdue. Turaki is making a seminal contribution to the discussion on theological methodology by articulating a clear evangelical methodology that engages and interacts with Christianity, ATR and worldviews in a "biblically grounded and theologically responsible" manner to "enable the gospel of Jesus Christ to become a powerful instrument for renewal and transformation in Africa." This theological method is consistent with the theological method called "theology from above" where the Scriptures and not culture or the ATR heritage shape our understanding of Christianity and the gospel.

Turaki's wisdom and biblical and theological prowess in handling this sensitive subject in a comprehensive and balanced manner is commendable. I endorse this important book for all who are concerned about sound theological training and a vibrant African church as well as those who care to do serious theological refection on matters related to African Traditional Religion, culture and Christianity.

James Nkansah-Obrempong, PhD
Professor of Theology and Ethics,
Dean, Nairobi Evangelical Graduate School of Theology,
Africa International University, Nairobi, Kenya
Vice Chair, World Evangelical Alliance Theological Commission

In this highly motivating book, Distinguished Professor Yusufu Turaki, a scholar and theologian of renown, has x-rayed African Traditional Religion through the lens of biblical theology. As a scholar, he takes the reader through the missionary exploits of how the gospel came to the shores of Africa, the way it was presented, and the challenges that accompanied those exploits. While reiterating the fundamentals of biblical theology and the exigency of Christians in Africa to unlearn certain African traditions that negate biblical truth, he stresses the need for us to embrace the infallible truth of God's power and communicable attributes and appropriate it. Professor Turaki stresses the need for believers in Christ to return to Scripture, the infallible word of God, as a guide for all issues of life. This book will be a great blessing to all those who want to remain on the right godly path in the course of our earthly spiritual pilgrimage, and to those who want to bring others on that path too.

Rev Stephen Baba Panya
President, Evangelical Church Winning All (ECWA)

Professor Yusufu Turaki's work, *Engaging Religions and Worldviews in Africa: A Christian Theological Method*, is a must-read by any theologian and Christian who wants to truly live his or her Christian life as an African and wants to meet the social and religious needs of fellow Africans such as "African social and religious values and institutions like, marriage, education, law, rites of passage, as well as age groups."

Turaki rightly makes very clear that if Christianity is to mean anything to both the traditional and modern African who still resorts to the African traditionalist and medicine or turns to African myths, practices and beliefs, when all else fails, the gospel of Christ must be presented in such a way that it meets the needs and expectations of the traditional modern African, just as African Traditional Religion has over the centuries met needs across the various African communities, past and present.

Turaki rightly stresses that for the African to see any meaning in Christianity and to embrace the gospel of Christ, the theologian-pastor must have a good grasp of biblical teachings and worldview along with traditional beliefs, attitudes, behaviors, and the social and religious practices of the African, and must be able to relate them to the traditional and modern African in a meaningful way. Failure to meet these needs and expectations in our modern day and age when Christianity in Africa is having ever more difficulty with Islam, means that "African converts to Christianity may well revert to their traditional religion in order to have their needs fulfilled and met," as is already happening. But this need not be, because Christianity is about the worship of the powerful, living and personal God that has invaded our world in human flesh to give humans life, and life abundantly. And Professor Turaki has done a good job in this book to develop an extensive biblical theology to help address these issues of real life with a view to meeting the needs of both the traditional and modern African without watering down the biblical teaching or the gospel of our Lord Jesus Christ. I therefore endorse this noble work in making the gospel of Christ down to earth on African soil.

Rev Pandang Yamsat, PhD
Executive Director,
Centre for Value and Attitudinal Reawakening, Jos, Nigeria

Engaging Religions and Worldviews in Africa

Engaging Religions and Worldviews in Africa

A Christian Theological Method

Yusufu Turaki

© 2020 Yusufu Turaki

Published 2020 by HippoBooks, an imprint of ACTS and Langham Publishing.

Africa Christian Textbooks (ACTS), TCNN, PMB 2020, Bukuru 930008, Plateau State, Nigeria.
www.actsnigeria.org

Langham Publishing, PO Box 296, Carlisle, Cumbria, CA3 9WZ, UK
www.langhampublishing.org

ISBNs:
978-1-78368-759-6 Print
978-1-78368-841-8 ePub
978-1-78368-842-5 Mobi
978-1-78368-843-2 PDF

Yusufu Turaki has asserted his right under the Copyright, Designs and Patents Act, 1988 to be identified as the Author of this work.

All rights reserved. No part of this publication may be reproduced, stored in a retrieval system or transmitted, in any form or by any means, electronic, mechanical, photocopying, recording or otherwise, without the prior written permission of the publisher or the Copyright Licensing Agency.

Requests to reuse content from Langham Publishing are processed through PLSclear. Please visit www.plsclear.com to complete your request.

All Scripture quotations, unless otherwise indicated, are taken from the Holy Bible, New International Version®, NIV®. Copyright ©1973, 1978, 1984, 2011 by Biblica, Inc.™ Used by permission of Zondervan.

Scripture quotations marked NKJV are taken from the New King James Version (NKJV). Copyright © 1982 by Thomas Nelson, Inc. Used by permission. All rights reserved.

Scripture quotations marked ESV are from The Holy Bible, English Standard Version® (ESV®), copyright © 2001 by Crossway, a publishing ministry of Good News Publishers. Used by permission. All rights reserved.

Scripture quotations marked NRSV are from the New Revised Standard Version Bible, copyright © 1989 National Council of the Churches of Christ in the United States of America. Used by permission. All rights reserved.

Scripture quotations marked GWT are taken from GOD'S WORD®, © 1995 God's Word to the Nations. Used by permission of God's Word Mission Society.

British Library Cataloguing-in-Publication Data
A catalogue record for this book is available from the British Library

ISBN: 978-1-78368-759-6

Cover & Book Design: projectluz.com

The publishers of this book actively support theological dialogue and an author's right to publish but do not necessarily endorse the views and opinions set forth here or in works referenced within this publication, nor guarantee technical and grammatical correctness. The publishers do not accept any responsibility or liability to persons or property as a consequence of the reading, use or interpretation of its published content.

Contents

Foreword xvii
Preface and Acknowledgements................................ xxi
Introduction xxiii
The Approach xxvii
Procedure xxxi
Definition of Terms xxxiii

Part I: Understanding Western Christianity and Worldviews

1　The Legacy of Western Christianity in Africa and the Need for an African Christian Theology................................. 3
2　Reactions to Missionary Christianity 27
3　Approaches and Typologies of African Theology 43
4　African Theological Issues 61

Part II: Towards an Understanding of African Traditional Religion

5　Various Approaches to the Study of Religion and Culture.......... 81
6　Defining Religion 109
7　On Studying African Traditional Religion 117
8　Fundamental Theological Beliefs.......................... 121
9　Fundamental Psychological Beliefs 135
10　Fundamental Philosophical Beliefs 139
11　Fundamental Moral and Ethical Laws...................... 151
12　Ethical and Moral Principles............................ 159
13　The Supreme Being 173
14　Gods, Divinities and Spirits: Monotheism or Polytheism 179
15　Communication With and From the Spirit World 189
16　The Acquisition of Power 201
17　The Exercise of Power 209
18　Being Human 217
19　The Meaning of Life.................................... 225

Part III: Engagement and Interaction between Christianity and the African Traditional Religion and Worldview

20 Introduction 231
21 Engaging with the Traditional Belief in Impersonal (Mystical) Powers 233
22 The Power of God's Sovereignty 247
23 Engaging with the Traditional Belief in Spirit Beings 253
24 Engaging with the Traditional Belief about the Origin of Spirit Beings 261
25 Engaging with the Traditional Belief and Good and Evil 269
26 Engaging with the Traditional Belief in Gods and Divinities .. 279
27 Engaging with the Traditional Belief in Ancestors 285
28 The Mediator: Jesus the Messiah 295
29 Engaging with the Traditional Belief in the Supreme Being .. 299
30 The Doctrine of God 303
31 Engaging with the Traditional Roots of Spiritual Idolatry 317
32 Engaging with the African Holistic Worldview 329
33 The Power and Authority of Jesus the Messiah 335
34 Engaging with the Traditional Communal Worldview 343
35 Engaging with Traditional Moral and Ethical Beliefs 351
36 Engaging with the Traditional Concept of Leadership 359
37 Engaging with Governance, Management and Administration 377
38 Engaging with the Need to Create a Responsible and Just Society .. 383
39 Engaging with Traditional Human Values 393
40 Engaging with the Doctrine of Man 405
41 Engaging with the Doctrine of Sin 417
42 Engaging with the Concept of Covenants 423
43 Biblical Theology 433
44 A Theological Framework of Religions and Cultures 439
45 To Sum Up 445
    Conclusion 451
    Bibliography 453

Foreword

For more than a generation Yusufu Turaki has been one of Africa's most distinguished and productive evangelical theologians. Here we have the fruit of his mature reflection on a principal crux of the African theological project, namely the appropriate way for African Christianity to understand and address Africa's traditional religious heritage.

Since one cannot understand Africa without understanding Africa's traditional heritage and, since the religious dimension of Africa's traditional culture affects all aspects of modern African life, Christian presence and witness in Africa cannot flourish within its context without a serious theological and practical engagement with these realities.

This is not Turaki's first endeavour in this field of inquiry. He has been engaging with these issues throughout his academic and ministry career. In so doing he has also been interacting with the considerable range of thinkers and literature in this field. Furthermore, within what otherwise has often been an ill-defined and poorly disciplined discussion, Turaki proposes a particular and fruitful way forward. In these pages Turaki is both commending and demonstrating a biblically grounded, theologically responsible methodology for a Christian understanding of African Traditional Religion. He seeks to show how Christianity can best address African Traditional Religion with informed realism, with scholarly depth and integrity, and with biblical faithfulness.

Having taken his first degree in Nigeria, Turaki then earned masters and doctoral degrees at leading academic institutions overseas. Thereafter he was long involved in the leadership of one of Africa's principal theological institutions, Jos ECWA Theological Seminary (JETS), and in the leadership of one of Africa's principal evangelical denominations, the Evangelical Church of West Africa (ECWA), now as, Evangelical Church Winning All (ECWA). In more recent years Turaki has also been engaged in international ministries and venues, including work with the Association of Evangelicals in Africa (AEA), the World Evangelical Alliance (WEA), and the Lausanne Movement (LCWE), as well as in extensive writing and teaching ministries.

At the beginning of this major contribution Turaki provides an in-depth study of the African traditional religious worldview. He is convinced that a thorough familiarity with the religious mindset of traditional Africa is essential for any effective Christian presence and witness in modern Africa. He first surveys both western and African scholarly approaches to traditional religion. Then he undertakes a detailed introduction to the foundational theological, psychological, philosophical, ethical and moral beliefs of African Traditional Religion, together with the relevant rituals, sacrifices, ceremonies, and festivals. He also emphasizes how those beliefs pervasively influence religious attitudes, practice and social behaviour throughout Africa today.

Turaki then turns to outline a Christian and biblical approach to the realities of African Traditional Religion in modern Africa. He discusses each major component of an African traditional worldview from this standpoint. In doing so Turaki emphasizes that the principal task of Christian reflection in Africa is not to understand Christianity from the perspective of African traditional culture and religion, but to understand African traditional culture and religion from the perspective of a Christian and biblical worldview, a method of engagement and interaction of religions and worldviews.

In this way Turaki is advocating a methodological approach that is meant as a deliberate alternative to many popular academic constructs current in African theological discussions. It is also an approach that promises sure light and welcome practical guidance for ordinary African Christian believers seeking to live out their biblical faith in a responsible manner within their African context.

By outlining a Christian worldview that provides step-by-step answers to Africa's traditional religious worldview, Turaki seeks to go beyond individual religious beliefs and practices to attend to the underlying mindset and thought-world of traditional Africa. He believes that it is at this level that we must understand traditional religion, and at this level that we must address its pervasive presence within modern African life. Only in this way can the gospel of Jesus Christ become the powerful instrument that it is meant to be for renewing and transforming Africa.

Within God's good purpose for Africa, African Christian believers must learn to approach their context with sensitive, informed, and caring understanding, assessed from within a Christian frame of reference. Turaki believes that the outcome of such a process will not only better ground and energize the vast and still growing Christian community on the continent, but also thereby bring good to modern Africa with all its difficulties and remarkable opportunities. By being faithful to a Christ-captivated mind, not least in engagement with African's traditional religious heritage, African Christianity has something vital to contribute to Africa's future. Turaki's work seeks to equip African Christian readers for this task.

This is a profoundly significant agenda, carried out with exceptional wisdom and insight. I am honoured to have known Yusufu Turaki for many years as a friend and esteemed colleague. It gives me much pleasure to commend wholeheartedly this major contribution to African theological reflection.

Paul Bowers
Managing Editor, BookNotes for Africa
Former International Director,
International Council for Evangelical Theological Education

Preface and Acknowledgements

The African theological enterprise has long been dominated by descriptive and comparative studies of Christianity and African Traditional Religion. Victor Turner, E. Bolaji Idowu and John S. Mbiti have made valuable contributions. However, there is an urgent need for a well-formulated theological method of engagement and interaction with religions and worldviews that is contextual and faithful to the Bible and Christian historical traditions and scholarship. Such a method is presented in this book.

I was encouraged to produce this book by David Waweru, the Chief Executive Officer of WordAlive Publishers, Nairobi, Kenya. It could be described as a revised edition of my *Christianity and African Gods: A Method in Theology* (1999), but it also includes elements from my later works, *The Unique Christ for Salvation: The Challenge of World Religions and Cultures* (2002, 2006) and *Foundations of African Traditional Religions and Worldview* (2002, 2006).

Professor Jesse N. K. Mugambi of the University of Nairobi, a renowned African theologian and author, also made recommendations with regard to the content and structure of the book. His critical evaluation and insights have added much value to this work. I am profoundly grateful to him for sharing his theological expertise.

The book not only offers a new conceptual and theoretical method and approach to the study of Christianity and African religions and worldviews, it also suggests ways in which Christianity as a system of teachings, beliefs and worldview can impact the worldview associated with African Traditional Religion. The importance of having such an impact is underscored by the work of Professors Andrew Walls, Lamin Sanneh, Kwame Bediako and Philip Jenkins, who have made it clear that the majority of Christians now live in the non-Western world and that Africa is emerging as a world centre of Christianity. That fact alone means that Africans need to engage seriously with both global and African religions and cultures, recognizing that the clash of religions in Africa is indeed a battle for the African mind. We need to understand how Christian missions, colonialism, African Traditional Religions and contemporary Christian trends have affected the modern African mind, and we need to work for transformation to a worldview that is both contextual and profoundly biblical.

It is hoped that the freshness, innovation and creativity of the approach presented in this book will continue to generate fresh theological discourse in Africa on Christianity and African Traditional Religion and worldviews and that it will also contribute to helping indigenous African Christian scholarship make a substantial contribution on a global scale.

Yusufu Turaki
Jos, Nigeria
January 2020

Introduction

I did my graduate studies in theology and social ethics in the United States of America in the mid-1970s at Boston University and returned to Nigeria in the early 1980s. My doctoral research was on the British colonial legacy in Northern Nigeria. This led me to identify other important legacies operating within the same geo-political region and environment, namely the Islamic legacy; the legacy of Christian missions; and the legacy of African Traditional Religion. Some of my work on these legacies is reflected in the Bibliography.

When I returned to Nigeria, I was given the task of pioneering a theological seminary in the city of Jos, Nigeria. I soon realized that I needed to rethink my Christian theology (founded on American Christian principles) by making an in-depth study of African Traditional Religion and worldviews. During major research in this field at Yale University in 1994, I became aware of the powerful legacy of African Traditional Religion and its influence on Christianity and Islam in Africa, as well as on modern African nation-states.

I taught four related courses at JETS: (1) Western and Non-Western Thought; (2) Man and Culture in Africa; (3) African Traditional Religion (ATR); and (4) Christian Doctrines. The primary objective of these courses was to relate the Christian faith and the Bible to African Traditional Religion, worldview and culture. During class discussions, important issues were often raised. These included issues concerning traditional religious beliefs and practices, as well as the religious and cultural life of traditional Africans in general. We discussed how the Bible and the Christian faith relates to these and how, as Christians, we could develop a biblical theology that would address the core religious and cultural values of traditional Africa. At that time, we did not have textbooks that could answer our questions, relevantly and comprehensively. The works of great African theologians, such as E. Bolaji Idowu and John S. Mbiti, were available but did not meet our needs as evangelical Christians who believe that in any theological enquiry and discourse we must recognize the centrality of the Bible, the Trinity, and the church and its mission.

There is a false assumption that African tradition, culture and religion are obsolete and have no influence over modern Africans. Some of the old institutions, social structures, and values have been replaced by colonialism and Christianity, but some have remained – not necessarily in institutions or social structures – but in the minds and in the worldview of Africans.

Traditional values therefore continue to exert a very powerful and pervasive influence over Africans, whether they are modernists or Christians. Some of these traditional values, cultures, and social institutions have been transformed into social formations and values that are neither traditional nor Western.

I am not advocating a return to the old traditions in order to escape present realities, but in an attempt to understand the traditions and their pervasive and profound influence upon Africans. We need to engage modern Africans in terms of these worldviews and values.

However studying African Traditional Religion alone is not enough. It must be complemented by a study of the impact of colonialism, Missionary Christianity and the secular global civilizing forces of the West. The West now has a new gospel – one of globalization through the civilizing forces of advanced science and technology, democracy, capitalism or market economy, mass communication and transport. Modern Africa is a mixture of the old African traditional values, institutions, religion, culture, and worldview; of Western colonialism, Christianity, modern Western values and philosophies, and the secular forces; and of new values, social structures, and institutions generated as a result of the interaction between civilizations such as the West, Christianity, and Islam. A modern African therefore has a new identity forged out of modernity. This African could be a Christian, or a non-Christian, or a traditionalist. Others might be neither traditionalist nor Christian nor Muslim. This is the Africa which we must address using Christian and biblical theology.

My students at JETS were fond of raising difficult theological questions about issues in African Traditional Religion and culture in relation to Christianity. The difficulty that we encountered then was our lack of proper knowledge of African Traditional Religion. We therefore had to study contemporary practical African experience in order to make up for these deficiencies. It was clear that knowledge of African traditions is essential for the task of developing and formulating a Christian theology that can adequately engage with both the old and the modern Africa. Furthermore, this background is necessary if we wish to help African Christians sort out which traditional religious beliefs, practices, and behaviours are in conflict with their Christian faith.

We observed that many African scholars and pioneers did not provide biblical and theological answers for Africans dealing with the modern realities of Africa. Unfortunately, western theology also did not adequately address the theological questions and issues arising from the Christian study of the African Traditional Religion and culture. Many African Christians have serious problems relating the Bible and the Christian faith to their traditional African religious system and their modern context. This means that manifestations of dual religious beliefs and practices are common among modern African Christians. Even after becoming Christians, many still hold to some of their "precious" traditional religious beliefs, practices and behaviours. They will consult traditional diviners, sorcerers, medicine men and women, and other specialists. If they lack sound knowledge of the Bible and Christian theology, it is easy to turn to the readily available beliefs and practices of their traditional theology or to modernism to make up for their lack of understanding. The same thing happens if they think that Christianity or modernity cannot meet their basic human needs. For this reason, we must not underestimate the power and influence of the traditional religious system and its beliefs, values, and practices upon Africans, even after they become Christians.

There may be similarities in some areas between Christianity and African Traditional Religion, especially with regard to spirituality, beliefs, religious forms, and practice, but the two have different religious purposes and theological foundations. These fine differences are significant. To accommodate the two or blur their distinctiveness is a disservice to each and demonstrates a lack of Christian and biblical scholarship.

For instance, in the African religious worldview, Jesus Christ can easily be identified as one of the many deities, divinities or gods, or even as one of the revered ancestors. Although Jesus Christ would certainly be worshipped, he would be venerated along with other competing divinities or gods. Thus, the divinity of Jesus Christ is not denied theologically but is upheld within a framework of religious pluralism. The worldview of some African Christians can easily accommodate Christian teachings about God, Jesus Christ, and the Holy Spirit, as well as other doctrines, alongside their traditional religious beliefs and practices. This accommodative traditional theology tends to deny the uniqueness of Jesus Christ, God, and the Holy Spirit. It is hoped that this book will enable us to address this.

Even though the influence of the African Traditional Religion and culture is profound and pervasive in modern Africa, many African Christians are not aware of the powerful influence it exerts over their lives. They live under its dominance every day and yet exhibit much ignorance about it. If we were to ask the ontological question: "What is the most pervasive and dominant reality in the African traditional worldview?" we would learn that Africa is rooted in spirit-power. This religious belief underscores religious life in both traditional and modern Africa. African Traditional Religion and culture are not relics or outdated, but are active and powerful in the lives of modern Africans. Even in modern Africa, then, the study of the African Traditional Religion is essential for African Christians.

Furthermore, Western secular beliefs of religious pluralism, cultural relativism, and modernity or post-modernity breed confusion because they also deny the uniqueness of Jesus Christ and the authority of the Bible. Missionary Christianity and modern philosophies both come from the West, but they are contradictory. For this reason, an analysis of Christianity in Africa must also include a thorough study of both Missionary Christianity and modern Western philosophies and values.

The Approach

Much has already been written about Christianity and African Traditional Religion. The bibliography of this work presents a variety of these approaches, methodologies, and typologies. However, this field has been dominated by the descriptive and comparative methods used in anthropology, sociology, and the scientific study of religion.

During the late 1970s at Boston University, USA, my good friend Professor Jacob Kehinde Olupona and I used to lament the fact that the study of Christianity and African Traditional Religion had yet to go beyond three scholars, Victor Turner, John S. Mbiti, and E. Bolaji Idowu. A generation later, it seemed that the students and graduates of these pioneers were continuing to follow their lead.

To test this hypothesis, we examined the research theses produced in religion and theology in African seminaries and universities. As suspected, this search revealed a preponderance of descriptive and comparative methods. Students were still looking for elements of similarity or dissimilarity between Christianity and African Traditional Religion, culture, or philosophy. Many comparative studies had been undertaken on topics such as concepts of God; salvation; religious rituals and practices; forms and modes of worship; spirituality and morality; angels and demons; intermediaries; ancestors; and religious festivals. Meanwhile the descriptive studies had focused predominantly on the impact of Missionary Christianity upon various social structures in Africa or on the impact of African cultures, religions, or worldviews on Christianity and the church. Such descriptive and comparative methods have value as they provide knowledge and understanding of traditional religion. However, they have been overused as they do not help African Christians to relate their Christian faith meaningfully to their religious past, heritage, and worldview.

The criticisms of African scholarship in religion and theology have oscillated between two extremes: that scholarship in Africa has been too Western, and that scholarship in Africa has been too African. Western scholarship is seen as being too rationalistic, too scientific, and too humanistic, with too many secularist ideas. This approach is regarded as betraying African authenticity. On the other hand, African scholarship has been accused of being too ideological, using the African culture, religion, or worldview to portray Africa in a better light. The early pioneers of "African Theology" sought to prove to the world that Africans had concepts such as God, history, and salvation. Consequently it is African concepts that have been promoted, rather than authentic, free scholarship. The desire to research African themes or topics has almost become a fetish as researchers seek to liberate African scholarship from the shackles of colonialism and to produce works on the African or the African Christian theology of this or that. Prefixing every form of scholarship with the word "African" is regarded as a sign of African authenticity. A scholar becomes a hero when the product of their scholarship can be labelled as "truly African." It may take a while before this ideology becomes moribund.

It seems as if African scholarship has overturned the era of the missionary presentation of the gospel of Jesus Christ. It is no longer the gospel and the Bible that confront Africa, but Africa that confronts the gospel and the Bible through her religious scholars. African scholars now seek to define the meaning of the gospel and the Bible so as to indicate how they differ from the missionaries. The missionaries' ideological interpretation of Africa has been replaced by the African ideological interpretations of the gospel and the Bible. One ideology has replaced the other. We have simply moved from one extreme to the other.

This is why there is a great need to look afresh at the methods of African scholarship in religion and Christianity. Both Western and African ideologies and their styles of theological discourse must be avoided, as must the dominant approaches of African scholarship, especially comparative analysis and description. The "Africanness" ideology in scholarship must also be put to one side as it will only divert our attention from engaging and interacting with the traditional African mind.

For this reason I advocate an approach that is deliberately different from the many popular academic techniques currently used in African theological discussions. This methodology is meant to help Christians who seek to live out their biblical faith in a responsible manner within their African context and to enable the gospel of Jesus Christ to become a powerful instrument for renewal and transformation in Africa (Rom 12:2).

We must begin with an in-depth study of the African traditional religious worldview. The traditional religious system needs to be defined and described, showing its foundational beliefs in theology, psychology, philosophy, ethics, and morality. In addition, we need to collate a relevant knowledge of traditional African rituals, sacrifices, ceremonies, and festivals. All this still has a profound influence on the moral judgments and religious attitudes and practices, as well as the social behaviour of Africans today.

With this understanding of the traditional religious system and its influence upon Africans, we need to outline and define a Christian and biblical approach to the realities of African Traditional Religion in modern Africa. Each major component of African traditional religious worldview must be analysed from this standpoint. The principal focus of this Christian reflection is not to understand Christianity from the perspective of African traditional culture and religion, but to understand African traditional culture and religion from the perspective of a Christian and biblical worldview. In this way, our approach will remain true to the apostolic preaching of the gospel of Jesus Christ.

This work, therefore, offers a new methodology, a fresh alternative: we will use our biblical worldview to engage and interact with the underlying mind-set and thought-world of African Traditional Religion.

Procedure

This will be a theological and biblical examination of African Traditional Religion within the context of modern Africa and western Christianity and secularism. As the primary focus is on Christianity, only incidental references will be made to modernity and Islam.

We shall begin by considering: first, the impact of modern western philosophies and values upon Christianity; second, the nature and impact of Missionary Christianity in Africa; third, the traditional religious beliefs, practices, and worldview; and finally, biblical teachings, worldview and Christian theology as tools for engaging, understanding, interpreting, and ultimately transforming the traditional African mind and religious worldview.

Definition of Terms

There are certain words and concepts that need to be defined.

African Traditional Religion refers to the totality of the traditional religious beliefs. This traditional religious system includes beliefs, religious practices, behaviour, spirituality, and worldview. It defines how a traditional African sees, understands, interprets, and lives life in general whether religious, cultural or social. Christianity as a religious system with its set of beliefs, and religious practices does not meet an empty African mind. This mind is neither dormant nor docile. It is already preoccupied with the African traditional religious thought and worldview. When it receives Christianity, it has the capacity to recast and transform it to fit into its own categories of thought and attitude. While biblical beliefs and practices may appear at times to be similar to those of the traditional religion, these commonalities or similarities do not in any way suggest "sameness" in religious meanings, realities, motivations, or expectations. The biblical and Christian religious system is different and distinct.

Biblical theology refers to the general teachings and principles of the Bible and is used interchangeably in this study with the term **Christian theology**. These terms refer to general Christian beliefs and teachings derived from biblical principles and foundations. The compound term **Biblical and Christian theology** refers to the body of religious beliefs, teachings and practices in Christianity which are derived from the Bible and are in contrast to those of African Traditional Religion.

African Christianity and **African Christian Theology** are terms that describe the general works of African scholars and theologians since the late 1950s on the topic of African Traditional Religion and Christianity in Africa. The Christianity that was planted in African soil grew to become African Christianity. It has taken on the characteristics of Africa in terms of its beliefs, cultures, practices, and even history and geography. Africans who embraced Christianity have adopted a variety of forms of Christian expression, some orthodox, some heretical, some syncretistic.

Modernity in Africa refers to new social formations and values as a result of the encounter with colonialism, formal education, and certain forms of western

Christianity. Westernized Africans have modern ideas that influence their attitudes, behaviour, and social and religious practices. These may conform to Western values and institutions or may exhibit characteristics that are neither Western nor traditional African. These ideas are not static, but dynamic. Social, cultural and religious values change, as do social institutions and societies, and ethnic or tribal nationalities. The Africa of yesterday is not the same as the Africa of today. The younger generations in Africa are quite different from the older generations. We talk about multi-religions, multi-cultures, and multi-ethnicity in Africa.

However, both religion and culture have characteristics which do not change. The material forms or institutions of the past might have changed or become extinct, but the values, beliefs, attitudes, behaviour or social and religious practices endure. Modern Africans may not worship idols or ancestors today as they used to do, but that does not mean that values and beliefs associated with these have vanished entirely. The core values still persist, influencing newer institutions and younger generations. This influence is not merely theoretical. It is pervasive and powerful, affecting Christianity and Christians alike in Africa.

Bibliocentric and **Christocentric**: All research and every inquiry is governed by a certain set of presuppositions, and these two terms form the guiding principles for this research. A student of mine, Matthew Michael, turned in a class term paper for a theology course, which gives a better definition to these two concepts. I quote parts of his term paper:

Bibliocentric as a term seeks to place

> the Bible as central and major source of biblical or Christian theology in Africa. It argues for the centrality and finality of the Bible in matters of theological investigation and enquiry. Even though references should be made to the culture, or the findings of social sciences, sciences and the humanities in the course of research or study, yet priority or prerogative must be given to the centrality and finality of the Bible to the Christian quest to proffer theological solutions to the various problems facing the African church.[1]

Michael continues:

---

1. Michael, "Foundational Biblical Principles," n.p.

> It is pertinent to note that by bibliocentrism I do not mean "Bibliolatry" or the worship of the scripture as some critics may presume, but the tailoring of all theological discussion, interpretation and understanding in order to dominantly reflect the Christian revelation as preserved in the Bible. The use of the Bible or scripture as springboard of a Christian theology arises not from some mystified, unknown or crucial superstitious beliefs surrounding the Bible, but that the Bible is open, accessible, authoritative and definitive to all matters of Christian theological reflection. The approach suggests that the Bible assumed its authority not on the basis of ecclesiastical decisions, but on the prima facie evidences of the pages of the Bible itself which attested to its claim to divine revelation, and the necessity of placing such a claim as the pendulum or fulcrum on which African theology must swing. Without such an authoritative reference or central point, Christian theology becomes merely a reflection of one's doubt or presuppositions and sentiments which are projected on the theological discourse as authoritative and final, or even eternal.[2]

The Bible must remain central in our theological method and discourse. Anything less is a betrayal of the Christian faith.

Christocentric is a term that

> stresses the thesis that African theological discussion must also adopt a dominant Christocentric theological agenda … the worship of Christ as Lord must be reflected in theological discussion by the centrality of Christ at every postulation and theological investigation. It is needful to observe that Christianity or the Christian faith is Christian to the degree by which it derives its authority or teaching from Christ. A culturocentric theology must give way to a Christian theology that has Christ as the motivation, goal and purpose of theological reflections.[3]

This statement also reinforces the need to centre our theological method in Jesus Christ, the Saviour of the world. Theologians like playing with words or symbols in order to convey the true meaning of a concept or a perception.

---

2. Michael, n.p.
3. Michael, n.p.

Some add value, while others take away! There is nothing wrong in seeing Jesus as an Ancestor or a Healer, so long as that does not distort the true meaning of Jesus Christ. Our goal is to ensure that the true meaning of concepts or perceptions is faithfully conveyed without any distortion.

It is important to remember that words that appear to be working today may become a problem another day. The problem of finding and using local words or symbols to convey biblical meanings is that their meanings can change. African theologians have attempted to build Christology on African concepts, such as, *ancestor*, *elder*, *brother*, *healer*, or *king*. Words such as *ancestor* or *healer* are not absolutes, but can be changed when better ones are available.

It is also important to realize that emphasizing Jesus Christ and the Bible does not mean that other major doctrinal themes can be ignored. No doctrinal theme must be given any lesser position than it was accorded in Scripture and in Christian teachings. The centrality of both the Bible and Jesus Christ in this study marks the difference between this work and those who make African culture and religion central in their research and writings. Africanizing or domesticating the Bible to the whims of Africans must be avoided. Rather, the Bible must address Africans and seek to transform and renew them (Rom 12:2).

Theology is but one's reflection or interpretation of one's belief. In 1985 I returned to my alma mater, Boston University, and visited my major professor. During our conversation, he made this profound statement, "There are professors in this university who profess to teach about God whom they don't know." There may be theologians and scholars who profess to research and to write theology for Christians about God, Jesus, the Bible, or about African Traditional Religion although they are not believers. Good scholarship, however, must not replace faith or commitment to the Bible, Jesus Christ and God.

Part I

Understanding Western Christianity and Worldviews

1

The Legacy of Western Christianity in Africa and the Need for an African Christian Theology

There were two waves of Western Christian influence on Africa. The first spanned the fifteenth and eighteenth centuries, and the second the nineteenth and twentieth centuries. Besides Christianity, there were other important western influences on Africa: colonialism and the western worldviews. Western worldviews had a profound influence upon Christianity in both the West and Africa. Western culture and philosophies impacted Christianity and society in the West and these ideas were then exported to Africa. However, since the fall of western colonialism and Christendom, Western Christianity has changed tremendously.

Missionary Christianity

Africa was influenced by two forms of Christianity: the older Palestinian, Mediterranean or Hellenistic Christianity which came directly from Jesus and his apostles who lived in Palestine; and the later Western Missionary Christianity. This form of Christianity came to Africa via Europe and North America, and the whites in diaspora in South Africa, Australia and New Zealand. It forms the largest sector of Christianity in Africa. The older form of Christianity was largely destroyed when Islam invaded North Africa in the middle of the seventh century. Although the Nubian Church was finally destroyed by conquering Muslims in the sixteenth century, the Coptic Church of Egypt and the Orthodox Church of Ethiopia have survived against all odds to date.

Our focus in this study is on Western Missionary Christianity in both colonial and post-colonial Africa. In our quest for an African theology it is important to understand the influence of both Western colonialism as well as Missionary Christianity.

Colonialism as a modern socio-political movement is an important subject on its own, but it also had strong implications for Christian missions in Africa. Western colonialism and Christianity influenced each other reciprocally, through cooperation and conflict. Both are products of the Western historical, social, political, economic and religious consciousness, and civilization. However, colonialism is quite distinct from Christian missions. Even though they shared or cooperated in some areas, they differed in their primary motive, goals, objectives, and interests. European expansionism and colonialism can be seen as a gradual historical process, developing from the Age of Discovery (explorers), to the Age of Mercantilism (merchants and traders), to the Age of Missions (missionaries), and to the Age of Empire Building (colonialists).[1] We are currently in the era of neo-colonialism. The colonial empires and nation states that ruled the world have been replaced by the corporations, such as the International Monetary Fund (IMF), the World Bank, multi-national corporations, the United Nations and other major power blocks and economic clubs. These institutions spread the new gospel of globalization through the civilizing forces of democracy, advanced science and technology, and market economy or capitalism.[2]

The prevailing Christian and social worldviews of the European and North American societies shaped the theory and practice of Christian missions, as well as the type of Christianity and the church structures that the missionaries planted in Africa. In searching for an authentic, relevant, and effective Christianity and church structures for modern Africa, we need therefore to examine the Christian worldviews of the North American and European Christian mission societies.

Emigrant Christianity was a by-product of the European spirit of expansion and colonization of the world. Although sometimes and in some places the differentiation is not quite clear, the contrast between colonialism and emigrant or Missionary Christianity must be kept in focus; otherwise one may regard Missionary Christianity as having been propelled by the spirit of colonialism

---

1. Turaki, *Theory and Practice*, 30–33.
2. Turaki, "Is Democracy the Ideal?," 156.

alone. Evangelical missions and missionary movements arose as an indictment of established Christianity that had neglected the Great Commission. Religious forces, such as revivals, felt mandated to evangelize the whole world, making disciples of every nation and bringing every soul into salvation in Christ Jesus. For most of the evangelical missions, this motive for missions was quite clear, even though they were sometimes influenced by the prevailing cultural and colonial milieu.[3]

The social and mission worldviews of the mission societies also reflected the historical background of the missionaries who brought Christianity to Africa. Inevitably the personal characteristics and qualities of both the pioneering and the subsequent missionaries were shaped by their prevailing Home Mission background. This, too, impacted the quality of Christianity in Africa. For this reason, it is very important that we pay close attention to the immediate social, religious, cultural, political and historical factors, events, ideas, and circumstances that exerted their influence on both the missionaries. This is fundamental to our understanding of the nature of the mission work and the quality of Christianity which Christian missions founded in Africa.[4]

For this reason, it is very important that we assess the instruments of both social and religious change, the philosophy, methods, strategies, techniques, and models that were used by the pioneering missionaries. Indeed the impact and consequences of those social and religious changes in Africa can only be properly evaluated in light of the philosophy and methods that were used.[5] Many missionary practices, beliefs, assumptions, and models of change in Africa are no longer relevant today and their continuity may pose problems to Christianity in modern Africa. For instance, the earlier general Missionary negativity towards African culture and personality robbed African Christianity of some valuable African foundations, such as the family unit, marriage, kinship, social and communal morality, ethics, and justice. Christianity in modern Africa is facing all kinds of crises and seems unable to cope because some of these African features were not utilized in establishing Christianity on African soil. Not everything in African culture, religion, and institutions was bad and Missionary Christianity has been criticized for throwing away the good aspects of African culture, religion, and institutions. These aspects could have been adapted and modified as key pillars for social and communal

---

3. Turaki, *Theory and Practice*, 33.
4. Turaki, 557.
5. Turaki, 557–558.

Christianity in Africa. Nonetheless, Christianity and colonialism did not wipe out everything African; some aspects have remained.[6]

The work of western Christian missions in Africa has come under severe criticism and attack from both Christians and non-Christians. The old missionary approach to the study of African Traditional Religion and culture raises pertinent questions on the nature of the missionary presentation of the gospel of Christ and the consequences of missionary work in modern Africa. The cross-cultural factor inherent in missions produced tensions between mission agencies and indigenous African Christians, especially in areas concerning the interpretation of the nature of Christianity and theology. Debates defining the relationship between the "Gospel and Culture" and African culture have been a major subject of discussions in missiology.[7]

The quest for authentic Christianity in Africa, then, must examine the philosophy, models, beliefs, assumptions, as well as the theory and practice of missions in an African setting. This approach may lead to a reconstruction of a Christian worldview and to church structures that are authentic, relevant, and effective in Africa.

The Problem of the Presentation and Transmission of the Gospel

Three scholars have dealt adequately with the subject of the transmission of the Christian faith into a foreign culture: (1) Lamin Sanneh in *Encountering the West: Christianity and the Global Cultural Process* (1993) and *Translating the Message: The Missionary Impact on Culture* (1989); (2) Andrew F. Walls in *The Missionary Movement in Christian History: Studies in the Transmission of Faith* (1996); and (3) Kwame Bediako in *Christianity in Africa: The Renewal of a Non-Western Religion* (1995). Each of these works addresses the problems and assesses whether what the missionaries did was valid.

Many African scholars criticize the methodology of Western missionaries and, as a result, the outcome of their work in Africa. The missionary who brought the gospel had a Western culture and worldview. This could be a mixture of biblical values, cultural Christianity, and the general cultural and social values of Western society. This "mixture" was transmitted to Africa. As a result, the Africans received more than the gospel from the missionaries. They also received Western culture and its worldviews, with all their positive and

---

6. Turaki, 558.
7. Turaki, 558.

negative characteristics. There is need therefore to examine the mode, form and content of the Christianity that they transmitted.

Sanneh's and Bediako's works mentioned above are very helpful in this area. If Western missionaries held a negative view of the African religious and cultural past, it is logical that they would refrain from using the traditional African worldview as a means of transmitting the gospel. Nonetheless they partially employed that worldview for, as both Sanneh and Walls observe, they used the traditional vernacular; the Scriptures were translated into African languages. Pioneer missionaries, however, failed to undertake a serious study of the African religious and cultural heritage. African theologians and scholars feel that the pre-Christian religious and cultural heritage could have been used by Western missionaries as means of presenting and transmitting the gospel.[8] Bediako asserts that the missionaries' narrow approach meant that they did not use the pervasive African religious and cultural worldview as a tool for a more effective gospel transmission. Shorter and Mbiti lament the fact that there was no dialogue between Christianity and traditional religion, and thus Christianity did not become aware of the wealth of African traditional spirituality.[9]

The Problem of the Reception of the Gospel

Other scholars have focused on the problem of the African reception of the gospel. The recipients of the transmitted Christianity also need to be examined critically. The African recipient was not simply a vacuum, but a person heavily loaded with both religious and cultural values and perspectives. The African received the gospel while standing on the shoulders of his African religious and cultural heritage.

The use of the vernacular meant that Africans were in a position to engage with the gospel, the Bible and Christianity from their own religious and cultural background. The freedom to do this meant that the outcome or the product was not always what the missionaries had expected.[10] Sanneh observes that the translation of the Christian Scriptures into the vernacular impacted both the receivers and the missionaries who brought the message. This occurred

---

8. Mbiti, *Concepts of God*; Shorter, *Dialogue with African*; Kibicho, "Continuity of the African Conception."

9. Shorter, *Dialogue with African*; Kibicho, "Continuity of the African Conception."

10. Sanneh, *Translating the Message*.

because "the receivers . . . not only heard but transformed and deepened the message in ways that often surprised and shocked the missionaries."[11]

The fact that the translation of the message of Christianity took place within the African culture and worldview explains the enduring presence and continuity of traditional religion among African converts.[12] Africans recast their own Christianity, whether it was properly understood or not into various African expressions of Christianity. The task for African theologians and scholars is to examine this recasting to ascertain how true it is to the Bible and how relevant it is to an African culture, worldview, and context.

Missionaries operated under the belief that there must be a *discontinuity* between Christianity and the African pre-Christian religious heritage. They insisted that African Christians must cut their ties with their African past. Thus, most Western missionaries rejected the African culture, worldview, and religious spirituality in their attempts to present the gospel of Christ to Africans. The study of the biographies of prominent pioneering missionaries would, of course, reveal exceptions as there were a few who were very different.

In modern Africa, Christianity has many faces or forms tainted by both the Western worldview and the traditional African worldview. Given this cultural mix imbedded in Missionary Christianity, pioneering African theologians and scholars took up the task of developing and formulating African Christian theology and identity.[13] When the African recipient engages with Western Missionary Christianity, he does so in order to sift what is truly the gospel and Christian and what is Western culture and worldview. However, the outcome may be African in nature but not necessarily biblical or Christian. This is why I cannot accept this methodology. I believe the Bible and Christian theology must engage and interact with the traditional African and his religion and worldview so that the outcome will be biblical and Christian by nature.

The Problem of Western Culture and Philosophy

Western culture and philosophy posed problems for the emergence of true and indigenous Christianity in Africa as they greatly influenced the Missionary Christianity that was brought to Africa from the West. The influence is still there, although the West is no longer the same. The West generally is

---

11. Sanneh.

12. Mbiti, *Concepts of God*; Shorter, *Dialogue with African*; Kibicho, "Continuity of the African."

13. Bediako, *Theology and Identity*, 1.

increasingly becoming non-Christian and those values which make it less Christian are also being imported to Africa and other parts of the world. We need to understand the nature of this change and the problem it poses for Christianity, not only in Africa but throughout the world.

The Historical Relationship between Western Culture and Christianity

The rise of modern states in Europe in the nineteenth century brought about the rise of European colonialism and ethnocentrism. After Martin Luther's Protestant Reformation and the rise of modern states in Europe, Christianity dominated the political, religious, and cultural life of Europe and the West for many centuries. It provided the worldview within which education, science and technology, capitalism or market economy, and democracy flourished. This was still true during the colonial era when colonial governments and the cultural components of the West ensured that Christianity expanded into the whole world.[14] Christianity made use of Western education, science and technology, literature, and medical work as a means of communication enabling the spread of the gospel of Christ to the nations of the world. Thus, during the colonial days, Western culture and Christianity enjoyed a happy relationship in which they reinforced each other in their quest for world dominance.[15]

This gave rise to Western ethnocentrism. Ethnocentricism is the tendency to look at the world primarily from the perspective of one's own ethnic culture. Many claim that ethnocentrism occurs in every society; ironically, ethnocentrism may be something that all cultures have in common. People often feel this occurring during what some call "culture shock." Ethnocentrism is "the technical name for the view of things in which one's own group is the center of everything," against which all other groups are judged.[16] Ethnocentrism often entails the belief that one's own race or ethnic group is the most important and/or that some or all aspects of its culture are superior to those of other groups. Within this ideology, individuals will judge other groups in relation to their own particular ethnic group or culture, especially with concern to language, behaviour, customs, and religion.

---

14. Son, "Cultural Relativism," 10.
15. Son, 10.
16. Wikipedia, https://en.wikipedia.org/wiki/Ethnocentrism.

The Fall of Western Christendom

Today Christianity and Western culture no longer hold the premier place in Western societies. Both colonialism and Missionary Christianity are being replaced by the new global civilizing forces, namely: (1) the rising power and influence of advanced science and technology; (2) the powerful influence of democratic systems of government; (3) the impact of capitalism and market economy; and (4) the revolutionary influence of communication and transport systems. These forces are presenting a new global gospel that is replacing Western colonialism.

By the mid-twentieth century, the Christianity that had influenced Western society and culture and that had given rise to colonialism and Missionary Christianity was losing its influence and power over Western society and culture. The political, social and religious forces which had controlled and held Western society together were crumbling, due in part to the works of cultural anthropologists who introduced pluralistic and relativistic views of culture, religions and values.[17]

Western culture and Christianity were greatly influenced by these modern Western philosophies, together with concepts such as the scientific empiricism, positivism, and materialism. These were very critical of both Western pride and arrogance (ethnocentrism) and Christianity. Culture and religion were regarded as suspect and biblical and Christian values were gradually eroded.

Embarrassment and guilt concerning the economic and political exploitation of the colonies grew. Christianity had not been critical enough of its evils and had, in fact, often benefitted from them.[18] Slavery and racism remained a sore in the Western Christian conscience. These evils of colonialism now tormented and haunted the Western psyche, provoking a powerful and critical apology for Western colonialism and Christianity.[19] The crisis in Western culture and Christianity, especially in missions, is also rooted in this Western guilt and its critical apology. Dr Son says that Western over-reaction to past mistakes of colonial exploitations and unfounded arrogance, the ensuing loss of pride and certainty in their own traditional heritage, growing tired of its own culture and loss of creativity, etc., seems to also have prepared an opening for the positive appreciation of other cultures. And not the least, the weakening of Christian influences on Western culture is responsible for it.[20]

---

17. Son, "Cultural Relativism," 10.
18. Son, 10.
19. Son, 11.
20. Son, 11.

The world no longer accepts the dominance and influence of Western ethnocentrism and Christianity. The West has been forced to acknowledge the validity and value of other cultures, traditions and religions.[21] This new philosophy of cultural relativism and religious pluralism provides the West with a powerful antidote to its guilt and shame. But this guilt trip is currently affecting Christianity adversely. Whereas once the West propagated Christianity worldwide, today the West is turning its back upon Christianity in all its modern cultural life. The decline of Christianity in the West casts a negative shadow over Christianity in the non-Western world. At the moment, militant Islam can terrorize and hold the West to ransom at will because the West is ashamed of its colonialism and Christian missionary activities.

Martin Jacques made the following remarks in an article in *The Guardian* on 17 February 2006:

> A continent that inflicted colonial brutality all over the globe for 200 years has little claim to the superiority of its values . . . because for around 200 years it dominated and colonized most of the world. Such was Europe's omnipotence that it never needed to take into account the sensibilities, beliefs and attitudes of those that it colonized, however sacred and sensitive they might have been. On the contrary, European countries imposed their rulers, religion, beliefs, language, racial hierarchy and customs on those to whom they were entirely alien. There is a profound hypocrisy – and deep historical ignorance – when Europeans complain about the problems posed by the ethnic and religious minorities in their midst, for that is exactly what European colonial rule meant for peoples around the world. With one crucial difference, of course: the white minorities ruled the rest, whereas Europe's new ethnic minorities are marginalised, excluded and castigated, as recent events have shown. But it is no longer possible for Europe to ignore the sensibilities of peoples with very different values, cultures and religions.[22]

Dr Son described what is going on in the contemporary West in the following words:

---

21. Son.
22. Martin Jacques, "Europe's Contempt for Other Cultures Can't Be Sustained," *The Guardian*, 17 Feb 2006, https://www.theguardian.com/world/2006/feb/17/muhammadcartoons. comment.

The fateful marriage between Christian faith and Western culture, however, is no longer as cozy today as it has been. Each has become an embarrassment rather than pride to the other, and none is entirely proud of itself either . . . Furthermore, the very culture that the faith has created and nourished is ever more strongly turning against it and disowning it. The two are no longer cherished partners and the worst-off party is Christianity. While the other partner remains as strong as ever, the survival of Western Christianity is threatened by increasing secularization coupled with rampant materialism and hedonism, as well as the onslaught of cultural relativism.[23]

Thus, the current state of Christianity in the West is quite different from that of the era of colonialism and Missionary Christianity. This social fact must be factored into any analysis of Western culture and Christianity. Furthermore, it is important that we examine the Western social factors and forces that pose this great challenge. Both culture and Christianity are seriously battling for survival.

Modern Philosophies, and Western Culture and Christianity

The change was political (the fall of colonialism), cultural (the fall of ethnocentrism), and religious (the fall of Christendom). But the breakdown of Western society also created new social forces, structures, and institutions. The modern philosophies of secularism, religious pluralism, cultural relativism, humanism, and hedonism emerged from the ashes. Modern religions such as neo-paganism, polytheistic religions, and new age religions also emerged. Global civilizing forces such as democracy, advanced science and technology, and capitalism have become entrenched.

As we consider the impact of modern Western philosophies such as dualism, secularism, pluralism, relativism and modernism on Christianity, it is necessary to consider the historical development of these philosophies in the West.

---

23. Son, "Cultural Relativism," 10.

The Influence of Dualism and the Dangers of Syncretism

Classical Greek dualism dominated western Christian theology from the age of the church fathers to the Enlightenment. Dualism as a philosophy had its roots in the ancient Greek concept of creation. The ancient Greeks assumed two eternal principles besides the rational God, namely, the eternal pre-existing matter that has no form or shape (matter) and the eternal principle of organization that gives form, structure or shape to things (ideas or forms). They argued that since only God is a rational (thinking) being, he created the world by acting as a craftsman putting these two eternal principles together, thus creating things out of both. God was the organizer, not the creator of matter or form. This view limits God because God is not the Sovereign Lord of the universe.

Later this grew into the Greek concept whereby form (idea) was regarded as divine and good, while matter or material was thought of as evil. Refined dualism states that there are two kinds of reality: material and immaterial; the physical world and the non-physical or spiritual world. Dualism as a worldview divides reality into two spheres: the secular, profane, or natural and the religious, sacred, or supernatural. It sees life as divided into two polarities, such as grace versus nature, church versus secular, soul versus body, spiritual versus material and theology versus philosophy.

This pagan Greek dualism was incorporated into medieval Christianity. The Christian scholars of the medieval period such as Augustine and Thomas Aquinas used Greek philosophy as a tool for interpreting and doing Christian theology. As a result, Greek philosophical influence turned Christianity, by and large, into a rational religion. Elements of this dualism can still be traced and identified in Christian theology and philosophy and therefore Christianity presents a view of life quite contrary to the holistic or organic biblical worldview. Missionary Christianity in Africa reflected this Western dualism and rationalism.

In some Western countries, one of the offshoots of Western dualism is the separation of church and state. As the state in the West has become increasingly secular, pluralist, and relativist, the sacred powers and influence of the church have increasingly been weakened. The secular state has taken centre stage, while the church has been relegated to the fringes of society. Over time, the role, status, and function of the state has become quite distinct from that of the church, partly as a result of the gradual change in worldviews and partly because of the immense corruption within the church when it was married to the state.

African worldviews, however, see life as holistic or organic, so dualistic interpretations of the Bible and the Christian worldview in Missionary Christianity gave Africans a wrong understanding of biblical teachings. Both the Bible and African beliefs regard the state and the church as one and the same. This Western view of the separation of church and state has huge socio-political and religious implications for Christianity in modern Africa. African Christians who have imbibed this Western conception find it very difficult to handle the relationship between the state and the church, especially where there is a dominant traditional or Islamic presence. This has weakened Christianity's influence on African society and has drastically weakened the ability of Christianity to act as an agent for transformation and social change. Other competing religions meanwhile, such as traditional religion and Islam, do not separate the state and religion, or faith and social life.

African scholars are very critical of the influence of Western culture and rationalism on Western Christianity. But the same criticism could be levied against African Christianity as some African scholars have also sought to use elements of African philosophy and culture (such as spiritualism) to interpret and do theology. In extreme cases, such cultural and philosophical interpretations of Christianity and theology lead to cultural and syncretistic Christianity.

What is syncretism?

> Syncretism is the process by which elements of one religion are assimilated into another religion resulting in a change in the fundamental tenets or nature of those religions. It is the union of two or more opposite beliefs, so that the synthesized form is a new thing. It is not always a total fusion, but may be a combination of separate segments that remain identifiable compartments . . . Syncretism of the Christian gospel occurs when critical or basic elements of the gospel are replaced by religious elements from the host culture. It often results from a tendency or attempt to undermine the uniqueness of the gospel as found in the Scriptures or the incarnate Son of God.[24]

Furthermore,

> Syncretism is usually associated with the process of communication. It can originate with either the sender or the receptor of the message. The sender may introduce syncretistic elements in a

---

24. S. R. Imbach in Elwell, *Concise Evangelical Dictionary*, 1062, http://mb-soft.com/believe/txc/syncreti.htm.

conscious attempt for relevance or by the presentation of a limited and distorted part of the message. It may happen unconsciously as the result of an inadequate or faulty grasp of the message. The receptor will interpret the message within the framework of his worldview. This may distort the data but fit his values . . . What is actually understood by words, symbols, or actions as expressed in creeds, or application to certain needs, is the test of the presence of syncretism. The receptor is the one who assigns meaning. It is therefore essential that the sender communicates with words or symbols that are not merely approximate equivalents, but dynamic equivalents of meaning . . . The communication of the gospel involves the transmission of a message with supra-cultural elements between a variety of cultures. This includes the disembodiment of the message from one cultural context and the re-embodiment of it in a different cultural context. . . . Cross-cultural communication of the gospel always involves at least three cultural contexts. The gospel message was originally given in a specific context. The receiver/sender assign meaning to that message in terms of his own context. The receptor seeks to understand the message within a third context.[25]

From these two broad definitions, it can be seen that syncretism can be both negative and positive. The positive is that it can deepen understanding and meaning. The negative aspect is that it can distort or change the meaning entirely. Although some scholars rule out syncretism as a problem, believing it is unavoidable as every form of interpretation or doing theology presupposes syncretistic elements, syncretism poses the problem that it may change the meaning of a belief, symbol, or ritual. Thus the meaning of some elements of the gospel of Christ may not reflect the truth of the gospel or the Bible.

The Influence of Secularism

Secularism has also profoundly affected Western society and Christianity and has great socio-political implications for Christianity in modern Africa.

Secularism is a philosophy that guarantees the autonomy of the state, society, institutions, individuals, fields of work, and powers from religion. It

---

25. S. R. Imbach in Elwell, 1062.

is the sociological process of the gradual removal of the influence of religion from both the state and society in order to create a religion-less state or society.

Secularism advocates that religion shall not interfere in the affairs of the society or state and that, likewise, the state shall not interfere in either personal or collective religious life. In other words, neither will dominate the other.

The Influence of Individualism and Human Rights

Because of the preoccupation of medieval thought with logic, metaphysics, law, and systematic theology, the study of the humanities was neglected until the fourteenth and fifteenth centuries. At that time, the Renaissance was simply a rebirth of interest in classical scholarship, and chiefly encouraged the study of the Greek and Latin writers of ancient times. This revival of scholarship was directed at those disciplines called the "humanities," especially languages, literature, poetry, history, and moral philosophy. Two fundamental beliefs emerged, namely, the claim to human autonomy; and the idea of human domination of nature through science and technology.[26] As a result the Renaissance gave birth to three philosophic concepts: humanism, individualism, and humankind's manipulation of non-human nature.

Humanism is

> the belief that human beings are autonomous. This means that human beings are their own source of meaning and authority . . . the authority of human beings is the final arbiter . . . human beings are regarded as actually creating their own nature. Man has the power to determine the very essence of his own being . . . In secular humanism, man is his own creator.[27]

Furthermore, humanism entails a commitment to the search for truth and morality through human means in support of human interests. In focusing on our capacity for self-determination, humanism rejects transcendental justifications, such as a dependence on faith, the supernatural, sacred texts, or religious creeds. Humanists endorse recognition of a universal morality based on the commonality of human nature.[28]

Humanism gave birth to the modern secular worldview: human autonomy. Freedom in humanism is "understood as the unlimited development of the

---

26. Jon Chapin, et al., *Introduction to a Christian Worldview*, 134.
27. Chapin, 131.
28. Wikipedia, https://en.wikipedia.org/wiki/Humanism.

human personality. The notion of human freedom is fundamental to the modern secular worldview."[29] Secular humanism or scientific humanism is based upon the belief in human autonomy, human self-creation, and human self-redemption.

Individualism is a moral, political, and social philosophy, which emphasizes individual liberty, the primary importance of the individual, and the "virtues of self-reliance" and "personal independence." Individualism embraces opposition to authority, and to all manner of controls over the individual, especially when exercised by the political state or "society." It is thus directly opposed to collectivism, which advocates subordination of the individual to the will of the society or community.[30]

The Renaissance also stimulated the desire in humankind to manipulate non-human nature. This gave rise to the philosophical doctrine of empiricism. Empiricism is the philosophical doctrine . . . of "testing" or "experimentation," and has taken on the more specific meaning that all human knowledge ultimately comes from the senses and from experience. Empiricism denies that humans have innate ideas or that anything is knowable without reference to experience. It is generally regarded as the heart of the modern scientific method, that present theories should be based on our observations of the world rather than on intuition or faith; that is, empirical research and a posteriori inductive reasoning rather than purely deductive logic.[31] The spirit of empirical science, which sees religion as a myth or superstition, has become quite dominant in Western society where religion is viewed as a relic of the primitive worldview.

During the eighteenth century, the Enlightenment thinkers also believed that any knowledge based on revelation was superfluous, deceptive, and dangerous to man. The spirit of this age exercised a great influence over many fields of culture, art, literature, politics, education, and also theology. "To be fully human was to be 'rational' in all fields of human life. By following the dictates of a reason unspoiled by faith, tradition, and dogma, true human fulfillment and happiness could be realized."[32]

The Enlightenment of the eighteenth century is usually referred to as the "Age of Reason." "The view of human reason as the source of all real knowledge became widespread . . . Autonomous human reason came increasingly to be

---

29. Chapin, *Introduction to a Christian Worldview*, 131.
30. Wikipedia, https://en.wikipedia.org/wiki/Individualism.
31. Wikipedia, https://en.wikipedia.org/wiki/Empiricism.
32. Chapin, *Introduction to a Christian Worldview*, 142.

seen as ushering in a new end of illumination. Vast hopes came to be vested in the power of reason to unlock the hidden truths of the world."[33]

During this time, the worship of human reason or rationality was placed above revelation, laws, and doctrines in religion. But Western scepticism and rebellion against Christianity has not discouraged the resurgence of religious beliefs in the non-Western world, where Hinduism, paganism and especially Islam thrive.

> Modern culture has developed in a distorted, lop-sided direction due to the exaggerated emphasis on scientific and technological control of nature, and unrestrained economic growth. The modern worldview has been reductionist in character: many of the rich and diverse possibilities for human cultural development which are rooted in the creation order have been stultified, due to the narrow preoccupation with material progress through science and technology. Divine norms for human life such as community and neighbourliness, ecological stewardship, social justice, artistic expression and so on, have been systematically violated.[34]

Even in the West, there was a reaction against the modern secularist and scientific worldview in the "counter-culture" and the romantic movements of the 1960s and 1970s. The abandoning of traditional morality and values, the rejection of the established authority and institutions, the emergence of the hippie-culture, rock music and the experimentation with alternative lifestyles and drugs, were just secularist protests and reactions against the scientific, rational, and humanist worldview.

These modern cultural protests and reactions, however, did not lead to a return to the Christian and biblical worldviews. Instead these secularization processes of Western society led to the rejection of anything Christian, biblical, supernatural or divine and led instead to the celebration of the age of human freedom and humanism, and later the emergence of neo-paganism, New Age Religions, cults, and hedonism.

Against this rich background of modern Western philosophies, how could the West understand the resurgent and vibrant forms and modes of Christianity in Africa and the non-Western world? The revival of religions and cultures in the non-Western world today debunks the secularist theories about society

---

33. Chapin, 140–141.
34. Chapin, 144.

and religion. Christianity, Islam and traditional religion reject the excesses of humanism, individualism and environmental degradation.

The Influence of Religious Pluralism and Cultural Relativism

The presentation of the gospel of Christ suffered a setback from the late 1950s to the 1970s on account of the debates arising from religious pluralism and cultural relativism.

In the West, cultural relativism and religious pluralism forced a paradigm shift. The West turned away from evangelizing other cultures or religions. The result is that it is no longer possible to present the teachings of Christianity, the Bible, the prophets, the apostles, Christian tradition, and especially the uniqueness of Jesus Christ to other religions and cultures.

What is religious pluralism? For pluralism to function and to be successful in defining the common good, all groups have to agree to a minimal consensus regarding shared values, which tie the different groups to society, and shared rules for conflict resolution between the groups.

The most important value is that of mutual respect and tolerance, so that different groups can coexist and interact without anyone being forced to assimilate to anyone else's position in conflicts that will naturally arise out of diverging interests and positions. These conflicts can only be resolved durably by dialogue which leads to compromise and to mutual understanding.

Religious pluralism is a loosely defined term concerning peaceful relations between different religions, and is used in a number of related ways:

- Religious pluralism describes "the worldview according to which one's own religion is not held to be the sole and exclusive source of truth," and thus recognizes "that at least some truths and true values exist in other religions."[35]
- Religious pluralism is used "sometimes as a synonym for ecumenism, i.e. the promotion of some level of unity, co-operation, and improved understanding between different religions or different denominations within a single religion."[36]

---

35. Wikipedia, https://en.wikipedia.org/wiki/Religious_pluralism, accessed 21 January 2020.

36. Wikipedia, https://en.wikipedia.org/wiki/Religious_pluralism, accessed 21 January 2020.

- Religious pluralism is sometimes used as a synonym for religious tolerance, which is a condition of peaceful co-existence between adherents of different religions or religious denominations.[37]

Extreme religious pluralists hold that no religion can claim to teach the only or absolute truth, arguing that religion is not literally the word of God, but rather is mankind's attempt to describe the word of God. Given man's finite and fallible nature, no religious text can absolutely describe God, or God's will, in absolute precision.[38]

These definitions are couched in Western thought and mean absolutely nothing to a militant religion such as the militant Islamist where, for example, you are either a Muslim or an infidel. You are either of *Dar al Islam* (house of Islam) or *Dar al Harb* (house of war).

However Dallas Willard asserts:

> Pluralism does not mean that everyone is equally right in what they think and do. It does not mean that we must agree with the views or adopt the practices of those of other persuasions. It does not mean that we must like those views or practices. It does not mean that we will not appropriately express our disagreement or dislike for other viewpoints. Pluralism also does not mean that we will not try, in respectful ways, to change the views or practices of others, by all appropriate means of persuasion, where we believe them to be mistaken. In fact, pluralism should, precisely, secure a social context in which full and free interchange of different views on life and reality can be conducted to the greatest advantage of all.[39]

Relativism is closely related to pluralism. It is the doctrine that ideas like knowledge, truth, and morality are relative. It is a denial of absolute truth which, taken to the extreme, leads to moral license and a denial of authority. Relativism expresses the view that the meaning and value of human beliefs and behaviours have no absolute reference. Relativists claim that humans understand and evaluate beliefs and behaviours only in terms of, for example, their historical and cultural context.[40]

---

37. Wikipedia, https://en.wikipedia.org/wiki/Religious_pluralism.
38. Wikipedia, https://en.wikipedia.org/wiki/Religious_pluralism.
39. Willard, "Being a Christian in a Pluralistic Society." http://www.dwillard.org/articles/individual/being-a-christian-in-a-pluralistic-society.
40. Wikipedia, https://en.wikipedia.org/wiki/Relativism.

The gospel of religious pluralism and cultural relativism is able to accommodate and accept non-Western religions and the rise of neo-paganism which are increasingly attracting people from the West. Westerners are turning in great numbers to the religions and cultures that Western ethnocentrism once abhorred and looked down upon. The world now faces the rise of Western non-religious global forces that have a profound influence upon Christianity and global society. The rebellion and scepticism make the West more vulnerable to the attacks of the resurgent militant religions such as Islam.

The Secular Global Civilizing Forces of the West

While Christianity is declining in the West, the West's modern civilizing forces continue to exert a powerful influence through advanced science and technology, democracy, capitalism, communications and transportation. Even though they had their roots in Christianity, these global forces have gained their independence and are now dominant across the globe. They no longer need Christianity and are ashamed to have been associated with it. Christianity is now seen as a relic that needs to be buried and forgotten.

Communication, transportation, consumerism, hedonism, humanism, democracy, freedom and rights are generating new global values that are fast displacing Christian values. Nations no longer need Christianity to become advanced scientifically, technologically, economically, and democratically. These forces are creating their own new cultures and religions.

The rise of these global civilizing forces in the West has threatened other cultures, civilizations and religions and has stirred up hostility and violence. Resurgent militant Islam is not only pitted against Christianity, but aims also to counteract the power and influence of these Western global civilizing forces. Western doctrines of human rights, democracy, the rule of law, religious freedom, and liberty are seen merely as the dictates and values of modern Western culture.

Post-Modernism and Religion in Western Society

Post-modernism stands as a challenge to Western culture, traditions, and Christianity. Charles Colson describes Western postmodernist mentality in the following words:

> Today's culture not only is post-Christian but also is rapidly becoming postmodernist, which means it is resistant not only to Christian truth claims but to any truth claims. Postmodernism

> rejects any notion of a universal, overarching truth and reduces all ideas to social constructions shaped by class, gender, and ethnicity... In postmodernism, there is no objective, universal truth; there is only the perspective of the group, whatever the group may be: African-Americans, women, gays, Hispanics, and the list goes on. In postmodernism, all viewpoints, all lifestyles, all beliefs and behaviors are regarded as equally valid.[41]

To this, B. H. Son adds that "life has no point. Nothing is sacred. Reverence is an unworthy relic of the past times; everything is a potential target for mockery. There are no honored models to shape behavior. The individual is alone and there are no route maps."[42]

Post-modernism is the birth of the "free human will." It has created a new "god." Humankind will determine everything and no one will submit to anyone, except self. The individual is an institution by itself, with itself and for itself. This means that everything that has been built in history, by an institution or authority must be dismantled, deconstructed, and reconstructed. Scepticism, narcissism and nihilism are the guiding principles.

Religion therefore has no real role to play in Western society but has been relegated to the shadows. Other global civilizing forces have displaced Christianity. "Technology and science are the most globalizing phenomena today along with market economy and the democratic system of government. And these form the core of modern life in almost every society in the world."[43] Dr Son goes on to describe this change:

> Unfortunately, however, the secularization process in the West has pushed the Christian faith as well as other related values also to the periphery. Art, literature, drama, music, etc., that have their origin in religious rites and enjoyed relatively high appreciation in the past, have all been pushed to the peripheries as luxuries of life, while money, physical force, political power, labour, and leisure have become the necessities of life and ascended to the center. The Enlightenment rationalism, development of natural science and technology, and the accompanying materialism and

---

41. Colson and Pearcey, *How Now Shall We Live?*, 23.
42. Son, "Cultural Relativism," 12.
43. Son, 12.

hedonism have deposed the faith that reigned on the cultural throne and usurped it.[44]

Although some thought that these global civilizing forces would replace religion and culture everywhere, it is happening only in the West. Religion and culture still occupy the centre of life and society in the non-Western world where the revival of Islam contrasts with the decline of Christianity in the West. What is it in our contemporary world that is driving the Muslim world and others into religious fundamentalism, militancy, violence, and terrorism? It is not religion as such which is declining, but Christianity and old Western ethnocentrism. The West is currently witnessing the rise of neo-paganism and the creation of a new post-modernist culture.

The Pagan Revival in the West
Soon after the counter-culture movements of the 1960s and 1970s, the West began to witness the revival of neo-paganism. When Western missionaries came to Africa with the gospel of Jesus Christ, Africans embraced Christianity and abandoned their pagan religions and practices. Today, African Christians see Westerners abandoning their Christianity and reviving those same pagan gods which their forefathers abandoned. Certainly, the pagan revival in the West is a great challenge to African Christianity.

Neo paganism and post modernism seek to answer questions such as: What lies beyond the grasp of science, technology, humanism, hedonism and materialism? What will replace Christianity and Western culture?

Western neo-pagan scholars prefer the extra-biblical and heretical literature of the early church, considering this more reliable than the Bible itself. Heretical and gnostic literature is more revered than the writings of the Apostles and the early church fathers. Christian teachings on topics such as marriage, male-female relationships, and authority have come under severe attack by neo-pagan theologians, homosexuals and feminists. Popular contemporary neo-pagan books are written in such a way as to discredit or ridicule Christianity, Jesus, the Apostles, and the early church fathers. Pagan books such as *The Da Vinci Code*, *The Expected One*, and *The Gospel of St Thomas* demonstrate the great influence of contemporary neo-paganism and its apologists in the West.

This new religion in the West is quite different from African Traditional Religion, older animism, or paganism. It is a modern religion born out of Western secularism, religious pluralism, cultural relativism, and post-

---

44. Son, 14–15.

modernism. Although it uses religious symbolism and spirituality, it is, in fact, a spiritual and cultural reaction to the Western scientific, technological, material, rational, hedonistic culture, as well as to the Christian approach to life. With its strong emphasis on individualism and human freedom, it is a return to simplistic humanism, self-intuition or insight, old fairy tales and folklores of pre-Christian Europe and North America, self-worship and nature worship. Neo-paganism also borrows freely from the spirituality of Eastern religions and animism as an alternative spirituality in protest against the Western secularist culture and the Christian faith and traditions.

Neo-paganism and the new age religions are propagated as the new spiritual and cultural liberators of the West. They provide the liberty to worship the free spirit of man, ancient folklores, and nature without any restraints or social guidelines. Yet, they are basically a search for inner human peace and harmony with nature.

Dennis Haack in his criticism of the book, *Drawing Down the Moon: Witches, Druids, Goddess-Worshippers, and Other Pagans in America Today*, written by Margot Adler (1979), has this to say:

> Adler gives us an in-depth, clearly written glimpse into a world of ritual, belief, and deep yearning for spirituality and personal meaning that for most of us is a world we know little or nothing about. "If you go far enough back," she writes, "all our ancestors practiced religions that had neither creeds nor dogmas, neither prophets nor holy books. These religions were based on the celebrations of the seasonal cycles of nature. They were based on what people did, as opposed to what people believed. It is these polytheistic religions of imminence that are being revived and re-created by Neo-Pagans today."[45]

Neopaganism, also known as contemporary paganism, describes a heterogeneous group of new religious movements, particularly those influenced by ancient, mainly pre-Christian and sometimes pre-Judaic religions. Often these are Indo-European in origin, but with a growing component inspired by other religions indigenous to Europe, such as Finno-Ugric, as well as those of other parts of the world. As the name implies, these religions are pagan in

---

45. Dennis Haack, "The Neo-Pagan Resurgence," 13, in *Critique* 4 (2005), https://ransomfellowship.org/wp-content/uploads/2016/10/Critique_2005_04.pdf.

nature, though their exact relationship to older forms of paganism is the source of much contention.[46]

Neopaganist beliefs and practices are extremely diverse. Some neopagans tend towards a syncretic melding of various religious practices, folk customs and ritual techniques. Reconstructionists, on the other hand, observe a specific historical religion to a degree that can border on historical reenactment. Still other neopagans practice a spirituality that is entirely modern in origin.[47]

In the USA, Wicca is the largest neopagan movement, and while itself heterogeneous, many adherents share a body of common precepts, including a reverence for nature or active ecology, goddess and/or horned god veneration, use of ancient mythologies, the belief in magic, and often the belief in reincarnation. Neopaganism may be defined as a "post-Christian" new religious movement (or, in the recent case of Judeo-Paganism, "post-Judaistic"), and is pronouncedly a modern phenomenon with its roots in early nineteenth-century Romanticism. Polytheistic or animistic traditions that survived into modern times relatively untouched by Christianity and Islam, like Shinto or Hinduism are not considered pagan nor neopagan. In some cases, notably in Icelandic Asatru, the revivalist movements may blend with surviving strains of pre-Christianization folklore. Other neopagans stress their connections with older forms of paganism in terms of an alleged "underground" continuity, but such claims are largely discredited.[48]

Neo-paganism in the West, then, must be understood within its socio-political context: (1) the fall of Western colonialism, ethnocentrism, and Christendom; (2) the influence of modern philosophies, such as secularism, cultural relativism, religious pluralism, and postmodernism; and (3) the rise of global civilizing forces, such as advanced science and technology, democracy, capitalism, communications, and transportation.

The forces of neo-paganism are not revival agents, as in Islam or Hinduism or African religions, but are deconstructionist and are bitter enemies of both Western culture and Christianity. They are essentially counter-culture or protest religions. Because Western Christianity has been dethroned, a religious vacuum has been created. Yet there is still an innate search for, and pursuit of purpose and meaning in life which haunts Western society. Individuals are searching for perfect human freedom, perfect expressions of humanism and hedonism, consumerism, materialism, and spirituality. They are looking for

---

46. Wikipedia, https://en.wikipedia.org/wiki/Modern_Paganism.
47. Wikipedia, https://en.wikipedia.org/wiki/Modern_Paganism.
48. Wikipedia, https://en.wikipedia.org/wiki/Modern_Paganism.

humane and friendly religions and lifestyles with humankind at the centre as gods or goddesses, religions that begin and end with humankind. They want to believe that there is no other authority, but themselves; no other sovereign, but themselves; no objective or external laws or constraints, but those created by humankind. There is no reference point outside their inner psyche. They are afraid that God is a male chauvinist, a racist, and an authoritarian. And so they are looking for a female god, or one who is both male and female, one who is non-racist, pluralist, relativist and postmodern. They are looking for simple, non-domineering gods that are very close to their own natures or, at least, close to the ones that their forebears once worshipped: the earth gods and goddesses, the polytheistic nature gods, Mother Earth. They do not want the chauvinistic and authoritarian God of the Christians and the Bible. They are not looking for the God who is out there beyond the heavens, aloof and out of touch with natural realities.

Certainly, Christianity still exists in the West but it is battling for survival. The state and society are in league and are ranged against Christianity; the forces of secularism, post-modernism, neo-paganism, hedonism, homosexuality, and materialism militate against Western culture and Christianity. The global civilizing forces are being used as carriers of its new gospel of neo-paganism and post-modernism.

This compounds the problem of the existing missionary legacy which has already left many social, theological, and ecclesiastical issues for the church in Africa to grapple with. We need to ask what our theological strategy should be both for the West facing neo-paganism and the decline of Christianity and also for Africa where Christianity is alive and vibrant and more and more people are becoming Christians.

2

Reactions to Missionary Christianity

By the 1950s Christianity had become a dominant religion alongside African Traditional Religion and Islam in Africa; by the late 1950s serious indigenous study into African Traditional Religion and its relationship with Christianity was beginning. It is very significant that African Christian theologians and scholars led this movement. Hitherto, the study of the traditional religion had been dominated by Western scholarship. Now African Christian scholarship applied new research methodologies, findings, interpretations, and applications to both Christianity and African Traditional Religion.

The primary focus of African Christian scholarship was the question of Western ethnocentrism, as expressed in slavery, colonialism, racism and Christian missions which had demeaned the African personality, culture and religion. As a result African scholars sought to deal with the twin issues of African identity and African freedom.

The quest for an African identity grew out of the experience of the liberated slaves in the Americas. Africans there or in the diasporas began to address the issue of identity, asking what it meant to be African within the context of slavery and racism in the white cultural hegemony. They addressed the issue of African identity through two social factors: culture and religion. These were the only means readily available to them whereby they could express themselves. They voiced their feelings in writings and songs, especially the Negro Spirituals. This movement culminated in *negritude* which had a profound influence on the early African scholars from Africa, especially those studying in the West who could identify with this quest for African identity.

The second issue of freedom from colonialism was gradually addressed by African nationalists. After the Berlin Conference in 1885, the African continent had been partitioned by the European nation-states. Western ethnocentrism and colonialism, however, sparked the issue of African independence and freedom and the African elites and nationalists of the 1940s and 1950s struggled through African culture and religion to make this a reality. Western education and Christianity played a role in these liberation struggles, as did the struggles of Africans in diaspora. The slaves had fought several wars in South America and the Caribbean in order to liberate themselves from their slave masters. Although Haiti in the Caribbean had become the first independent country for slaves from the diaspora, other liberation movements took place in the West Indies and along the northern coast of South America in Venezuela, Guyana and Brazil.

These quests for African identity and political freedom dominated the thinking and writings of African nationalists and scholars. Although they addressed the question of identity, another important question was not vigorously pursued: they neglected the question of what it meant to be a *free* African. They did not search for answers to questions such as: How should Africa be developed and transformed? How should independent Africa develop, transform, and organize its peoples, societies, and environment? What values and institutions should Africans adopt for better development and transformation? Issues of good leadership and good governance were ignored as a result of the overemphasis on the quest for African freedom and identity. As a result the independent African states failed to develop and transform their peoples and their environment because they did not have concrete agendas for development and transformation.

Meanwhile African scholarship focused largely on the African identity, ignoring issues of political freedom. In their attempts to rehabilitate the African personality, culture and religion after Western colonialism, slavery and racism, the ideologies of negritude, nationalism, and pan-Africanism were born.

The lack of scholarship and the lack of an ideology for development and transformation meant that neo-colonialism was able to entrench Western values and to stifle African indigenous values, creativity, and innovations through Western global civilizing forces, such as advanced science and technology, market economy and capitalism, democratic systems of government, and communications and transportation. Thus, unfortunately, the West dictated how Africa should be developed and how it should organize itself politically and economically.

This background is very important if we are to understand the reactions to Missionary Christianity in Africa. Missionary Christianity, of course, was also very Western. African expressions of Christianity, therefore, also had to grapple with it. Some protested against the forms, structures and culture which they believed were generally based on a derogatory definition of African personality, cultures, and religions. They felt these were influenced by the inferior socio-political role and status of Africans within Western colonial systems. Some African Christians broke away from Missionary Christianity on the grounds of culture, while others reacted to its doctrines. This meant that Christian instructions (the dos and don'ts with regard to teachings, practices, rituals and ceremonies) were rejected by some Africans who questioned the missionary teachings about polygamy, the use of drums and dancing, the drinking of beer, the eating of some meats and foods, and the wearing of certain clothing or paraphernalia. Intense conflict about these matters between some missionaries and Africans led to schisms and to the founding of independent African churches.[1] Interestingly, the proliferation of African independent churches in Southern Africa is much higher than in the rest of Africa as a result of Apartheid (forced separation of races based upon colour).

Africans argued that the Christianity that was brought to Africa by colonial masters, immigrants, or missionaries could hardly develop a relevant African understanding and interpretation of the Bible and Christianity. Neither, they complained, could the socio-political, cultural, and theological issues affecting Africans under the colonial rule be adequately addressed by Missionary Christianity.

Similar attitudes had been expressed already by colonial anthropologists who suggested that Christianity was not suitable or relevant to the African way of life. They argued that Christianity detribalized or denationalized Africans or that Christianity anglicized Africans, making them less African.[2] They also argued that Christianity and Western education were agents of cultural imperialism or destruction. F. D. Morel even suggested that Islam was better suited to the African way of life than Christianity.[3] These colonial anthropologists developed guiding tribal profiles – usually derogatory and repugnant – as to how the colonial masters should treat and handle the various African tribes.

Some Africans in diaspora (in the Americas) also reacted against Missionary Christianity, Western colonialism and cultural imperialism, rejecting racial theories of colour, intelligence, superiority and inferiority, as

---

1. Barrett, *Schism and Renewal*; Sundkler, *Bantu Prophets in South Africa*; Ndiokwere, *Prophecy and Revolution*; Omoni, "Colonial Policies."
2. Kingsley, *West African Studies*; Morel, *Nigeria*.
3. Morel, *Nigeria*, 230.

well as its classification of races, culture and civilization.[4] In reaction, Africans sought to promote "blackness" as a philosophy and to promote "Africanness" with its own culture, religion and personality.

Theologia Africana

The result of these attitudes was a quest for an African theology, a "post-missionary Christianity," distinct from that of Missionary Christianity – *Theologia Africana*.

Bediako observed that the question of African theological identity is "the key to understanding the concerns of Christian theology in modern Africa and in the Second Century AD."[5] He asserted that the primary agenda of modern African Theology must be "the meaning of the pre-Christian heritage as a prime concern." He stated, "There is no issue so crucial as the understanding of this heightened interest in the African pre-Christian religious tradition, if Africa's theologians are to be correctly interpreted and their achievement duly recognized."[6] This seems to suggest that he felt that Missionary Christianity had undermined African understandings and expressions of Christianity and that these needed to be rehabilitated.

Bediako's view was that African Theology should become "something of a dialogue between the African Christian scholar and the perennial religions and spiritualities of Africa."[7] Despite Bediako's suggestion that "the meaning of the pre-Christian heritage" should be a primary focus in doing theology in Africa, no comprehensive and well-defined African biblical and theological worldview has been developed. Not all African theologians and scholars saw the necessity of this dialogue. Byang H. Kato and other evangelicals preferred to place the emphasis on doing biblical theology in order to provide a good biblical theology for Africa. The debate was between biblical hermeneutics and cultural hermeneutics, not the engagement and interaction between the two.

Doing theology in Africa, therefore, was compounded by three major problems: the continuing pervasive presence of the African pre-Christian religious tradition which exerts a powerful influence over the lives of Africans; the powerful influence of Western culture, philosophies and forms of Western

---

4. Blyden, *Christianity, Islam and the Negro Race*, 1887; Curtin, "Scientific Racism"; Bolt, *Victorian Attitude to Race*.
5. Bediako, *Theology and Identity*, 1.
6. Bediako, 1.
7. Bediako, 1.

Christianity; and the need to choose an effective and relevant theological method. Any theology that can transform the African mind will have to go beyond dialogue to serious engagement and interaction between Christianity and African Traditional Religion.

The desire of African theologians and scholars to develop their own distinct African theology met with strong criticism from both Christian and non-Christian scholars. Christian scholars reflected their deep concerns about how this noble goal of developing African theology could be "achieved without injury to the integrity of the Gospel."[8] The fear of heresy and syncretism loomed very large. This was because the comparative methods and dialogue approaches sought to keep Christianity and African Traditional Religion equal, but distinct. It was not seen as necessary that they should engage or interact.

Non-Christians, p'Bitek[9] and Mazrui[10] also criticized African theology for "Christianizing African religious traditions."[11] They criticized Mbiti, Idowu and other pioneers for using Western philosophical and Christian thought to define and interpret African Traditional Religion and culture. They reasoned that the result of this work was at best syncretistic and not truly African. Because these scholars looked at Missionary Christianity in the same way as they looked at colonization, they may not have valued the transforming power of the gospel of Jesus Christ and the Bible, regarding it merely as bewitchment.

Bediako outlines the overriding focus, orientation and approach of the early pioneers of African theology:

> In my remarks on the early flowering of African theology in the decades of the 1960s and 1970s, I noted that the African theological quest then resolved itself into an "indigenization" of Christianity and the church which was achieved by a process of Christianization of the pre-Christian past. The process was as much about rehabilitating African identity as it was about affirming a Christian commitment. It is curious indeed that whilst that era of African theology was obviously seeking to achieve Christian ends, that is, the indigenization of the church, it seemed to be doing so with rather scant attention to what might be described as "areas of traditional Christian doctrine," which as Adrian Hastings

---

8. Tinou, *Theological Task*, 50–51.
9. p'Bitek, *African Religions in Western Scholarship*.
10. Mazrui, *Political Values*.
11. Bediako, *Theology and Identity*, 9–10.

commented in 1976, disappeared or were marginalized for not being "reflected in the African past."¹²

Commenting further on this era, Bediako states:

> Thus the task of theology in Africa has altered. The struggle for the indigenisation of the church by the Christianisation of the Christian heritage is past. Obviously this topic will continue to be discussed in some places and also written about, but as a trend in theological reflection, it is over. The African theology of the earlier era has had no small part to play in ensuring that the debate should now rage over the abiding relevance of the old religions in the transition to the new in Christianity. African Traditional Religion has been a serious preparation for the gospel in Africa and forms the major religious substratum for the idiom and existential experience of Christianity in African life.¹³

From the late 1950s to the 1970s, African theologians and scholars made great strides in researching and defining the nature of African Traditional Religion. In response to these questions of Christian identity, African freedom, and theology and also as to what to do with the pre-Christian African religious and cultural heritage in Africa, pioneering African theologians and scholars sought to correct Western notions in the following areas.¹⁴

Africans have an enduring history: Western scholars portrayed Africans as having no history. The historical works by Diop of Senegal, by the School of History of Ibadan University in Nigeria and by Fourah Bay College in Freetown, Sierra Leone stand in stark contrast to this assumption. Extensive research into ancient history has revealed that Africans had advanced civilizations and empires until they were eclipsed by Western slavery and colonialism in the seventeenth and eighteenth centuries.

Africans have dignity, worth, honour and identity: Western colonial masters and missionaries generally presented Africans as primitive, childish, racially inferior, and backward. The revival of African culture, the dignity of the African personality, and the beauty of blackness were promoted to uplift the profile and status of the black person.

Africans have civilized cultures, religions, traditions, and societies: The works of Western anthropologists defined African cultures, worldview, and

---

12. Bediako, *Christianity in Africa*, 82–83.
13. Bediako, 82–83.
14. Diop, *African Origin of Civilization*.

personality as primitive, inferior and backward. The promotion of the African philosophy of negritude and the African identity, personality, and culture became major themes that boosted African nationalism and Pan-Africanism in the late 1940s and the 1950s.

An African can be a scholar, a scientist, an administrator, a politician, and a theologian:[15] F. D. Gossett gave an extensive description of the portrayal of an African in social Darwinian scholarship.[16] The intelligence of the African was questioned and Africans were ranked at the bottom of the human civilization scale. On account of this and many other racial depictions of Africans, the quest to prove that Africans are a civilized people became the overriding "cultural agenda." Thus African theologians developed forms of theology that sought to be distinctively African. Africa demonstrated its criticisms of Missionary Christianity in research, writing and documentation.

In these, the missionary influence was criticized for its paternalistic nature and its Western cultural hegemony. The missionaries' typical indigenization philosophy of self-propagation, self-support, and self-governance was severely criticized as paternalistic. In reality, the missionary products in Africa had functioned in a parent-child relationship.[17] Furthermore, these indigenous leaders were not well-trained theologically or groomed in church administration and in relating the Christian faith and life to African culture, religion, and society. This meant that they were ill-prepared and ill-equipped to handle the rapid socio-cultural or political changes in Africa and were unable to confront the traditional and modern African mind with the gospel of Christ.

Because the missionary approach to Africa had generally denigrated and negated African religion and culture, it had not developed relevant theological and missiological principles of engagement and interaction with African Traditional Religion and culture. They had failed to develop a relevant biblical theology. African theologians and scholars responded to these apparent failures and weaknesses by developing and formulating their own African theology.[18] As a result, we have a variety of approaches, theologies and typologies.

The late 1960s and the 1970s then were devoted to addressing African theological problems and modern issues resulting from colonialism and Missionary Christianity. The primary focus was the development of an indigenous African theology. This was an attempt at understanding the essence

---

15. Irele, "African Scholar"; Turaki, *British Colonial Legacy*.
16. Gossett, *Race*.
17. Bediako, *Christianity in Africa*.
18. Boulaga, *Christianity without Fetishes*; Ela, *African Cry*, and *My Faith as an African*.

of Christianity and interpreting that understanding through the thought categories of Africans. Although it was accepted as crucial that Africans must develop their own indigenous theology, the primary focus was on correcting the mistakes of colonialism and Missionary Christianity. The focus of the pioneers, therefore, was on finding, defining, promoting, and defending the relics of traditional religion and culture and on rehabilitating or integrating these into Christianity.

They contributed immensely to renewed interest in African Traditional Religion, culture, and philosophy so that these were seen to be comparable to Christianity and Western theology and philosophy. African philosophy, culture, and worldview were established as "prolegomena" to understanding and interpreting Christianity and the Holy Scriptures in Africa. In fact, so much time was spent on identifying the African pre-Christian heritage or defining African identity that very little attention was paid to addressing and engaging the traditional African mind and the emerging modern African mind with the gospel of Christ. Neither the traditional mind nor the modern mind was thus renewed or transformed by biblical teachings and Christian theology.

The cultural agenda also did not focus on engagement and interaction between Christianity and African Traditional Religion, but instead focused on a descriptive-comparative analysis and dialogue. Most of the early pioneers of African theology (such as Harry Sawyerr, Bolaji Idowu, John S. Mbiti) were advocates of this approach, and it was their research findings and conclusions in comparative religions, cultural anthropology and philosophy that were used to develop an African theology. The need to formulate theological subjects, such as an African theology of marriage, worship, community, God, the Holy Spirit, Jesus Christ, and the church was strongly advocated.

The overriding emphasis of this approach seems to give credence to an assumption that the only "good" Christianity or theology for Africa was one that had been developed or formulated through the African culture and worldview. The goal was to make Christianity and theology more African and less Western. An indigenous African theology, then, was said to be one which was produced using African thought, religious, and cultural categories. It was a theology produced within context, reflecting the richness of the African pre-Christian heritage. These theological works seem to be motivated and guided more by the cultural agenda and the political ideology of the nationalist era than by the Bible. The pitfalls, snares and trappings in African theology are couched in cultural and political ideologies, so that the dangers of being less biblical and Christian can be glossed over and exaggerated and inflated interpretations and conclusions can be drawn. The religious and cultural sensitivities, as manifested in the works of some of these African scholars and theologians, did not allow for any serious evaluation, analysis, or criticism to ascertain their accuracy and their theological soundness in relation to the Bible. It did not allow for serious theological engagement and interaction between Christianity and African Traditional Religion. As a result this exercise did not always produce sound biblical and Christian guidelines.

Early Pioneers and Trends in African Theology

At this point it would be wise to stop and note the names and theories of pioneers who sought to provide a good definition and understanding of the nature of African Traditional Religion from the perspective of cultural anthropology.

The works of Edwin Smith, Edward Tylor, J. V. Taylor, Plecides Tempels, G. Parrinder and Benjamin C. Ray elevated African Traditional Religion to the level of a study discipline which had much to offer cultural anthropology. The approach used by these scholars can variously be called anthropological, sociological or scientific and their serious academic and scholarly research created a great deal of interest in African Traditional Religion.

Pioneering theologians and scholars then used this cultural anthropology to develop an African theology. The early works of Edward Blyden and much later the works of J. B. Danquah, Harry Sawyerr, E. W. Fashole-Luke, E. Bolaji Idowu and John S. Mbiti ushered in the era of the African voice and scholarship with regard to African Traditional Religion.

After the pioneers of African theology, a new crop of African scholars focused on how Africa should be developed and transformed. Questions of development, transformation, organization, education, society, institutions, leadership, and governance dominated theological research and discourse.

What follows is an outline of the major philosophy and thrust of each movement, its pioneers, its publications and its impact on the quest for an authentic African theology. We are using as the basis for our discussion the valuable work *Historical Context of Theological Discourse in Africa* by Valentin Dedji.

The Impact of the Negritude Movement

Edward W. Blyden was the father of "Negritude" (Blackness). Arising from Africa's struggle against Western cultural imperialism and racism, this movement sought to extol the virtues of black civilization by promoting the concepts of "Blackness" and of the "Negro personality." While Marcus

Garvey of the West Indies asserted his influence, the leading personalities in this movement were Leopold Sedar Senghor of Senegal, Franz Fanon of West Indies, Aime Cesaire and Julius Nyerere of Tanzania.

Dedji states, "Negritude asserts authenticity which eventually expresses itself as a radical negation: rejection of racial humiliation, rebellion against the rationality of domination, and revolt against the whole colonialist system."[19] Negritude became a revolutionary movement pitted against foreign domination: political, cultural and religious.

The movement took root among French-speaking Africans who debated the theme of Black African culture between 1945 and 1960. Significant achievements were made through the founding of *Société Africaine de Culture* (SAC) and *Présence Africaine* (1947) and Cheikh Anta Diop published his book *Nation Négre et Culture* in 1956. The Cultural Revolution triggered by negritude influenced church leaders such as Vincent Mulago, Alexis Kagame, Tharcisse Tshibangu, Robert Sartre, Meinrad Hebga and Engelbert Mveng. In 1956 about eleven black priests from Africa and the diaspora published *Des Pretres Noirs s'interrogent*, which dealt with the problem of inculturation. This publication can be regarded as the first manifesto of African Theology.[20]

The Impact of Placide Tempels

Father Placide Tempels published his book *La Philosophie Bantoue* (Bantu Philosophy) which greatly influenced young African theologians at the Faculty of Catholic Theology at Kinshasa in the Democratic Republic of the Congo. Catholic theologians, such as Tshibangu, Mulago, Kagame, Lufuluabo, Malula, Tchidimbo, Hebga, Sanon, and others including Mveng, Ngindu-Mushete, Eboussi Boulaga, Mudimbe, Ntabona, and Jean-Marc Ela, pioneered the theology of inculturation.

The major impact of Tempels's work in Bantu philosophy was that it showed the possibility of dialogue between cultures. Tempels saw "vital force" as the unifying notion underlying a Bantu cosmology, ethics, and ritual. He pointed out that the African quest for life, fertility (fatherhood and motherhood) and its yearning for communion with other beings were common to all other peoples.[21] Tempels's works provide the impetus to young African theologians

---

19. Dedji, *Historical Context of Theological Discourse in Africa*, 13.
20. Dedji. 14.
21. Dedji. 14.

wishing to explore how to relate Christian theological categories to African culture, religion, and worldview.

The Inadequacy of Adaptation

Roman Catholic priests developed a theology of "adaptation" that was merely Africanization or indigenization of some forms of Missionary Christianity. This concept was later seen as inadequate because it did not deal with the whole religious life of African civilization. It simply adapted some aspects of African worldviews to Western Christian views.[22]

The theology of "incarnation" then replaced "adaptation." Incarnation involved "immersing Christianity in African culture [so that] just as Jesus became man, so must Christianity become African."[23]

Dedji points out two events that were significant in ushering in theological debates on the continent of Africa: the founding of the Protestant All Africa Conference of Churches (AACC) in 1963 by the World Council of Churches (WCC) and the theological conferences hosted by the Catholic University at Kinshasa from 1954. Through the AACC, the Ecumenical Association of African Theologians (EAAT) was established. This proves the impact of negritude and Pan-Africanism within anglophone Africa.

Pan-Africanism had these objectives: "*unification* of all black people, commitment to the empowerment of black people and the liberation of black people."[24] Pan-Africanism gave "all people of African descent a sense of identity, self-determination and emancipation." It also "provided the relevant context for (Anglophone) African theologians to formulate theological constructs on Africanisation and liberation."[25] Dedji lists the following as the leading theologians of the anglophone group: John S. Mbiti, Jesse Mugambi and Zablon Nthamburi (Kenya); Charles Nyamiti and Laurenti Magesa (Tanzania); John Pobee, Kwesi Dickson, Peter Sarpong and Kwame Bediako (Ghana); Bolaji Idowu, Eugene Uzuku and Justin Ukpong (Nigeria); Harry Sawyerr (Sierra Leone); and Patrick Kalilombe (Malawi). Their works cover various theological themes, including the Bible, African religions, inculturation, liberation, ecumenism, Christology, ecclesiology.

---

22. Dedji, 15.
23. Dedji, 17.
24. Dedji, 19.
25. Dedji, 19.

Just as the Roman Catholic Church was uneasy about the theologies of adaptation and incarnation, so too the evangelicals were uneasy about the outcomes of the study of African religion by the pioneers who were mainly from the AACC and WCC. The World Evangelical Fellowship (WEF) established its Africa office as the Association of Evangelicals of Africa and Madagascar (AEAM) in Nairobi, Kenya, in the early 1960s. The evangelical contributions to the debate on African theology were led by Byang H. Kato of Nigeria, Samuel Odunaike of Nigeria, Tokunboh Adeyemo of Nigeria, Rene Daidanso of Chad, Isaac Zokoue of Central African Republic and Tite Tienou of Burkina Faso. They emphasized the centrality and primacy of the Bible, Christology and missions in doing theology in Africa.

Theological Discourse in South Africa

South Africa has the largest white population in Africa. In 1948 Afrikaners took power and imposed "Apartheid," a philosophy of "separate development" of the races. This meant that the whites, blacks and coloureds were not allowed to mix but were to develop separately. The Blacks were the hardest hit by these obnoxious policies. De Gruchy "identified five types of theology born in the struggle against Apartheid": (1) confessing, (2) black, (3) liberation, (4) womanist or feminist, and (5) prophetic or *kairos* theologies.[26]

*Confessing and prophetic/*kairos *theologies* expressed their concern as to whether faith and obedience lay behind the historic creeds and confessions which were expressed in particular situations. They urged that it was not enough for Christians just to confess their faith and creeds, they must also act upon them. For example, the Christian confession of justice or love must result in people showing acts of justice or love. Both Blacks and Whites in South Africa were called upon to act "now" (*kairos*) against the injustices of Apartheid in the light of their Christian faith and the confessions of their creeds. This movement in South Africa was greatly influenced by the works of the German theologians Karl Barth and Dietrich Bonhoeffer whose struggle against Nazism seemed to echo the struggle against Apartheid.

Black and liberation theologies were developed as the Blacks in South Africa reflected on the Israelite experience of slavery in Egypt and their great deliverance by Yahweh. They saw this as similar to the experience of the Blacks under Apartheid. Simeon Maimela defines Black theology as "a conscious and systematic theological reflection on black experience which is characterized

---

26. Dedji, 20.

by oppression and suffering in white racist societies in North America and South Africa."[27] The murder of Steve Biko in 1976 gave the Black Consciousness Movement (BCM) a radical political posture.

Dedji suggests that this movement had two phases. The first phase was from early 1970s to 1977 when it was banned by the Apartheid regime in South Africa. The movement sought to conscientize the Blacks to their oppressive situation and to translate that into political action for their liberation. The leading figures of the first movement of Black theology were Mans Buthelezi, Bongajalo Gaba, Mokgethi Motlhabi, Desmond Tutu, Allan Boesak and Simeon Maimela.[28]

The second phase of Black theology began in the early 1980s. The Institute for Contextual Theology (ICT) set up the Black Theology Task Force which used a Marxist analysis of the South African Society. This took the form of a race-analyst approach, a class-analyst approach and the middle-ground approach of holding race and class together in creative tension. *The Unquestionable Right to Be Free*, which was published in 1986, also included the feminist perspectives on women's issues. *A Journal of Black Theology in South Africa* regularly published the theological views of the era. Dedji listed the following as leading personalities: Itumeleng Mosala, Buti Tlhagale, Takatso Mofokeng and Frank Chikane.

African feminist/"womanist" theologies. The Ecumenical Association of Third World Theologians (EATWOT), established in 1976, gave women a theological voice during the fifth conference in New Delhi in 1981. Feminist theology was defined as: "a critical theology of liberation engaged in the reconstruction of theology and religion in the service of the transformation process, in the specificity of many contexts in which women live . . . feminism is concerned about a different consciousness, a radically transformed perspective which questions social, cultural, political and religious traditions and calls for structural change in all these spheres."[29]

Women's issues included, "the struggle for full and democratic rights for all, economic equality and the securing of women's rights in marriage, revised inheritance laws and the removal of violence against women."[30] These views were aired by the Circle of Concerned African Women Theologians in the face of African traditional culture which was regarded as oppressing women in the

---

27. Simeon Maimela, as quoted by Dedji, 23.
28. Dedji, 23.
29. Dedji, 26.
30. Dedji, 27.

African patriarchal society and male-dominated churches. The experience of women within these structures of oppression informed their understanding of Christology and theology in general, for instance presenting Jesus Christ as the liberator of both women and men.[31] Leading women theologians were Mercy Oduyoye, Elizabeth Amoah, Louise Tappa and Alice Walker.

The Association of Evangelicals in Africa (AEA), formerly AEAM, established the Pan African Women Association (PACWA) as an arm of the organization to deal with women's issues in both the church and African society. Rev Mrs Judith Mbugua of Kenya, Dr Mrs Mary Lar of Nigeria, Mrs Naomi Famonure of Nigeria, Mrs E. Chombo of Malawi, and Mrs E. Sanderson of Zimbabwe were among its leading personalities.

"Inculturation" and "liberation" themes. The Pan African Conference of Third World Theologians (EATWOT II) which was held in Accra, Ghana in 1977 brought together Protestants and Roman Catholics, Anglophone and Francophone theologians. At the conference different theological approaches were apparent: one admitted the inherent values in the traditional religions, seeing them as a preparation for the gospel; another promoted dialogue as a critical theology arising from contact with the Bible and from openness to African realities; and Black theology took the Black experience of oppression and the struggle for liberation in South Africa very seriously.[32]

Dedji identified two theological trends: "inculturation theology" which embraced both the Roman Catholic "incarnation" and the Protestant "indigenization" (Africanization), and "African liberation theology." He listed the following as key proponents of inculturation theology: John S. Mbiti, Harry Sawyerr, Bolaji E. Idowu, Kwesi Dickson, and Fashole-Luke. Proponents of liberation theology include Jean-Marc Ela, Engelbert Mveng, Laurenti Magesa. African women theologians include Mercy Oduyoye, Teresa Okure, Louise Tappa, Bette Ekanya, Therese Souza, Rosemary Edet, Rose Zoe-Obianga and others.[33]

The Moratorium Debate

This addressed the question of the continued presence of Christian missions in Africa. African political independence from its colonial masters encouraged

---

31. Dedji, 28.
32. Dedji, 30.
33. Dedji, 31.

Christians to reflect the same independence. This was a call for "missionaries [to] go home."

The AACC debated the issue of moratorium at two levels: the search for cultural authenticity (Africanization) and integration; and the quest for human development, dignity, justice, and peace. This led to the desire to halt external support, through both financial aid and personnel, to African churches from the West. It also called into question the Western theology of mission in Africa.

The Missionary Church in Africa had created denominationalism which posed a great problem for African Church unity, hence the need for some form of ecumenism. The call for a moratorium raised the following issues: the meaning of catholicity (the universality of the church); fellowship (the relationship between missions and Africans churches); liberation, and authenticity. How could Africans set about achieving these objectives without hurting the West?

The Theology of Reconstruction

The prognosis for contemporary socio-political issues in Africa was not good. Africa needed a new direction. In 1991 the AACC coined the concept of a "theology of reconstruction" at Mombasa, Kenya. Jose Chipenda, the then General Secretary of AACC, used the metaphor of "crossroads" to define both the era and the quest for a new direction: "African churches are at the crossroads between the promises of the future and problems with very grave implications."[34] Mugambi who helped to entrench this new direction defined the problem of the African Church and proffered solutions in reconstruction and social transformation. "Reconstruction was now applied not only to African countries and cultures ravished by colonization, but also to churches embedded in inappropriate socio-ecclesial structures and inadequate theological thinking. Reconstruction was therefore seen as a necessity for all African societies and churches."[35]

---

34. Dedji, 37.
35. Mugambi as quoted in Dedji, 38.

3

Approaches and Typologies of African Theology

With this awareness of the historical context of the theological discourse in Africa, we can move on to examine the various methodologies that African theologians and scholars have used in studying traditional religion and culture as well as some of the methods used in relating the Bible, the gospel of Christ and Christianity to traditional religion.

Indigenization

The indigenization principle dealt mainly with the cultural contextualization of Christianity. Christianity could be rejected on cultural grounds if it appeared more Western than African. Their desire for cultural expression was causing many Africans to reject Christianity so Western Missionary Christianity must be indigenized.

This became the rallying cry of some of the pioneering African theologians and scholars, especially from the late 1940s to the 1960s. Their primary objective was to strip Christianity in Africa of all its Western trappings and to replace them with what is African. These advocates strongly believed that the Christianity brought into Africa was shaped by Western culture and that African culture should replace Western culture. They also believed that Africans would understand Christianity much better if it were fully indigenized. The overriding interest of a cultural agenda tended to make the African theological exercise look more like a cultural replacement with African culture replacing the Western culture that had dominated Christianity on African soil.

African advocates believed that Christianity must be cast in new African constructs so as to remove its foreignness and strangeness. All categories of language and thought must be stripped of Western thought and replaced by

African thought categories. Christian worship in its mode, form, content, music, liturgy, prayers, and places of worship should be given African castings. This African theological movement of indigenization was strong during the late 1950s and the early 1960s, and the leading figure at that time was Professor E. Bolaji Idowu of Nigeria.[1]

The merit of this movement was that it highlighted the fact that Africans do not have to abandon their culture and become Western in outlook in order to embrace Christianity. All that is necessary is for Africans to embrace in faith Jesus the Messiah as their Lord and Saviour. In other words, only the "seed" of Christianity needed to be planted in African soil. When it germinated, it would grow into African Christianity.

Africanization

Closely related to the indigenization principle is the "Africanization" principle: mission and the church should be Africanized and controlled by Africans. Africans must be seen to be in charge. They must control the mission policies that affected their destiny. The focus here was mainly on personnel, administration and church structures. The cry was that more Africans needed to be trained so that they could take over the work from Western missionaries.

These twin ideas of indigenization and Africanization were motivated by the nationalist movements from the late 1940s to the early 1960s. The Trusteeship and Mandate doctrines of the League of Nations and later of the United Nations impressed upon colonial masters the need to prepare their colonies for independence and to hand over political power to nationals. The influence of these nationalist doctrines and the aspirations of Africans in the political realm made inroads into the church and mission circles in Africa. Political independence and the issues of "identity and theology" became the primary motivating factors. Africans in the church and on the mission field sought to have some measure of autonomy from Western control.

However, these twin movements did not in any way address the central and primary African theological problem. They merely focused upon cultural definitions of Christianity and on African participation in the Christianization process. Although Missionary Christianity decided in some cases to hand over the mission work and churches so that Africans could then be seen to be in charge, Africans were not necessarily in a position to create and produce an indigenous African theology. The Christian faith within the African context

---

1. Idowu, *Towards an Indigenous Church*.

needed to develop a relevant and biblical theology that could address African cultural, religious, and contextual questions.

Contextualization

Contextualization can mean many things. As a tool of doing theology in Africa, it focused principally on making the essence of Christianity relevant and understood within the African context.

The question arose as to what one should emphasize in pursuit of contextualization. Is it the context (Africa) or Christianity (a possible mixture of the gospel, Holy Scriptures and Western cultural Christianity) or the text (the gospel and the Holy Scriptures)? Some theologians seemed to emphasize the African context (Africa's worldview, culture, religion, traditional and social values, and institutions), while others emphasized the text. The theological task faced challenges brought by the impact of the pioneering cultural agenda and political ideology,[2] by the need to incorporate the pre-Christian African heritage,[3] and by the primary importance of biblical theology.[4]

In moving from the text to the context, it was essential that the essence of Christianity from the Holy Scriptures must be preserved and transmitted accurately even as one seeks to be relevant to the recipient context. If the text is obscure and difficult to understand, then the task of the theologian is to simplify it without losing its true meaning. If it is the context that poses a problem, then the context has to be studied and understood so as to determine what mode and form of the contents of the text should be transmitted and how this transmission should be undertaken.

It is therefore important to note that contextualization as a theological method is very complex. Whatever hinders understanding, whether from Western or African cultural baggage or from the biblical text, should be dealt with through the principles of biblical and cultural hermeneutics or interpretation. Sanneh emphasized the critical cultural factor in translation which affected both the receivers and the missionaries, as well as the "meaning" which emerged from the process of translation. Both "subjective" and "objective"

---

2. Sanneh, *Encountering the West*.
3. Bediako, *Theology and Identity*.
4. Kato, *Theological Pitfalls in Africa*.

factors operated.⁵ Bediako stressed the significance of the vernacular, the need to read or hear the Bible in one's mother tongue.⁶

This theological movement came to Africa in the early 1970s and dominated the 1980s and 1990s. However, the search for *Theologia Africana* or African theology and the application of these principles of contextualization has not as yet given us a final word. Instead it has highlighted the need for better theological methods.

Theologians have come up with different answers as to how we should apply contextualization:

Inculturation

Catholic theologians took inculturation very seriously. Through the Paulines Publishers based in Nairobi, Kenya, Catholic theologians published many research works in this area. These covered various aspects of Christian life: Christology, marriage, culture, religion, theology, mission, etc. The following statements were made:

> The Synod considers inculturation an urgent priority in the life of the particular Churches, for a firm rooting of the Gospel in Africa. It is a requirement for evangelization, a path towards full evangelization, and one of the greatest challenges for the Church on the Continent on the eve of the Third Millennium.⁷

> Through inculturation the Church makes the Gospel incarnate in different cultures and at the same time introduces peoples, together with their cultures, into her own community.⁸

> On the one hand the penetration of the Gospel into a given sociocultural milieu gives inner faithfulness to the spiritual qualities and gifts proper to each people . . . strengthens these qualities, perfects them and restores them in Christ. On the other hand, the Church assimilates these values, when they are compatible with the Gospel, to deepen understanding of Christ's message and give it more effective expression in the liturgy and

---

5. Sanneh, *Translating the Message.*
6. Bediako, *Christianity in Africa.*
7. Catholic Documents, *Church in Africa*, no. 58.
8. Catholic Documents, *Redemptoris Missio*, 52.

in the many different aspects of the life of the community of believers.⁹

This double movement in the work of inculturation thus expresses one of the component elements of the mystery of the incarnation.¹⁰

There were other theologians who emphasized that inculturation must reduce both the messenger and the message into communicable and understandable categories. They sought first of all to acculturate the gospel carriers into the receiving culture and context, and second to interpret the Scriptures and Christianity into the language and cultural categories of the receiving people. These two approaches were undertaken to ensure clearer understanding and interpretation. John Pobee advocates *skenosis*, which means, "the tabernacling of the Word in culture" (see John 1:14, "the Word became flesh and lived for a while among us"). This was a form of incarnational theology.¹¹

Biblical Theology

Biblical theology as forged by the evangelicals emphasized two principles, namely, the centrality and the inerrancy of the Bible as a tool for doing theology in Africa.

The major concern of Byang H. Kato, a leading figure in this approach, was "the use of sources other than the Scriptures as of equal standing with the revealed Word of God."¹² Kato advocated and promoted the centrality and inerrancy of the Bible, biblical theology and worldview as the prolegomena to the study of religions and cultures. He also sought to protect "the Absoluteness of the revelation of Jesus Christ" as revealed in the Bible from the ravages of universalism and "liberal theology." Kato defended and promoted the belief in the unique Christ for the salvation of the whole world.

In so doing, he was responding to the views of some liberal Western theologians who argued that "universal grace" is cosmic, embracing the entire humanity and that God alone can mediate this universal grace, through his universal Spirit or through his Cosmic Christ who is not necessarily the historical Christ. The unique Christ for salvation which Christianity

---

9. Catholic Documents, Vatican Council II, *Gaudium es Spes*, 58.
10. John Paul II, *Apostolic Exhortation Catechesi Tradendae*, 16 Oct. 1979, 1319.
11. Pobee, *West Africa*.
12. Dedji, *Reconstruction and Renewal*, 174.

preaches makes no sense. Liberal African theologians suggested that a plural and comparable salvation, similar to that in Christianity, could be found in traditional religions. The theology of African "intermediaries" asserted that God has mediators between himself and the Africans, thus affirming the plurality of salvation. For African theologians and scholars, the emphasis on the "universal grace" was focused within the African Traditional Religion itself and not in individuals, as Western universalism asserted.

The question of Jesus the Messiah being the only mediator of this universal grace is at the heart of Kato's theological discourse. Kato challenged the African theologians who accepted the liberal Western view in his doctoral dissertation (later published as *Theological Pitfalls in Africa*) at Dallas Theological Seminary. The liberal theological view was relatively new on the continent of Africa, so Kato used the term "incipient universalism." Dr Kato believed that this teaching did not originate from Africa but from the West and that it was just beginning to take root in Africa. He sought to maintain the purity of biblical theology and thus approached his works as an African Christian apologist against universalism and syncretism. His views on this universalism of salvation and grace were firm, assertive, direct, and authoritative.

Kato's arguments are picked up by Dr Ken Gnanakan: "But the question is to do with the availability of salvation directly through this grace and without the explicit work of Jesus Christ."[13] He then answered this question as follows:

> This grace is not available in religions because of their status as religions, but because of people to whom God wants to make his grace available. Wherever people are present, God's grace must also be present, particularly if grace is of God demonstrated despite sin. But this grace is not operative through religion, but wholly through Jesus Christ, towards whom God's grace must point.[14]

Because of his fierce criticism of the works of Professor E. Bolaji Idowu, Professor John S. Mbiti and other scholars of traditional religion, Kato was thought to be anti-African religion and culture. However, he also denounced and rejected the cultural imperialism and missionary paternalism of Western Christianity in Africa. Furthermore, he appreciated and promoted the study of African culture, religion and philosophy as prerequisites for the development and formulation of a biblically based theology and worldview, believing this

---

13. Gnanakan, *Pluralistic Predicament*, 210.
14. Gnanakan, 210.

would provide a means of addressing and evaluating African religions and cultures and facilitate the development of a sound, evangelical theological education for the training of African theologians, pastors and church leaders.

Beyond the debate of the possibility of salvation outside the church and Jesus Christ is the current emphasis on "gospel and culture." The focus of this approach is on the study of religion or culture and how the gospel relates to both. It does not deal with the questions of salvation per se, but with the translatability of the gospel of Christ. The gospel has to be made intelligible both by understanding and by communication and therefore it has to be made intelligible by expression and communication in a given cultural context.[15]

Critics of Kato fault him in this area. They argue that his attitude, style and application of the gospel of Christ to African Traditional Religion and culture were "biblicist," that he turned the Bible into an idol. He was also accused of advocating a discontinuity between Christianity and the African Traditional Religion and cultures and that his framework did not allow for "culturally rooted questions."[16] These assertions and many others totally misrepresent Kato's theological agenda for Africa.

While his opponents emphasized the use of traditional religion and culture as the basis for doing theology in Africa, for Kato the primary tool for doing theology was the Holy Bible and its inerrancy. He argued that the Holy Bible addresses and challenges the African Traditional Religion and cultures with its claims. He proposed a methodology of relating the gospel of Christ to traditional religion and culture and can only be faulted for being out of step with the popular methodology which was rooted in a cultural agenda and political ideology: he dared to challenge the liberal tendencies of African theology. He subscribed to a tradition which was very unpopular with the leading pioneers of African theology: one which came from the "evangelical wing" with a very strong background in American fundamentalism.

Kato had four major concerns: (1) the African cultural and religious revolutions and revivals which seemed to negate the gospel of Christ; (2) African nationalism and protests against Christianity as the "white man's" religion; (3) the fact that the majority of African Christians lacked sound biblical and theological understanding of the Holy Bible and Christianity in general; and (4) the dominance and influence of African religion and culture over African Christianity. He saw himself as leading a crusade against what

---
15. Bediako, *Theology and Identity*; Sanneh, *Encountering the West*.
16. Bediako, *Theology and Identity*.

most African theologians promoted on the continent of Africa. He foresaw the dangers of heresy, syncretism, and spiritism.

Unfortunately, Kato did not live long enough to take up the second theological task which he had set himself: a discussion on the relationship between the gospel and culture. Nonetheless many have hailed Kato as a great African theologian. Paul Bowers states:

> [Kato] was the first African evangelical to attempt to engage with the African intellectual world, to participate in the principle intellectual project of African Christianity in his day. And the first to provide a published contribution in that effort. For this alone he deserves exceptional credit, for this alone to be highly honoured amongst us. Indeed it is just this particular contribution, his challenge to intellectual engagement, that I want to single out.[17]

Bowers lists a number of others who have written about the immense contribution made by Kato to the development of African Christian Theology: George Foxall, Christiana Bremen, Tite Tienou, Tokunboh Adeyemo, Yusufu Turaki and Keith Ferdinando.[18]

Professor Kwame Bediako has taken up the mantle of Kato's second task, namely, the question of the "gospel and culture." His christocentric faith gives him the liberty to approach the pre-Christian religious heritage and to create a theological synthesis of the traditional religious worldview and the Christian worldview. Bediako believes that a Christian must hold to the primacy of the Bible and Jesus Christ in doing theology in Africa if he is to be faithful to the Christian faith. When liberal African scholars focus on African religion and culture as the means of achieving this, both religious and cultural agendas as motivating principles seem to relegate the Bible and its theology to the background.

Liberation Theology

The *Theory of Dependecia* was developed in Latin America in reaction to the underdevelopment of Latin America and the colonies by Europe and North America. The political and economic imbalance between the metropolitan countries (developed) and the provinces (underdeveloped) gave rise to political and economic theories of *dependecia* (dependency). The proponents of Liberation theology used Marxist analysis to expose political, economic,

---

17. Bowers, "Christian Intellectual Responsibilities in Modern Africa," 91.
18. Bowers, "Christian Intellectual Responsibilities."

theological, and cultural oppression, as well as class struggles in Latin America. Liberation theology became the emancipation tool.

Liberation theology had limited application in Africa, except in South Africa where racist apartheid was dominant and powerful. The rest of Africa was more preoccupied with cultural matters, emancipation, and the Africanization of Christianity. However, wars of liberation were fought in Algeria, South Africa, Angola, Mozambique, the Western Sahara, and Sudan.

Liberation theologians read the Bible, highlighting liberating and emancipation themes, predominantly the exodus experience of the Israelites under Egyptian slavery. Jesus was read as a revolutionary paradigm and model. These scholars focused on the oppressed needing a liberating theological tool in order to overthrow their oppressors or tyrants. Western theology and ecclesiology were seen as oppressive tools used to subjugate the non-Western world and needed to be replaced by liberation theology. This called for self-theological praxis: throw away anything foreign and replace it with your own. The outcome was the rejection of Western theology, ecclesiology and values.

Black Theology

Black theology was developed in the United States of America as a means of confronting slavery and racism between the late 1950s and the early 1970s. Led by James Cone, Robert Doetis and others, it became a theological tool for addressing racial discrimination, as well as the political, economic and cultural oppression of Blacks in America. Feminist theology and Black theology were quite similar in their aspirations as they were both concerned with defining the oppressors and the oppressed. They developed strategies of emancipation in order to fight oppression, discrimination, prejudice, bias, and differential treatment based upon colour, race, or gender.

The form of racism in the United States was quite similar to that of Apartheid in South Africa. However, Black theology as developed in South Africa focused more on raising the Black people's awareness of their oppression and their depressing socio-political and economic situation. It encouraged them to seek the ways and means to liberate themselves from the shackles of Apartheid. The Christian theology as propounded by the Afrikaner Dutch Reformed Church was rejected on the grounds that it was a racist theology that denied the basic Blacks in South Africa their human, cultural, political, and economic rights.[19]

---

19. Turaki, *The Future of South Africa*.

Feminist Theology

In similar vein, gender oppression of women as a distinct group over the centuries gave rise to Feminist theology. Christian theology has been diagnosed by Marxian analysts as a tool of oppression against both Blacks and women. Male chauvinism and male dominance have been challenged by Feminist theology, and women theologians are now rewriting theology so that it is gender sensitive and liberating for women.

Reconstruction and Renewal Theology

Valentin Dedji listed the following as proponents of the theology of reconstruction and renewal: Jesse Mugambi, Ka Mana, Kwame Bediako and Jean-Marc Ela.[20] Dedji states:

> During the 1960s and '70s, African Christian theology had emphasized "liberation" which was then necessary for extrication from colonial servitude, but the church had been relatively silent on the need for social transformation and reconstruction. Reconstruction was now applied not only to African countries and cultures ravished by colonization, but also to churches embedded in "inappropriate" socio-ecclesiastical structures and "inadequate" theological thinking. "Reconstruction" was therefore seen as a necessity for all African societies and churches.[21]

As a leader in the field, Mugambi, as quoted by Dedji, stated that reconstruction and renewal theology "endeavors to revitalize African traditional cultural values, myths and symbols in order to reconstruct them in symbiosis with the biblical message and to re-cast them to meet the needs of African churches and societies."[22] Mugambi calls this project re-mythologization. The "theologian thus engaged discerns new symbols and new metaphors in which to recast the central Message of the Gospel."[23]

Ka Mana's reconstruction and renewal theology states:

> What is fundamentally at stake in the theology of reconstruction in Africa is to train anti-crisis human beings who are equipped with new rational, ethical and spiritual principles. Therefore, the

---

20. Dedji, *Reconstruction and Renewal*.
21. Dedji, 38.
22. Dedji, 38.
23. Dedji, 45.

challenge is an urgency to engage in a double responsibility that is at the heart of the mission of churches for the renewal and the reconstruction of Africa: to re-evangelise the institutions and structures that determine the existence of our societies today, and to re-orient the framework of our imaginaire according to the fundamental exigencies of the human condition that the Word of God reveals and proposes.[24]

Reconstruction and renewal theology aims at addressing the tragic modern situations of African theology with regard to institutions, ecclesiology, political crises, social crises, economic crises, ethnic violence, tribal and racial conflict. It seeks to find, develop and apply a theology that can address these crises relevantly and effectively.

A Christian Worldview

The various theological approaches in Africa were all aimed at developing a coherent Christian understanding and interpretation of Christianity and the Holy Scriptures within the African context. Reformed theologians and philosophers, especially from South Africa, called for the development of a comprehensive "Christian worldview" for Africa.[25]

Van der Walt defines a worldview as "an integrated, interpretative set of confessional perspectives on reality which underlies, shapes and motivates and gives direction and meaning to human activity."[26] We see, understand and interpret our world and life in general from the perspective of our worldview. The Christian worldview seeks to emphasize a way of seeing, understanding, interpreting, and approaching the totality of human life from the perspective of Christian history and biblical principles and values. It is an attempt to develop a definite understanding of what Christianity and the Bible teach about all human activity and endeavours. In short, it relates the Christian faith to real life situations and to all human learning and art. A Christian biblical worldview is dynamic and subject to the contingencies of human life which challenge it, causing it to be deepened or weakened. The Holy Scriptures, the Holy Spirit, and the experience of the church in history are the "measure" of any theology or worldview produced in Africa. They are the constant source from which

---

24. Dedji, 93.
25. Van der Walt, *Liberating Message*.
26. Van der Walt, 39.

a Christian worldview can be developed, strengthened, renewed, motivated, and challenged.

The Holy Scriptures therefore also shed light onto our cultures and religions. African religion, tradition and culture are the indigenous building material or straw used in building up an African Christian worldview. But this worldview can only be credible and authentic if it is built under the authority of the Holy Scriptures and the guiding light of the Holy Spirit.

Christianity in Africa has "come of age"; it is no longer foreign, but indeed an African religion.[27] However, for Christianity to be authentic in Africa, there are many questions regarding its biblical foundations, its relevance, and its effectiveness in the midst of the many socio-cultural and political problems facing Africa. Christianity's continued influence on the continent of Africa depends very much upon its ability to address, adequately and effectively, not just the traditional but also the modern Africa. Africa today is replete with crises: economic, political, ethnic, racial, tribal, social, cultural, religious, and educational. This requires us to develop a comprehensive Christian worldview, or in the words of Paul G. Hiebert, a Holistic theology that "deals with all areas of life."[28]

Hiebert warns that there is a danger of returning "to a Christianized form of animism." This warning bell rings louder than ever in Africa today and the Christianization of the pre-Christian African religious heritage by African theology needs to be examined in the light of this warning. Tienou gave a similar warning, "But if the purpose of Christian theologizing on our continent is to revitalize traditional religion and validate it from the Bible, then this will not be acceptable to any person committed to God as He has revealed Himself in the Scriptures."[29]

Translating the Christian Message

Lamin Sanneh reasserted the primary importance of the translation principle in the transmission of the Christian faith. He states:

> That Christianity, from its origins, identified itself with the need to translate out of Aramaic and Hebrew and from that position came to exert a dual force in its historical development. One was

---

27. Sanneh, *Translating the Message*, and *Encountering the West*; Bediako, *Theology and Identity*.

28. Hiebert, *Anthropological Reflections*, 198.

29. Tienou, *Theological Task of the Church in Africa*, 28.

the resolve to relativize its Judaic roots, with the consequence that it promoted significant aspects of those roots. The other was to destigmatise Gentile culture and adopt that culture as a natural extension of the life of the new religion.[30]

The successful key is the vernacular translation. Sanneh emphasizes by stating that, "missionary adoption of the vernacular, therefore, was tantamount to adopting indigenous cultural criteria for the message, a piece of radical indigenization far greater than the standard portrayal of mission as Western cultural imperialism."[31]

Andrew Walls has contributed immensely to the work of establishing the vernacular as an important factor in the translation of Christian history.[32] Both he and Sanneh have shown the significance of the principle of translation in establishing a Christian missionary enterprise and also in providing a very powerful critique of secular criticism of Christianity.

The translation principle is a very powerful mission tool in Christian evangelization and in the planting of Christianity in various cultural settings around the world. As illustrated in the work by Sanneh and Wells, translation has contributed immensely to establishing the historical validity and the positive contribution of the mission enterprise to world Christianity. Furthermore, the translation principle has also affirmed and vindicated the status and identity of the recipients of the gospel around the world through their immense contributions to world Christianity. The translation principle is both a very powerful tool for transmitting the gospel, and for doing theology.

Bediako reminded us of the value of Africans reading the Scriptures in their mother tongues. This, too, he says, makes Christianity an African religion.

African Theology and Identity

Christianity, therefore, is not just the religion of the white man; it can also be an authentically African religion. As already suggested, Bediako is both the chief interpreter of African theology and an advocate for the "quest for African Christian identity, theology and integration."

> African theologians have set about demonstrating that the African religious experience and heritage were not illusory and they

---

30. Sanneh, *Translating the Message*, 1.
31. Sanneh, 3.
32. Walls, *Missionary Movement*.

should have formed the vehicle for conveying the Gospel verities to Africa . . . It was vital for the African's self-respect that this kind of rehabilitation of his religious heritage should take place.[33]

He goes on to add:

To the extent that African Theology's attempt at "rehabilitating Africa's rich cultural heritage and religious consciousness" has been made as a self-consciously Christian and theological effort, it can be said to have been an endeavour to demonstrate the true character of African Christian identity.[34]

There are serious concerns about the theological methods used and the output of African theology in these decades. Critics have observed the weakness in neglecting the primary mission agenda of the gospel, and the very high premium placed on the cultural and the ideological agenda. The discourse has seemed to elevate and exalt the historical, cultural tradition and the pre-Christian heritage above the biblical and doctrinal matters of Christianity. These should not be opposing extremes but complementary strengths, under the supreme and final authority of the Scriptures.

Those searching for a Christian identity must be aware that its roots lie in the motives of the cultural agenda and of political ideology, especially its "liberal theological roots." It is important that African Traditional Religion and culture be rescued from the caricature drawn by Western ethnocentrism, but in pursuing this we cannot afford to ignore the primacy and authority of Scriptures.

The quest to integrate the biblical data and the gospel of Christ with the pre-Christian heritage must take place under the overriding authority and the guiding light of the Bible and the Holy Spirit. Those doing theology in Africa must know Christian theology and doctrines and must be committed to the mission agenda of the church and the gospel of Christ. Tienou summed it up when he stressed the primary importance of the "biblical interpretation in Africa," "teaching and discipleship," that "the church must become the center for theological instruction and discussion" and our "basic motivation must be our obedience to our Lord and Savior, Jesus Christ."[35]

In a similar vein, Hiebert asserts:

---

33. Bediako, *Theology and Identity*, 2.
34. Bediako, 3.
35. Tienou, *Theological Task of the Church in Africa*, 50–51.

All theologies had to be tested against the Gospel as it had been revealed in Scripture and given to the apostles and elders. The test was made by the church and its leaders acting as a hermeneutical community. Paul checked his message with the apostles (Gal 2:2). The Jerusalem conference was an example of such a process.[36]

He continues:

Interpretation and application of Scripture in everyday life was not just a personal matter. Ultimately, the church as a whole acted as a hermeneutical community. Believers needed others to help them detect their personal biases, of which they themselves were often unaware, just as they needed others to help them see the sins they did not want to admit to themselves.[37]

The church in Africa needs to subject the theologies produced by Africans over the past few decades to critical biblical scrutiny. Commitment to faith and spirituality cannot be secondary. Theology is not just an academic exercise, but a reflection of practical faith expressed in a theological language. The task of theology is to strengthen, to edify and to build up the Christian faith, commitment, loyalty, and responsibility in the body of Christ, the church.

Historiography: The Imperative of Africans Telling Their Own Story

In their research into the history of Christianity in Africa, Ogbu Kalu and Diane Stinton emphasized the significance and the necessity of Africans telling their own story.[38] African church history, as seen from the perspective of outsiders, misses the input from the practitioners themselves. Missionary historiography of the origins and growth of Christianity in Africa has in most cases underplayed the vital role played by Africans in the process. During studies on the work of the Faith Mission Agency in the 1980s, I saw that the archival records of missionary itinerancy, evangelization, language studies, mission and church planting generally emphasized and recorded the activities of the white missionaries, while the vital role played by their African colleagues was not mentioned. On the other hand, in her doctoral dissertation on the work of SIM in Nigeria, Ruth Cox includes extensive interviews and studies

---

36. Hiebert, *Anthropological Reflections*, 95.
37. Hiebert, 100.
38. Kalu, *African Christianity*; Stinton, *Jesus of Africa*.

concerning the significant role played by Africans in planting Christianity in their home areas.[39]

Africans telling their own story about Christianity in Africa gives us their perspectives, rooted in their own understanding of Christianity. This reveals a variety of forms of Christianity depending on their locality and context, for Christianity is, after all, rooted in the diversity of the human race and geography. Nonetheless, all these localized expressions of Christianity must be subjected to the tests and standards of the church as a hermeneutical community.

The Prosperity Gospel: Wealth, Health and Miracles

The revival and resurgence of African cultures after independence in the 1960s has already led to the emergence of various new religious cults, neo-paganism and syncretism. Although Africa also has home-grown neo-paganism, religious cults and syncretism, Western neo-paganism and American Prosperity Pentecostalism are part of a new religious wave which entered Africa in the mid-1970s. This has serious theological implications for Christianity worldwide and especially for modern Africa.

Let me consider one of these, without intending to demean this group in any way. The American Prosperity Pentecostalism is rapidly eclipsing the older and more established Pentecostal church. Because of the global power of television and money, these American churches have also exported their ecclesiology, theology, worship, music, rituals and lifestyle to African city churches especially. Their theology can easily be adapted to suit traditional African religious beliefs and worldview. Their emphasis on prosperity, wealth, health, miracles, and wonders resonates with traditional African spirituality and social life. It also resonates with the African conception of spirit-power. It is very difficult for the older denominations to maintain their traditional forms of worship, music, rituals, and lifestyles in the wake of these new Western religious forces. African Christianity has to assess these new entrants and the impact of their teachings on Africans and African Christian theology.

As has already been stated, Western neo-colonialism has already conditioned, shaped and moulded the modern African mind. Western media has enlarged the African appetites and consumerism has inflamed African passions and pleasures into inordinate greed and lust. Western junk culture dominates the youth and feeds the minds of the wretched poor. The "higher culture" becomes the fascination of the elites. Africa's overwhelming orientation

---

39. Cox, "The Lord's Work."

is towards the West. Market economy and democracy are the bait set to trap the politicians and the rich. The African is bombarded with that which destroys not only the African identity and freedom, but even African Christianity.

The African traditional religious worldview and spirituality provided the religious foundations through which Christianity was understood and accepted. Christianity in Africa reflects the way Africans generally see, understand and interpret. This, however, enables Africans to create new forms and expressions of Christianity and Christianization. This will be different from that of other cultures and regions of the world. However, not every form of Christian expression is authentic, biblical, or even culturally relevant in an African setting. Not every theological experiment, teaching and model is sound. The believing Christian community has the duty of ascertaining what is acceptable and what is not. Every cultural understanding, interpretation and expression is not necessarily valid. These too have to be authenticated by the believing Christian community.

By being true to itself and to its spiritual understanding of the Scriptures and apostolic Christianity, the believing Christian community must set guidelines. Only sound biblical hermeneutics, exegesis, and theological methods can help guard against the errors, heresies and syncretism which could lead to the emergence of new cults and neo-paganism.

4

African Theological Issues

Western ethnocentric caricatures of traditional religion and culture evoked reaction and response, especially from the pioneering African theologians and scholars. Western terminologies, such as "primitive, savage, native, tribe, paganism, heathenism, fetishism, animism, idolatry, juju, mana, vital force, ancestor worship" were usually rejected by Africans.[1] These terms served simply to heighten controversies over the nature, form and status of African Traditional Religion and culture.[2]

The early pioneers of African theology, such as J. B. Danquah of Ghana, E. Bolaji Idowu of Nigeria and John S. Mbiti of Kenya, set out to prove that Africans worship "One God." They interpreted African religion in "monotheistic" terms and integrated the African religious past with Christianity.[3]

Different scholars have emphasized different things in the study of African Traditional Religion. For example, Laurenti Magesa seeks to capture the morality of traditional religion: "The promotion of life is the criterion of African morality. This is life in its fullness, the mystique of life."[4] Magesa uses this theme to analyze the transmission of the life force, the enemies of life, the restoration of the force of life, and the political ethics of Africa.

As is evident from the bibliography, many scholars have contributed to this discussion on the religious, anthropological, cultural and theological issues prevalent in African Christianity. Included in the bibliography are the works of those who pioneered African studies in these areas. Not all of the important theological issues which these African scholars sought to address can be discussed here; some will only be mentioned in passing and none will

---

1. Westerlund, *African Religion*, 28.
2. Cole, "Christian and African."
3. Ray, *African Religions*.
4. Magesa, *African Religion*, 8.

be discussed exhaustively. Nonetheless we must note the theological issues that endure and these will form the background for our discussion.

The Knowledge of God

African perceptions of God are rooted in the theological concept of revelation. Those who did not have a clear understanding of revelation in theology assumed that Africans did not have a concept of God. The early pioneers of African theology did extensive research to prove them wrong.

Generally speaking, human beings have an innate perception of the existence of God. For example, human beings are able to deduce from nature the possible existence of God. Classical theologians and philosophers also came up with an idea of God based on reason and logic. Therefore, a general knowledge of the existence of God is available to all human beings.

African theologians and scholars recorded that the African understanding of God was based on their belief in the existence of God as the creator of all things. Africans acknowledged that his attributes of purity, infinity, eternity, immutability, omnipresence, sovereignty, and providence set him above humans. And, the evidence shows, Africans accepted humankind's dependence on God as the provider of all good things including rain, many children, prosperity, health, and long life.[5] It is clear that some of the attributes of God in traditional religion are anthropomorphic or metaphorical. God is being described in human terms or forms and not necessarily from God's self-disclosure. Religion was viewed as a human phenomenon and the study of African Traditional Religion focused primarily on its religious beliefs, practices, rituals, ceremonies, and rituals.

The African perception enables people to define God theologically as the universal God of every human race, tribe, language, or nation. God as one creator established the solidarity and universality of all humanity and the universe. This theological approach, therefore, regards the god of African Traditional Religion as the same as the Lord Yahweh, the God of Abraham, Isaac and Jacob, of the Hebrew religion in the Bible. It suggests we do not have multiple creators or gods, but one sovereign Lord of the universe. The biblical phrase, "Nevertheless He did not leave Himself without witness" (Acts 14:17a NKJV) is still often quoted to prove the universality of God, his creative activities, presence, and revelation in the African Traditional Religion.

---

5. Nyirongo, *Gods of Africa*.

The early pioneers of African theology were very comfortable with this religion of creation theology because it was rooted in general theology which was common to all humanity. But they were uncomfortable with redemption theology as it is rooted in God's revelation of Jesus Christ. The revelation of God in Jesus Christ rivals the revelation of God in the ancestors. It is hard for Africans to give up their ancestors for Jesus Christ and to identify with the observation that Jesus Christ takes the place of ancestors.[6]

However, general revelation does not carry with it any salvific quality with regard to the fall of mankind into sin. Salvation is only found in special revelation. The correct biblical concept of God is that he is both creator and redeemer. Both these attributes of God must be reflected in our African theological discourse. Yet, the emphasis of African theology on the theology of universal creation was not balanced by an emphasis on the biblical theology of the fall, sin and redemption. Very little, if any, attention has ever been given to the concept of God as redeemer or to the revelation that the fall of man and creation altered God's creation and that God's attribute of love necessitated the use of his redemptive power and authority over his entire creation, as is shown in Jesus Christ and his redemptive work on the cross.

Human experiences are, of course, valid and have value within general revelation and human self-experience. They can be "the schoolmaster" (Gal 3:24 KJV) that leads to a salvific experience of Jesus Christ. However, only specific revelation fulfils the short-comings of general revelation. Just as Jesus Christ fulfils all the Old Testament prophecies and promises and the Jewish religious sacrifices and festivals (as explained in the book of Hebrews), he also fulfils African traditional expectations, African hopes and African religious sacrifices and festivals. The Hebraic model which related the gospel of Jesus Christ to Judaism can also be used to relate the gospel of Jesus Christ to African Traditional Religion.

On close examination of the recorded religious beliefs, practices, and behaviour of traditional Africans, one has to wonder whether their "evidences" are God's revelation of himself, his self-disclosure, or whether they are humankind's inventions or projections. Do Africans in their traditional religions derive knowledge of God through revelation or through human intuition, perception, or self-understanding?

Further questions also arise: What is the content of this knowledge of God? In what ways do Africans respond to this knowledge? Although the traditional concepts and attributes of God as stated by the African pioneering theologians

---

6. Nyamiti, *Christ as Our Ancestor*.

and scholars are comparable to those of Christianity and other religions, it is clear that in traditional religious thought, the meanings and import of these terms has to be measured by the traditional religious system itself. They cannot be interpreted using Christian theological categories, for then they will lose their traditional meanings and authenticity. Some of the early pioneers of African theology did just that: they tried to use Christian theological categories to formulate and interpret the traditional concepts and attributes of God. Their conclusions usually differed from those formulated from the traditional African point of view. African theology has been criticized on this score by scholars such as Okot p'Bitek and Ali Mazrui, as already mentioned.

Salvation

Creation theology raised a crucial theological issue when it suggested that the Christian and biblical concept of salvation in Jesus the Messiah is also found in the African Traditional Religion. Is this not reading too much of Christianity into the traditional religion?

This theology suggests that God has equally important "intermediaries" or "mediators" like Jesus in Christianity between himself and humankind in the traditional religion. But are the intermediaries or mediators in the traditional religion of special revelation? Has God revealed himself in the ancestor(s)? If indeed God has instituted a valid and authentic means of salvation and intermediaries in the traditional religion, then the logical conclusion is that Africans have no need of the Christian and biblical offer of salvation and mediation through Jesus the Messiah.

It is important to state at this point that the traditional religious system does have its own definition of salvation and what it takes to obtain such a salvation, although religions differ in their claims.

The most important theological issue in this concept of salvation in African theology, however, is the *equality of all religions*. Some African theologians and scholars assert that salvation is not the exclusive reserve of Christianity, but that it is possible to find salvation outside the church and Jesus Christ. This view is ultimately informed by the modern philosophies of religious pluralism or parity of all religions and is deeply rooted in creation theology based upon general revelation. The suggestion of parity between the traditional religions and Christianity means the Christian concept of salvation is interpreted as "of another kind," which must be held as equal to the one found in the traditional concept of salvation. This is an acceptance of *universal grace without Jesus Christ* or the *universalism of salvation without Christ*.

The suggestion is that "universal grace" within traditional religions simply refers to God's general creation and dealings with all humanity. For example, God's gift of the sun, air, water and so forth is for all humanity. Jesus Christ in this conception is not necessarily the cause and effect of this "universal grace," but God alone, who is the Father of not only humanity in general (individuals) but also of the religions and cultures of all peoples in the world. All these arguments are rooted in creation theology and general revelation alone.

Ken Gnanakan states the issue: "But the question is to do with the availability of salvation directly through this grace and without the explicit work of Jesus Christ."[7] He explains:

> This grace is not available in religions because of their status as religions, but because of people whom God wants to make his grace available. Wherever people are present, God's grace must also be present, particularly if grace of God is demonstrated despite sin. But this grace is not operative *through religion*, but wholly *through Jesus Christ*, towards whom God's grace must point.[8]

We can understand why some theologians and scholars present one type of theology against the other. The theological concepts of salvation and worship as propounded by some African theologians and scholars are generally based only on the theological understanding of God as creator. Adeyemo in *Salvation in African Tradition* gives a Christian response to such views.

The major emphasis of salvation in Jesus Christ is eternal life; salvation means obtaining eternal life. Yet, in Christianity, eternal life can never be earned; it is a gift of God through Jesus Christ. There is no such quest for eternal life in traditional religion. Research reveals that the traditional African quest is for the immortal name. A person seeks to have his or her name immortalized through some action, such as "good deeds." (Laurenti Magesa differs from this understanding and stresses the African quest is for "life force." Others say that this is the quest for "well-being.")

Because creation theology chronologically precedes redemption theology, Christianity can still propagate its claims of salvation in Jesus Christ alone to Africans. In the garden of Eden, sin brought about death and loss of life and altered God's relationship with humankind and creation. Humans cannot talk about salvation and worship of God as if nothing has happened between them

---

7. Gnanakan, *Pluralistic Predicament*, 210.
8. Gnanakan, 210.

and God in history. Salvation and worship are rooted in both the redemptive power of God's response to sin, which has been revealed both in creation and in the cross of Christ. If we accept a plurality of means of salvation offered by one God, then God is being misrepresented or misinterpreted. God cannot offer two equally valid means of salvation or two valid and equal truths. This would suggest we are confused about God's eternal attribute of being eternally true and the unique Christ for salvation as claimed by Christians seems to make no sense.

This theological confusion will be resolved when we have a proper understanding of the human sources of knowledge. Human beings acquire knowledge through their common sense and through the use of reason and senses. Knowledge can also be revealed by the spirit beings and, of course, revelation knowledge of God is revealed by God. Many scholars discuss religious ideas without stating their sources despite the fact that this leads to confusion.

Pre-Christian Religious Heritage

The African pre-Christian religious heritage is African Traditional Religion. But how does the gospel of Jesus Christ relate to this traditional religion? Is it in the same way the gospel of Christ related to Judaism or the Old Testament?

The fundamental issue here is whether there is a continuity or discontinuity between traditional religion and culture and Christianity. The opinions of African theologians and scholars differ remarkably in this area and it has featured prominently in the African theological discourse. These differences reflect their theological traditions, persuasions, and methodologies. Some see continuity, while others see discontinuity, depending upon what they mean by continuity or discontinuity. The discontinuity model asserts that "the Christian faith possessed its own set of beliefs distinct from the belief system of traditional religion; accordingly, to accept the former was to reject the latter."[9] The continuity model asserts that the traditional religious heritage is preparatory to the acceptance of the Christian. Some theologians and scholars hold to both continuity and discontinuity. They believe that there are some elements in traditional religion that continue in Christianity and some that discontinue.

Scholars who take a continuity view of the gospel of Christ have two views on the relationship between Christianity and the pre-Christian African

---

9. Bediako, *Christianity in Africa*, 69.

heritage. Some hold to the view that continuity between the pre-Christian African heritage and Christianity makes the continued presentation and proclamation of the unique Christ for salvation unnecessary in Africa. That which is comparable in the traditional religion can replace the gospel of Christ and the Bible, because what Christianity has and offers as salvation is already present in the traditional religion. In this case, the real theological issue is not that of continuity but of the equality of all religions, as we noted in the previous section.

The other view of continuity, asserted by Bediako, holds that the pre-Christian African heritage is preparatory to the gospel. Traditional Africans have a religious worldview and a religious language, which provide a "pre-understanding" or "self-understanding." This provides the basis of religious discourse and dialogue between traditional Africans and Christianity. The Christian gospel is understood from this "pre-knowledge." This view of continuity suggests neither comparative religions nor religious pluralism. It implies a religious pre-understanding through language, knowledge and "spirituality" without which no meaningful theological discourse and dialogue could take place between the two religions. The continuity of the traditional religious spirituality and the Christian religious spirituality promotes understanding.[10]

However, Bediako asserts that both the pre-Christian African heritage and Christianity must submit their spirituality and theology to the ultimate authority of the Bible and the Holy Spirit. The real theological issue is not so much one of continuity or discontinuity, but the need to accept the authority and lordship of Jesus Christ and his Word over both religious worldviews (old and new). Christ does not negate our past or our background, but he redeems, transforms and fulfils it. When we use our pre-Christian religious heritage material for doing African theology, this theological process must be brought under the guiding light of the Holy Spirit, the Word of God and the wisdom of God. This will enable us to see both what is good and what is evil. We will retain what agrees with the Bible and keep out what contradicts the teachings of the Bible. If the Word of God is the standard, we cannot compromise or reject any of its truth. The underlying theological quest in this area is the "need to discover all that the Bible is saying in order to come to grips with the widest

---

10. Shorter, *Dialogue with African*; Kibicho, "Continuity of the African"; Bediako, *Christianity in Africa*.

circle of God's dealings with humankind in his redemptive plans to establish his Kingdom."[11]

As always, the problem is a result of a lack of clear definition and understanding of the difference between general and special revelation in Jesus Christ. The prophets and the Old Testament prophesied the coming of Jesus Christ. When he came, Jesus said that he had not come to destroy prophecy, but to fulfil it. The arguments about continuity or discontinuity did not arise as Jesus did not negate religion or culture, but offered something better. Instead of destroying or eradicating the religion or culture, he renewed and transformed them. The book of Hebrews gives an excellent model of how the gospel of Christ related to Judaism and the Old Testament and the same principles can be used to address or relate the gospel of Jesus Christ to traditional religion. The gospel of Jesus Christ and the Bible as special revelations of God address the entire realm of African Traditional Religion and culture. What has been transformed by Jesus Christ and his gospel replaces that which is old, just as the old covenant was replaced by our Lord's new covenant when he came. The good needs to be renewed or transformed. Bad elements must go.

The next debate relates to which elements in traditional religion and culture should be retained and which should go. Much of this debate is a reaction to the general negation of African culture and the demeaning of traditional religion. The entire corpus of traditional religion and its cultic practices cannot be demeaned or held in low esteem just because they stand in creation theology and general revelation, like all other religions in the world. To describe one religion as higher and the other as lower, or one civilized and the other primitive is a reflection of ethnocentrism arising from a lack of understanding and knowledge. Christians believe that, after the fall and especially after the events at the Tower of Babel in Genesis 11, all human religion and culture are in a fallen state and stand in need of renewal, regeneration, recreation, redemption, and transformation.

Cultural and Ideological Agenda

We have seen that during the pioneering era of African theology, the greatest motivating factors for doing indigenous theology in Africa were the cultural and the political factors: the quest for African identity and African freedom.

As a result of this dominant pursuit, primary theological issues of missions, doctrinal matters, biblical interpretations, and theology were relegated to the

---

11. Gnanakan, *Pluralistic Predicament*, 222–223.

background. Much still needs to be done in order to answer questions like these: What is the primary mission of the church in Africa? What dominant and primary theological issues should engage African theologians and scholars? How does African theology address the traditional mind and modern African realities?

However, if meaningful change, renewal, and transformation are to take place in Africa, we have to begin by revisiting the issue of education. The colonial model of education and its product of colonial mentality, culture, and worldview oriented Africans away from African realities. In consequence, Africans look outward to the West and copy wholesale Western values, hypothesis, models, and assumptions of socio-political and economic development. When Africans failed to formulate a theology of development and transformation, this meant that post-colonial Africa was driven by the ideology of Western neo-colonialism with devastating consequences for African societies and nations.

This does not mean that Africans are not well educated or that they lack natural resources or the expertise of social scientists; there is simply a lack of vision for society and for how to organize themselves. There is a lack of knowledge about the potential and creative use of land on the one hand, and the potential and creative use of labour on the other. The secret of a viable society lies in the innovative use of both. If education does not lead to this, such education is misplaced. However, colonial education taught conformity, not innovation, creativity, renewal, and transformation. It aimed to maintain colonial institutions, structures, and values. But Africans need to know what to do with God-given land and their environment: how to develop it and use it to create a new society and a new nation. They also needed to know about the strength of God-given labour in man and how to develop labour skills that could transform their land, environment, society, and nation and how to use these to enhance the quality of human life.

This is what was missing in the quest for African identity, African freedom and subsequently African theology. There was no theology of development and transformation of Africa although we needed to transform the land, the environment, and our labour. The African person and African society needed to be transformed.

In Genesis it is recorded that God prepared the uninhabited land and made it good for man to dwell in. The garden of Eden was given to humans as a gift. When they lost it as a result of the fall and sin, God still promised humankind land through Abraham. Land, therefore, occupies a prominent place in the life of humankind here on earth. We have failed as Africans because we did not study the Bible in depth and draw out basic principles for building this land, this labour (human and mechanical skills), and the human person (enhancing the quality of human life).

Two theological concepts are important in our consideration of this subject: *imago Dei* (image of God) and *dominium* (man as maker and cultivator).

Imago Dei is a biblical concept which indicates both humanity's relation to God and also the relation of humanity to the non-human creation. Because they are created in God's image, human beings should live in the community of man and woman, brother and sister, in families, "tribes," and peoples and nations.

> As God's image, humanity is to rule with care over the non-human creation (land) and in this way share in the preservation of earthly creation and further its development. Humankind as a whole has been created in God's image without distinction of sex, class or race.[12]

Dominium speaks of the responsibility of humanity towards the non-human creation (land) and has two aspects: humanity as the maker (*homo faber*) and also humanity as the cultivator.[13] This covers labour and the development of human skills, including mechanical skills. As an intelligent being created in the image of God, man can use his intelligence to become innovative, enhancing his labour and augmenting his skills through mechanical means. Where manual labour is limited because it depends upon human or animal strength, mechanical inventions go beyond labour. They are the innovations and creativity of labour. Technology is, therefore, a substitute for human labour.

Africans need to abandon the mentality of conformity and maintenance education, of walking in the white man's shoes and of the blind and uncritical assimilation of Western models of socio-political and economic development. We need to go back to the basics – to the land and labour. These simple principles in the Bible can be used by Africans to create viable and sustainable societies.

Theological Methodology

We have observed that the approaches, attitudes, and methodologies of African theologians and scholars differ remarkably. These differences reflect their theological traditions, persuasions and orientations.

There is no scholarship that is not based upon a belief or a presupposition. The methodology and the end-product of any research or writing reveal one's

---

12. Turaki, "Institutionalisation of the Inferior Status," 338.
13. Turaki, 338.

belief. A methodology is like a door that has its own exit. If one enters by one door, one will leave only by its equivalent exit. Sometimes, though, we read the works of African theologians and scholars who say they believe in the authority of the Bible and the lordship of Jesus Christ, but whose research conclusions seem to contradict their faith and beliefs. This is because the assumptions and values of their methodologies forced them to arrive at conclusions that were at variance with their beliefs. The heart believed differently from the head, as it were. (By the way, we find this contradiction among African modernists too. Their modernist beliefs are often at variance with their affinity and attachment to traditional practices.)

The other extreme is the use of random Bible texts and Christian doctrines to address traditional religion and culture. Although the goal of this approach is to transform the African worldview with the biblical and Christian worldview, it fails to develop and formulate a comprehensive and coherent biblical teaching and Christian theology that can engage, interact with and address traditional religion, culture, and modern Africa. African Christians need good theological guidelines concerning their traditional religious beliefs and practices. We need a thorough knowledge of both the traditional religion and the Bible and Christianity, not merely random ideas. It is dangerous for ignorant people to write a theology, either of Christianity or of traditional religion.

The theological methodology which has dominated in Africa has been the comparative study of religions using various anthropological, phenomenological, cultural, and sociological approaches, such as historical and descriptive methods. It is noticeable, however, that the majority of theologians and scholars of African theology used the Bible and Christian theology only as secondary to their primary tools and methodologies. Most major and influential works in African theology were not written from the perspective of a sound biblical theology and worldview, but from the perspective of African Traditional Religion and culture. This theology was then used to engage and even evangelize African Christians. Sadly, when something does not strengthen or edify the Christian faith, it can be used to weaken it.

There are areas which we must mention in passing here, although they will be dealt with later in more detail.

Worship of Divinities and Spirits

African theologians and scholars have generally agreed that Africans revere and worship divinities both as ends in themselves and as intermediaries.

Some are of the opinion that ultimately all worship is accorded to God, even though God is not worshipped directly, but only through intermediaries. There are others who are of the opinion that the worship of intermediaries is an end in itself and that therefore African worship can be called idolatry, since it is not God who is being worshipped.

Whether God is worshipped directly or not does not change the fact that the entire religious corpus of African traditional Religion lies under general revelation. Traditionalists do not see any problem here. However, because Christian scholars and theologians have knowledge of the special revelation of God in Jesus Christ and the Bible, they read this knowledge into their interpretations of traditional religion. The term "intermediary" or "mediator" is a Christian one which has been projected into the traditional religion. We need to interpret traditional religion, not from Christian perspectives, but from those of the traditional religion itself.

Ancestors

Ancestors hold a place of pre-eminence in traditional society. Much has been written about their place, status and role, as can be gleaned from the works of Willoughby, *The Soul of the Bantu*; Tempels, *La Philosophie Bantoue (Bantu Philosophy)*; Parrinder, *African Traditional Religion*; Mbiti, *Introduction to African Religion*; Nyamiti, *Christ as Our Ancestor*.

African theologians and scholars differ considerably about whether or not the recognition of ancestors with sacrifices and offerings is reverence or actual worship. If they are not worshipped, they are at least highly revered. The emotional attachment which some of the African theologians and scholars have to their ancestors tends to colour or weaken their discourse.

Some African theologians, like Magesa, Bujo, Pobee and Bediako, have sought to give the African ancestors a christological definition, exploring ways in which they can be incorporated or rehabilitated into African Christianity. We need to remind ourselves that a religious understanding of the position of ancestors in traditional religion is based on a theological position. Theologically, the ancestors fall under creation theology based upon general revelation. They do not occupy any place under the special revelation, but served a religious function prior to God's special revelation in Jesus Christ. Because they do not carry any salvific value, they themselves stand in need of God's redemption as offered in Jesus Christ. Whatever role ancestors had in traditional society is transformed and made obsolete at God's revelation in Jesus Christ. Jesus Christ stands at the other side of revelation and of redemption theology.

At best, ancestors may be compared with the Hebrew forebears. The Old Testament shows that the Israelites did not worship their patriarchs or ancestors. Only Yahweh, the Lord, was worshipped. Ancestors were revered but were never even described as "intermediaries" or "mediators." Prophets and priests were designated by the Lord, Yahweh, as his representatives before the people. Once the office of priesthood and prophecy were established in Israel, the heads of families no longer even performed the role of the family priests.

Idolatry and Worship

African theologians and scholars have also exhibited divergent views in their study of traditional worship. Some are sympathetic to worship in traditional religion and have claimed that African religion is not idolatrous. They claim that idolatry is denied by Africans themselves; that intermediaries are not gods; that Africans never worshipped man-made objects; and that sacrifices to ancestors are symbols of fellowship.[14]

However, the issue here is not what some Africans think, but what the Bible says about all world religions. The Bible definitions of idols and idolatry are quite clear. The Pentateuch defines the relationship between Yahweh, the Lord God, and other gods, especially the Egyptian and Canaanite gods. The Gospels define the relationship between the Lord Jesus Christ and the Graeco-Roman gods. It is God's special revelation of himself, the Bible, and Jesus Christ which in effect classify worship in traditional religion as idolatry.

Spiritual and Power Encounter

Spiritual powers and forces lie behind every form of human religion, and African Traditional Religion is no exception. As we study traditional religion, it becomes evident that the phenomenon of spiritual-power is dominant and pervasive. Traditional religious beliefs, practices, and behaviours are greatly influenced by the presence of spirit-powers and forces. Human dealings with spirit beings, divinities, gods, ancestors, and specialists involve extensive use of and manifestations of spiritual and mystical powers and forces. Spirit-powers are therefore seen to be present in traditional practices, rituals, ceremonies, festivals, initiation rites or rites of passage, sacrifices or offerings, covenants, and vows or oath taking.

---

14. Nyirongo, *Gods of Africa*.

The cultural and political agenda of African theology has downplayed the significance of this important theological issue. Some African scholars have treated traditional religion as a "cultural system" and, as a result, tend to ignore the theological issue of the spirit-power encounter. Yet many testimonies about this phenomenon in traditional Africa reveal that pioneering missionaries and early African converts encountered such spirit-powers. As Christianity seeks to enlarge its foothold on African soil, this issue will have to be addressed adequately. In its evangelizing and transforming mission in Africa, Christianity must prepare itself for spirit-encounter with traditional religion.

Polygamy

There are apparently irreconcilable views on this aspect of African culture and religion. Missionary Christianity in Africa itself held divergent views on the question of polygamy. Some rejected polygamy in favour of monogamy, while some allowed limited practice of polygamy. Shorter and Hillman have written extensively on marriage and polygamy in Africa.[15] They reviewed the dogmatic positions of Western missionaries on African polygamy and proposed that Christians undertake a serious and careful study in this area. O'Donovan writes: "Polygamy (literally polygyny) is a difficult problem in Africa. Since it involves the commitment and responsibilities of marriage, it is not the same issue as sexual immorality or adultery." He also states that "there are strong cultural arguments in support of polygamy in African society" and that "polygamy makes sense from a traditional African point of view."[16]

The questions of baptism, church membership, and church practices compound the problem of polygamy. The whole matter rests upon what church practice is being adopted in the light of biblical understanding and the historical experience of the church. The church in Africa does indeed need to examine this question of polygamy as divergent and conflicting views will create theological problems for Christianity in Africa. In 1997, for example, I was called upon to mediate the conflict over polygamy between a national church and the newer Western missionaries in a certain African country. These new and young Western missionaries were advocating that the national church should relax its stand on baptism and church membership for polygamists. Their arguments were based upon new understanding of biblical teachings on these matters. They opined that the pioneering and older Western missionaries

---

15. Shorter, *African Culture*; Hillman, *Polygamy Reconsidered*.
16. O'Donovan, *Biblical Christianity*, 288.

were wrong in dogmatizing about the matter. The national church, however, argued that the new, young, Western missionaries were not greater than their forefathers who had brought Christianity to Africa. Furthermore, they argued that the marriage dogmas of the pioneering and older missionaries had been accepted and had become part of their own culture. African Christians who have embraced the norm of monogamy would find it difficult to allow polygamy, even if it were to be sanctioned by the church. To change from that stance would create serious social and Christian problems and crises. The problem was that of theological correctness versus cultural correctness.

A study suggests that missionary positions on polygamy have changed almost every ten years as a result of new understanding and social changes. Some missionaries advocated that a converted polygamist should send away all his later wives, leaving only the first one, while others advised that the convert should choose one wife and send the rest away. In some missionary churches, polygamists were not allowed. Although later polygamists were tolerated and allowed to sit at the back, they could not be baptized or take Holy Communion or take church membership. Later, the practice of sending a polygamist away was stopped altogether and they were allowed to attend church in the hope that, as they heard the word of God, this might bring about change. Gradually, some churches allowed polygamists to attend regularly and even allowed some limited church membership. When Africans took over the mantle of leadership from Western missionaries, some African church leaders were sympathetic and tolerated polygamists in church while others broke away from the missionary church to found their own as a result of attitudes to polygamy. Today doctrine differs from church to church.

In the Old Testament it is stated as a fact that polygamy was practiced among the Israelites, but this is not a value judgment about whether it was good or bad. Polygamy, divorce, and remarriage arose as result of sin in this fallen world. They were not the original purposes of marriage that God intended at the beginning. They are not the norms but indicate a fallen human culture that stands in need of redemption. We learn the true meaning of marriage through the teachings of Jesus and the apostles.

The issue of polygamy is not a cardinal foundation of Christian faith that can cause a Christian to lose his salvation in Jesus Christ. Nonetheless, the church as a community of believers will have to depend upon the guiding light of the Holy Spirit and the Word of God to determine issues relating to the practice. Meanwhile, individual theological positions must respect the communal understanding of the church. Church dogmas on borderline issues like this are time-bound and might change with the passage of time. Where individuals differ from their church on this matter, they still have to respect the view of their church.

African theologians need to develop a Christian theology of marriage based upon biblical teachings, church history, and the African traditional background so that current church practices on marriage, re-marriage, divorce, and polygamy can be evaluated.

Denominational and Ecumenical Issues

Dedji stated that the nineteenth-century missionary movement in Africa involved a multiplicity of missionary societies which "resulted in a wide range variety of ecclesiastical forms and doctrinal emphases in African Christianity."[17] To minimize conflicts among these mission agencies, the colonial masters developed a zoning policy of allocating mission stations according to regions, districts, tribes, and missions. Where mission agencies founded denominations, in most cases these still follow the same tribal or regional lines. Denominationalism therefore created a situation of rivalry, antagonism, competition and conflict between and within missionary societies and the churches that were founded in Africa.

Regions and ethnic groups that received mission agencies earlier also gained a head-start with regard to Christianity and Western education. This meant greater access into the colonial and missionary institutions and it changed the religious and power equations among African people groups. Some people groups that had been despised and thought of as weak before colonialism and missions became powerful and dominant as a result of these benefits. Much of the socio-political, economic and religious conflict and violence in African countries is rooted in this change in the balance of power.

Because the church in Africa is so divided along denominational lines, some African theologians have called for a new ecumenism as a solution. Professor Mugambi, who has devoted his life to addressing these ecumenical issues, states:

> Theologians as teachers of faith within and between their respective churches have a moral duty to educate the Christian community on the necessity of Ecumenism for the successful witness of the church to the world. A divided church will remain scandalous to the people. A differentiated church will manifest the richness of

---

17. Dedji, *Reconstruction and Renewal*, 63.

human response to the gospel, provided that the differences in ecclesiology are mutually recognized and respected.[18]

Mugambi proposed that this new ecumenism must transcend denominationalism and ethnicity and tribalism and that it must be "other-centred, constructive, inclusive, collaborative, amiable, attractive, appreciative, progressive, and sensitive as opposed to the negative values: self-centred, destructive, exclusive, competitive, combative, repulsive, deprecating, retrogressive and insensitive."[19]

This ecumenical quest has met with difficulties as a result of the great doctrinal rivalry between World Council of Churches (WCC) with its All Africa Council of Churches (AACC) and the World Evangelical Fellowship (WEF) with its Association of Evangelicals in Africa (AEA).[20] The doctrinal and theological differences between WCC and WEF have inflamed the rivalry between AACC and AEA in Africa.

These factors will be addressed in later chapters as we consider the messianic community of believers, but concrete theological solutions must be found to solve the issues of denominationalism, tribalism, racism, and ethnicity in modern Africa.

The Relevance of Christianity in Africa

Some Africans have suggested that the African gods are angry at African prostitution with Western religion and culture, hence Africa's crisis of identity and dignity. They believe that salvation for Africa lies either in its repentance and return to reverence for African divinities or gods, religion and culture or in the need to embrace a religion or culture that is a better "fit" for Africans than Christianity.

Many opponents of Christianity assert that Western Christianity cannot be allowed to supplant the traditional revered religion and culture and have raised the question of the relevance of Christianity in Africa. Some have reasoned that it is a relic of Western colonialism and that Africa must rid itself of this colonial, white man's religion. They believe that the Christ of the Bible cannot be allowed to assume prominence or supremacy over the revered African divinities or deities of its traditional religion.

---

18. Mugambi as quoted in Dedji, 64.
19. Mugambi as quoted in Dedji, 68.
20. Breman, *Association of Evangelicals in Africa*.

Other opponents have argued that Islam is the only "saviour" of Africa in view of the "atrocities" of the Western colonial Christianity in Africa and the backwardness of traditional religion and culture. They argue that Islam is best suited to Africa in that it can easily be adapted and made relevant to African context. These assertions are made in spite of abundant evidence of Islamic colonialism, slave raiding, slave trade, and slavery in Africa over almost fifteen centuries. It is still argued that it is Christianity that "destabilizes, denationalizes, detribalizes and anglicizes" Africans. Professor Ali A. Mazrui's term, "a triple heritage" (Islam, ATR, and Christianity), propagates these old views of colonial anthropologists. His documentary film, *The Africans: A Triple Heritage*, asserts the inferiority of Christianity and the superiority of Islam over both traditional religion and Christianity.

If Christianity cannot meet or solve the problems of modern Africa, then there is something wrong with its presentation to Africa. Pagan, barbaric Europe was transformed by the Christian gospel. Despite the current decline of Christianity in the West, its society is still greatly influenced by biblical and Christian values.

Christianity can only become an African religion when the African's mind and intellectual life are renewed and transformed.

There are many more theological issues which could be raised. However, these few provide a good introduction to some of the theological issues that are still relevant in Africa today and which need a comprehensive Christian theological approach and study. These five chapters have revealed the need for relevant *theological methodology*. The next chapter presents some specific examples on how to approach the study of religion and culture in general. There are important principles that can be gleaned.

Part II

Towards an Understanding of African Traditional Religion

5

Various Approaches to the Study of Religion and Culture

There are various ways of relating the Bible and the gospel of Christ to the study of religion and culture. The primary objective of this chapter is to indicate some of the methods that have been developed. We shall consider the work of a few theologians in order to highlight their theological methods and the light they can shed on our understanding and approach to the study of traditional religion in general. There is a lot that we can learn from them.

A Theology of Religion: Ken R. Gnanakan

In his book, *The Pluralistic Predicament*, Ken Gnanakan developed a simple method which is worth our consideration. Here is a summary of it:

1. A theology of religions will need to begin with a commitment to God as Creator of heaven and earth. This commitment will ascertain that we consider the widest circle of God's dealings with humankind, accepting all men and women as made in the image of God. There is therefore an inherent spirituality in all humankind.

2. Although all humankind is the creation of God and therefore belongs to God, the Bible clearly underlines the influence of Satan and his forces within all creation. Hence, all "spiritual" activity is not necessarily of God. There is sufficient evidence, directly and indirectly, to reveal the work of Satan drawing men and women further away from God.

3. The Bible depicts men and women as sinful and fallen. Subsequently, they have been distanced from God. Yet, in the fact of their being made in the image of God, there is within

every human being this inherent "religionness" which gifts them with the capacity to know God. It is this religionness that leads to religion. In this sense, religion is a necessity. We do not mean that religion is necessarily good. Being created by God, the pressure of the divine impels all humanity to get back to the Creator. However, men and women being made in the image of God are also capable of setting their own direction.

4. Since religion is a consequence of the religionness of humankind directing them towards God, God has revealed himself in a limited way in religions. Whether this is to be seen as "general" or "preparatory" revelation, God is active even in religions, not in order to transform them, but to convict and to draw men and women into a true relationship with Him. The Holy Spirit is active, convicting men and women of their sin and revealing the truth and grace of the Lord Jesus Christ.

5. Although we may speak of God revealing himself to religious people even outside of Jesus Christ, this revelation does not directly bring salvation. It points towards, even leads towards salvation. It has pre-salvific significance, preparing people to accept the grace and truth of God. A person or a community may genuinely experience the revelation of God outside of Jesus Christ, but the test of its genuineness is that the Holy Spirit will lead the individual or the community to an encounter with the Lord Jesus Christ, through whom alone salvation is available for all who believe.

6. There is therefore continuity between the religionness of humankind and the revelation of God in Jesus Christ. This is not the same continuity as in the case of Israel's history and its fulfillment in Jesus Christ. It is purely the continuity based on our creationality, from which people can be drawn further towards an experience of a new creationality in Christ. Evangelism and dialogue based on this continuity will be a more positive involvement in the lives of men and women searching for God in many different directions.

7. There is only one decisive revelation of God available to the entire world and this is the revelation through the Lord Jesus Christ. Although this final revelation has already been made known to us in the historic event of Jesus's life, death and resurrection,

the world is yet to fully come face to face with God's grace and judgment in his ultimate triumph at the climax of history.[1]

Gnanakan argued that the Bible has given us an adequate definition of world religions and cultures and that therefore a theology of religion can be developed from the Scriptures. The Bible is the final authority in any Christian pronouncement and a good Christian theology must be grounded in the normative principles of the Bible, even if the definitions recorded are not exhaustive. These principles must take precedence over all our interpretations of and presuppositions about traditional religions and cultures.

The Bible makes categorical pronouncements about world religions and cultures. It deals with both creation theology (general revelation) and redemption theology (specific revelation) and is the story of how God has "engaged" with humankind and the religions and cultures of the world. When we put together all that the Bible has to say, we can reconstruct a comprehensive biblical view on all non-Jewish religions and cultures and will find abundant guidance on how to handle the non-Jewish religions and cultures and, therefore, also the African religious and cultural past.

Both the Old and the New Testament provide models for us. The Pentateuch (five books of Moses) outlines how God addressed the questions of the Egyptian and Canaanite religions and cultures in contrast with that of the Israelites. Similarly, the Acts of the Apostles and the epistles in the New Testament outline the apostolic approach to the Graeco-Roman religions and cultures. The religions of the Canaanites, the Philistines, the Assyrians, the Babylonians, the Medes, the Persians, the Egyptians, the Ethiopians, the Greeks, and the Romans as described in the Bible all bear striking resemblances to African religions. They have a similar, although not identical, nature, form, status, classification, and essence. The revelations of the Bible therefore apply as much to African Traditional Religion as to those ancient religions. These same models show how the gospel of Jesus Christ can transform African Traditional Religion.

This biblical perspective is available to theologians and scholars from various backgrounds. No one is prevented from understanding, interpreting, and applying the Bible and Christian theology to their own religious and cultural heritage. Even non-Christians are free to approach the Bible and to arrive at conclusions rooted in the traditional beliefs that they held prior to their encountering the Bible and Christian theology.

---

1. Gnanakan, *Pluralistic Predicament*, 225–227.

The issue of the African pre-Christian religious heritage and its continuity with Christianity has been prominent in the African theological discourse for the past three decades. Most theologians sympathetic to the African religious past assume that the Bible alone is not sufficient to deal with African religious and cultural questions. They believe that what is necessary for doing theology in Africa is knowledge of this African religious past, together with knowledge of its cultural elements. The conclusions they draw from their scientific and theological studies of world traditional religions and cultures therefore differ from those of the Bible. Their presuppositions, biases, theological traditions and methodologies make it difficult for them to appreciate the Bible's wisdom. However, by neglecting to use the Bible as the ultimate and primary textbook on the definition and place of world religions and cultures before God, they have robbed us of sound biblical and theological scholarship in Africa. As a result Africa lacks a strong biblical theology of African Traditional Religion.

A Holistic Theology: Paul E. Hiebert

Paul Hiebert addressed the problem of the Platonic dualism of the West. This rationalistic, dualistic, and scientific theology results in a worldview which excludes the supernatural phenomenon in human history and experience. Instead, the West makes a strong distinction between "Cosmic History" and "Natural History." He describes the Western two-tiered view of reality in the following words:

> How did this two-tiered worldview emerge in the West? Belief in the middle level began to die in the seventeenth and eighteenth centuries with the growing acceptance of a Platonic dualism and of a science based on materialistic naturalism. The result was the secularization of science and the mystification of religion. Science dealt with the empirical world using mechanistic analogies, leaving religion to handle other-worldly matters, often in terms of organic analogies. Science was based on the certitudes of sense experience, experimentation and proof. Religion was left with faith in visions, dreams and inner feelings. Science sought order in natural laws. Religion was brought in to deal with miracles and exceptions to the natural order, but these decreased as scientific knowledge expanded.[2]

---

2. Hiebert, *Anthropological Reflections*, 196–197.

Hiebert presented his views in a diagram:[3]

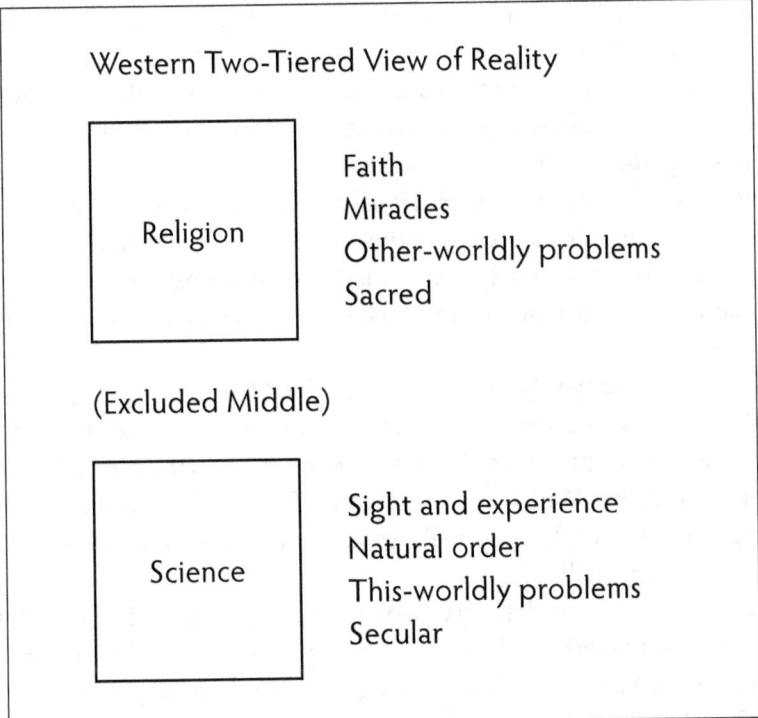

Hiebert argues that it was the secularizing forces in Western history that led to the "flaw of the excluded middle" in the Western worldview. Yet this ignored and excluded "middle" is necessary if we are to deal with problems of life, such as "the uncertainty of the future, the crises of present life and the unknowns of the past."

This "flaw of the excluded middle" is a crucial theological issue in modern Africa, especially within circles which have had or still have a predominantly Western missionary influence. Hiebert's diagram makes it clear that theology in modern Africa has, in the main, been developed from the "top level," and that it is based upon a Western worldview. The spirit-power phenomenon in the "middle level" is simply ignored. In fact, many missionaries coming from the West or trained in the West had no answers to the problems of the middle level within their Christian worldview. Yet this is the foundation of traditional religion and ignoring it hinders the effective presentation of the gospel in non-

---

3. Hiebert, 198.

Western societies.[4] Our theological method of engagement and interaction therefore must take the African spiritual and supernatural phenomena very seriously. At the moment most of the theology being developed at this level is from the grassroots through independent churches and movements in Africa.

Everyday life still reflects the same spiritual, social, and cultural worldviews seen in the nations of the Bible, and these cannot be ignored when we seek to present the gospel of Christ with "power."

However, Hiebert warns of two dangers: "Secularism," which denies "the reality of the spiritual realm in the events of human life and reduces the reality of this world to purely materialistic explanations"; and "a return to a Christianized form of animism in which spirits and magic are used to explain everything."[5]

The second danger is very relevant to the African context for it is very prevalent in African expressions of Christianity. There are already dangerous manifestations of Christianized animism in reaction to the secularism of the modern worldview. When African converts feel that biblical and Christian theology does not explain the realities in life, they fall back into traditional theology and spirituality.

When fully developed, the six theological components of Hiebert's holistic philiosophy – Trinitarian Theology, Theology of Creation and Redemption, Theology of the Kingdom of God, Theology of Power, Theology of Discernment, and a Theology of Suffering and Death – can adequately address all aspects of human life. This theology is an alternative "to the worldviews offered by consumerism, animism and New Age theology." Hiebert suggests that, in order to guard against these and similar views,

> we must formulate clear theological guidelines rooted in Scripture. To chart a course through the turbulent seas of our times we need a theology of healing, exorcism, provision and guidance. Such a theology, dealing with God's work in our daily lives, must be part of our broader theological understandings of God, creation, sin, the cross, judgment and redemption.[6]

This calls for serious study of the spirit-power phenomenon in Africa as it speaks directly to the spiritual, social, and cultural needs of Africans. Given the fact that African traditional religious and cultural worldviews emphasize

---

4. Hiebert, 198.
5. Hiebert, 200.
6. Hiebert, 228.

the pervasive presence of spirit beings, powers and forces, Hiebert's proposal has much value for African theology.

A Theology of Culture and Ethnicity: Bennie J. van der Walt

In his book, *Afrocentric or Eurocentric?: Our Task in a Multicultural South Africa*, B. J. van der Walt addresses the question of "world cultural diversity" from a biblical perspective. He emphasizes that we must understand the impact of a "cultural interpretation" of life. Such knowledge can help us apply biblical teachings to the theological and spiritual needs of specific cultures.

Our major problems in Africa are ethnicity, racism and tribalism. From research, it is clear that the conclusions and interpretations of African theology are heavily burdened by cultural and political agendas, whether "Afrocentrism" or "Eurocentrism." Van der Walt's study exposes the cultural agenda and the political ideology which has dominated African theology for the past three decades.

Ethnocentrism stems directly from our cultural definitions of people who are different from us. The way we treat others is based on our ethnic, racial or tribal prejudices, biases, and stereotypes. Van der Walt's treatment of "Afrocentrism and Eurocentrism" sheds light on multicultural interactions in modern Africa which affect our understanding and interpretation of religions and cultures, and even of Christianity.

He uses creation theology to explain the origins of this diversity in ethnicity and cultures. "Our first point of departure is the biblical perspective that God reveals Himself as well as information about creation to all people and nations (Rom 1:19–20)."[7] This revelation is called "creational revelation."

> Our second point is that in their different cultures all human beings, whether they are aware of it or not, are answerable to God's creational revelation. These answers can be given in obedience or disobedience. And because all humans are sinful, the cultures they create are usually of a mixed nature.[8]

> Our third point emphasizes the four basic relationships into which God has created all human beings: (1) in relation to himself/ herself, (2) to his/her fellow human beings, (3) to nature and (4)

---

7. Van der Walt, *Afrocentric or Eurocentric?*, 14, http://www.socialtheology.com/docs/afrocentric-or-eurocentric-000097.pdf.

8. Van der Walt, *Afrocentric or Eurocentric?*, 14.

to God. These four relationships should be in balance.... the different cultures tend to overemphasise one of these relationships, regarding it as more basic or real than the other three.[9]

On the African continent the relationship to one's fellow human beings is of paramount importance.... The community has priority above the "individual."... The word to describe this viewpoint is *communalism*.

Western culture does exactly the opposite: it stresses the importance of the individual. Being human does not mean to be in community, but implies to be independent, on one's own.... This viewpoint is described as *individualism* because it absolutises the individual. Each of these ... cultures (... Africa and the West) contains an element of truth because it emphasises a real relationship. But at the same time it contains an error, a misconception, because they overemphasise one of the ... relationships at the cost of the other.[10]

Van der Walt is fully aware of the danger of generalization and oversimplification. He therefore elaborates on Western and African perspectives as follows:

1. The Relationship between Self and Community
Van der Walt argues that it is difficult for Africans to understand human individuality, because in Africa the "individual" only exists in a community. The person is a reflection of the community. "I am, because we are."[11] The West finds it difficult to understand and appreciate genuine community, because it views a community simply as a collection of independent individuals. Their community is an expression of the individual will. "We are, because I am."

2. Relationship with God

> From their perspective in which the community receives all the emphasis, Africans also see their relationship towards God as something communal.... it was unthinkable for Africans to regard religion as something requiring *a personal* decision.

---

9. Van der Walt, 14.
10. Van der Walt, 15.
11. Van der Walt, 18.

If we compare this with the West, we again find a totally different perspective. From its starting point of individualism the relationship towards God is regarded as something individual requiring personal conversion, confession of guilt, faith and finally also personal salvation.[12]

3. Relationship with Nature

From its communalistic perspective Africa views nature as a reflection of the community. Something physical (such as a mountain), a plant (for example a tree) or an animal (for instance a bull) may symbolise a clan or a group. From a Western angle, nature, however, is regarded as an object. The question is how it can be used to the individual's advantage.[13]

Van der Walt seeks to show that our cultural interpretations of reality can lead to undue emphasis on certain areas, while we neglect other equally important areas of life. Our religious and philosophical worldviews are usually developed along the lines of our cultural idolatry, that which we emphasise above God. As a result we become preoccupied with our own corrupted cultural view of the world around us.

The dominance of this cultural agenda in African theology cannot be overemphasized. Africa is plagued with racial, ethnic, tribal or denominational wars, and conflicts. Even when Africans (or any other human groups) view life holistically within their context, in almost all cases such a view of life is partial and parochial. This segmented view of life results in ethnocentrism. The pursuit of one thing at the expense of others, especially when its basis is ethnocentric, causes us to develop a defective and deceptive view of life in relation to others.

One of the greatest needs of Christians in Africa is to develop a strong theology of others, a relational theology on how human beings can live with others in the light of the Bible. We need a theology that transcends ethnicity and embraces a new messianic community of believers and the world community. Basic relationships and alienations must be addressed by the cross of Christ which brings reconciliation and restoration to all broken relationships.

Africa's issues of race, ethnicity, tribes, and denominations cannot be addressed adequately simply by using the traditional African concept of communal life. Biblical teachings and a biblical worldview are needed to

---

12. Van der Walt, 18.
13. Van der Walt, 19.

provide a balance. Christian communal values and principles are needed to transform the traditional African kinship and communal values.

The Gospel and the African Pre-Christian Heritage: Kwame Bediako

Kwame Bediako has written extensively and has contributed substantially to the historical study of Christianity in Africa. We have already talked about his work, but it is worthy of further attention.

Referring to Bediako's assessment of the task of African Christian theology, Dedji states, "The essence of the quest for an African Christian theology as it appears throughout Bediako's writings is to translate faith in Jesus Christ to suit the tongue, style, genius, character and the culture of African peoples."[14]

Those who wish to study Bediako's work may not be able to follow his line of thought properly if they do not have a sufficient knowledge of the development of the thinking and of the theological corpus of both the World Council of Churches (WCC) and All Africa Council of Churches (AACC) from the 1960s to the 1980s. The theological terms and concepts which Bediako used developed from the theologies of these two organizations. These themes were the basis of theological discourses at conferences across the continent of Africa during those years. Bediako took these theological concerns and issues and articulated them better than others.

Bediako stressed that both Africa's pre-Christian traditional religious heritage and its present Christian identity were important. He urged African theologians and scholars to take "The African religious past as a prime theological issue."

As a result he set out to define the following major theological issues:

- "What is African Christianity?" It is a non-Western religion.[15]
- "What is African Theology?" It is both a process and a product of African theological enterprise.[16]
- "What is African Christian identity?" It is a cultural and spiritual continuity between Africa's pre-Christian traditional religious heritage and present African Christianity.[17]
- "What is the African theological method?" It is a hermeneutic of identity, to liberate and to integrate the African religious past,

---

14. Dedji, *Reconstruction and Renewal*, 194.
15. Bediako, *Christianity in Africa*.
16. Bediako, "Understanding African Theology."
17. Bediako, *Theology and Identity*; *Christianity in Africa*; "Understanding African Theology."

to provide an African re-interpretation of African pre-Christian religious tradition, to clarify the nature and meaning of African Christian identity.[18]

- "What does it mean to be African and Christian?" It is a Christian self-definition and self-understanding, a unified vision and an integration of the "old" and the "new" in African religious consciousness.[19]
- "What is the nature, the form and the mode of the encounter between the gospel/Christ/Scriptures and African tradition/consciousness?" The encounter between the Christian gospel and the African experience is a mutual one. It involves "rooting the Christian faith in African consciousness" so that "dialogue is possible between the Gospel and African tradition." Because the Scriptures are being translated "in the categories of local languages, idioms and worldviews," they can "become our story" and, through them, we are linked to the Old Testament "saints" through Christ.[20]

Although the entire theological corpus of Bediako has yet to be critically evaluated by African theologians and scholars, clearly his interpretation of African theology and African Christianity is central to his arguments. Bediako anchors his historical and cultural interpretations upon the historical experience of the universal church, the historical African experience of Christianity, and the African understanding and interpretation of the Bible. The Holy Spirit must guide the theological process.

What is important for us is Bediako's emphasis on Africa's pre-Christian traditional religious heritage:

(1) His definitions and interpretations of African theology, African Christianity, Christian identity, and Africa's pre-Christian religious heritage;

(2) His methodology or approach to the study of African theology and African Christianity as subjects of study and to African theologians and scholars as theological practitioners; his use of the primal religious heritage and its cultural and spiritual categories; his use of African theology as both process and product of African theological method; and his use of the gospel and Scriptures as methodological tools;

---

18. Bediako, "Understanding African Theology."
19. Bediako, *Christianity in Africa*; "Understanding African Theology."
20. Bediako, *Christianity in Africa*.

(3) His theological motivation, priority, and agenda in developing and formulating "theology and identity" in Africa in relation to the overall mission of the church in Africa.

In order for us to grasp what Bediako was saying, we must once again remind ourselves that all religions and cultures of the world fall under the category of general revelation, whereas the Bible and Jesus Christ fall under special revelation as God's self-disclosure to all mankind.

Bediako's major concern was that Missionary Christianity in Africa emphasized only redemption theology based upon special revelation and did not recognize the value of the traditional revelation. Instead, the missionaries condemned it, demeaned it and did not consider theological discourse with it. They rejected it as a tool for doing theology because they failed to see "much continuity in relationship" between Africa's pre-Christian religious heritage and Christianity. They did not see it as "a preparation of the gospel," but instead emphasized discontinuity.

Bediako observed that that which Western missionaries saw as demeaning and "unworthy," "now occupies a centre of academic stage." This African religious past "is not so much a chronological past, as an 'ontological' past."[21] Bediako stated:

> The point of the theological importance of such an ontological past consists in the fact that it belongs together with the profession of the Christian faith in giving account of the same entity, namely, the history of the religious consciousness of the African Christian. It is in this sense that the theological concern with the pre-Christian religious heritage becomes an effort aimed at clarifying the nature and meaning of African Christian identity.[22]

This position can be stated in much stronger terms: "The quest for African Christian theologies amounts to attempting to make clear the fact that conversion to Christianity must be coupled with cultural continuity."[23]

Bediako lamented missionary exclusion of any possibility of "preparation for Christianity" in the African Traditional Religions. This resulted in the exclusion of the "pre-Christian memory in African Christian consciousness" which he described in the following words: "For theological consciousness presupposes religious tradition and tradition requires memory and memory

---

21. Bediako, "Understanding African Theology," 3.
22. Bediako, 3.
23. Bediako, 4.

is integral to identity: without memory we have no past and if we have no past, then we lose our identity."[24]

Bediako argued that our Christian identity as Africans is tied to this religious heritage and that its "relationship of continuity" must be emphasized "rather than discontinuity with Christian belief":

> At the heart of the new theological method would be the issue of identity, which would itself be perceived as a theological category, which would therefore entail confronting constantly the question as to how far the "old" and the "new" in African religious consciousness could become integrated into a unified vision of what it meant to be African and Christian. The issue of identity in turn forced the theologian to become the locus of this struggle for integration through a dialogue which, if it was to be authentic, was bound to become personal and so infinitely more intense.[25]

He believed that a suitable theological method would yield "Christian self-definition," since the African scholar would be engaged in "a dialogue" with "the perennial religions and spiritualities of Africa."[26] Accordingly, African Christian experience emerged as not much more than a refinement of their experience of the "old" religion and the vindication and affirmation of African self-hood which, at the start, had been conceived as the task of the church, later came to be entrusted to the revitalisation of the "old" religions, with their "God-given heritage of indigenous spiritual and cultural treasures."[27]

When Bediako talked about the integration or synthesis of the African pre-Christian religious heritage with Christianity, he simply meant merging the two forms of revelation: creation theology and redemption theology, general revelation and special revelation. He stated "that it is important to recognize the integration of African Christian experience as a religious reality in its own right. Christ has effectively become the integrating reality and power linking the 'old' and the 'new' in the African experience."[28] The term "encounter" captures Bediako's intentions. The coming together of Christianity with African Traditional Religion is that of encounter as one faith system encounters the other with its claims of truth.

---

24. Bediako, 4.
25. Bediako, 5.
26. Bediako, 5.
27. Bediako, 5.
28. Bediako, 6.

This is described as follows.

> Consequently, the task of African theology, came to consist, not in "indigenising" Christianity, or theology as such, but rather, in letting the Christian gospel encounter, as well as be shaped by, the African experience.... The overall goal of African theology then, was to seek to show that there were genuinely and specifically *African* contributions – derived from the twin heritage of African Christianity, namely, the African primal tradition and the African experience of the Christian gospel – to be made to the theology of the universal Church.[29]

Bediako believed the objective of "encounter" has been achieved:

> African theology has succeeded by and large in providing an African re-interpretation of African pre-Christian religious tradition in ways which have ensured that the pursuit of a creative, constructive and perhaps also a self-critical, theological enterprise in Africa is not viable, but in fact distinctively possible, as a variant of the universal and continuing encounter of the Christian faith with the realities of human societies and their histories.[30]

He suggested that Christian Scriptures provided a further link between the two religious traditions, through the translation of Scripture into the vernacular.[31] Although he recognized that Scripture stands under redemption theology based upon special revelation and that Africa pre-Christian religious heritage stands under creation theology based upon general revelation, Bediako stated that

> the centrality of Scripture translation points to the significance of African pre-Christian religious cultures, as a "valid carriage not only for the divine revelation," but also for providing the medium of Christian apprehension.... Indeed, the possession of the Christian Scriptures in African languages, which could probably be regarded as the single most important element of Western missionary legacy in Africa – in some cases, the Scriptures becoming the foundation for a new literary culture which did not exist previously – ensured that there did take place an effectual

---

29. Bediako, 6.
30. Bediako, 6.
31. Bediako, *Christianity in Africa*.

rooting of the Christian faith in African consciousness. This, in turn, ensured also that a deep and authentic dialogue would ensue between the gospel and African tradition, authentic in so far as it would take place, not in the terms of a foreign language or of an alien culture, but in the categories of local languages, idioms and worldviews.[32]

Bediako saw that the primal religious worldview could become a very useful tool for doing theology. Underscoring the great value and the significance of primal religions and the primal worldview to Christianity and theology in Africa, he argued that primal religions and primal worldview have an affinity with Christianity (phenomenological affinity). He said

> that this special relationship of primal religions with Christianity and the possibility of "affinities" between the primal and Christian traditions could have far-reaching significance for our understanding of the nature of the Christian faith itself.... [if] there is only a minimal "paradigm-shift" as we pass from the spiritual universe of primal religions into the spiritual environment of the Christian faith ("this is what we have been waiting for"), then one would want to pursue the matter by asking how the primal imagination might bring its own "peculiar gifts" to the shaping of Christian affirmation. The issue becomes even more pressing if Christian thought has hitherto been moulded by a worldview from which the "living forces" of the primal imagination seem to have been expelled.[33]

He argued furthermore that primal religions and the primal worldview are significant for Christian theology:

> Consequently, this modern theology [Western] appears to have lost touch with and to be incapable of answering to, the crucial issues which lie at the heart of human existence, issues which are essentially religious: questions of human identity, community, ecological equilibrium and justice. Because primal worldviews are fundamentally religious, the primal imagination restores to theology the crucial dimensions of living religiously for which

---

32. Bediako, "Understanding African Theology," 7.
33. Bediako, *Christianity in Africa*, 96.

the theologian needs make no apology. The primal imagination may help us restore the ancient unity of theology and spirituality.[34]

He went on to question how Christians could treat primal religion lightly when the history of Christian expansion showed that "it is primal religions which underlie the Christian faith of the vast majority of Christians of all ages and all nations."[35]

We need to understand that Bediako was giving an historical analysis and not a theological one. African pre-Christian religious heritage is viewed as an historical religious system. Hence his query as to why one valuable historical piece should be thrown away. Many think differently, seeing the matter strictly in theological terms.

From the tone of Bediako's arguments, it is clear that he emphasized what he called "African existentialism," that is, African self-understanding. He believed that an African scholar or theologian who does theology on the African continent must be "culturally existential," knowing the pre-Christian religious heritage. In other words, the African cultural and religious self-understanding provides an opportunity to shape the form and nature of African Christianity.

The shaping of African Christian self-expression can be effected either by the conscientious theologian who knows the art of doing theology or by ordinary people whose everyday life and experience provides self-understanding and self-interpretation of their Christian experience. While practitioners (theologians) invent theology, the ordinary people live out theology which grows out of their everyday experience.

This approach values both the process and the product of theology, provided that it is African. Doing theology is not just concerned with the subject of Christianity or the Bible, it is also concerned with whether the act of doing Christian theology utilizes the Christian worldview as rooted in the Bible. It suggested that Africans are producing theology, anyway, without questions concerning the quality, authenticity, orthodoxy, or heresy of the theological method or the product. As a result, varied stories of Christianity are told in African idioms.

Bediako used two Christian principles to describe this: christocentric faith and the Bible. He believed in the sufficiency of a christocentric faith which

---

34. Bediako, 96.
35. Bediako, 105.

could be open to interaction with both the Bible and the pre-Christian cultural heritage. This could lead to a possible theological synthesis.

A christocentric faith is rooted in redemption theology or the Bible, but not in African Traditional Religion. This means that the African Christian must first of all believe in Jesus Christ; be baptized and taught the teachings of Christ and apostles; and be rooted and grounded in the Holy Scriptures, the Christian faith, and some fundamental doctrines before being able to make a valid "existential" Christian theological pronouncement. A theological product must reflect this faith and belief in Jesus Christ and his gospel. Otherwise, the individual may respond in ignorance of Christian teachings and values, perhaps without ever having been transformed through the process of engagement and interaction with the Christian and biblical worldview. Self-understanding and self-interpretation are usually devoid of any sound biblical understanding and in such a situation theological heresy or syncretism is a real possibility. What is lacking in this methodology is the theology of revelation. Historical or sociological analysis will not be able to clarify our understanding.

In considering his work, we must also examine Bediako's interpretation of African theology and the works of E. Bolaji Idowu, John S. Mbiti, Mulago wa Cikala Musharhamina and Byang H. Kato.

In studying African theologians, Bediako considered why the interest, the meaning and the investigation of the pre-Christian African religious heritage should be a prime concern to modern African theology. He concluded:

> It is arguable that by developing their interest in the African pre-Christian religious heritage into a major theological concern, Africa's theologians have moved in the direction anticipated by some for Christian theology in Africa in the post-missionary era. . . . Theology in Africa has to interpret this Christ in terms that are relevant and essential to African existence.[36]

He goes on to say:

> It is worth noting that the very writers who have been preoccupied with the nature and meaning of the African religious past are the ones who have been just as concerned to explore ways in which African *Christian* experience may establish its identity within African life itself and in the Church worldwide . . . the African theologian's concern with the traditional religions of Africa must

---

36. Bediako, *Theology and Identity*, 3.

find its fullest interpretation within the framework of *Christian* theology.[37]

Bediako believed in the historical method. He suggested that the first task was to establish "a religious model for the study of the 'religion' of African religions." He was convinced that "African primal religions form part of the common spiritual heritage of mankind."[38] He regarded the second task as being the need to establish "an organic view of Christian history." He pointed out that the historical Christian experience of Africa is never isolated from the universal history of the church. The African Christian experience is a reflection of this universal Christianity.

> If one maintains an organic view of Christian history, then the study of the variety of modern African responses to the gospel of Christ in relation to, say, earlier patterns, is legitimate. It allows us to examine and appreciate some urges of "essential Christianity" as these manifest themselves in different cultural contexts. The "particular" is within the "universal," and by studying the dynamics of African Christian self-understanding and earlier responses in other historical milieu, each in its own context, we are also learning something about Christian self-understanding as a whole. . . . Looked at from the perspective of an organic view of Christian history, therefore, the encounter of the Christian faith with the African religious heritage ceases to be the meeting between *Western* culture and *African* values.[39]

In pursuit of historical examples, Bediako chose to study the "beginnings of Hellenistic Christianity in the early Roman Empire" which he said "offers the most instructive parallels to the modern African context." Bediako felt that Hellenistic Christianity had not been given sufficient prominence in historical studies on the early church although they too had faced problems as a result of pre-Christian beliefs.

He noted that then too there were two factions: those who advocated continuity and those who advocated discontinuity. As he examined how both factions handled this question theologically, Bediako identified two prime concerns, the questions of "identity" and "theology." He believed that Hellenistic Christianity accepted that Christian theology and identity were

---

37. Bediako, 5.
38. Bediako, 6.
39. Bediako, 6.

rooted in continuity, integration, or synthesis, and urged modern African theology to draw lessons and insights from them. This "ancient analogue" could inspire modern African theology, since its theological agenda and prime concern was similar to those of African theology.

The second historical pattern he noted in the theological writings of the early African church fathers was the question of orthodoxy and dogma. This emerged from the theological need to interpret and apply the Bible correctly for the Graeco-Roman-African society. If one were to focus solely on questions of identity and theology based upon the concepts of continuity, integration, and synthesis, questions of doctrines, orthodoxy, heresies, and apologetics which were also equally important, would be ignored. However the early church fathers showed that both issues of identity and doctrinal issues, apologetics and theological orthodoxy were important.

African theology had not included this second theological and historical trend of early Hellenistic Christianity in its theological schema. Redemption theology or special theology has been downplayed. We in Africa must maintain a balance between identity and theology on the one hand, and dogma, apologetics, and orthodoxy on the other. General revelation (or creation theology) and special revelation (or redemption theology) are complementary. Both were essential historical products of Hellenistic Christianity.

Of the four theologians whose work Bediako examined, Kato alone belonged to the theological school of discontinuity. Kato would have agreed with the second historical trend noted in Hellenistic Christianity, the theological school of orthodoxy and apologetics, rather than with the school of identity and theology. His style was polemical and apologetic, typical of the one wing of Hellenistic Christianity, while that of Idowu, Mbiti and Mulago was in keeping with the school of continuity, identity and theology. Kato used the Bible and evangelicalism as his starting points, not culture or traditional religious heritage as the others did. In short, Kato's theological strength was in special revelation and redemption theology, while the others favoured general revelation and creation theology.

Bediako's theological analysis, in which he pitted Kato against the other three, reveals a repugnance of Kato's theological views and tradition. This strong aversion was unfortunate because Kato's position was as well rooted in Hellenistic Christianity as the others' position was. Kato's polemics and apologetics were rooted in Christian orthodoxy which seeks to deal with theological heresy and biblical doctrines. Bediako's criticism of Kato reveals his weakness in addressing the possibility of heresy in African theology.

Hellenistic Christianity was not only theology and identity, but also orthodoxy and apologetics.

Kato's biblical challenge and stance in African theology should not be ignored nor underrated given the decline of Western Christianity and the rise of neo-paganism in the West. Not all evangelicals would agree with Kato's style and strong convictions, but they all agree with his affirmation of the centrality of the Bible in doing theology for the church in Africa and in the need for Christian doctrines and apologetics in Africa.

The greatest contemporary threat to Christianity in Africa comes from Western forms of Christianity and Western modern philosophies (secularism, religious pluralism, and cultural relativism) and neo-paganism. It is imperative that the church in Africa develop a sound method of biblical theology that will take on and meet the concerns of African Christianity, in the areas of authentic Christian doctrines, biblical orthodoxy, apologetics, heresy, and syncretism. This second concern of Hellenistic Christianity is still relevant. In our pursuit of relevance, "identity and theology" must not ignore the other equally important pursuit of orthodoxy, dogma, and apologetics as weapons against heresy and syncretism.

African Traditional Religion feels very comfortable with a Christianity that limits itself to cultural and traditional analysis only. However, Redemption theology has concerns about issues of orthodoxy, dogma, apologetics, heresy, and syncretism. One cannot simply ignore the difference between creation and special theology.

Not all theologians will agree with Bediako's theological views. However, Bediako's emphasis on the enduring African religious past cannot be ignored nor taken lightly. He was able to raise questions of "theology and identity" in Africa to the level of theological discourse. How we approach our religious heritage in theological enterprise must be a matter of priority. A biblically based theology of religions and cultures must be developed. It must maintain a balance between historical and cultural concerns, on the one hand, and doctrinal, apologetic, orthodox, heretical, and syncretistic concerns on the other. Historical analysis must be balanced by theological analysis.

A Biblical Theology of Traditional African Religion (ATR): Richard J. Gehman

Richard J. Gehman, in his book *African Traditional Religion in Biblical Perspective*, sought to emphasize two major elements: ATR as traditionally practiced in Africa and ATR as interpreted by the Holy Bible, with the aim of "examining carefully some of the crucial issues in ATR in the spotlight of God's Word so that we may discern between truth and error."[40]

Gehman placed African Traditional Religion under general revelation or creation theology. He reasoned that the "truth and error in ATR is representative of all non-Christian religions throughout the world."

> In biblical perspective, this book affirms that the fundamental elements of ATR are not unique to Africa. Belief in God, divinities, spirits, ancestors, magic, witchcraft and sorcery are universal. They have been believed and practised by peoples around the world from antiquity past until the present. By demonstrating that these beliefs are universal, the study shall avoid any temptation to single out ATR as uniquely in error or unusually rich in religious understanding. The African peoples are one with mankind who are all made in the image of God and have all rebelled against their Creator.[41]

Gehman confirmed that putting African Traditional Religion into biblical perspective was the whole reason for his writing his book. He argued that a biblical view of traditional religion must hold to both the positive and the negative elements presented by Scripture.

Biblical Elements in Traditional Religion

Gehman found that African Traditional Religion contained some scripturally sound elements such as the following:

- one true and living God, sovereign and eternal;
- the creation of man in the image of God;
- the revelation of God to man:
    general revelation (in nature and in conscience);
    special revelation (primeval revelation, biblical revelation, Jesus Christ);
- traditions of revelation passed down by generations:
    Canaanites;
    Philistines;
    Mesopotamians;
    Cush, Mizram and Put.

---

40. Gehman, *African Traditional Religion*, 10–11.
41. Gehman, 12.

He also listed some negative elements that Scripture records, such as that:

- all mankind is in rebellion against God;
- man attempts to deify the creature;
- man suppresses the truth revealed to him by God;
- man is uniformly described as without God, without goodness and without hope;
- man is subject to demonic influences.

According to Gehman, humankind is not divided into good and bad, but corrupt motives, self-centred attitudes and sinful behaviour.

Gehman's theological method is deeply rooted in the evangelical perspective. He stated that the basic presuppositions of his book include the following: (1) "The belief in the divine inspiration and infallible authority of the Bible for all faith and conduct is the one fundamental presupposition which is the foundation for this book." (Ps 119:89; Isa 40:8; Matt 5:17; Luke 24:27, 44; John 10:35; 17:17; 1 Cor 2:12–13; 2 Tim 3:15–17; 1 Pet 1:10–11; 2 Pet 1:21; Rev 22:18–19.) (2) We acknowledge the general revelation of God, given to all men in nature and conscience which is not sufficient for salvation, but which leaves men without excuse (Rom 1:18–20; 2:14–16). We therefore accept all truth wherever it is found as being derived from common grace. (3) We affirm that all men, by virtue of their Adamic nature, are sinners in rebellion against the Triune God and living under God's wrath (Rom 3:9–18; 5:12–21). (4) We further believe that salvation from eternal condemnation is a free gift of grace, received alone through faith in Jesus Christ (Rom 3:21–22; Eph 2:1–10). (5) We acknowledge the existence of a personal devil and spirit beings that, in their fallen state, can molest and harm unbelievers (Eph 2:2; 6:12). But we also affirm our faith in the omnipotent God whose power is infinitely greater than any creature and who pledges to preserve his children from all evil (Rom 8:31–39). (6) We are bound by Scripture to believe in both heaven and hell; hell where all unrepentant sinners shall be banished from God's presence and judged by his wrath in conscious torment forever and heaven where God's people, sinners redeemed by the blood of the Lamb by grace through personal faith in Christ, shall live forever in conscious fellowship with God (Matt 8:12; 25:41; Rev 21:27).[42]

Gehman believed that one must approach the study of ATR committed to God and believing in the redemptive work of Christ on the cross by which salvation is offered to all humankind, to peoples of all religions.

---

42. Gehman, 27–28.

Gehman's theological method becomes critically important to our study when he addresses the theological issue: "The relationship of Biblical Christianity to African Traditional Religion." In his analysis of various theological approaches to this matter, he grouped them as follows: (1) those who stress the continuity between Christianity and other religions, (2) those who emphasize discontinuity, and (3) those who teach a biblical continuity-discontinuity. He outlines these three positions as follows:

Continuity

Gehman asserts that:

> Throughout most of church history, continuity between Christianity and world religions has not been the emphasis. This was so because the goal of mission was to preach the gospel, call people to repent, baptize converts, build churches and extend the lordship of Christ and the uniqueness of biblical revelation ... The emphasis was more on discontinuity than on continuity.[43]

In modern times the situation has changed and today there are many scholars who stress continuity in their writings. Gehman listed liberal Protestants, Roman Catholics and humanists that hold this position:

> Some teach that every religion says basically the same thing. All religions deal with ultimate reality. Others teach that world religions are all a manifestation of the Divine Life and they represent the religious development of the human race, with Christianity at the apex of the evolution of religion. Many theologians believe that world religions are preparatory for and lead to the Christian faith. Others believe that Christianity shares with all other religions something of divine revelation and man's response to that revelation. Some emphasize the relative value of each religion for each adherent. And still others admit that while there are serious differences between world religions, they all stand side by side in their practical religious experience.[44]

Gehman listed Hegel, Ernst Troeltsch, Arnold Toynbee and Wilfred Cantwell Smith as leading historians and philosophers who uphold continuity.

---

43. Gehman, 245.
44. Gehman, 246.

Similarly, he listed Karl Rahner, John Mbiti and Bolaji Idowu as leading liberal Christian theologians who also uphold this same view. After a very brief analysis of the works of Mbiti and Idowu and a few others, Gehman concluded by saying:

> Thus we find in Africa the stress on continuity, finding in African Traditional Religion elements of truth, practical evidence that the Eternal Logos has been lighting the peoples of the world. They do not deny that error may exist in ATR. No one who holds to continuity denies the existence of evil in the various world religions. But the emphasis is on finding truth, not error. The relationship is positive, not negative. The relationship of ATR to Christianity is that of law and grace. Just as the law prepared people for the grace of Christ manifest in the New Testament, so ATR has prepared men and women to embrace Jesus Christ.[45]

However Gehman pointed out some problems with this view of continuity:

> The Scriptures simply do not stress the positive relationship between biblical faith and other religions.
>
> Converts from non-Christian religions do not recognize that their old religion prepared them for Christianity. Nor do the adherents of other religions acknowledge that their religions are a preparation for conversion to Christianity. Adherents of other religions and Christian converts from those religions see discontinuity, not continuity.
>
> This extreme emphasis on continuity is contrary to the orthodoxy of the historic Christian church. The theology of continuity is rooted in the skepticism of the modern era since the enlightenment and is fostered by those who deny the uniqueness of Christ and biblical revelation.[46]

The theological debates on continuity and discontinuity were referred to in the analysis of Kwame Bediako. There is no need to repeat the arguments here.

---

45. Gehman, 250.
46. Gehman, 250–251.

Discontinuity

Gehman seemed to suggest that discontinuity is the reaction of neo-orthodoxy led by Karl Barth and others (including Hendrik Kraemer) against the "Hegelian notion of evolution in religion with Christianity being the most perfect religion." Quotations from Karl Barth and Hendrik Kraemer were presented in support of this:

From Karl Barth:

> Jesus Christ does not fulfill and improve all the different attempts of man to think of God. But as the self-offering and self-manifestation of God replaces and completely outbids those attempts, putting them in the shadows to which they belong.[47]

From Hendrik Kraemer:

> Theologically speaking, "nature," "reason" and "history" do not, if we want to think stringently, afford preambles [an introductory portion], avenues or lines of development towards the realm of grace and truth as manifested in Jesus Christ. There are, to be sure, longings and apperceptions [clear understanding] in the religious life of mankind outside the sphere of the Christian revelation . . . but it is misleading to describe the religious pilgrimage of mankind as a preparation or a leading up to a so-called consummation or fulfillment in Christ.[48]

Biblical Continuity-Discontinuity

Gehman stated:

> Biblically speaking, there is in fact a measure of continuity between ATR and Christianity which is ignored or down-played by the Barthians. But it would also appear to us that the discontinuity between ATR and Christianity is so great that we cannot truly speak of mere continuity between the two. We can only speak of a biblical Continuity-Discontinuity.[49]

---

47. Barth, *Christ and Adam*, 80.
48. Kraemer, *Christian Message in a Non-Christian World*, 2–3.
49. Gehman, *African Traditional Religion*, 253.

Gehman outlined this position as follows:

Biblical discontinuity is evident in the differences between ATR and Christianity:

- ATR's belief in man and sin contrasts with Christianity;
- ATR's understanding of salvation contrasts with that of the gospel;
- The relationship between ethics and religion is in sharp contrast;
- ATR is a degeneration of biblical revelation: "But ATR is fundamentally more than a preparation for the gospel. It is the result of Man's fall away from God."[50]
- Converts from ATR stress discontinuity, not continuity;
- Christianity is not a fulfilment of ATR.[51]

However, both the Christian faith and ATR are a fulfilment of humankind's desire. This means that it provides valuable points of contact.

Gehman concluded his analysis as follows:

> Continuity, therefore, has its roots in a low view of Scripture and a high opinion of man's moral character. Discontinuity in its Barthian form is a reaction to the idea of continuity of liberal theologians. A biblical continuity-discontinuity seeks to maintain both emphases of Scripture properly balanced. There must be discontinuity because of man's sinful rebellion against God. There must, however, be some measure of continuity because of general revelation given to all men through nature and conscience.[52]

Gehman's objective was to help African Christians develop

> mature Christian thinking about African Traditional Religion. As Christians we need to think "Christianly," and this means biblical thinking. Not only do we need a correct factual understanding of ATR both in the past and the present, but we also need a Christian discernment of the true origin and nature of ATR through the study of the Bible. [We] shall, therefore, seek to evaluate traditional religion in such a way that we can preserve that which is true and good; at the same time we need to reject any error found in ATR.[53]

---

50. Gehman, 253.
51. Gehman, 253.
52. Gehman, 268.
53. Gehman, 10–11.

Gehman's method is worth our consideration. "Scripture becomes the normative standard whereby we judge truth and error"[54] in all religions and in our case, African Traditional Religion. The good aspects of ATR can be utilized and incorporated into Christianity, while the bad aspects can be thrown out. It is unfortunate that Gehman did not discuss the level of engagement and interaction.

In this chapter we have examined a few representative examples of the approaches and methodologies used by African theologians and scholars in approaching African Traditional Religion. These scholars provide a background for the entire study and introduce us to a variety of theological methodologies which have been developed as research tools for approaching the study of religions and cultures. Learning from them will enrich our approach to the study of African Traditional Religion and culture in general.

Two things emerged very strongly in the course of this chapter: that the Bible and Christian theology must be used as primary, not secondary, research tools; and that we need to have a thorough knowledge and understanding of traditional religion and worldview.

---

54. Gehman, xii.

6

Defining Religion

One of the major difficulties faced in this study was the choice of literature. Since the classics of the pioneers such as Idowu and Mbiti, comparative, anthropological, phenomenological, historical, and descriptive methods have continued to dominate the scene. The few works that do use theological and biblical methods are not comprehensive, systematic or coherent. Although some have set out to study the traditional religion and worldview from a comprehensive biblical point of view, the knowledge gained has generally yet to be formulated and developed. Much of the biblical theology is lacking in perspective. Attempts have, however, been made in certain areas, such as polygamy, Christology, ethics and philosophy, enculturation, and contextualization.

There are, however, a few useful books included in the bibliography. However, the most helpful of all is Philip M. Steyne's work and his study provides the background information for this chapter. I have then interpreted the views and ideas that were gathered in order to develop a method whereby one can undertake a systematic examination of the interaction between Christianity and African Traditional Religion.

We need to start by defining what we mean by religion. This is particularly important as some of the earliest visitors to Africa denied that Africans had any religion at all because the system of worship they encountered did not match the system of mosques and churches with which they were familiar. Moreover, it also did not seem to be characterized by the familiar features of prayer and praise to a Supreme Being and professions of faith and trust in him.

Later anthropologists and scholars described African Traditional Religion as primitive and asserted that it represented the earliest form of religion, from which all others had evolved. "This was a reference to religion in its earliest forms among mankind – assuming an evolutionary trend. This idea was soon laid to rest by the more disciplined anthropologists."[1] Terms such as fetishism, animism, and paganism were bandied about, but did little to advance an understanding of the nature of African Traditional Religion.

Religion has been defined from various perspectives: anthropological, sociological, phenomenological, psychological, and theological.[2] However, any definition of religion involves five aspects. The first of these provides a general functional definition of religion, the others define and interpret the fundamental theological, psychological, philosophical and ethical or moral beliefs.

A Functional Definition of Religion

A functional definition of religion is necessary in order to apply the theological method to the study of African Traditional Religion and worldview.

The study of African religion and culture has matured and various classifications of African religions have emerged. Most scholars have noted that there are four key areas in the African religious system: (1) the belief in the Supreme Being, or God; (2) the belief in the lesser spirit beings or divinities; (3) the cult of ancestors; and (4) the use of magic, charms, amulets, and spiritual forces. As a result of this classification, some scholars have labelled African religion as "polytheism," the worship of many gods. African scholars, such as Professor Idowu, rejected some aspects of this classification, preferring the term "diffused monotheism." Monotheism simply means the worship of one God. This debate about whether African religion is an example of "polytheism" or "monotheism" continues as new insights are gained.

Religion as a Theory of Meaning

Benjamin C. Ray, after studying the nature and form of African religions, suggested this was the best way to approach and understand African religions. He wanted to be able to describe and understand the meaning of the religious phenomenon – ceremonies, and rituals.

He suggested there are three concepts: archetypal symbols, ritual, and community. By "archetypal symbols," he meant, "sacred images, whether they be gods, ancestors, sacred actions, or things, which make up the traditional universe." He further states:

---

1. Cole, "Christian and African," 3.
2. Glock and Hammond, *Beyond the Classic?*

> Such images, enshrined and communicated in myth and ritual, provide a network of symbolic forms, uniting social, ecological and conceptual elements into locally bounded cultural systems. They give order to experience by framing the world in terms of sacred figures and patterns. Thus encapsulated within a local universe of archetypal form, traditional African thought tends to abolish both time and chance by shaping experience to interrelated moral and ritual patterns.[3]

Ray suggested that these symbols provide us with the religious worldview of African Traditional Religion. The "archetypal symbols" are "models for behaviour as well as modes of thought." Through them the religious practitioners can "re-enact the deeds of the gods, to become possessed by divinities, to manipulate sacred objects, to speak sacred words." They can "conform experience to normative patterns of meaning and thereby . . . control and renew the shape and destiny of the world." In the light of this, people should be able to understand what the religious practitioners are doing.

Ray described the role of "ritual" as follows:

> The ritual sphere is the sphere par excellence where the world as lived and the world as imagined become fused together, transformed into one reality. Through ritual, man transcends himself and communicates directly with the divine. The coming of the divine to man and of man to divinity happens repeatedly with equal validity on almost every ritual occasion. The experience of salvation is thus a present reality, not a future event. The passage from the profane to the sacred, from man to divinity, from moral conflict to moral unity occurs Here and Now. In short, almost every African ritual is a salvation event in which human experience is re-created and renewed in the all-important ritual Present.[4]

Ray's concept of "community" can be defined in the following way:

> Archetypal symbols express a community's past and they structure collective rites for corporate benefit. In the traditional context religion cannot be a purely personal affair; the relation to the sacred is, first of all, a communal one. Ritual specialists, priests,

---

3. Ray, *African Religions*, 17.
4. Ray, 17.

prophets, diviners and kings are the servants of the community and their role is to mediate the sacred to the people. The life of priests and kings is bound up with the life of the societies they serve; rites which "strengthen" them and "strengthen" the people as a whole. African ritual has a specifically social-functional character and this is clearly recognized by the participants themselves. Every sacrifice is a re-creation of the group's solidarity, every rite of passage a reforging of the corporate life.[5]

This understanding of religious ritual as a corporate event rules out any suggestion of an individualistic understanding of a religious practice. Religion is a corporate or communal affair.

Ray defined African religion from the perspective of "seeing religion as a meaning system" which sees "man as a symbolizing, conceptualizing, meaning-seeking animal."[6] From this conception, one can deduce that meaning is imbedded in religious rituals, practices or ceremonies. Getting to the true meaning is of paramount importance in studying or understanding religion. The chief advocate of this view is Clifford Geertz who defined religion as:

> (1) a system of symbols which acts to (2) establish powerful, pervasive and long-lasting moods and motivations in men (3) by formulating conceptions of general order of existence and (4) clothing these conceptions with such an aura of actuality that (5) the moods and motivations seem uniquely realistic.[7]

Geertz also defined religion "as a cultural system." Defining religion from this perspective alone would be grossly inadequate. Most anthropological and sociological definitions of religion focus on the meaning of religion, and on religion as a cultural system. However, religion is more than just "a theory of meaning" or just "a cultural system"; it is also "a theory of being" or ontology. This concept is essential to balance and strengthen the religious definitions of both Ray and Geertz.

Religion as Explanation, Prediction, Control and Communion

Robin Horton interpreted definitions like the ones above as referring to "a system of theory and associated practice directed to the comprehension and

---

5. Ray, 17.
6. Morgan, "Religion and Culture," 363.
7. Geertz, *Interpretations of Cultures*, 89.

practical control of events in the everyday space-time world."[8] However, Horton argued that one element of religion was missing and he therefore added "communion." By communion, he means "a set of personal relationships with the being or beings postulated by the theory – relationships which are entered into by the human partners as ends in themselves."

But Horton felt that the above definition was still missing something, and so he introduced the additional concept of manipulation. He defined religious manipulation as "a social relationship in which one partner treats the other as a means to achieving an ulterior end." Manipulation is thus almost the opposite of communion, where "one partner treats the other as an end in himself or herself." Horton showed "that in religious as in purely human relationships, there is a wide range of variation between these two poles, with more or less pure 'manipulation' at one extreme, more or less pure 'communion' at the other and a great many combinations lying between them."[9]

Thus Horton suggested that religion can explain, predict, control, manipulate, and also have communal characteristics.

Religion as a Theory of Being

Bolaji Idowu's definition of religion focuses on it as a theory of being. This is very similar to Horton's idea of communion. Idowu states that religion

> results from man's spontaneous awareness of a Living Power, "Wholly Other" and infinitely greater than himself, a power of mystery because unseen, yet a present and urgent reality, seeking to bring man into communion with Himself . . . Religion, in its essence, is the means by which God as a Spirit and man's essential self communicate.[10]

Commenting on this theory of being, Steyne stated: "Religion may then be defined as essentially a search for a relationship to and with the supernatural."[11]

---

8. Horton, *Pattern of Thought*, 5.
9. Horton, 5.
10. Idowu, *African Traditional Religion*, 75.
11. Steyne, *Gods of Power*, 24.

Religion as Feeling, Behaviour and Beliefs

Terms like "being" and "meaning" are, however, rather abstract. So Steyne summarized his understanding of religion in more concrete terms. According to him, religion is associated with three categories of human experience: feelings, behaviour, and beliefs. He explains these as follows:

> Feelings may be manifested in thrills, exaltation, awe, exhilaration and occupation with internal sensations. Examples of religious behavior include rites, rituals, and customs and socially mandated behavior patterns. And these behavior patterns are motivated by beliefs. These include beliefs in spirits outside of men, conceived of as more powerful than man and as controlling all those elements in life upon which he lays stress. These beliefs are interconnected with and related to physiological facts such as birth, reproduction, disease, death; to man's encounter with the forces of nature and his relationship to his fellow man. The ensuing behavior patterns may show that man has a sense of control, confidence and well-being. Or, on the other hand, they may show that he feels fear, uncertainty, confidence, or even frustration.[12]

All of these feelings, behaviours, and beliefs have a goal and purpose and so Steyne listed some definite functions of religion. Religion, he said,

1. Provides order and cohesion to society through belief in and practice of common values and beliefs.

2. Relates adherents to a source of power beyond themselves and thereby creates a sense of well-being.

3. Provides symbolic solutions to fundamental human problems.

4. Offers access to counter-forces for both the mysterious and other dimensions beyond normal control.

5. Postulates an explanation for vexing human problems.

6. Validates society's value system.

7. Reduces fear and anxiety and so alleviates the helplessness of the human condition.

8. Provides a source of help for man's substantive needs.

9. Gives life meaning and quality by steering life to the sacred.

---

12. Steyne, 25.

10. Calls people beyond themselves to an ideal.

11. Provides distinctives that establish an identity.

12. Holds out hope for maturation and thus mastery in the face of human frailty.[13]

Steyne summarized this long list by saying that religion provides a system of belief and practice to deal with the struggles and problems of human life; deals with man's sense of powerlessness and the feelings he derives from what he believes; gives man a sense of order and understanding which provides him with a measure of security and a sense of control, however limited, over the tenuousness of human existence.[14]

People want a religion that they can use to meet their needs and which can provide for their wishes. This combination of human interests and the use of religion are summarized by Steyne, who ultimately defined religion as

> an awareness of and reaction to a living power; an ultimate concern which qualifies all other concerns, which contains the answer to the question of the meaning of life; a way of honoring oneself (by elevating symbols which signify man's devotion to a people group); a means to maintain courage (by conceiving of benevolent powers worthy of worship); a way of exploitation whereby deities bribe man and man in turn bribes deities (and thus a system to placate gods, which subjugate people); an impulse to discover what is right and what is wrong and a search for security, success and happiness.[15]

---

13. Steyne, 31.
14. Steyne, 31–32.
15. Steyne, 27–28.

7

On Studying African Traditional Religion

The study of African religion by African theologians is a relatively young discipline. Before the 1970s the field was dominated by Western anthropologists and scholars whose works provide useful background material and consequently have been included in the bibliography. Reference will be made to some of them when appropriate.

There is, however, a dearth of creative and innovative works. The study of African Traditional Religion has attracted all kinds of scholars, anthropologists, sociologists, theologians, missionaries, and Africanists. However, none of them presents a comprehensive theological systematization.

In attempting to develop a systematic and comprehensive method of studying the traditional religious system and worldview, I found that the most useful book was *Gods of Power: A Study of the Beliefs and Practices of Animists* by Philip M. Steyne. His comprehensive and systematic approach shaped my own understanding and interpretation of African Traditional Religion and its worldview and will provide a guiding light as we attempt to interpret religious and theological themes within the traditional religion of Africa. Yet I have to set off in humility, admitting that I shall not be able to bring everything that is known to bear on this study.

We shall not examine religious institutions and their roles in traditional Africa, or religious practices, or the religious phenomenon and its meaning and purpose in traditional Africa. As the bibliography shows, many scholars have already done a great deal of work in all these areas. Rather, our goal is to ascertain which traditional religious and social values, beliefs and practices shaped the mind and worldview of traditional Africa and also which ones are still influencing modern Africa.

Many scholars have observed that the concept of communion with and worship of the Supreme Being (and other divinities) is not as fully developed in African Traditional Religion as it is in Christianity. They suggest that African religion does not emphasize prayer and praise to God, nor professions of faith and trust in him. Instead Africans are concerned with securing their place and well-being in the face of "the contingent and the incalculable" and with manipulating and using religion for their own benefit.[1]

It appears then that African religious beliefs, practices, rituals, sacrifices, and ceremonies suggest that Africans are preoccupied with security and well-being in their dealings with the spirit beings and the mystical, mysterious and unseen powers which surround them. Some scholars have even suggested that Africans have a utilitarian approach to religion, that they are more interested in what they can get out than in what they can contribute. However, further examination of the role and function of religion in African society may give us another perspective on the social psychology of African religious life.

It is clear that any understanding of African Traditional Religion must incorporate at least the following dimensions, which together make up the traditional religious worldview:

> *personal*: what religion means to believers; their expectations, feelings, and behaviour;
>
> *sociocultural*: the communal aspects of religion and what they mean to both individuals and the community;
>
> *phenomenal*: the all-encompassing meaning of religion in terms of beliefs, behaviour, feelings, and practices to the religious practitioners and community;
>
> *supernatural*: how life revolves around and is totally integrated with the realm of spirits and the supernatural.

Steyne argued that the traditional African religious system addresses social and psychological needs extremely well. It provides "meaning and usefulness" to its adherents; and "order and cohesion" to society. It relates its adherents "to a source of power beyond themselves" and relates "everyone and everything to their influence." It explains human life "fairly adequately by providing satisfactory answers for vexing human problems." It addresses "the personal welfare of its devotees," reducing "their fear and anxiety" and giving them a fair understanding of life in general. It provides for people's "daily physical

---

1. Gehman, *African Traditional Religion*; Steyne, *Gods of Power*; Magesa, *African Religion*.

needs" through invoking "supernatural powers" to provide such things as rain, fertility and health. It teaches "that all of life is sacred because all of life is spiritual," and for this reason "the spirit world must be respected and treated well with cautionary ritual, since spirits interpenetrate the total fabric of life." It creates "identity" and "solidarity in community" and by so doing produces "spiritually oriented people" and enables "its practitioners to communicate with the supernatural and thus achieve a measure of control over power sources."[2]

African Traditional Religion is not a "cognitively oriented system" with esoteric doctrines, and strict rules or regulations. Rather, it is a very existential and experiential religion that is "more felt than understood." This is what makes it very powerful.

Anyone introducing a new religion needs to be aware that the traditional religious system will persist if the new religion fails to address the social and psychological needs which were satisfied by the older religion. In order to introduce a new religion effectively, therefore, one must know the theological foundations of the traditional religious system and how to apply the message of the new religion to meet the needs of individuals and communities. Considering this helps us to understand why a traditional religion will persist, regardless of whether the new beliefs being introduced are those of Christianity, Islam, or modernity.

The truth of this observation is confirmed by the great variety of African expressions of Christianity and Islam and modernity. Despite the fact that colonialism and Christianity might have destroyed the religious and social institutions, the invariant traditional beliefs and worldview live on in the minds of Africans. The worldview of the traditional religious system has an enduring influence on the minds, attitudes, behaviour and social practice of Africans.[3] If Christianity is to transform the African mind, it has to address these traditional religious beliefs and this worldview.

Many African scholars have focused on purely descriptive analyses of religious acts and their functions and meanings (phenomenology). In most cases, little attention has been paid to the theological, psychological, philosophical, and moral or ethical beliefs that influence such acts and practices. This is what I will attempt to address in the hope of contributing to an understanding of the religious and social role and function of each belief, and why these persist.

---

2. Steyne, *Gods of Power*, 31.
3. Mbiti, *Concepts of God*; Kibicho, "Continuity of the African."

8

Fundamental Theological Beliefs

Even though the traditional institutions and structures that harboured, strengthened, and reinforced traditional religious beliefs and practices may have been destroyed by colonialism, Christianity, Islam, or modernity, some elements of these religious beliefs and practices have endured. These may be modified and adapted, but the religious beliefs endure in the minds of people.

Christianity cannot effectively address Africans if it has a shallow understanding of who or what an African is in terms of his beliefs, personality and way of life. To be authentic and relevant in their message, African Christians must have a thorough knowledge of the African terrain. Africans do not abandon all their beliefs or culture or way of life when they become Christians. Christianity does not negate their Africanness, but affirms, renews and transforms it, promoting and even defending it. The Christian faith and biblical teachings give the African a new compass to chart the course of life within an African context, culture, worldview and society. Africans must be able to see that Christianity and biblical teachings are relevant to the African context.

Any meaningful or effective approach to the theology of African Traditional Religion and its accompanying worldview must begin with its fundamental beliefs. Scholars have done extensive case studies of various people-groups in Africa which confirm that there are fundamental beliefs throughout Africa, even though they may be expressed differently from region to region, or from people to people. Africans believe in: impersonal (mystical) powers; spirit beings; divinities/gods; a Supreme Being; and a hierarchy of spiritual beings and powers. These fundamental tenets have shaped the minds and worldviews of Africans and they persist unchanging even in modern Africa.

From his study of Edwin Smith, Victor B. Cole identified four foundational principles of African Traditional Religion: (1) *mysterium tremendum*; (2) dynamism or magic; (3) spiritism; and (4) awareness of God. In his definition of animism, Steyne identified the same categories: (1) belief in impersonal power; (2) belief in spirit beings; (3) belief in gods, and (4) belief in one supreme God.[1]

According to Smith, magic came into being when humankind tried to "control and conciliate the awareness of the mysterious power at work in the world" and when an African was "faced with the contingent and the incalculable." Smith understood that the African seeks "practical ends in both his magic and his religion; he seeks to use the mysterious powers of nature for his benefit, or at least he tries to ward off the harm that they may cause him."[2] The manifestation of these magic powers is what Smith called dynamism (power). Smith saw this dynamism as religion since it was directed to "a power superior to man." This is what we shall call the *power phenomenon*.

Closely related is the African belief "in psychic beings that are intelligent, purposive and personal as opposed to impersonal potency at work in dynamism." This is what Smith called spiritism and what we shall call the *spirit phenomenon*.

Lastly, the awareness of God was also identified. Some of the pioneering anthropologists and missionaries denied that Africans had any awareness of God. The works of Danquah, Idowu, Mbiti and many others, however, "argued convincingly for this sense of awareness."

Let us examine each aspect of these foundational religious beliefs in turn to see how they influence the African mind and worldview.

Belief in Impersonal (Mystical) Powers

Scholar after scholar has documented beliefs in the supernatural, mystical, impersonal, and unseen powers among people-groups across Africa. It is believed that everything that exists is infused with this impersonal, mystical power which lies behind the material, the physical, and the visible. Since this impersonal power is not visible, it may be supernatural, spiritual, or mystical, but it is a reality.

This impersonal power has been given various names. Edwin Smith called it the *mysterium tremendum* and stated that this phenomenon was "played upon, defined and rationalized by myths and creeds and put to use through

---

1. Steyne, *Gods of Power*.
2. Edwin Smith quoted in Cole, "Christian and African," 3.

control and conciliation."³ It has also been referred to as *mana*, the life force, vital force, the life essence, and dynamism.

The source of this power is not always known, but it is usually attributed to the activities of mysterious higher powers, whether personal or impersonal, which generate or deposit power in things or objects. The potency, efficacy, and durability of this power can vary from object to object and from place to place. Some objects are inherently imputed more power than others, that is, they are always assumed to be more naturally endowed with power than others are.

The traditional African is fully aware of the overwhelming presence of the mystical, mysterious and unseen powers and forces at work in the world. Creation, nature and everything that exists is infused with this impersonal power. African beliefs and practices of witchcraft, divination, and sorcery are rooted in this understanding. Medicine men and women, diviners, and seers use the impersonal powers associated with natural objects, plants, and animals for medicine, magic, charms, and amulets. Some believe that the mysterious powers embedded in objects can be extracted for specific uses. They believe that mysterious powers can be transmitted through certain objects or by purely spiritual means to specific destinations. However, they believe that these powers can also be contagious, transmitted through contact with objects carrying or mediating such powers.

These impersonal powers can be used for both good and evil. The existence of wicked human beings and wicked spirit beings, who have access to the mysterious powers, makes life full of uncertainties – rife with unpredictable wickedness and evil and dangerous to human beings. Thus traditional Africans who believe in the presence of dominating impersonal powers feel that they are at the mercy of users of these powers. The attitudes of African Christians to witchcraft, sorcery, and divination are based on their belief in these powers. The practical realities of their daily experiences are thus structured and rooted in these traditional beliefs; Africans see and experience their power and efficacy in their daily life. Christianity, Islam and modernity have all encountered this traditional belief and its worldview.

Christians must recognize that the theological foundation of the traditional African belief in these forces is power spirituality. Power spirituality generates attitudes, feelings, behaviours, and social and religious practices which must be understood and addressed. The Bible and its teachings must be applied to the root of this belief.

---

3. Smith in Cole, 3.

Traditional Africans need a picture of the Christian worldview which contains answers to power spirituality. They need to know why they should believe what the Bible says and how the power described in the Bible differs from their power spirituality. We must match belief with belief, worldview with worldview, spiritual power with spiritual power. In defining our Christian approach, therefore we must ask:

- How do we apply the message of the Bible and the gospel of Christ to the nature of this power spirituality and its impact or influence upon man?
- How do we apply the message of the Bible and the gospel of Christ to all the practices, feelings, attitudes, rituals, rites, and ceremonies that traditional Africa has developed from this power spirituality?
- When a traditional African confronts Christian categories such as the power of the blood of Christ; the power of Christ; the power of the Holy Spirit; the power of God; the power of prayer in the name of Jesus, how are these spiritual powers understood theologically?

However, our theological approach must go beyond merely matching biblical texts with specific traditional beliefs. When a belief in the potency of these powers is condemned as demonic or satanic, people in traditional Africa need to know why these powers are regarded as such. The new spiritual power must be seen to work, otherwise it will be dropped for a better one, or the individual will simply go back to the old which they have seen to work. People will only agree to abandon their belief in traditional power spirituality if they know that the spiritual power that is being offered in Christianity is superior to the one they know. The difference between the two is, of course, what lies behind their contents. It is the source of religious and spiritual power that makes Christianity different: the power of the Triune God (Father, Son and Holy Spirit).

Belief in Spirit Beings

Mystical power is not the only mysterious force in traditional African belief. The spirit world of African people is very densely populated with spirit beings, spirits, and the living-dead or spirits of the ancestors.[4] These are "psychic beings that are intelligent, purposive and personal as opposed to the impersonal

---

4. Mbiti, *African Religions*.

potency at work in dynamism."⁵ This aspect of African belief we call the *spirit phenomenon*.

This is different from the *power phenomenon*. However, there is a very close relationship between spirit beings and the mystical or impersonal powers and forces. Like those powers, spirits are believed to inhabit certain trees, rocks or mountains, caves, rivers, lakes, forests, burial grounds, animals, human beings, the skies, the ground and other sites, carved or moulded objects, charms, amulets – the list is endless.

Spirits are ranked hierarchically in accordance with their power and the role they play in the ontological order in the spirit world.⁶ First in the hierarchy is the Creator, thereafter are the deities, the object-embodied spirits, the ancestors' spirits, and other miscellaneous spirits that are non-human. Humans stand between this host of spirits and the world of nature.⁷

Spirit beings are usually categorized as either the spirits of the dead elders (the ancestors, who are close to humans and serve as their custodians) or non-human spirit beings. They can also be classified as good or evil, depending on whether they use the powers with which they are endowed to achieve positive or negative goals, to bring blessings or curses. Africans believe that evil spirits are always associated with Satan. The spirit world or the realm of the supernatural is, in a sense, a battleground of spirits and powers that use their mystical and spiritual powers to influence the course of human life. The spirit world also evokes belief in life after death, future rewards, future punishment, and reincarnation.

Spirit beings can be malicious or capricious, and so one must be wise and tactful in one's dealings with them to avoid angering, provoking, or injuring them. If humans knew how to master and control the realm of the spirit world, the world would be a much happier place. Consequently if one wishes to be successful, or even merely to enjoy well-being, it is important to consult human specialists with experience of and access to mystical powers. These specialists include medicine men, rainmakers, mediums, diviners, sorcerers, magicians, witches, and any others who have the ability to manipulate spirit beings so that they serve humans, or vice-versa.

Other sources of safety and protection in a world dominated by the spirit beings and powers include religious rites, reverence for ancestors, symbolic totems and adherence to taboos, rituals, superstitions, and customs. Some,

---

5. Cole, "Christian and African," 3.
6. Oji, *Ikpu Alu* [Atonement].
7. Ikenga-Metuh, *Comparative Studies*.

if not all of these are needed for guidance and protection. Africans think that believing in spirit beings also means believing in the possibility of spirit possession and in the need to practice exorcism. The *bori* dance in Hausaland (West Africa) is a social practice that deals with spiritism, health, healing, and exorcism.

Traditional African concepts of reality and destiny are deeply rooted in this spirit world, as the activities and actions of spirit beings are believed to govern all social and spiritual phenomena. Spirits define, mould, shape, and condition the life of traditional Africans. For this reason, the way Africans interpret, and apply this belief is bound to affect their worldview and their understanding of any new religion introduced to them. Traditional Africans are overwhelmed by the presence of spirit beings in life and need to know why they should believe what the Bible says about spirits when it is different from their traditional beliefs.

The attributes and moral character of God, the Spirit of God, the Holy Spirit, Satan, angels, demons, and ancestors must consequently be clearly explained. The differences between these spirit beings must be clarified, as well as how they differ from the mystical, mysterious or impersonal powers and forces of traditional religion. Because the traditional holistic view of life puts all these spirit beings into one "communal basket," the holiness and transcendence of God can easily be devalued.

Biblical texts condemning involvement with spirits and demonic activities abound. But our theological approach must move beyond matching biblical texts with specific beliefs in spirit beings. We must address why such a belief exists and why Africans get involved with spirits. We also need to explain why the Bible condemns our involvement with spirit beings. African Christians can benefit greatly from their traditional spirituality if it is renewed and transformed by the gospel of Christ and sound teaching.

African Pagan Spirituality

When we combine the concepts of *power phenomenon* and *spirit phenomenon* we get *spirit-power*, a dominant spirituality in traditional religion.[8] We might call this African pagan spirituality, for want of a better term. The word "pagan" is not used pejoratively to demean African spirituality, but descriptively to describe a distinctive type of spirituality.

---

8. Turaki, *Techniques of African Pagan*.

These two basic categories, power phenomenon and spirit phenomenon, are related. We have noted that the term "power phenomenon" refers to the unseen forces, to supernatural powers. "Spirit phenomenon," we learned on the other hand, refers to spirit beings which can exert a spiritual influence over humans or nature. They are distinct from the impersonal powers and forces and can cause the supernatural powers to perform miracles.

This twin belief is the key to our understanding of traditional African spirituality and its profound influence and effect upon traditional African life.

In African pagan spirituality there is only one supreme reality – *spirit-power*. Both spirit and supernatural power are dominant in what lies behind the physical reality. The material world of nature is not actually real, but the spirit world, the supernatural, the invisible, the hidden, the unseen and the mysterious is real. The activities and actions of spirit beings are believed to govern all social and spiritual phenomena. This spiritual reality also provides the means of communication with the spirit world, as well as the acquisition and exercise of spiritual powers. Various methods, techniques, and means of communicating with and by spirit beings have been developed within this African pagan spirituality.

The most interesting debate in African pagan spirituality is the location of this spirit-power which can manifest itself as both personal and impersonal power. Some suggest it is located in the Supreme Being or in spirit beings in general. Others see it as being located in nature, the material world, or the human world. In dealing with spirit-power, some use gods or divinities, while some use nature or creatures. God is not distinguishable from this spirit-power as the emphasis is not on differentiation or transcendence, but on harmony and balance. Depending on one's understanding and interpretation, the Supreme Being can be both personal and impersonal. Reality is seen as holistic organism, uniting all things in creation.

African pagan spirituality is people-centred. People seek to possess spirit-power in order to acquire something beneficial. There is no religion for the sake of religion or altruism. The ultimate goal of religion is each person's own happiness and goodness. Thus, religious rituals, ceremonies, techniques, methods are all simply means to obtain personal happiness and a good life through spirit-power.

Since spirit-power is very real, it dominates the psyche, the mind, and the thought world of traditional Africans. Traditional religion, neo-paganism, religious cults, and new forms of religious movements all make use of this power. There are many who become Christians and yet maintain allegiance to it. Yet satanic and demonic activities dominate this spirit-power and can exercise tremendous spirit-power over human beings and societies. We must differentiate between this spirit-power and the Supreme Being, between spirit-powers and the Holy Spirit and angels even though they may have similar manifestations. Even in church and Christian gatherings it is very easy to imitate the works of the Holy Spirit through miracles, healings, wonders and signs. Imitation must be detected through spiritual discernment. Spirit-powers are inferior to Christ-power and to the Holy Spirit.

Belief in Many Divinities

African Traditional Religion in some parts of Africa has an elaborate pantheon of divinities. The Yoruba of Nigeria, for example, are known to have several hundred divinities. But this is not the case in Southern Africa or in some parts of West Africa. Some African ethnic groups do not seem to have any divinities, while others have no special shrines or places of worship associated with divinities or a Supreme Being.

In those places in Africa that have divinities, each divinity has its specific area of influence and control. Some of them were originally mythological figures from African legends, primordial histories, and cosmologies; some were tribal heroes or heroines. However, divinities are usually associated with different aspects of life, society, and community. There are, for example, divinities of the sea or the waters, of rain and thunder, of fertility, of health or sickness, of planting or harvest as well as tribal, clan, or family deities. African divinities can take the forms of mountains, rivers, forests, mother earth, the sun, the moon, the stars, and ancestors. The plurality of divinities with their varying powers, their influence, their hierarchy, and their territory, even within one ethnic group or community, clearly indicates that traditional religious thought is open to religious pluralism, accommodation, tolerance, assimilation, and adaptation.

Some African scholars no longer accept the term polytheism (worship of many gods) as being applicable to African Traditional Religion and prefer the term "divinities" or "deities" to "gods."[9] To them, the term "idolatry" is a derogatory misnomer. The debate in African theology about whether African divinities are worshipped as gods or whether they are only intermediaries or mediators is inconclusive. Some have argued that Africans do not worship either their divinities or their ancestors but only God or, rather, that God is worshipped through them. In terms of this argument, sacrifices, offerings, and

---

9. Idowu, *Olodumare*; Mbiti, *Prayers of African Religion*.

prayers are not directed to the divinities or the ancestors themselves, but are directed ultimately to God. This kind of interpretation removes the stigma of idolatry.

However, such arguments are simply Christians talking among themselves, reading or projecting Christian concepts of "intermediaries" or "mediators" into African Traditional Religion. This is the result of using comparative analysis methodology in the study of religions. Comparative analysis is simply descriptive; it is not theological. If African theologians and scholars want to remove the stigma of Western scholarship that demeaned traditional religion, that is understandable, but their response ought to be theologically correct. It is theologically impossible to compare African Traditional Religion with the biblical revelation and the Christian gospel. Traditional religion can only be measured under a theological discourse within general revelation, although the Bible provides a specially revealed definition of some of the religious elements found in African Traditional Religion. The Bible and the gospel of Christ challenge and offer to transform traditional religion. For instance, the Bible speaks out strongly against the nature and practice of idolatry.

The introduction of Christianity and other monotheistic religions, such as Islam, may have added what is called "henotheism" to the African worldview. Henotheism is the worship of one god without denying the existence of other gods and reveals African dualism and pluralism. Traditional beliefs can accommodate the worship of the Christian God along with other gods without creating any serious theological crisis for the believer. A plurality of gods or divinities permits a plurality of beliefs, practices and behaviours in one religion. This belief also allows for the accommodation, adaptation, and domestication of new gods or divinities into the old religion. An accommodative religious belief can hold two opposing views without any conflict. For example, pluralism has the ability to hold to both what Jesus stands for and what the ancestors stand for. Many worship Jesus Christ plus their ancestral beliefs.

In presenting the gospel of Christ and biblical teachings to traditional Africans, this fundamental theological belief concerning the plurality and hierarchy of divinities or gods, together with its religious and social role in traditional society, must be understood. Any attempt to introduce Christian categories into Africa, such as Jesus Christ as God the Son, the Holy Spirit as the Spirit of God and God as the Father, must be explained clearly. The traditional African can easily understand or interpret them on the basis of traditional theological beliefs, simply assigning Father, Son and Holy Spirit each a place in the pantheon of gods or divinities and their hierarchy.

Because traditional religion already had a fundamental theology and a worldview, our task is to get to its theological foundations and roots through theological engagement and discourse. We must acknowledge the traditional belief in many divinities or gods and understand why such a belief is held. The acceptance of the gospel of Christ and the Bible must be evident in transformed attitudes, feelings, behaviours and practices. Without this evidence, it is clear that assent to Christ or biblical teachings has not touched the heart.

Belief in a Supreme Being

Some of the pioneering anthropologists and missionaries denied that Africans had any perception of God. They were wrong. It has been firmly established that Africans do have a concept or awareness of a universal God and Creator.[10]

Idowu calls the Yoruba religion "diffused monotheism."[11] This means that the Yoruba were originally monotheistic, but that over the centuries a proliferation of divinities overshadowed the earlier monotheistic beliefs and practices. Similar ideas of diffused monotheism are scattered across the continent of Africa. As a biblical scholar, Idowu knew that after the fall sin gradually diffused man's knowledge of God. His idea reflects the statement by the apostle Paul in Romans 1 that, even though humankind knew God, people abandoned that knowledge to worship the creatures instead of God.

The overwhelming burden of evidence suggests that, even though Africans generally have an awareness of and a belief in a Supreme Being, this Being is not worshipped exclusively and directly. Instead, lesser spirit beings dominate the everyday religious life of traditional Africans. They receive the sacrifices, offerings, and prayers offered directly. Only in some parts of Africa is the Supreme Being mentioned in prayers, songs, and some religious ceremonies.

Because they have this attitude to God, people generally turn to impersonal powers, divinities, ancestors, and spirit beings for help. God is only mentioned, remembered, or approached occasionally. The God who is above the lesser gods seems "not to be intimately involved or concerned with man's affairs and world. Instead, men seek out the lesser powers to meet their desires."[12] This fosters a form of spirituality that does not make for intimacy with God and that hinders the development of a strong Christian spirituality based on an intimate relationship with God. Spirituality without a strong sense of God's

---

10. Idowu, *Olodumare*; Mbiti, *Concepts of God*.
11. Idowu, *Olodumare*.
12. Steyne, *Gods of Power*, 35.

sovereignty over one's life weakens the concept of holiness, righteousness and the strong commitment to godly things and practices.

The problem is compounded if the Christian triune God appears not to be as powerful and as active in human affairs as the traditional African spirits, ancestors, mystical powers and forces. Belief in God can falter if the Christian priests, pastors, bishops, and teachers do not seem to be as powerful or as active as the traditional African specialists.

Our task is to get to the root of this traditional theological belief in the Supreme Being to examine its influence over traditional Africans. We are not just trying to affirm a concept, awareness or perception of God. If God is seen to be absent or not engaged in the daily affairs of man, this affects humankind spiritually. We know that humankind's rebellion and disobedience to God resulted in a broken relationship, an alienation from God. After the fall, humankind lost intimacy, communion, and fellowship with God, and so turned to the worship of spirit beings and supernatural powers. In the absence of God, spirit-power as a form of spirituality will dominate the life of traditional Africans. Yet Christ's power through the cross and through the resurrection has broken the power of these spirit beings and spirit powers. This Christ-power must be used to confront and to overcome the traditional belief in spirit-power. Paul explained this in these words:

> And having disarmed the powers and authorities, he made a public spectacle of them, triumphing over them by the cross. (Col 2:15)

> For though we live in the world, we do not wage war as the world does. The weapons we fight with are not the weapons of the world. On the contrary, they have divine power to demolish strongholds. We demolish arguments and every pretension that sets itself up against the knowledge of God, and we take captive every thought to make it obedient to Christ. (2 Cor 10:3–5)

Belief in a Hierarchy of Spiritual Beings and Powers

Traditional Africans believe in the hierarchy of spirit beings and powers. The Supreme Being enjoys the highest and greatest position, while gods (or divinities) occupy a lesser position. Next come spirit beings, whose authority, power, influence and legitimacy depend upon their position within the ontological order of being. However, it is important to note that this hierarchy is a fluid one, where the distinction between spirits may be vague and their powers diffuse.

Spirit beings dispense and control the effects of spiritual and mystical powers and forces, and influence the morality and ethics of human societies.[13] Traditional Africans respond to these spirit beings according to each spirit's place in the spiritual hierarchy, their power and influence, territoriality, legitimacy, and role. Because God seems to be so far away, traditional Africans deal intimately with the lesser spirit beings and supernatural powers that are closer to them. An African saying states, "You know only the one whom you see." Africans know and deal only with those who are involved in the realities of their lives. The presence of witchcraft and witches, the preponderance of demonic activities and the curses of gods, spirits, and evil people cause many Africans to seek help, not from God who seems to them to be out of touch with reality, but from whatever can grant immediate relief or provide a solution. There are certain things which they feel God cannot do, so he is not needed. Instead one can go to those who are ever ready to grant requests, to those presumed higher and more influential than oneself who are ready to help.

These traditional principles of power, authority, and legitimacy have a profound influence on the African conception of spirituality. Many Christians leave the church and their pastors to seek spiritual help from witch doctors, spirit mediums and wizards. When African Christians fear witchcraft or even worship the spirits of the dead or ancestors, they do so as a result of practical experience. This is the reality of life that surrounds them. Unless they know that they can be liberated from such powers and fears, they cannot leave the traditional way and beliefs no matter how much they are involved with Christianity. Unless the power of the cross of Christ is seen and felt to be superior to that of the spirits, powers and ancestors, some will battle to leave the old way of beliefs and life.

Even when traditional Africans embrace Christianity, the Christian God, Jesus Christ, the Holy Spirit, Satan, angels, demons, and ancestors may be treated theologically in accordance with their assumed hierarchy or status. Alternatively, they may be placed in one "basket" and treated accordingly.

Paul, however, once again reminds us that the hierarchy of powers is subject to Christ's power:

> And his incomparably great power for us who believe. That power is the same as the mighty strength he exerted when he raised Christ from the dead and seated him at his right hand in the heavenly realms, far above all rule and authority, power and

---

13. Ikenga-Metuh, *Comparative Studies*.

dominion, and every name that is invoked, not only in the present age but also in the one to come. And God placed all things under his feet and appointed him to be head over everything for the church, which is his body, the fullness of him who fills everything in every way. (Eph 1:19–23)

Therefore God exalted him to the highest place and gave him the name that is above every name, that at the name of Jesus every knee should bow, in heaven and on earth and under the earth, and every tongue acknowledge that Jesus Christ is Lord, to the glory of God the Father. (Phil 2:9–11)

9

Fundamental Psychological Beliefs

If we were to reduce the motivation behind African Traditional Religion to psychology or primitiveness alone, it would reveal that we do not have a deep theological understanding of the definition of religion.[1] Theology or beliefs may arouse or assuage a variety of psychological feelings. Besides religious or spiritual motivation, there are real psychological elements in religious practices and behaviour.

The African religious mentality is loaded with emotions and feelings arising from their combination of beliefs, rituals, festivals, and ceremonies. An African becomes pragmatic and proactive, confronting life with spirit-power or else perishing. However, traditional life is not all fear and anxiety, nor is it totally fatalistic or totally manipulative. Life has both its negatives and positives. Philip Steyne identifies five core psychological feelings that dominate the traditional religious mind and worldview. The first four exert a negative impact upon life, while the last one gives a positive and dynamic ray of hope.[2]

1. The dominant fear of mysterious or mystical powers and forces, the power of spirit beings, gods, divinities, ancestors and wicked or evil forces.

Anxiety and fear are rooted in the belief in spirit-power. The knowledge and belief that such spirit-power exists generates strong emotions, feelings, attitudes, behaviours, and practices. It is believed that only a superior spirit-power can allay these. If Christ's power is not seen, the African mind will not be renewed and the new biblical worldview will not replace the old worldview that generates anxiety and fear and that person will continue to feel and behave as before.

---

1. Hountondji, *African Philosophy*; Horton, *Pattern of Thought*.
2. Steyne, *Gods of Power*, 48.

2. The absence of consolation, peace and comfort and the presence of evil and wickedness in the world.

Spirit-power generates a sense of the presence of evil and wickedness in the world. This takes away consolation, peace and comfort. Human beings are saddled with the problem of removing this sense of evil or succumbing to it. Traditional Africans are fully aware of the devastating impact of spirit-power and believe that deliverance can come only from a source that can generate its own spirit-power, much stronger than the one dominating the scene. Only a stronger spirit or power can bring consolation, peace and comfort. Without this superior spirit-power, the feelings, attitudes, behaviours and practices will continue. Christianity's task is to present the reality that Jesus Christ is a superior Spirit-Power who has defeated and conquered all principalities and powers. The Christ-power of the cross and resurrection can remove anxiety and fear.

3. Little differentiation between good and evil or lack of clear-cut boundaries in ethics and morality, attitudes, behaviour and social practice.

The traditional worldview is holistic or organic and only differentiates between the spiritual and matter, or the spirit and nature. It lacks clear boundaries between good and evil. Imagine the attitude, behaviour, and practice of someone who cannot distinguish between good and evil, between the spirits and supernatural powers, between God and spirit-powers, or between the role of Jesus Christ and that of ancestors.

4. A fatalistic approach to life which cripples initiative, hope and endurance as one's destiny has been determined by spiritual and mystical powers and forces.

Fatalism is state of hopelessness. Imagine dealing with people who are perpetually in a state of *fait-accompli*, knowing that a situation cannot be changed. They desire liberation, but it will take a strong man to change the situation or destiny. In this situation, people look for one who can promise hope and new destiny.

5. A search for a means to manipulate things or beings to achieve some measurable ends.

In a situation of need, people become pragmatists. They act using certain means to change their situation or destiny. Let us consider some of these psychological beliefs.

Fundamental Psychological Beliefs

The Presence of Fear and the Absence of Consolation

The presence of fear or dread in traditional religion is caused by the strong and pervasive belief in the impersonal, mystical, and spiritual powers and forces. How can one have peace and comfort when one lives in the midst of unseen, unpredictable, and dreadful mystical or mysterious powers and forces, which are controlled by malicious and capricious spirits and human beings? Traditional religious practices in the form of rites, rituals, and ceremonies help only to reinforce, heighten, or consolidate such beliefs, not to bring lasting consolation, comfort, and peace. The repetitive nature of these rites, rituals, and ceremonies adds more dread and fear.

If it is to be effective, Christianity must address Africans at this psychological level. The gospel, in presenting Christ's power, plays a key role in allaying, assuaging or removing these fears.

Little Differentiation between Good and Evil

The gods and spirit beings exhibit contradictory characteristics, suggesting they are both good and evil. On account of this, it is difficult to make any distinction between good and evil. The manifestations of sorcery, witchcraft and fate create more problems and compound the issue of good and evil in life. If the boundaries between good and evil are undifferentiated, this makes for difficult ethical and moral practices and considerations. Attitudes, behaviours, and social practices can hardly be clearly defined.

Christianity, on the other hand, is very clear in terms of what is good and what is evil. Ethics and morality govern attitude, behaviour and practice.

The Belief in Fatalism

When one is subjected to dominant powers that are superior, one tends to resign oneself to fate. Evil and fatalism abound. Where evil predominates, fatalism takes over. One's lot or destiny has already been settled by the powers that be. This breeds hopelessness and meaninglessness. It stifles initiative and discourages action. If what I am, or if what I will do has already been predetermined, serious ethical and moral problems arise.

Christianity brings "good news" of hope, life, and a new beginning.

The Quest for Control

The search for a means to control and manipulate the powers dominates traditional Africa. Humans are on the lookout for allies among these unpredictable and capricious spirit beings, gods, and even among other people. Humans need such allies for their survival, but the spiritual beings need humankind for their survival as well.

Laurenti Magesa in his book *African Religion: The Moral Traditions of Abundant Life* (1998) has a dominant view which emphasizes the African quest for life force. He states that the only dominant "ideology" or reason for living that an African has is the quest for life force. If the primary goal in life is pursuit of life force, then the search for a means to obtain it becomes frantic. This pursuit becomes the dominant goal of African life, morality, and ethics. A traditional African turns to rites, rituals, ceremonies, sacrifices, and offerings as a means of communication, control, manipulation, fellowship, communion, and affinity with the spirit world, spirits, divinities, ancestors, and gods. African religious mentality, spirituality, and behaviour are shaped by this religious worldview and psychology.

When Africans become Christians, things do not change immediately and these attitudes may persist, influencing Christian teachings. Sin, spirituality, and power are understood in the light of rituals, ceremonies, religious exuberance, and religious ecstasy. The Christian message is that dealing with sin involves more than these. It involves the cross of Christ, and our consequent redemption, sanctification, deliverance, and repentance with forgiveness.

10

Fundamental Philosophical Beliefs

Traditional Africa must be understood not only in terms of its religious beliefs and practices but also in terms of the philosophical beliefs and practices which underlie the traditional worldview and its moral laws. There is always an interaction between a society's philosophy (its understanding of the world or worldview), and its fundamental theological beliefs with their corresponding religious practices, behaviours, and feelings. This is why it is important to examine the philosophical foundations that influence modern Africa, Christianity and Islam.

Turner's Categories of Traditional Worldview

Bediako identified the following six categories of traditional worldview in the works of Harold W. Turner.[1]

1. Kinship with Nature

Humankind has an affinity or "sense of kinship with nature, in which animals and plants, no less than human beings, have their own spiritual existence and place in the universe, as interdependent parts of a whole." On account of this belief, "any object of the natural environment may enter into a totemic spiritual relationship with human beings or become tutelary and guardian spirits whilst the environment itself is used realistically and unsentimentally but with profound respect and reverence and without exploitation."

---

1. Bediako, *Christianity in Africa*, 93–95.

2. A Sense of Awe

There is a "deep sense that man is finite, weak and impure or sinful and stands in need of a power not his own." This opens humans up to the possibility of religious beliefs and practices.

3. Belief in Transcendent Spirit Beings and Powers

This is the "conviction that humankind is not alone in the universe, for there is a spiritual world of powers or beings more powerful and ultimate than itself." This conviction encourages humans to seek affinity with the spiritual powers that are beyond them.

4. Communication with the Spirit-World

There is a "belief that man can enter into relationship with the benevolent spirit-world and so share in its powers and blessings and receive protection from evil forces by these transcendent helpers." This leads humankind to develop means of communication with the spirit world.

5. Creation of an Ancestors' Cult

There is an "acute sense of the reality of the afterlife, a conviction which explains the important place of ancestors or the living dead in many primal religions." The total life and existence of traditional Africans is deeply rooted in this ancestral belief.

6. Harmony between the Physical and Spiritual Worlds

The physical and spiritual worlds are not separate, but are one and interdependent. This means there is a holistic view of life.

Steyne's Basic Philosophical Foundations

In his study of animism, Steyne outlined five philosophical foundations of the traditional worldview.[2] If we combine Turner's philosophical categories with those of Steyne, we can formulate a comprehensive philosophical system that will throw light on the interpretation of traditional religion and culture. Steyne's

---

2. Steyne, *Gods of Power*.

five basic categories are holism, spiritualism, dynamism, communalism, and fatalism.

The combination of the African theological beliefs and these basic philosophical beliefs creates a powerful and pervasive religious and cultural worldview that dominates and moulds African thought.

Holism

Holism refers to a state of complex interdependency, in which each part of an organism has a function. Philosophically, holism is the term for the view that life is more than the sum of its parts. Steyne defined the concept in the following way:

> The world interacts with itself. The sky, the spirits, the earth, the physical world, the living, and the deceased all act, interact, and react in consort. One works on the other and one part can't exist nor be explained without the other. The universe, the spirit world and man are all part of the same fabric. Each needs the other to activate it.[3]

This view of the world means that there are no clear boundaries between the physical and the spiritual dimensions of life. There is also no sharp distinction between secular and religious activities, between one's work and one's community responsibilities – they are "all knit together in a whole [so that man] feels at one with his world."[4]

The same idea was also expressed by Bediako:

> Man lives in a sacramental universe where there is no sharp dichotomy between the physical and the spiritual. The physical acts as a vehicle for spiritual power whilst the physical realm is held to be patterned on the model of the spiritual world beyond.[5]

It is easy to see how Western dualism creates serious theological problems for traditional Africans who have an organic or holistic view of life. Because nature, humanity and the spirit world constitute one fluid coherent unit, there are clearly pantheistic elements in African holism. In fact, nature is defined as:

---

3. Steyne, 58.
4. Steyne, 59.
5. Bediako, *Christianity in Africa*, 95.

This visible material world or universe, comprising both living and non-living things, visible and invisible powers, plants and animals, the inanimate and the natural phenomena, like lightning and thunder, all centred around man. The spirit world is all the same tacitly understood as inclusive in nature.[6]

Thus, nature includes both the impersonal or mysterious powers and spirit beings. Bediako showed how this leads to pantheism:

[Humankind has] a sense of kinship with nature, in which animals and plants, no less than human beings, had their own spiritual existence and place in the universe, as interdependent parts of a whole. [On account of this belief,] any object of the natural environment may enter into a totemic spiritual relationship with human beings or become tutelary and guardian spirits whilst the environment itself is used realistically and unsentimentally but with profound respect and reverence and without exploitation.[7]

Africans do not live in a confused world of non-integrated parts. Life is mysterious, but it is part of a whole. That whole is governed by the law of harmony, which aims to maintain a state of agreement or peacefulness. The traditional African seeks to live in harmony and to balance his life in a harmonious and peaceful existence with his entire world and especially with the spirit world.

The traditional concept of harmony relates to cosmic order. Here, the spirit world and the world of nature combine together harmoniously as one spirit-power. When the spirit acts upon matter or nature, the product is spirit-power or supernatural power. Even though the supernatural is not seen, it is felt and its visible deeds in nature are observable. So spirit-power works through nature. The physical activities of the humans or spirit beings have consequences upon the balance or harmony in the cosmos.

This holistic view does not distinguish between the sacred and the secular and, as a consequence, traditional religion and worldviews do not have creeds. Beliefs do not have to be learned, but are caught, passed on, and lived.

Traditional religion has a clearer understanding of this spirit-power than most Christians have, but this link is clearly revealed in the Bible. The ground or earth or cosmos was also cursed by God on account of the fall of Adam and Eve in the Garden of Eden. Sin as a spiritual phenomenon has both physical

---

6. Oji, *Ikpu Alu* [Atonement], 15.
7. Bediako, *Christianity in Africa*, 95.

and spiritual consequences. It affects not only our human nature, but also our environment. But most grievous of all is its impact on the spiritual aspect of life. It is this understanding that leads to the concept of the restoration of harmony through blood sacrifices and other rituals that we see in traditional religion. Some Africans will cherish their beliefs in traditional spirit-power even when they become Christians unless this belief is replaced by Christ-power.

The law of harmony covers the theological questions of reconciliation, restoration, reverence, awe, a sense of wonder, accompanying sacrifices and offerings, ceremonies, rituals, and worship. Moral and ethical questions are also raised in the area of the relationship between the humans and spirit beings. With whom and what should one seek to live in harmony, in peace, in fellowship and communion? The theology of redemption and reconciliation in the work of Christ on the cross becomes more meaningful as it addresses these questions of cosmic harmony.

Christianity in Africa must address this holistic worldview. It is not facing a specific religious belief, but a philosophical worldview that covers the totality of life, both in the human world and in the spirit world.

Spiritualism (Spirit-Phenomenon)

In the previous section we stated that traditional beliefs do not distinguish between the material and the spiritual worlds. It might be truer to say that traditional Africans regard this world in essence as spiritual rather than material and life as saturated with supernatural possibilities. Spiritualism in this sense is spirit phenomenon. Spiritualism is defined by Steyne as follows:

> The whole universe is interconnected through the will and the power contained in both animate and inanimate objects. Everything man is, does, handles, projects, and interacts with is interpenetrated with the spiritual. His sociocultural structures, down to their finest details, are under the control of the spiritual powers or forces. Nothing in man's environment escapes the influence or the manipulation of the spirit world. The world is more spiritual than it is physical and it is spiritually upheld.[8]

The whole creation is replete with the dominant and pervasive presence of impersonal powers and forces, spirit beings, many divinities, and gods. It

---

8. Steyne, *Gods of Power*, 37.

becomes imperative for humans to maintain good relationships with these spirits, gods, and ancestors in order to secure favour.

> Man is related to and dependent upon the unseen. For this reason, all of life is to be understood spiritually. The correct response to any situation is spiritual, whether the matter is a family affair, sickness, or ceremonial practice.[9]

Thus, in African traditional philosophy, answers to questions about meaning in life (the "why" questions) are always dominated by a spiritual emphasis. When trouble comes in the form of disease, natural disasters, or untimely death, traditional Africans look beyond the obvious physical causes and consult religious specialists to find the ultimate spiritual cause. In old Africa, before doing anything, Africans would consult the oracles in order to obtain divine answers; the Jews of the Old Testament did the same thing.

This philosophy both draws on and supports the pantheistic or polytheistic theology. The law of the spirit is a universal principle which governs universal events and unseen powers and mysteries. It affects the destiny, the well-being, and the general life of individual human beings, as well as the lives of people-groups or families, clans, communities, and tribes. It manifests itself in and through the spirits, human beings, and inanimate objects. It defines the reality of the African worldview and is pervasive, hidden, unexplainable, unpredictable, powerful, and awesome. This law is reflected in the moral laws and religious practices that govern the interrelationship and integration of spirit beings and humans in the traditional spirit world.

African spirituality is rooted in this understanding of life. It is not an understanding of how the Holy Spirit works in human life, but of cosmic spirits and their spirit-power. Christianity must examine the theology of this traditional spiritual worldview that is so similar to that of the Bible and must formulate a Christian theology of spirit-power which is rooted in the cross and the resurrection of Christ.

Dynamism (Power Phenomenon)

Dynamism is both a belief and a philosophy of power or supernatural power. When we combine spiritual phenomenon and power phenomenon, we get spirit-power. Power-consciousness therefore is very strong in traditional belief and philosophy.

---

9. Steyne, 59.

When one views the world in terms of holism and spiritualism, one's natural response is to look for ways to establish communication with the spirit and supernatural world. And because spirit beings cannot easily be reached by ordinary people and because supernatural powers are impersonal, unseen, and unpredictable, this desire to have access to them is so that one can obtain spirit-power. Steyne described this in the following words:

> A life without power is not worth living . . . Power offers man control of his uncertain world. The search for and acquisition of power supersedes any commitment to ethics or morality. Whatever is empowering is right.[10]

Power can be obtained in a variety of ways, some of which Steyne listed:

> Ritual manipulation . . . in the form of sacrifices, offerings, taboos, charms, fetishes, ceremonies, even witchcraft and sorcery… The power may also be secured by the laying on of hands or by encountering a spirit being, either directly or through ritual means. The power may be transmitted through contact with persons of superior religious status or by using clothing or something previously associated with such a person. How it is secured is a secondary concern. It must be acquired whatever the cost.[11]

This all-consuming need for power exerts an enormous influence on morality and ethics and on the relationship between humans and spirit beings and supernatural powers or forces. It also affects how traditional Africans assess the potency or efficacy of a new religion or ritual practice.

A powerless Christianity can hardly make an impact in a society so pregnant with dynamism or spirit-power. The lack of a good and relevant Christian theology of Christ-power has driven many Christians back to traditional spirit-power.

Communalism

If everything that exists is in an organic (holistic) relation to everything else that exists, as discussed earlier, then the same applies to human interactions. People are not individuals, living in a state of independence, but are part of a community, living in relationships and interdependence. In contrast to the

---

10. Steyne, 60.
11. Steyne, 60.

Western approach, one does not claim personal rights and freedoms, but rather one fulfils communal obligations and duties. Van der Walt lists some forty characteristics of African communalism that contrast with Western individualism.[12] These characteristics can be summarized as communal self-respect, interdependence, the survival of the community, group assurance, cooperation and harmony, affiliation, and shared duties. This concept of community is not restricted to the community of human beings alone, but embraces a communal attitude to the world of the spirits and ancestors as well as to the world of nature. People in their human world live in relationship with the world of spirit phenomenon and power phenomenon.

Communalism in relation to fellow humans

The fact that African traditional societies were organized around the basic social unit of kinship or lineage is very important in understanding African concepts of community, religious beliefs, behaviours, practices, morality, ethics and ethnicity.

A traditional African community consisted of clans with different histories, emblems and taboos, as well as sub-clans and kindred (a lineage system). Villages were generally occupied by kin, although some might include people who did not belong to the principal group in the village. At the next level of organization was the household, which consisted of a small social group of parents and children.[13]

At the root of kinship is a belief in a shared common progenitor or ancestor. Genealogical relationships and the legend or tradition of the founding ancestor provide the philosophical basis of unity in a clan, lineage, or even for a whole tribe. Stories of heroes and their great exploits bring pride and prestige to the members of a lineage, clan, or tribe. Each clan or lineage has its own name, identity, and social function in a community. Each lineage is differentiated from others by symbolic means (totems) and is assigned a corporate function or social role. For example, one lineage or clan may be the custodian of religious affairs, while another is responsible for warfare, and another for hunting. Each lineage comprises of a number of families or households that may consist of children, parents, grandparents, uncles, aunts, brothers and sisters and other immediate relatives. The most powerful principle of social organization is the concept of brotherhood, and all members have affinity, loyalty, and obligations to the blood-community.

---

12. Van der Walt, *Afrocentric or Eurocentric?*
13. Meek, *Northern Tribes of Nigeria.*

The kinship system provides the principles of social differentiation and social organization that guide communal life. It also regulates social behaviour and attitudes as well as structuring social interaction. Religious and social norms and codes of behaviour govern interactions among kinsfolk and also how kinsfolk relate to outsiders and to strangers.

The fragmenting effects of this social differentiation are countered by social institutions that unite and coordinate the various sectors of kinship-based communities. These institutions include communal festivals and feasts, hunting expeditions, and wars as well as the religious rites that accompany births, initiations, marriages, deaths, and sickness. The festivals, feasts and ceremonies are usually accompanied by much eating and drinking, dancing, and singing, and these social activities create and strengthen social ties. Working together in such corporate contexts inculcates social responsibility and accountability. The exogamous marriage system also creates a network of kinsfolk with binding ties.

This system of relationships has been seriously disrupted by the introduction of universal religions such as Christianity, Islam, and modernism. It has also been affected by the re-alignment of tribal units in the new colonial states. The integration of tribal groups into modern African states did not eradicate kinship but incorporated it. This has resulted in many social and political problems, including fears, suspicions, rivalries, tensions, and conflicts among the various ethnic and tribal groups within colonial and post-colonial Africa.

Communalism in relation to ancestors and the spirit world

The human community is not only intimately related to its living members, but also to the community of ancestors who now live in the past as well as those still to be born. The life of the community of the living is controlled, maintained, and protected by the community of ancestors who now live in the spirit world. Communal life is therefore ancestrally inbred. Steyne observes that outside of this ancestral kinship "there lies no possibility of life" and that "personhood is meaningless" apart from these ancestral kinship and relationships.[14]

The belief in the continuity of community life has important implications for the traditional view of marriage:

> Man is only man in relationship, as he participates in family and community life ... Marriage is more than a physical relationship. It has eternal consequences. Not to marry is to cease living now

---

14. Steyne, *Gods of Power*.

and in the hereafter. Marriage establishes essentials in life and in death. Begetting children guarantees eternal life. Not only do children provide for the reincarnation of the ancestors, they also sustain the ancestors through prescribed rituals such as sacrifices and offerings.[15]

This concept of "eternal life" through marriage needs to be modified. Both marriage to beget children or engaging in a memorable heroic act are steps toward achieving an immortalized name. The quest is not for "eternal life" as in Christianity, but for an "immortal name." Traditional Africans give a memorable or immortalized name the highest value.

The communal perspective also has important implications with regard to the spirit world that permeates everyday existence. If humans are part of a holistic community with the spirit world and the supernatural world, it is very important to avoid offending the spirits or powers. However should one offend either, the responsibility is not solely one's own but is shared by the community to which one belongs, for one is the product of one's family, clan, and tribe and of the spirits (i.e. of the community). This traditional belief results in a denial of responsibility for one's own actions and has serious consequences for morality and ethics in Africa.

Communalism in relation to nature

The law of holism, which was presented earlier, stresses that everything is part of an organic whole. People seek to understand the mysterious forces that lie behind the natural or power phenomenon. Because the power phenomenon connects humans to the natural world, any natural object may carry a message that needs to be deciphered. Nature provides a vast array of contact points with both the world of the spirit and the world of the supernatural.

For instance, totemism is one expression of this relationship to nature through a totem object:

> In totemism certain taboos apply to the totem animal(s) and/or plant(s). Totem objects are not to be killed, spoken of by name, eaten, or even looked at in some cases. They elicit feelings of brotherliness. They are believed to have souls of similar nature to man's. They may be emblematic of abstract and emotional attitudes claimed by a group of people.[16]

---

15. Steyne, 66.
16. Steyne, 70.

The belief in totemism sets apart some animals or plants for kinship affinity, and religious or medicinal purposes. The potency, value, and efficacy of each are determined by its nature, which can be enhanced or reduced by other objects nearby. Animals and birds for sacrifices, objects for offerings, and ritual or ceremonial sites or groves are carefully selected on the basis of their religious value and efficacy.

When traditional Africans are caught up in dealing with these kinship matters, their ancestors, the spirit world, and the world of nature, their dealings with God take second place. Africans regard a blood-relationship as sacred, and kinship values are rooted in a blood-relationship that develops a very strong affinity with, obligations to and loyalties towards the kinship community. Tribalism, ethnicity and racism reflect the negative side of these. Their adverse consequences are reflected in communal and social sins with regard to the treatment of strangers or outsiders, and in spiritual idolatry aimed at maintaining loyalty to the ancestors, spirits, divinities, and their worship.

All forms of communitarian ethics are derived from this traditional concept of the community of blood-relationship. The task for Christianity is to present the context of this communal network of relationships. It has to handle the issues of kinship values, such as loyalty, affinity, and obligations based upon blood-relationships. Christianity must also address the issue of the exclusion of outsiders or strangers as a result of the emphasis on blood-relationships.

Fatalism

The concepts of destiny and fate in the traditional worldview are closely related to the belief in spirit beings and mysterious powers. Destiny is the belief that the position, place, and status of individuals or groups have been predetermined by some external, spiritual power or supernatural power. Fate is similar in that it means that certain events are predetermined to happen. The end result is fatalism. Fatalism is "a doctrine which states that events are fixed in advance for all time in such a manner that human beings are powerless to change them."[17]

The traditional belief is that one's destiny cannot be changed and that it should be accepted readily. Any attempt to change it will have devastating consequences. Nonetheless, one can be hindered from fulfilling one's destiny by others or by spirit-powers. This is where the concept of fate comes in. Fate is the outcome of predetermined evil against an individual, a community, or an age by the spirit-powers. Spirit beings and supernatural powers control the

---

17. *Webster's New Collegiate Dictionary* (Springfield, MA: G. & C. Merriam, 1977).

world of fate, and God does not seem to be active in protecting man against evil activities by these spirit-powers. One has to find one's own protection and security.

Traditional Africans therefore look for spirit-powers that can counteract the fate that attacks them. They dread spirit-power attacks and seek to avoid them at all cost, fearful that someone or some spirit-powers might hinder them from realizing their destiny.

The task for Christianity is to understand the African fatalistic worldview that is rooted in the mystery of evil. The apparent lack of active protection from God has great theological implications. The sovereignty and power of God over all of his creation needs to be fully explained so as to counteract the anxiety and the fear of fate, evil, and wickedness which is being experienced.

11

Fundamental Moral and Ethical Laws

The traditional African moral and ethical system is complex and problematic. For this reason, we must consider the fundamental moral and ethical laws separately from the ethical and moral principles.

Magesa and Tempels reduce the fundamental moral laws to one which Tempels regards as "vital force," and Magesa refers to as "life force." Both mean the same thing. For Magesa, the foundation for African morality is "the promotion of life." Ethics revolves around "the transmission of life force, the enemies of life, the restoration of the force of life, and the 'political' ethics of Africa."[1]

The fundamental moral laws are deeply rooted in the theological and philosophical principles which have been discussed previously. It seems that five major moral laws can be derived from these:

1. Holism finds expression in the law of harmony;

2. Spiritualism finds expression in the law of the spirit;

3. Dynamism finds expression in the law of power;

4. Communalism finds expression in the law of kinship;

5. Fatalism finds expression in the law of destiny.

Nonetheless these laws are interdependent. An action that may seem inexplicable in terms of one law may make sense when all the moral laws are considered together.

---

1. Magesa, *African Religion*, 8.

The Law of Harmony

The traditional African holistic worldview holds in cosmic harmony the spirit world, nature, and the human world, regarding the natural, ontological, social, and spiritual orders as interdependent. The law of harmony holds them in balance and defines the place of humans in relationship to all spirit beings and the supernatural world. The greatest duty of human beings is to learn to live in balance and harmony with the spirit world (spirit phenomenon) and the world of nature (power phenomenon).

Any distortion of or damage to this cosmic harmony has disastrous consequences and results in human suffering. Two main things can disrupt this cosmic harmony. The first is the unpredictable attitudes and behaviour of the agents of the spirit world, those spirit beings who dispense powers to humans and who saturate nature with spirit-power. They may or may not respond to the demands, requests, and needs of the humans. The second source of disruption is any breach in the relationship between people and their benevolent spirits or any of the supernatural powers imbedded in nature, institutions or things. Such a breach may arise as a result of sins of omission or commission (for example, failure to observe prohibitions, abominations, or taboos). The punishment for misbehaving is a moral sanction mediated by the spirit beings or supernatural powers. The traditional African believes that morality and ethics are controlled by spirit beings and supernatural powers and not by humans.

When disharmony or alienation occurs, there is a need for reconciliation, for the restoration of fellowship between humans and the spirit or supernatural world. It is up to humans to take the necessary steps to achieve this through sacrifices and offerings and also through the observance of taboos. "The idea of reconciliation – the need to restore harmony, brings balance or equilibrium back to man's experience of his world – is very much a part of man's religious experience."[2]

The law of harmony is not concerned with tolerance or equality, with issues of "right" or "just" attitudes or practices, but only with what will hold things in balance. Thus, answers to ethical questions do not focus on the morality of the action but on the morality of the goal. In traditional Africa, an action or behaviour is only termed bad or inappropriate if it does not lead to cosmic order or harmony and any means is justified in the pursuit of balance and harmony.

By contrast, in Christian ethics, morality is understood to be universal and to transcend the community. The reason for the difference is that the moral goal in Christianity is not the re-establishment of cosmic harmony or conformity

---

2. Steyne, *Gods of Power*, 135.

to a moral order but conformity to the image of Christ and his moral law. If immoral action is required to achieve a goal, that goal is not legitimate. Our moral goal is to please God himself and to live at peace with God who judges our inner motives (Prov 16:1–3; Acts 24:16). Our obedience to the will of God is a moral standard: "Does the LORD delight in burnt offerings and sacrifices, as much as in obeying the LORD? To obey is better than sacrifice and to heed than the fat of rams" (1 Sam 15:22).

In Christianity, moreover, God is seen as the only true source of peace and harmony. Any pursuit of harmony from sources apart from him and his moral law is futile. Whereas sin resulted in the fall of humankind and the fall of nature, the cross of Christ is the basis of reconciliation and harmony between God and humankind, person and person, as well as between humankind and nature. It even enables one to be reconciled with oneself! This new human harmony is reflected in the messianic community, the church. Christian communitarian values and ethics will maintain harmony and peace, broker reconciliation and provide for repentance and forgiveness within humanity.

The Law of the Spirit

The traditional African conception of reality is deeply rooted in the law of the spirit (spirit phenomenon). Reality does not consist of what is apparent. Things are not accepted at face value; their essence or hidden nature is wrapped up in the spiritual web of reality. Events and actions are controlled, guided, and caused by unseen spiritual powers. Thus, it is in the hiddenness of things that one looks to find causes. The question to ask is not "why" or "how," but "who or what is behind what is happening?"

The law of the spirit reflects the belief that the world is spiritual in essence, dynamic with mystical and spirit activities and full of mystical powers and forces. This belief is not a source of comfort, but of fear for it makes it difficult to distinguish between good and evil, and fatalism dominates life. The good that comes one's way is usually associated with the Creator or with benevolent spirits or the ancestors. The bad things in life come from evil spirits and human beings or as a punishment from the gods, divinities or the Supreme Being for breaking cosmic harmony or communal taboos. "Catastrophes, natural disasters, diseases, untimely death and other exigencies of life are all evaluated spiritually."[3]

---

3. Steyne, 37.

The result is a constant quest for consolation, peace, and comfort or, in other words, a quest for spiritual meaning through supernatural and spiritual powers. Traditional Africans have myriad spirit beings from whom they may find spiritual meaning. When personal resources fail, religious specialists can be consulted to divine the spiritual meaning of what is happening through dreams, visions, vision quests, divination, or ordeals. As a result, medicine men and women, diviners, ritualists, and spiritists hold an important position in an African society. People go to them to inquire about their own destiny, fate, and welfare, as well as about the destiny and well-being of others, families, clans, or tribes.

This quest for meaning is rooted in expediency, existentialism, and pragmatism. Therefore, a moral action or behaviour is one which is undertaken to find spiritual meaning. The focus of this action is on achieving success for oneself, one's kinship community, clan, or tribe in relation to the will of the higher spirit beings. This preoccupation with spiritual matters is not generally a sign of true spirituality, but is rather the pursuit of information to achieve a specific end by the use of any suitable spirit-power. In traditional Africa, the pursuit of spiritual meaning tends to take precedence over moral obedience to the will of the Creator.

By contrast, the moral end or goal in Christianity is not a spiritual quest to acquire understanding of what is happening to us, but to do the will of God and to please him. Christians believe that the true meaning and purpose of life and being are rooted only in God who is the Eternal Spirit and not in lesser spirit beings or in subordinate spirit-powers. Meaning in life is derived from one's relationship with God himself as the only source of spiritual meaning, purpose and power.

The Law of Power

The pursuit of spiritual meaning merges into the pursuit of mystical or supernatural powers. Because traditional Africans believe very strongly that their destiny and well-being are controlled and manipulated by supernatural or unseen mysterious powers, they embark on a quest for power so that they can control and manipulate the spirit-powers for their own benefit.

To achieve this they consult specialists who have special means of gaining access to these spirit-powers. These specialists use rituals, divination, ceremonies, sacrifices, incantations, symbolism, witchcraft, sorcery, charms, fetishes, as well as white and black magic. The search for more potent and powerful spiritual agents and supernatural powers is a strong driving force.

Although power is distributed among the unseen mysterious beings, some are more powerful or influential than others.

An action or behaviour is only termed bad or inappropriate if it does not lead to finding spiritual and mystical powers to deal with the problems in life. In Christianity, we recognize that God is the only source of legitimate power and that he sustains his creation through his power. Any powers obtained from sources other than him are illegitimate.

The Law of Kinship

The law of kinship derives from communalism, the belief that protection, meaning, identity and status are rooted in the kinship community or blood-group. The community has its origin and centre in ancestry and kinship and is therefore governed by kinship values, loyalty, affinity, and obligations. Kinship provides both ideological identity and security.

This means that every behaviour pattern is conceived of in terms of kinship relations. The community can only survive if it has good relationships with the world of nature and the spirit world. Thus it strives to maintain harmony with the world around it, pursuing spiritual meaning with the spirit world and seeking mystical and spirit powers for its own security and survival. Members of the kinship community have a moral obligation to maintain specific patterns of conduct, to fulfil expected social roles, and to conform to societal values. Traditions are received from the ancestors, the elders and the community and these must be maintained without being changed. One passes them on intact to the next generation. Any disregard of these has spiritual ramifications and will give offense to the spirit world. To break relationships or disregard custom is to sin.[4]

Conforming to convention is a strong moral and ethical principle. Therefore kinship-interest, group-interest, territorial-interest, tribal-interest, or racial-interest takes precedence over every other social and ethical consideration. One cannot form a community with strangers or outsiders because one has no blood ties, no ancestral affinity with them. Strangers or outsiders cannot expect to be treated in accordance with the moral and ethical principles that prevail within the kinship community. The in-group ethic shuts its eyes and heart against outsiders. There are no universal standards and, as a result tribalism, ethnicity, or racism is prevalent.

---

4. Steyne.

African traditional life is dominated by communitarian values and ethics, not by the individualism of Western ethics. The African's conception of sin, shame, guilt, transgression, and accountability is rooted in these communal values that exclude those who do not belong. The fact that Missionary Christianity challenged these values, instead of transforming them, has left Africa with all manner of crises, especially ethnic genocide. Many of the atrocities committed against fellow Africans reflect social and communal sins.

The greatest challenge for Christianity and biblical teaching lies in incorporating, renewing, and transforming the traditional kinship values of affinity, obligation, and loyalty to create an all-inclusive new community in the body of Christ. This new humanity, that embraces all races, tribes, languages, peoples, and nations, can give the old values a new meaning, purpose, and motivation in Christ Jesus.

The Law of Destiny

The concepts of destiny and fate are closely related. Destiny is the belief that the position, place, and status of individuals or groups have been predetermined by some external, supernatural power or spiritual being. Fate means that certain events are predetermined.

The traditional worldview considers that one's destiny is both a gift and a decree from the Creator. One is born with, or is given at birth, a destiny or a guardian spirit which will accompany one throughout one's life. Families and groups also have their own unique destiny decreed by the Creator. If one wishes to know one's destiny, one can consult diviners and other spiritual resources.

If traditional Africans believe that others or spirit powers are hindering them from realizing their destiny, they will pursue power to counteract such attacks. This can result in serious social conflict between individuals or people groups.

Individuals or groups can also manipulate this concept of destiny. Certain people ascribe to themselves a superior destiny and consign others to an inferior role. Both these roles are then regarded as fixed and unchangeable, and so castes and social classes develop. Even though these distinctions are man-made, they may get religious and social sanction. Humans have usurped the role and function of God and the spirit powers in determining the destiny or fate of others. When this occurs, there is great potential for social conflict. Over the years in modern Africa certain ethnic groups have claimed that they are from a superior human stock and are thus destined to rule over and control others. This may have been simply by self-proclamation or because their colonial masters designated them as "natural rulers." The status quo and the principles governing succession and leadership were interpreted in terms of this decreed destiny, and this has created the potential for serious political crises in post-colonial Africa. Identifying caste systems with destiny in modern Africa has also had devastating consequences, with some groups being denied political participation and representation. Where such beliefs have been challenged, there has been tension, violence, and conflict.

African Christians who have a shallow knowledge of the teachings of the Bible and Christian theology can be subjected to negative influences. Traditional African spirituality is saturated with spirit-power, either of spirit beings or of cosmic powers. Fate and evil in all its physical manifestations are powerful. Christ-power is the biblical answer to this traditional quest for spirit-power, but Christians must know what they are facing before they can deal with it effectively.

12

Ethical and Moral Principles

This chapter examines how the traditional beliefs and ethical values influence attitudes, behaviours, and social practices of individuals, communities, tribes, or institutions in Africa.

Basic Moral Principles
Moral Pursuit Takes Precedence over Moral Behaviour and Moral Consequences

In traditional African ethics, the principle of moral pursuit reigns supreme. What counts is not how one behaves, but the moral pursuit, goal, or end that needs to be achieved. This means that the private social behaviour of the person or group is secondary and irrelevant.

An action is motivated by an individual or from within a group primarily to serve an exclusive self-interest. Other moral considerations can be laid aside so that the goal can be achieved. All that matters is that this moral behaviour is legitimate within the kinship community. The actions must be sanctioned by the individual, group, or tribe, but not necessarily by an external or a strange authority. Thus, moral action or behaviour is limited and does not have universal application.

Steyne explains moral pursuit in these words:

> Without physical and spiritual power, man will not have fame, status, wealth, health, sexual vigor or influence in society. The acquisition of life force unashamedly serves selfish ends and, therefore, it may be acquired by any means, good or bad. Morality is not the ultimate consideration; but the acquisition of life force is. Therefore, any means of securing life force is condoned, if not sanctioned. Magic, ritual means, stealth, robbery, sacrifice

and even killing are all accepted. The cosmos is manipulated by whatever means necessary to acquire and guarantee security, happiness and success, without reference to any objective standard of morality. Immorality and unethical activity may always be covered (if not expiated) with impunity by ritual means.[1]

Unless moral action or behaviour is rooted in a moral standard or principle, moral pursuit becomes moral relativism. This is what has happened in modern African states. They are not ruled by universal values. Instead individuals and tribal groups function in terms of moral relativism. This means that each tribe's moral pursuits are in competition with and may clash with those of other tribes or people groups.

In Christianity, there is a moral norm; moral action or behaviour is judged by God who is himself a moral and ethical personality and who is the moral standard and the moral judge (Ps 94:12–23; Col 3:17, 23–24). Moral pursuit becomes doing the ultimate will of God and nothing less.

Kinship Takes Precedence over Strangers and Outsiders

In traditional Africa, the principle of moral kinship operates within its sphere of influence in a defined community, territory, group, class, tribe, or a race. Loyalty, affinity, and obligations apply only within the kinship community which is given preferential treatment. In all matters, the pursuit of the kinship community takes precedence over the interests of others. In this context, ethical relativism abounds.

Because of age-old alienation and broken relationships, individuals and tribes or communities have no respect for anyone outside of their own community or tribe. Strangers are excluded and are treated differently. When people with an exclusive tribal mentality or kinship values are brought together, their variant moral pursuits and ethical beliefs ignite conflict, crisis, and violence. This is the root of many grievous social evils and sins, for example tribalism, racism, and denominationalism, within modern African nation-states. Even the management of national institutions and Christian denominations can be plunged into crisis because they are dominated by ethnic groups or classes of people who regard others as outsiders and treat them accordingly.

---

1. Steyne, *Gods of Power*, 162.

This is destroying African nation-states. A new ethical structure and new moral and ethical principles are desperately needed.

Communal Moral Accountability Is Superior to Inner or Personal Morality

Because communal moral accountability is rooted in kinship values based upon blood relationship, personal responsibility and accountability fall away. Group or tribal values, good or bad, govern the attitudes or practices of the individual or group and become the norm. The political or religious behaviour of many African individuals within African nation-states is determined by these communal values even though these values may be out of step with the universal or national values, ideals, and objectives. "Blood is thicker than water." Individuals or groups often feel a greater affinity with and a greater obligation or loyalty to tribal or kinship values and pursuits than to the overarching national or institutional values and objectives. Sometimes this results in churches and nation-states becoming ungovernable because communal or kinship values hold them to ransom.

In many African nation-states, the individual, ethnic group, or tribe takes no responsibility for moral behaviour. They believe that their moral actions are rooted in the communal moral accountability. Moral actions are always seen as legitimate if they were taken on behalf of the kinship community to bring about its good or harmony. Moral judgments by outsiders on moral actions taken on behalf of a kinship community have no legitimacy.

A wrong or guilt may be imputed to an individual by a kinship community, a clan, or a tribe and yet the inner moral principle will still vindicate the individual. There is no personal moral conscience. Individuals can always excuse failures on the grounds that they were not personal. It is the kinship community that has a moral conscience or moral accountability, not the individual. Moral compliance is all that matters for individuals.

Instead, responsibility belongs to the group. Individuals can lay a charge against the kinship community that caused them to do wrong by appealing to the spirit world for help through ritual means such as moral ordeals and oath-taking. In this context, the personal moral conscience defies communal morality by appealing to an undefined external moral standard. The ritual connects the individual to an outside spiritual authority higher than that of the community or religious group. This is why people known to have broken communal laws seek the help of spirit-powers. So, for example, criminals in African societies practice all kinds of rituals to ensure their success in their criminal activities. Some even go to Christian priests to solicit prayers before embarking upon their criminal activities. Pen-robbers bribe their kinship communities by lavishing their loot upon them.

This type of ethical thinking is explained by Steyne:

> Concepts of propriety do exist and are maintained by fear of spirit world recriminations in the face of default. When the restraints of the spirit world are removed during special rites or celebrations, the resulting ethical conduct is depravity itself. The spirits may be cheated with impunity, bribed to overlook human debauchery or deflected with counter medicines such as indulgences.[2]

It is important to state here that the traditional societies do have moral laws, values, and maxims which define acts as good or evil and thus govern social life, behaviour and social practice. Even though at times individuals seem not to blame themselves for their moral failures, they know that, when they violate the prescribed moral codes or taboos, they and possibly their communities will be punished for their misdeeds.

Modern African is being torn apart by divergent and contradictory ethical and moral traditions: traditional kinship moral values and obligations, Western moral and ethical values and Christian or Muslim religious values that moderate the life of their adherents. There is no personal moral direction and so a person may make a personal existential moral judgment which may not conform to any of these competing moral traditions. For example, a head of state may lodge billions of dollars taken from the government treasury in a foreign account, thus impoverishing his people and nation. This does not reflect Western, or Christian, or even African kinship values. This is moral bankruptcy.

The soul of the modern African is divided. The African is neither totally traditional nor totally modern, neither committed Christian nor committed traditionalist. The mixing of Western moral values and institutions with traditional values and institutions in African nation-states has produced outrageous moral and ethical values that are destroying both the people and their nation-states. When we look across the continent of Africa we can see that everywhere:

> The fundamental objectives and directive principles of state policy as stated in the Constitution seem not to guide national and state policy-making. The conduct of public officers and of the operators of the private sectors has revealed a serious lack of honesty, hard work, humility and humaneness. The attainment of self-reliance in

---

2. Steyne, *Gods of Power*, 163.

political economy has continued to be a mirage owing to wholesale adoption of foreign values, institutions and consumption patterns and endemic corruption. Furthermore, national and individual life have not been significantly moderated by the national ethical structure as contained in the Constitutions and in the tenets of religion and African morality.[3]

The Christian believes that each individual is personally accountable before God, the Chief Judge (Rom 2:1–16; 14:12). No inner personal or communal morality can stand against the moral laws of God.

Moral Fear and Moral Power Dominate Attitudes, Behaviour and Social Practices, Ethics and Morality

The fear of the power of the tribe, the community or the majority over certain issues greatly influences how people behave and how issues are resolved. The principle of moral fear operates under the moral principle that "might is right." Rules do not apply to the mighty, but for the weak all rules are binding. The mighty rule with power, and the weak must obey in fear. This can destroy justice, equality and freedom.

The principles of moral power and moral fear are pervasive in traditional society as a result of the dominant presence of the mystical and mysterious powers and forces, as well as the hierarchy of beings. Battles for power generate fear and uncertainty. One must always side with the strong if one wants to win; one must be on the winning side.

This reveals a great deal about the moral and ethical attitudes of the traditional African in dealing with the spirit world and the powers that be. The strong have no regard for the weak, and the weak have vowed never to submit to the strong. We hear of civil wars, ethnic cleansing and civil strife everywhere in Africa. Most relations within African nation-states are governed by the dictates of the moral power of the majority or the strong and by the consequent fears of the weak. The majority have imposed democracy but in reality it is the dictatorship of the majority. Insecurity, instability, crisis, and chaos result.

Christianity teaches that all moral beings, strong and weak, are under the judgment of God's moral laws. God is impartial and his judgments are based upon universal truth.

---

3. Philips and Turaki, "An Evaluation of Nigeria's Ethical Structure," 1.

The Pursuit of a Good Life or Security Dominates Ethical and Moral Behaviour

Many scholars have observed that the traditional religions are anthropocentric in nature. This means that they regard humankind as the centre of everything. Dealings with the spirit world are not undertaken for their sake, but for one's own. Religious practices, rituals, and ceremonies are done in order to ensure well-being and security. The will of humankind dominates and one seeks to manipulate things to one's advantage.

In societies where poverty reigns, where resources are few, and where individuals face deprivation or hardship, people tend to pursue the good life or security at the expense of good moral behaviour or ethics. In an insecure environment or a corrupt society characterized by conflict and mistrust, a new form of ethics or attitudes is developed that is neither traditionally African, nor Western, nor Christian. Most politicians or elites in African nation-states act unethically or irresponsibly in order to pursue the good life or to ensure their own security. Treasuries of African countries, companies and institutions are emptied or depleted in pursuit of personal or group life with no concern for the communities or the nation. An African leader will steal billions of dollars from a poor nation and lodge them in a Western Bank. Traditional African kinship values cannot sanction these practices, nor can Western ethical values. And yet such actions are committed with impunity in Africa as a result of a broken spiritual relationship and alienation. Such a person is alienated from traditional society with its values and also from the modern values of a nation-state, Christianity or Islam.

Pragmatically, the African uses the modern African context to formulate new values. This pursuit of security in the volatile and unstable African nation-states is the driving force behind the unprecedented corruption, moral decadence, and indiscipline that is rampant across Africa. The focus is not on building a good society or nation, but on personal and parochial success. However, this is an invitation to disaster, conflict, crisis, and violence. The society suffers.

Those who loot the government, companies, churches, or institutions for the benefit of their communities or tribes regard their actions as heroic and commendable. They are not ashamed, but are proud of what they have done. Communities or tribes dispense honorific titles and recognition for those sons and daughters who have helped their communities or tribes, even though this has been done through dubious and relativistic means. Outsiders may scoff, but insiders hail the act. Such morality encourages corruption and the dominance of one group over others.

The ultimate personal or tribal good would be to create a well-managed, viable, and peaceful society. However, many modern Africans, despite being well-educated in Western arts and sciences, have no concept of society. They are a terrible mixture of the colonial mentality and the traditional mentality. Despite the wealth of their education, they do not know how to organize an environment where they can stay and live at peace. They do not know how to fix the water system, electricity, roads, farms, health, or the economy. The African personality and character and society needs to be renewed and transformed. African nation-states are in need of serious rehabilitation, reconstruction, and transformation.

There are two things that influence the development of character traits, attitudes, and social practices: human nature and culture.[4] All humanity inherits a common nature but culture is learned and becomes specific and peculiar to a group of people. Human beings absorb and develop their own culture through learning, enculturation, and socialization. This means that different groups of people do not practice, or believe the same things. Thus, a human being has both an inherited human nature and a learned, specific group culture. Both the people group and the personality reflect a learned culture.

This explains why individuals or ethnic groups have a hidden programme which impacts on their behaviour, practice and beliefs. When human beings interact, they do so in terms of their character traits as individuals and as members of specific people groups. They behave in the way they were raised culturally. They bring into the society, nation or institution their own way of seeing, of understanding, of interpreting and of applying things. Because the practices and behaviours of individuals from different cultural groups will be different, conflict, misunderstanding, and problems may result.

Africans urgently need to address this intolerance that refuses to recognize differences between individual personalities or cultural differences among people groups. Humanity developed its culture, religion, ethics and morality in brokenness and alienation, without God. Because human culture and religion are fallen and sinful, they generate spirit-power that leads to communal and social sins and conflict. Whenever humanity comes together, it is ridden with anxiety and fear of others. This, in turn, leads to crisis, conflict and violence.

Sin, Shame and Guilt in Africa

The concepts of sin, shame and guilt are difficult to define in traditional Africa. To help us do so, imagine that a forbidden object is touched. This means that a wrong has been committed. A forbidden object has its own sanctions which

---

4. Turaki, *Unique Christ*.

fall on anyone who touches it. The evil consequences may affect the person or that person's community, although punishment may be averted by ritual or sacrifice.

However, communal punishment for touching a forbidden object will only be imposed if one is seen or found out. So long as the forbidden act is hidden and has no adverse public consequences, one is free. But if a plague or a visible curse results or if by divination a culprit is found, that person carries the weight of punishment along with his or her people. We find similar examples in the Bible: when Achan took the forbidden object, he was found out by the casting of lots. He and his entire family were killed and everything of theirs was burnt (Josh 7:1–26).

Guilt only arises when an act is realized to be a transgression. An offence has been committed against both the law and the law-giver. Having transgressed, I am a sinner or a transgressor. I have moved from acting wrongly to being in a state of wrong. I feel guilty because I am reminded that I have broken the law and that I will be punished.

Shame, on the other hand, only occurs if one is seen or caught touching a forbidden object. Then shame is felt by the person, their household, and their people. The person or community suffers from a state of being in the wrong. Shame is therefore a state of being, not an act. Without exposure or self-awareness or self-realization, the one who has done wrong does not feel shame.

Guilt, then, is doing while shame is being. Shame is more prominent than guilt. Many scholars have alluded to the fact that African society is a "shame" society, but not a "guilt" society. Because the wrong is committed against the community, because the community is sinned against, shame is community-induced. There is only a communal moral conscience. The inner personal moral principle may see nothing wrong with the act, although in the eyes of the community a trespass has been committed. Shame comes upon one only because one has been seen or caught, not because one feels guilty.

Shame is not regarded as a state or condition of being in a despicable moral state, affecting the totality of our being. Therefore when we marvel at the fact that some people are not ashamed of their deeds or acts, it is simply because we are looking for the wrong thing in the wrong place.

African traditional societies do not have written moral codes that can impose sanctions if the codes are broken. However, they do have taboos, customs, and traditions that serve as moral codes. Generally, traditional Africans are law-abiding because breaking traditional laws carries such severe punishments, sometimes death or excommunication. Conformity is the norm and there are few rebels in society. Certainly, traditional Africans know when the laws have been broken and they also know the judgments. Philip Steyne made a revealing connection between traditional guilt and sin in reference to God:

> Guilt is not an offence against a holy God who does not and cannot tolerate sin. Sin has no effect on God. There is no objective standard, so there is no question of transgressing his law. Man alone is the loser when he sins and yet if he can find and perform the right ritual, he can circumvent all the consequences of his sin.[5]

What is the basis of morality and spirituality, if "morality or ethical conduct is not prerequisite for being worthy or being effective in this religious system?" Steyne argued that neither is "necessary for spirituality or for practicing religious rituals." In traditional religion:

> Morality, goodness and virtue have no bearing on being a worthy practitioner of the faith. The most immoral person is totally capable of giving good religious counsel and performing the rituals required for positive spirit response. The key to wisdom is not the fear of God, but rather knowledge of the secrets, which spell out how to manipulate the spirit world successfully. One who has mastered these techniques and proved to be successful is revered and honored, apart from moral and ethical considerations.[6]

This argument does not mean that the traditional individual fails to understand wrong acts or evil deeds. Individuals are aware of the principle of punishment or retribution if laws are broken. However, a religious practice or ritual can be used as a means of escape from punishment or to shield one from any moral consequences. This approach to moral and ethical issues means that goodness and virtue or purity and holiness are not the moral and ethical norm. The norm is to conform to the correct ritual and correct religious practice. This is ethics at the level of outward acts or deeds, and not an inner purity of motive or disposition. Having the right religious formula is far more important than the right moral attitude.

The pursuit of power brings better results than right moral behaviour. So long as results are obtained, right moral behaviour or ethics can be forgotten. This is why honest, faithful, and sincere Africans are often scolded by their tribes for refusing to do something that would benefit the tribe. This is why

---

5. Steyne, *Gods of Power*, 164.
6. Steyne, 164.

good people are rejected in politics: they are useless because they do not bring political and economic booty to their tribes. What counts in politics and economics is the ability to make others do what you want, regardless of morality. In many African societies and nations, the dominant social values are influence and power, not honesty, sincerity, or integrity. Tribal and party politics look for men and women of influence and power to advance their cause and not for men and women of integrity.

These traditional moral and ethical foundations are different from Christian morality and ethics which are based upon Scripture and the revealed will of God.

> But the LORD said to Samuel, "Do not consider his appearance or his height, for I have rejected him. The LORD does not look at the things people look at. People look at the outward appearance, but the LORD looks at the heart." (1 Sam 16:7)

God judges the heart, the inner motives. This teaches that morality is imbedded in the very act itself. The criterion is not just on doing, but also on being. Christianity looks for men and women of integrity, honesty, and sincerity. The "right" religious ritual or practice is not the moral criterion in Christianity. If right religious practice is to have any meaning and approval, it has to be because it has a godly motive and inner disposition.

One may ask why it is that in Africa people who hold public or private offices do not seem to have a cultivated and principled godly lifestyle based upon goodness, virtue, purity, integrity, holiness, hard work, and humanity. The simple answer is that many do not understand sin, shame, and guilt. The state's moral and ethical code is not binding because it comes from the outside world and not from the kinship community. Hence it is regarded as lacking legitimacy and authority. The traditional definition of and the traditional attitudes to these concepts contributes to African ethical and moral relativism.

Kinship and Communal Morality

We must return to the topic of the law of kinship because it is the most powerful and the most pervasive of moral laws in traditional Africa. It is the queen of African moral laws!

The law of kinship defines in unequivocal terms who are the "insiders" and the "outsiders." This means there are two types of morality: a code of morality and ethics for insiders (the community, the tribe) and a second code of morality and ethics for outsiders (strangers). Those who belong are treated preferentially. This morality and ethics is determined, not by any universal principles, but by the principles of kinship.

This ancestral foundation of morality and ethics rules out what is personal and what is outside of the community. Kinship systems, families, clans, ethnic groups and tribes, or races exhibit particular moral and ethical characteristics. The moral norm or the golden rule here is that "Blood is thicker than water," what belongs to your blood-group is yours and takes precedence over what is not from your blood-group. Blood-group interest is regarded as better than self-interest and altruism. One must take care of what belongs to one's blood-group first before considering outsiders.

In the kinship system, the place of an individual is also well-defined. The individual receives life and existence from these kinship foundations. The individual does not exist for self and has no personal social life or right to determine an own course of life, as in Western individualism. Individualism for its own sake is regarded as an aberration.

It is further believed that religion, morality and ethics cannot be located outside of ancestry, outside of the blood-group or blood-community. No external, objective or transcendent source can provide these. Religion and ethics are communal, particular to the group, not universal. The application of moral laws derived from the cosmos, the spirit world, the gods, and the divinities is therefore limited. Even though these laws come from the gods, their interpretation and application are limited as they are given communitarian values, interpretations, and applications. It is accepted that the moral laws of the other kinship communities will be governed by their own set of moral laws. These may be similar or different, but each community has its own authority and legitimacy. The overriding ethical principle is relativism and not universalism.

Modern national constitutions with their ethical and moral codes, as well as the codes of Christianity, Islam or modernity, can easily be brushed aside when they come into conflict with these kinship values and interests. Universal or modern state values are regarded as lying outside of this moral law and may at times even be regarded as working against kinship morality and ethics. These new values, together with those of Christianity and Islam, do not moderate the behaviour, attitudes and practices of individuals or groups. In fact, their legitimacy and authority are often questioned. Cases abound where ethnic groups make unnecessary demands on their sons and daughters, demanding that they comply with the wishes and the interests of their blood-group and blood-community rather than with the universal and nation-state values.

Biblical Christianity has to transform this traditional law of kinship by presenting the message of a messianic community and of Christian communitarian ethics that transcend ethnic or racial boundaries.

The Place of Outsiders or Strangers

The problem most Africans have within African nation-states is that of acceptance of others from different tribes, communities, or religions. Anything outside of the kinship system is labelled as being from the "outside world." The outside world is regarded as a territory that is owned by no human group, but by an impersonal group such as a government, an institution, a denomination or a company. Foreign institutions are "neutral grounds" or "battle fields" where kinship or tribal rules do not apply. There, might is right and the end justifies the means. No one can claim absolute ownership of them; they can be seized by whoever is strong enough to do so. Consequently, the outside world is characterized by war, rivalry, competition, intrigues, manipulations, wit, and stratagems.

When the colonial masters created new states in Africa, the accompanying colonial institutions were usually seen as belonging to the outside world. This meant that these institutions could become spoils and booty. What they possessed could be taken by force. Ethnic groups or tribes in colonial governments and institutions saw themselves as competitors or warriors seeking domination so they could get as much as they could for the sake of their kinship groups. Rights of dominance and discrimination, the preferential and differential treatment of others, and the control of colonial goods were defined in terms of relativistic kinship, tribal, racial, and religious beliefs.

This is still true in modern Africa. In the absence of universal and national values and ideals, these sub-national values have been used to run and to govern modern African nation-states. Communities, tribes and races still strive to dominate, control, and determine the course in the new states. The group must stamp its identity and dominance on others. This is not an individual decision; it comes from the group. Excluding others from political participation and representation has reflected the morality and ethics of kinship, the tribe, and the race or religion. The fear of political and economic power or dominance has often led to tensions and conflicts which have been aggravated by modern political, economic, cultural, religious, and social factors.

The law of outsiders or strangers has been adequately addressed in Scripture. In the Old Testament the Israelites were commanded by God to take special care of strangers because the Israelites themselves had once been strangers in Egypt. Their experience of slavery and their maltreatment in Egypt was to serve as a lesson on how to provide better treatment to the stranger in their midst. They were to love the strangers (Lev 19:34); provide for them (Deut 10:18); share the leftovers with them (Deut 24:19–22); treat them fairly (Deut 24:14, 17); allow them to share in religious festivals (Deut 16:11, 14) and allow them to hear the law (Deut 31:12).

In the New Testament the question of the religious and moral status of the stranger is also addressed. The Gentiles were uncircumcised strangers (aliens), without the law, without God, without Christ, without covenants of promise, and outside of the commonwealth of Israel. However, they had been brought near by the blood of Christ (Eph 2:11–13). The dividing wall, the barrier or enmity between Jews and Gentiles was abolished and destroyed through the cross.

The cross of Christ created a new humanity, the messianic community or the church. In Christ ethnicity, racism, and tribalism have been abolished. All become one in Christ. Hostility, enmity, divisions, prejudices, discrimination, biases, and stereotypes have been annulled by the law of Christ. The broken relationships that characterize human communities, tribes, or races have been healed in Christ. If God is sovereign, all human beings can live in solidarity. People will still belong to tribes, races, peoples, and language groups, but there will be no tribalism, racism, and prejudice.

Moral Consciousness

Ikenga-Metuh stated that the Creator built a "moral conscience" into Africans. He defined moral conscience in the following words:

> This moral conscience pronounces judgments on the goodness or badness of any action and directs him to choose the right course of action and even reproaches him if he chooses to do the wrong thing. This means in effect that most of his deliberate actions are in fact moral actions regardless of whether the norms governing such actions are taboos, customs, social, religious or moral rules.[7]

He then listed three basic types of moral faults in traditional morality and ethics:

---

7. Ikenga-Metuh, *Comparative Studies*, 244.

Bad behaviour consists of breaches of rules of etiquette and social conventions and other minor faults which are generally condemned but carry no specific sanctions.

Bad deeds are sins properly so called. They are deliberate transgressions of serious moral norms of the society. They have three qualities: they are deliberate; they flout the laws of the land and they carry some social or mystical sanctions or both.

Taboos or prohibitions are forbidden and are abominations... Their infringement threatens the natural order and the very existence of society... They are mainly ritual or religious offences believed to disrupt relationship with the supernatural forces... These are either voluntary or involuntary breaches with grave consequences on both individuals and the entire society... An abomination can be contained only by physically or ritually removing the cause of the breach or pre-empting its effect.[8]

These three categories may differ from place to place and from one ethnic group to another, but the three types are always represented.

Moral laws are communitarian terms, limited by kinship, although they are derived from the cosmos, the spirit world, the gods and the divinities. For example, when someone talks about ethical and moral terms such as love, kindness, justice, goodness, faithfulness, they do not imagine that these are to be applied universally. The same is true of religious codes, duties and obligations, authority and legitimacy, and principles. Traditional religion binds one with very strong ties of affinity, loyalty and obligation.

The overriding ethical principle is relativism and not universalism.

---

8. Ikenga-Metuh, 250–252.

13

The Supreme Being

The traditional concept of God is complex and thus difficult to explain and interpret accurately. One therefore needs to take all the variables into consideration and weigh the possible influence of each on a particular concept or idea. Most scholars, however, tend to seize on one or two points on which they then base their interpretations and conclusions. The result is that they invariably present only partial and inconclusive answers and solutions.

A Supreme Being (God) stands at the top of the hierarchy of spiritual beings. Below him are ranged lesser divinities, ordinary spirits, and ancestral spirits. The traditional religious system does not seem to have clear, specific criteria which distinguish between gods, divinities, and spirits according to their nature, form, status and hierarchy, roles or functions, or even in terms of the religious practices associated with each category. The borders of some of the categories are fluid and diffused.

The traditional philosophical principles of holism and spiritualism mean that the belief in a Supreme Being is undifferentiated from the belief in other gods, divinities, and spirits. The transcendence and holiness of God is not as clear cut as in Christianity or Islam.

Theologically, the belief in the Supreme Being falls under creation theology. The traditional knowledge of God comes from general revelation which includes nature, human intuition, and innate awareness or perception.

A Shared Belief

It is not necessary to prove to Africans that God exists. They are abundantly aware that there is a Supreme Being, even though some Western scholars argued that traditional Africans had no concept of God. Responding to these critics, Idowu and Mbiti insisted that their research showed that traditional religion generally has a concept and an awareness of God comparable to that of Christianity and Islam. They interpreted the God of traditional Africa as being absolutely transcendent, having the same characteristics and attributes as the God of Christianity. This transcendence creates a chasm between God and the lesser beings, gods, divinities, and spirits. It is argued that even though traditional Africans believe that God exists, he is remote. He is not involved in their everyday affairs. God is aloof, "wholly other," and unapproachable.

Further support for the idea of a common understanding of God is provided by the fact that missionaries and Bible translators have successfully used traditional African concepts and ideas about God to transmit the gospel message to Africans. If such common ground were lacking, communication would be difficult. There are striking similarities between the practices, rituals, ceremonies, and cultures of the Old Testament and the traditional religious frameworks.

Sanneh, Walls, Bediako, and Gehman all stressed the significance of this commonality. Scholars like Bediako argue that dialogue between Christianity and traditional religion is possible. Some scholars see this dialogue in terms of religious pluralism and cultural relativism; others see it in terms of finding similarities or dissimilarities (comparative religion); others see it in terms of finding contact points for sharing or explaining Christianity to the traditional mind. It is important to stress, however, that the commonality of the theological framework does not mean that the theological foundations are the same or that the two religions have the same theological message or meaning.

In their desire to defend their people against the charge of having no concept of God, Idowu and Mbiti may have fallen into the trap of using Western philosophical and theological terms to define and interpret traditional concepts of the Supreme Being. Critics insist that the picture of God that has emerged from this new theological reconstruction is in reality neither traditional nor Christian. He is a new "god of philosophers."[1]

A Hidden Difference

While it is generally agreed that there are some similarities between the traditional African concept of God and the biblical, Christian concept of God, these concepts are rooted in radically different theological foundations. One stands in general revelation and its discourse about God is based upon creation theology whereby God is principally a creator. Conversely, the biblical concept

---

1. Ikenga-Metuh, *Comparative Studies*.

of God is grounded in special revelation and redemption theology where God is both creator and redeemer.

Consequently, although it is important to recognize that traditional language and concepts can be used to convey the gospel meaningfully to Africans, the problem that arises is how to prevent the channel from affecting the message that is heard. Traditional language and concepts have been shaped by a powerful worldview. The task for Christianity in Africa is to present and proclaim the contents of the gospel in such a way that Africans will internalize the message, the meaning, and the essence of the gospel and be able to distinguish it from the channel through which it comes.

If we are to understand the hidden differences between the concepts of God, we need to focus on the theological context of traditional African beliefs.

A Holistic Understanding

Any understanding of the contents of traditional African concepts must be rooted within the entire religious corpus of traditional religion and its unified religious worldview. The concept of God does not exist in isolation. Let us use the categories identified in an earlier chapter to help us consider aspects of the traditional African conception of God that have been ignored by some African scholars.

Influence of the Holistic or Organic Worldview

As pointed out previously, the holistic or organic worldview regards all things as operating together as a whole. Natural objects, animals, the spirits, the living and the dead are all part of an intricate web of beings. No sharp distinction is drawn between the sacred and the profane, between secular concerns and religious concerns, or between people's professions and their community responsibilities. Thus the traditional African belief in God is no different from the belief in impersonal mystical powers, spirits, the gods, and other divinities. There may be a hierarchical status, roles, and functions, but there is no absolute differentiation. The spirit beings and the material and spirit worlds act in harmony. God's transcendence, that marks his absolute holiness and separation from all other spirit beings, is diffused in the traditional spiritual worldview. When theologians and scholars analyse the hierarchy of spirit beings and characterize God in terms of absolute transcendence or remoteness, they are doing violence to the view of the holistic nature of the universe.

Scholars have assumed that the traditional view of a transcendent, remote God arises because Africans do not seem to have active dealings with the Supreme Being in their everyday life, as they do with the lesser spirit beings. Shouldn't the holistic view of life have produced an active God in traditional Africa? The answer to this question seems to lie in the African conception of God's status, role, and function within the traditional holistic community of the gods, the divinities, and the ancestors. God's involvement or non-involvement in the everyday life of the people should not be interpreted exclusively in terms of his transcendence (holiness), as some scholars would have us believe, but also in terms of his communal religious function as part of a hierarchy.

Influence of the Spiritual Worldview

The spiritual view of the universe is also holistic in that it regards everything in life as being influenced by or responding to the world of spirits. Spiritual powers lie behind every act or action in life and the meaning of life can be interpreted in spiritual terms.

Traditional African myths and legends assume that the Supreme Being has assigned duties and responsibilities to many lesser spirit beings, gods, and divinities, each of which has its own place, status, duty, and territory in the cosmic community. Their active presence in everyday life means that they have a closer affinity to humans than God does. God is acknowledged and is believed to exist, but his role and function mean that he is neither as close nor as feared as the spirit beings that are present in everyday life.

Some African scholars, such as Idowu, assert that the gods, spirits, and divinities are manifestations of God and that they serve as intermediaries or mediators between God and human beings. They claim that God is worshipped indirectly through these intermediaries. But this theology of intermediaries falls short both of biblical standards and of a true understanding of African Traditional Religion where the question of a direct or indirect approach to the worship of God does not even arise. Rather, the assumption is that if God is active behind the various gods and divinities, he is automatically also approached when they are approached. Both the Supreme Being and the lesser beings are part of the same cosmic community. God can be approached directly, but very often this is not considered necessary.

The theological concept of an intermediary or mediator is fundamentally Christian. It refers to Jesus Christ in his salvific or redemptive relationship to both God and humans. "For there is one God and one mediator between God and mankind, the man Christ Jesus, who gave himself as a ransom for all people" (1 Tim 2:5-6). To suggest that the divinities, ancestors or gods in traditional religion are intermediaries or mediators is an example of projection. Traditional religion itself would not have seen or defined them from this perspective.

We need to define the role of the divinities or ancestors within the context of traditional religion. Given the dominant spirit phenomenon in traditional belief, the role and place of spirit beings is well defined. In the hierarchy of spirit beings, the lesser spirit beings occupy a lower position than God. They are also much closer to humans and their daily affairs. An African uses these spirit beings to obtain spirit-power. Africans will do anything that the divinities or spirit beings ask, provided that they will obtain this spirit-power or life force. However, this does not imply worship. This is a search for the good life or life force, but not for redemption.

Influence of the Power-Conscious Worldview

The pursuit of power also influences African beliefs about the Supreme Being, gods, divinities, and spirit beings and their role and function within the cosmic community. Within traditional religion, the focus is on meeting one's needs. Given that most of the things humans need fall within the sphere of authority of lesser beings, there is no need for traditional Africans to go to God or bother him, unless the lesser beings prove inadequate. It is very difficult to differentiate between powers that belong to God and those that belong to lesser beings.

It is important at this stage to address the issue of whether the traditional worldview conceives of God as a Supreme Being or merely as an impersonal Supreme Power. The answer is that in the traditional conception God has both personal and impersonal attributes. Because spirit-power includes both personal and impersonal powers, God can manifest himself as a personal power or an impersonal power.

On the one hand, the attributes of God are usually described in personal terms. When Africans address mountains, rivers, woodcarvings or clay figurines, the sun, stars, or moon, they believe that the associated gods or divinities can hear them. The deities are thought of anthropomorphically, that is they are imagined with human forms and human attributes. This means that higher beings may delegate power to them.

On the other hand, because the traditional conception of power in the universe is diffused and undifferentiated, those who speak of the God of traditional Africa as an impersonal power are also correct. The role of impersonal and mystical powers in the traditional worldview means that serious consideration must be given to the possibility of the existence of a Supreme Power behind all spirit beings as well as the physical and the material world.

The traditional African conception of God is not narrowly defined. God may be viewed in a pantheistic, or polytheistic, or anthropomorphic manner, as a Supreme Power or a Supreme Being.

Influence of the Communal Worldview

The traditional community is held together holistically, spiritually, dynamically, and communally in a network that defines their relationships, roles, and functions. This sense of community extends beyond the local community into a world community of beings and non-beings whose interactions reflect cosmic harmony or cosmic disorder.

God, too, has an assigned place both in the local community and in the cosmic community of spirit beings. Communal religious life revolves around lesser beings who receive communal and personal prayers, sacrifices, offerings, gifts, and even worship. Unless the lesser beings have failed to meet the needs of the community, God is usually not bothered. God therefore appears to be remote or transcendent, not in an absolute ontological sense, but in terms of his place and function in the hierarchy of being. Whatever is given to lesser beings is conceived of as being indirectly given to him. Whatever is received from the immediate lesser beings is also indirectly received from him. The function of the gods or divinities which are designated as intermediary must be interpreted within this communal worldview where every being has an assigned place, role, and function.

14

Gods, Divinities and Spirits: Monotheism or Polytheism

African theologians and scholars claim that the space between God and human beings is filled with a hierarchy of gods, divinities, and spirits, who are sometimes described as intermediaries. These beings give humans aid and guidance in the mundane matters of everyday life. Some divinities are "self-sufficient and act independently of the Supreme Being," some have "the same attributes as the Supreme Being," and some are assigned territories or "special spheres of concern."[1]

Although some scholars talk of the transcendence of the Supreme Being in traditional religion in terms of "space," it is the aloofness of the Supreme Being from human affairs which is being described, not his holiness. Others think that it is out of the traditional respect a lesser person has for a higher person that one must go through an intermediary, much as Roman Catholics use saints and Mother Mary to take their prayers to God.

But it is necessary to begin by reopening the old debate as to whether African Traditional Religions practice monotheism or polytheism.

Belief in a myriad of spirit beings existing within a hierarchy is not unique to African Traditional Religion. A parallel can be found in biblical teaching regarding angels and evil spirits. The theological issue here concerns the status of these beings in relation to humans and to the Supreme Being, and whether or not they are accorded worship. A belief in angels does not necessarily lead to the worship of angels. Likewise, the African belief in spirit beings does not necessarily lead to the worship of spirit beings.

As mentioned previously African scholars, such as Idowu and Mbiti, were horrified that the label "polytheistic" was applied to Traditional African

---

1. Steyne, *Gods of Power*, 75.

Religion. They regarded it as demeaning and insisted that traditional beliefs were monotheistic. They argued that all the other divinities and spirit beings are merely intermediaries between the Supreme Being and humanity, and that God is thus worshipped indirectly. Unfortunately, their view represented a gross oversimplification of the traditional African worldview. Bediako charged that these scholars failed to adequately engage with the dimension of unity and multiplicity in African Traditional Religion. The reason for this failure was that these theologians had set themselves the goal of:

> Drawing together the total African religious experience into a coherent and meaningful pattern . . . focused unduly on the African sense of God, making it continuous with the received Western account of God in terms of monotheism . . . [leaving] what goes on in actual daily religious life and practice – in the company of divinities, ubiquitous spirits, ancestors – virtually untouched.[2]

The holistic view of the pervasiveness of spiritual power and its presence in all phenomena makes it difficult for traditional Africans to distinguish their dealings with spirits, divinities, and gods from their dealings with the Supreme Being. The worship that is offered is undifferentiated, inclusive and mixed, with God and the lesser beings acknowledged in the same act of worship. If God, the gods, the divinities, and the ancestors are all members of the hierarchical cosmic community, it can be assumed that God is also being worshipped when lesser beings are worshipped. Unfortunately, however, there is abundant evidence that in most instances God is simply ignored and the worship of the traditional gods, divinities and spirit beings is seen as an end in itself.

Such inclusive and mixed worship of God and lesser beings is exactly what the Bible condemns as idolatry. Whenever the Jews worshipped other gods as well as the Lord Yahweh, they were accused of idolatry and polytheism. Knowledge that a supreme God exists is not enough to constitute monotheism. The offering of worship to anything other than the one true God violates the first two commandments in the Decalogue:

> You shall have no other gods before me. You shall not make for yourself an image in the form of anything in heaven above, or on

---

2. Bediako, *Christianity in Africa*, 97.

the earth beneath or in the waters below. You shall not bow down
to them or worship them. (Exod 20:3–5a)

The many African divinities can be regarded as being a result of humanity's rebellion against God. When people reject absolute worship, service, and obedience to God (Rom 1), they turn to man-made divinities, gods, and spirits. The existence of this host of lesser beings is a product of this rebellion and involves the worship of creatures or creation instead of God. By offering worship to lesser deities, African Traditional Religion is idolatrous, as are all non-biblical religions.

Polytheism and Harmony

The number of deities involved means that traditional religion is undoubtedly also polytheistic. While Bediako dismissed Idowu and Mbiti's attempt to emphasize the monotheistic elements in Traditional African Religion, he did not deny that there are links between biblical theology and traditional religion. They share common convictions that the law of harmony that should exist in the universe has been broken and that some spirit beings may be evil.

A Universe of Conflict

Bediako saw links between Christianity and traditional religions in the very multiplicity of deities and in the fact that the harmony that should exist in the universe is lacking:

> Idowu's irritation with the multiplicity of divinities which swarm all over the place must be noted and, rather than reducing divinities into attributes or manifestations of God, recognize them as they are actually treated in normal religious practice, as entities which operate as ends in themselves. It would then be acknowledged that the spiritual universe of African primal religion is not . . . a neat hierarchy of divine beings and spirit-forces held in unitary harmony. The African primal world can be conceived of as a universe of distributed power, perhaps even fragmented power; it is as much a universe of conflict as the rest of the fallen world in that it is a world not of one Centre, God, but many centres; the unity and multiplicity of the Transcendental in the African world also reveals a deep ambivalence. It is this ambivalence to which

a creative Christian engagement must answer and do so in terms of the primal imagination itself.³

This same lack of harmony is clearly evident in this description of the nature of the divinities:

> The divinities do not necessarily act in concert with one another and may sometimes act in opposition. They may be played off against each other, so that they respond jealously. The devotee must act with great care lest any other divinities be alienated. These divinities are thought to have full power to act as they please. Man cannot be sure of their responses either, as they seem to act with great caprice. They can bring man success or cause failure. They can act in anger, or be vengeful, downright mean, or hardhearted. Man must bear the consequences and seek ways to restore cordial relations. Divinities are thought to have human appetites, which must be fed and human passions, which must be appeased. They are placated with different kinds of offerings and sacrifices, each prescribed for the occasion.⁴

When theologians debate these matters without using theology itself as the tool of analysis, they forget that African Traditional Religion is rooted in general revelation and therefore stands separate from the special revelation which Christians have in the Bible and Jesus Christ. To equate revelation and tradition is to deny biblical inspiration and God's special revelation. When this theological premise is denied, all religions and all cultures will be treated alike. Then every theology must be lumped together as general revelation and the theological discourse must take place within creation theology. The theological aspect of God as Redeemer would be brushed aside.

In African Traditional Religion it is up to humans to perform the rituals needed to restore the harmony that should exist between the physical and the spirit worlds. Christians, by contrast, would argue that the Supreme Being took the action to restore that equilibrium, in the miracle of incarnation and the cross of Christ.

---

3. Bediako, *Christianity in Africa*, 99–100.
4. Steyne, *Gods of Power*, 75.

Evil Spirits

The lack of harmony in the spirit world is not merely caused by disagreements among spirits. There are also spirits that are actually evil. The origin and nature of these evil spirits is shrouded in mystery but, most commonly, they are associated with humans. There is a common traditional belief that:

> Certain deceased people become evil spirits during the improper dispatch of the body in funeral rites, through breaking the tribal custom, an abnormal death or improper ritual performances in life ... [They] are to be feared because of the mischief they create, the terror they spread and the destruction they work.[5]

These evil spirits can possess people and inflict all kinds of diseases and sufferings, although they can be exorcised or appeased through sacrifices and offerings as in the Hausa *bori* dance.

The wicked or evil spirits in African Traditional Religion are the equivalent of the fallen angels in the Bible. These are the angels who fell along with Satan and were cast out of heaven by God. They are variously described as "unclean spirits," "familiar spirits," "demons," "principalities," and "powers." The traditional African belief is that these spirits have certain powers that can actually be put to use to help human beings achieve certain goals. The dominance of spirit-power in African spirituality is rooted in this conception.

Polytheism and Power

The most potent attribute of all spirit beings is power, although they do not necessarily possess this power inherently. They may simply be channels for the powers delegated to them by higher beings in which case they are only responsible for certain functions. This concept of delegation makes it very difficult to distinguish between the powers that belong specifically to the Supreme Being and those that belong to lesser beings. It is also difficult to tell at what point these beings cease to act on behalf of the Supreme Being and start to act on their own behalf.

Because human beings are by nature powerless, they need to find the guardian gods, divinities, and spirit beings that will help them to gain access to the spirit world that is the source of all power. We have seen that the pursuit of power and the quest to understand the spiritual meaning of events takes precedence over all other considerations: "whatever is empowering is right"

---

5. Steyne, 78.

and "a powerless religion is valueless." It is acceptable to go to any god, divinity, or spirit being who is believed to be able to deliver the goods.

Traditional Africans know that they are dealing with powers other than the Supreme Being. They also know that in almost all cases the spirit beings they approach have sufficient power in themselves to meet their needs without any reference to the Supreme Being. In some cases, the power or help obtained is even contrary to what the Supreme Being would have wanted. Gods are known to have acted defiantly!

The morality of the spirit who is being approached and the morality of the worshipper are irrelevant in this search for power. The worshipper does not even need to have much knowledge about the spirit being with whom he or she is dealing. All that is important is the correct rituals or the right customs. When these are observed properly, the needed power will automatically be granted. (We used the word "worshipper" simply for want of a better word to refer to the one who is soliciting spirit-powers.)

Finding gods and divinities is rather like window-shopping. While dealing with one god, one keeps one's eyes open for another god who may have something greater or more powerful to offer. One will worship or solicit the one who makes the best offer, whether this be a minor divinity, a major one, or even the Supreme Being himself. This means that someone who professes to worship or solicit one divinity may still be seen worshipping or soliciting another. An individual does not have one standard God, but may interact with many gods, many divinities, and many spirit beings.

Polytheism, the Spirit World and the Kinship Community

Certain divinities or gods are primarily thought of in terms of their relationship to certain communities or categories of people.

Personal, Household, and Tribal Gods

Individuals, households, clans, or tribes may have their own divinities who act as protectors over the total welfare of the home. These are the benefactors of the individual members of the household. They are accorded sacrifices, prayers, and worship; they are consulted for guidance and information about what the future holds; they are asked to bring luck. However if humans do not approach them correctly, they may reap disaster.

A household or tribal god is usually represented by a stone, metal, or wooden idol. People are aware that the idol is not the god; rather, "the object is understood to be the husk providing a contact point – a representation of what is spirit in essence."[6] Gehman quoted Idowu as saying that "the Yoruba do not bow down to the wood and the stone, but only before the wood and the stone, which are emblems of the divinities."[7] In the Yoruba religion, idols almost always represent a spirit or a divinity distinct from the Supreme God. The fact that an idol has been constructed and that the spirit worshipped is not the Supreme God means that this kind of worship is idolatrous in biblical terms.

The Spirits of the Ancestors

Belief in the ancestors is the most fundamental religious tenet governing African religion, culture, customs, life, and meaning. Some refer to it as the "the cult of the ancestors" and speak of worship or veneration of the ancestors. There is, however, disagreement about whether recognition of ancestors with sacrifices and offerings reflects mere respect or whether it is equivalent to actual worship.[8] It is difficult to distinguish as reverence and worship can take place in one act.

While there may be public institutions or communal assemblies associated with the ancestors, in general the rituals are private and kinship-based. Only members of a family, a household, a clan, or a tribe may take part, for only the children of the deceased ancestor have the right of access. This right is rooted in the concept of the fatherhood of the ancestor. He is the progenitor or the original seed of the lineage, the clan, or the tribe and his life is transmitted to all who proceed from his loins. He is the life-source of all his descendants and the basis of their unity, community, and existence. Like a father, he loves, cares for, protects, blesses, advises, and has authority. Consequently, he also commands reverence, respect, loyalty, and veneration. But a father also has negative powers: he is the one who curses and brings misfortune in response to any act of disobedience or to any wrongdoing done to him personally or to anyone of his seed. When the one who has done wrong repents, the father forgives and takes away the curse. The father retains these functions after death; in fact, the potency of fatherhood increases at death.

Moral conduct and a "holy" life will please the ancestors; conversely, misconduct and impurity will result in curses that bring evil and misfortune. Thus the living descendants of an ancestor approach him reverently, seeking

---

6. Steyne, *Gods of Power*, 78.
7. Idowu quoted in Gehman, *African Traditional Religion*, 132.
8. Fortes and Dieterlen, *African Systems of Thought*, 126.

blessings and protection as well as forgiveness when they have done wrong. Normally, such requests are accompanied by libations or sacrifices at his tomb or some other fixed place.

When misfortune strikes, those affected must examine their conduct toward their kinsfolk and neighbours to see whether some duties and obligations have not been fulfilled.[9] Any sin or moral wrong must be atoned for, often through the sacrifice of an animal or fowl although some offenses also require the payment of fines. Peacemaking ceremonies and treaties include oaths and vows, which are usually sealed by blood sacrifices. Forgiveness takes effect immediately after restitution or reconciliation and the quarrels between individuals, families, or communities are settled.

When someone dies and is about to join the ancestors, they may be "requested to take greetings or requests to the previously departed. But communication does not end there. The deceased will again communicate with the living in this present life."[10] In an attempt to avoid unpleasant communication, some groups have developed elaborate burial ceremonies and rituals that must be followed to facilitate the onward journey of the deceased to the city of the dead. These memorial ceremonies may take place over a period of time, ranging from six months to a year or more. These rituals protect the living from the harm that the angry spirit of the deceased might wreak; an improper burial might result in an ancestral spirit lingering in the vicinity, haunting the family, taking revenge on enemies, and generally making life miserable.

The relationship between the living and the ancestors also shapes matters of daily life. It has led to customs, superstitions, social laws, regulations, and taboos that define the general order of existence in a given society. Some Africans, for example, would not think of eating or drinking without giving a token offering to the ancestors.[11] The relationship has also led to the formulation of concepts of good and evil, morality, ethics, and justice that are strictly kinship based. This is the original source of ethnic or tribal values.

It is clear that belief in ancestral spirits profoundly influences the practices, behaviours, and attitudes of ethnic groups, tribes, clans, and families. Gehman's list of some of the types of relationship that exist between the living and their ancestors summarizes much of what has been said in this chapter:

---

9. Cole, "Christian and African."
10. Steyne, *Gods of Power*, 80.
11. Steyne, 80.

As senior elders of the clan, the ancestors function as the guardians of the family traditions and life.

When the living fail to follow the customs of the fathers, it becomes the duty of the ancestors to correct their errors.

As elders, the ancestors serve as the owners of the land, fertilizing the earth and causing the food to grow.

The living dead receive requests and offerings from the living.

The ancestral spirits may also serve as intermediaries between man and God.

The living dead become a source of comfort to the living, which are always conscious of their presence.

The living dead communicate with the living through revelations, dreams, calamity, ecstasy and trance, possession, prophecy, and divination.[12]

There seems to be no clear-cut distinction between the role and functions of the Supreme Being and those of gods, divinities, and spirits. At times it is even difficult to differentiate between religious practices and social practices, particularly in matters relating to the ancestors.

While it is important to understand these aspects of traditional religion within their cultural context and to try to distinguish the cultural from the religious, our understanding must stand under the authority of the Bible. The Bible clearly categorizes the traditional religions of the world as idolatry. The numerous lesser gods, divinities and spirits who receive worship fall under the biblical definition of unclean spirits, demons, idols, and the gods of the nations. The task for Christian theologians is to develop a theology of worship and spirituality that adequately addresses the significance of the spiritual beings, powers and forces that lie behind traditional religious beliefs.

---

12. Gehman, *African Traditional Religion*, 134.

15

Communication With and From the Spirit World

It is often assumed that contact with colonialism, Christianity, Islam, and modernity wiped out the traditional religion and worldview. This is not so. True, some of the religious and traditional institutions were affected as a result of their encounter with these new ways of thinking. However, although some of these structures and institutions might not have survived, traditional spirituality with its power consciousness, beliefs, practices, and worldview has endured. Its continuing influence means that it is essential for us to gain a thorough knowledge of this powerful traditional mind. People need to see beyond religion and worship and uncover what traditional Africans actually do with the spirit world and the supernatural world.

It is not surprising that the knowledge that the whole world is full of spirits that control their destinies gives traditional Africans a strong desire to communicate with this spirit world about the general maintenance of harmony in the world and about their own specific needs.

Traditional Africans believe that the law of cosmic harmony works to maintain a spiritual equilibrium or balance between the human and spirit worlds. But the desired harmony is constantly under attack. The human world is unstable, chaotic, vulnerable, fragile, and subject to invasion and the caprices of the more powerful gods and spirits. A continual effort is required to restore it, to repair breached relationships and to achieve reconciliation. Traditional religion thus had to address the question of how fellowship, communion, harmony, and equilibrium were to be maintained between humans and the world of spirits and gods.

This prompts further questions such as "How does one know whether one is in good standing with the gods?" and "How does one know that things have gone wrong? And if things have indeed gone wrong, how can they be put right? How can breached relations between the gods or spirits and humanity be restored?" and even, "What is necessary for maintaining fellowship, communion, peace, and harmony?" In order to answer these questions humans have to communicate with the spirit world.

Communication with the Spirit World

The discussion that follows does not attempt to distinguish between which practices are religious and which are social. Nor does the discussion mean to imply that all traditional practices are suspect: there is both good and evil in the traditional religious worldview. The purpose is to enable African Christians to identify the sources of their moral and social behaviour.

Taboos

In the African tradition taboos govern numerous aspects of social, cultural, and religious life. They operate at different levels: some reflect common sense prohibitions, others sanction authority and institutions, still others relate to levels of hierarchy or social status and to mystical and spiritual powers. They govern such things as sacred places, land use, the manner in which festivals or special days are celebrated, what animals may be eaten, marriage and procreation, relationships with the ancestors, and the roles of males, females, fathers, mothers, and children. In other words, they set out the codes of conduct or the "do's and don'ts" of the community. They are sacred moral codes that prescribe the social, customary and religious behaviour required to maintain cosmic harmony. They are tools for sociocultural and religious conditioning, maintaining the social order and the harmony and structures of meanings and worldviews.

Steyne defined a taboo as follows:

> Taboo is the place where the spirit world meets social and religious custom. Taboo enforces the concept of the sacred. It is a prohibition against touching, saying, being or doing something, for fear of harm being inflicted by "the mystic dangerousness of a particular object," or supernatural power. Certain objects, persons, places, and times are forbidden because they are associated with supernatural powers . . . Taboo is a scheme of systematized fear that excites and promotes awe and respect, as well as a sense of "awe-fullness." It is one of the strongest checks on man's behavior

in both traditional and contemporary society, motivating him to maintain harmony and balance with his environment. Its many rules and regulations encourage him to keep on the narrow path of custom. In a very real sense, taboo is a prohibition imposed by social and religious custom, as a protective measure against deviancy. Not to observe taboo issues in a judgment involving dire consequences, even death. By proscribing behavior on certain occasions and respecting certain objects and people – what to see, what to touch, with whom to associate, where and what to attend or avoid or use – taboo safeguards and protects a people's accepted physical, social and metaphysical systems. Taboo confirms and supports their worldview. Taboo is a legal system which dictates how life shall be lived in order to realize salvation and blessings . . . It is an all encompassing system calling on the spirit world to either validate, restrict or censure human behavior.[1]

Religious Festivals, Rituals and Ceremonies

Numerous sacred feasts and rituals have always regulated the religious and social life of traditional Africa. Some of these were communal and cyclical and took place at fixed times as determined by the calendar. Thus new moons were celebrated, as were the beginnings of the rainy or planting season, of the harvest season, of the new yams festivals and of the hunting season. Others were only performed as the need arose. These included rites of passage (birth, initiation, marriage, and death), rainmaking, and purification rites. Depending on the occasion, ceremonies included meals, dance, music using a variety of instruments (drums, animal horns, trumpets, as well as vocal and choral groups), chants, incantations, storytelling, recitation, drama, sacrifices, offerings, and parades in honour of deities, ancestors, or heroes/heroines.[2]

These traditional rituals and ceremonies have a number of functions, some of which are primarily emotional. Steyne described them as "a codified expression of belief and emotion, demonstrating faith" and reminds us that:

> In a sense, the more ritualized a religious system is, the less the walking by faith is necessary. The converse is also true. Both approaches are religiously valid because in both cases faith is what

---

1. Steyne, *Gods of Power*, 141–142.
2. Steyne.

sustains the system. However, the more ritualized the religious system is, the more loyal its devotees are. Ritual sustains and generates the myth underlying the belief system, while it also binds people together socially, psychologically, and physically as they participate. Shared activities such as dancing, clapping hands, singing, reciting liturgies, praying, carrying burdens, sacrificing and performing ceremonies of various sorts all serve to reinforce collective sentiments . . . They are cathartic and therapeutic experiences, producing a sense of well-being and assuring the participants that their religious faith is correctly placed.[3]

Rituals can serve as an outlet for certain forms of behaviour. In certain ritual practices, norms of morality and ethics are relaxed and what are "normally considered aberrant behavior forms are exhibited, such as reversal of sex roles, sexual license, drunkenness, drug use, humor, laughter, free speech, glossolalia, etc."[4]

Rituals are also a means of maintaining harmony or restoring relationships and communication between humans and the spirit and mystical world. Steyne was speaking of this when he defined a ceremony as "a sacred rite, a formal act or series of acts prescribed by ritual" and went on to say:

> Ceremony is a visual demonstration of a reciprocal affirmation of recognition, responsibility, and accountability of deity to devotee and of devotee to deity (spirit). Spirit beings need living devotees who will give them recognition by worshiping them through various rites. These rites include sacrifices and offerings, incantations and prayers, acts of veneration, like burning of incense or feeding the deities. When the spirit beings are neglected, they in turn refuse to perform their responsibilities to their devotees. The spirit beings generally communicate their displeasure through calamities, dreams and/or visions and refusal to answer prayers.[5]

Steyne listed the following purposes of ceremonies:

> Renewing, strengthening and in some cases restoring bonds between devotees or worshipers and spirit beings (deities, spirits, ancestors); maintaining filial relations between spirits and

---

3. Steyne, 95.
4. Steyne, 95.
5. Steyne, 97.

devotees; and uniting worshipers or devotees and spirit beings in a common bond of reciprocity.

Controlling or gaining favor from the spirit world; preventing trouble, calamity and general distress of the devotee group; fulfilling and meeting what the spirit world expects, requires and even demands; maintaining harmony with the spirit world; securing success and victory for the performers.

Providing socio-psychological affirmation for the participants; confirming patterns and feelings of loyalty to the deity (spirit, god, and ancestor); establishing common bonds of loyalty and a common goal among devotees; producing psychological well-being in the devotee; building moral and self-perpetuation.

Serving as a social control mechanism in society by establishing patterns of loyalty and prescribing parameters of acceptable conduct; integrating people into the religious system, the framework of sociocultural customs and meeting the socio-psychological needs of man.[6]

All these religious and social practices generate a social and spiritual worldview that shapes and moulds the traditional African mind. This has been passed on from generation to generation, and it is this traditional mind that encounters Christianity, Islam, or modernity.

The Jewish religion, whose festivals are described in the Pentateuch, had many festivals and ceremonies that were similar to those of traditional religions. The Christian church, too, has a calendar of annual feasts. However, the important difference is that worship and ceremony in Judaism and Christianity do not emphasize the manipulation of gods or the search for power and well-being. Instead they celebrate the blessings, grace, and mercy of God and God is worshipped.

When comparing traditional feasts and Christian feasts and deciding what elements should or should not be retained, Christian theologians need to explore the meaning of the traditional festivals, feasts and the cyclical calendar. They need to be aware of the religious beliefs, the worldview, and the spiritual powers that lie behind them.

---

6. Steyne, 97.

Sacrifices and Offerings

The maintenance of harmony may also require sacrifices and offerings to spirit beings. Offerings are gifts that are given voluntarily, while sacrifices are gifts that are required to atone for wrongs that have been done. Specific offerings and sacrifices are prescribed for specific occasions.

The things presented as offerings and sacrifices generally have a close affinity with the one who is sacrificing, thus signifying the giving up of something for the sake of another. They may include "cereals or other vegetable life, prepared food and/or drink, animal victims, sometimes human life, and other objects." When it comes to sacrifice, the object for sacrifice may be determined by custom or by divination, but the shedding of blood is an essential element.[7]

The concept of sacrifices and offerings is common to traditional religion. Although their overriding concern is the pursuit of harmony, there are also other purposes:

- Paying homage to the Gods
- Bribing the gods with a gift so that they will act favorably to the donors
- Maintaining communion between giver and receiver
- Feeding the gods, who in turn will provide blessings and protection
- Establishing and maintaining communication with the spirit world
- Appeasing the spirit world
- Seeking the help of the spirit world in time of need
- Blinding the spirit world to some taboo infraction
- Removing any possible guilt arising out of fear lest insufficient recognition has been given or appeasement made to the spirit world
- Removing sickness that has been sent as a judgment by the spirit world
- Sending off the dead or welcoming them into important communal ceremonies
- Restoring relationships among opposing individuals, families and tribes
- Mending broken relationships with the spirit world, the ancestors or the gods
- Purifying or cleansing through acts of consecration[8]

---

7. Steyne.
8. Steyne, 137–138.

Many parallels exist between the Israelite practices of the Old Testament and those of the African Traditional Religions. Both, for example, laid considerable emphasis on sacrifices and offerings. However, it is important that Christians realize there are major differences too:

> The OT sacrifices were specifically prescribed by God and received their meaning from the Lord's covenant relationship with Israel – whatever their superficial resemblances to pagan sacrifices. They indeed include the idea of a gift, but this is accompanied by such other values as dedication, communion, propitiation (appeasing God's judicial wrath against sin) and restitution.[9]

Communication from the Spirit World

At times a direct communication from the spirits may be necessary. This may occur because an individual has unwittingly breached the law of harmony, but direct communication from the spirit beings is also required if one is to satisfy the quest for power. Humans need to know where to acquire power, and how to discover their own destiny or that of their community. Such communication is generally sought through dreams, visions, vision quests, and divination.

Dreams

Africans take dreams seriously because dreams are the chief sources of revelation from the spirit world. Dreams enable the living to receive guidance, commands, good messages of blessing, or even bad omens and warnings. There is also a belief that in sleep the human soul can leave the body and travel to other places, especially in the spiritual realms. This enables the living to communicate with the gods, the spirits and the dead.

Dreams or night visions are recognized as an important means of divine communication in the Bible but it is clear that the interpretation of dreams is only possible with God's guidance. Joseph, Jacob's favourite son, dreamed (Gen 37:6-9; 40:8, 12-13, 18-19; 41:25-32) and Daniel dreamed in Babylon (Dan 2:19, 27-45; 4:19-27; 7:16). Some of these dreams were difficult to interpret, but God used them to make theological statements. God also used dreams to provide guidance, as with Joseph, the husband of Mary in the Gospels. Mosaic law laid down the death penalty for those who claimed to have received divine

---

9. *NIV Study Bible*, 145.

messages in dreams but whose words proved false (Deut 13:1–5; see also Jer 23:25–32; 29:8–9 and Zech 10:2).

Visions

The *Eerdmans Bible Dictionary* defines a vision as:

> A supernatural visual manifestation, which may also involve the aural, that serves as a divine revelation of something otherwise secret. Visions are closely related to such other revelatory phenomena as dreams and journeys through heaven and hell. Nearly every religious tradition, ancient or modern, contains traditions of visions experienced by holy men and women.[10]

In visions, unlike dreams, people "perceive an event as external to their own senses, something which imposes itself upon the mind." In traditional religion, visions have great significance and "bring guidance, warnings and promises of blessings."[11]

Vision Quests (Spirit Possession)

Traditional believers undertake vision quests when they use rituals and ascetic practices in order to induce a spirit to take possession of them. The Hausa *bori* dance is a typical example of this. The means of inducing spirit possession include,

> meditative and contemplative exercises, self-inflicted tortures ([including] jumping from heights, walking on burning coals, thrusting skewers into cheeks and tongue), using drugs, dancing, drumming, chanting [and] singing oneself into a frenzy.[12]

A person thus possessed can make contact or communicate with the spirit world and may receive ecstatic experiences, glossolalia, unusual visions, and dreams. "The indwelling spirit is also thought to be the personal guardian of the possessed."[13] This practice is also associated with keeping totem animals whose spirits are said to possess persons.

---

10. *Eerdmans Bible Dictionary*, 1040.
11. Steyne, *Gods of Power*, 126.
12. Steyne, 127–128.
13. Steyne, 127.

The Bible condemns this religious practice of associating with "familiar spirits."

Divination

Steyne defined divination as "a technique with which to interpret phenomena of nature and occult spirits," while the *Eerdmans Bible Dictionary* defines it as "the art of determining the future or ascertaining the divine will."[14] The traditional belief that anything that happens must have a definite spiritual cause means that the use of divination is widespread in Africa. The reasons for undertaking divination include the following:

> To find out about one's future, destiny, well-being and what may possibly happen to oneself, one's family, clan, or tribe;
>
> To establish contact with the sources of mystical and spiritual powers that can be tapped to meet one's needs;
>
> To find out how to protect oneself and one's community from the evil activities of witches and sorcerers and unseen, unpredictable mystical and spirit powers;
>
> To gain power, confidence, assurance and boldness in facing the challenges of life and triumph over them through esoteric and mystical powers;
>
> To overcome human limitations, finitude, impotence, dependence, contingency by knowing how they function and affect;
>
> To be able to receive and interpret messages from the spirit world for both personal and communal well-being and to maintain harmony between humans and the spirits or gods.[15]

The Bible mentions a number of forms of divination, some of which have also been traditionally practiced in Africa. These include throwing objects and examining their position when they fall (Ezek 21:21), examining the entrails of animals (Ezek 21:21), and consulting the dead (Ezek 21:21; Lev 19:31). The Bible strongly condemns divination as fraudulent (Ezek 13:6–7) and an abomination (Deut 18:11–12). In the Old Testament, divination was punishable by death (Lev 20:6, 27). The reason for this condemnation is that "Divination

---

14. *Eerdmans Bible Dictionary*, 287.
15. Steyne, 131–132.

is a pagan counterpart of prophecy. Divination is by demonic power, whereas genuine prophecy is by the Spirit of God. God, therefore, detests divination of any kind."[16] Fleming both warns and admonishes:

> Divination, witchcraft and all these associated practices are contrary to the ways of God, not only because they depend on evil spiritual powers for their operation, but also they are a denial of faith. True believers walk humbly with their God, accepting that, no matter what the circumstances, God is still in control of their affairs. Having been saved by faith, they now live by faith (Gal 2:20; Eph 4:17–24; Col 1:11–13; Heb 11:6). Jesus Christ has triumphed over all the unseen powers of evil and through him believers too can triumph (Eph 1:19–21; 2:6; Col 2:8–10; 3:1–3).[17]

Ordeals

In exceptional circumstances communication from the spirit world is sought through trial by ordeal:

> [An ordeal] is a test used to determine the guilt or innocence of someone who is suspected of some violation of custom or taboo. Essentially, the practice of ordeal assumes guilt. It is assumed that because the spirit world is on the side of truth, a person who is innocent will be granted supernatural power to supersede any dangerous or painful test. Even if the test is not dangerous or painful in itself, if the suspect is guilty, supernatural power will supposedly bring the required judgment to bear. In some cases it is assumed that the inward life will validate the outward behavior. Therefore the innocent have nothing to fear, but the guilty will not escape the punishment due them.[18]

The primary goal of an ordeal was to ascertain innocence or guilt with regard to moral behaviour or a questionable act. Since human knowledge is limited, judgment has to be left in the hands of the gods or of lesser beings who speak through their oracles.

---

16. Watkins, *Complete Christian Dictionary*, 189–190.
17. Fleming, *Bridge Bible Directory*, 271.
18. Steyne, *Gods of Power*, 132.

The most common of these were ordeals through oath taking, through boiling oil and the use of hot articles and fire, through poison, as well as through divination and sorcery. However, certain ordeals could only be administered by particular oracles, and people would travel long distances to reach the renowned oracles that could administer them. One such was the famous Arochukwu oracle of the Igbo in eastern Nigeria, while the Bifa oracle of the Gong people in Central Nigeria was used as a means of settling disputes within and between communities. After the chief priest had performed certain rituals, the person was asked to sit on a particular standing stone. If one were innocent, the stone would flatten with a thundering sound, allowing the person to sit. If one were guilty, the stone would sharpen like a piercing arrow, making it impossible for the guilty person to sit down.

There are references to ordeals in the Bible (Num 5:11–31; Jer 8:14; 9:15; 23:15). However, these were only permitted under God's watchful eye.

Rules concerning taboos, religious festivals and sacrifices were laid down in Exodus, Numbers, Leviticus, and Deuteronomy. These were given to the Israelites as they moved into the land of the Canaanites, whose religion also had these features. But the religion of the Canaanites was an abomination to the Lord God, Yahweh and the Israelites were forbidden to copy their religious beliefs and their practices.

The attitude of the Lord God Yahweh to the Canaanite religion and culture should be our theological norm and model.

Professional Communicators with the Spirit World

The complex nature and the variety of the African traditional beliefs and practices, especially in relation to the spirit world, produced what we may call African specialists or professionals. These are the people to turn to for help when one is trying to communicate with the spirit world.

A victim, the person who is experiencing misfortune, may appeal to a shaman, witchdoctor, prophet, priest, medicine man or woman, or a worker of evil (a sorcerer or witch). All of these are believed to have the extraordinary skills and powers needed to deal with problems and to know the secrets and mysteries of the gods, spirits, powers, and human beings.

Specialists use spiritual and mystical powers and life force to enhance the well-being of individuals and the community. They also develop and conduct effective and meaningful rituals to ensure the harmony, balance, and peace of individuals and communities; to exercise control over the spirit world and human society; and to communicate with the spirit world.

The services of these traditional specialists are eagerly sought by traditional Africans, seeking to protect themselves from the menacing and capricious activities of spirit beings, witches, wizards, sorcerers, as well as natural disasters or calamities, diseases, human weaknesses and various forms of human suffering, and death.

Each profession has its set of beliefs, rules and regulations, practices, and rituals. Some specialists use mystical and spirit powers, some ordinary human ingenuity and wisdom, while some are cheats or deceivers.

African pagan spirituality still has a profound and pervasive influence on Christianity, Islam and modernity in Africa. Many traditional beliefs, rituals, and ceremonies have been carried over into African expressions of Christianity. When Africans become Christians, their basic human needs remain the same, and may even increase in intensity. What is different is how the religious beliefs, rituals, and ceremonies are used to address these needs.

In their comparative studies most African scholars have ignored the significance of the spiritual powers and forces in traditional religion and culture. Yet since its arrival in Africa, Christianity has encountered these spiritual powers and has been engaged in a spiritual warfare with them (see Eph 6). Neglecting the role played by these spirit-powers in traditional Africa has produced a shallow Christian theology that does not adequately address the issues of spiritual and mystical powers and forces.

If a relevant Christian and biblical theology is to be developed, the totality of traditional African beliefs, practices, rituals, and ceremonies associated with communication between divinities and spirit beings and humans has to be studied thoroughly, together with what the Bible teaches about non-Jewish religions.

16

The Acquisition of Power

Traditional religion is a religion of power and mystery. Spirit-power forms the basis of African pagan spirituality. In examining the theological basis of the Supreme Being and the numerous subordinate gods, divinities, and spirit beings, the concept of power and the need to acquire it has often been mentioned.

The Need for Power

We have already discussed the concept of *mysterium tremendum*, the life force, the mystical, impersonal, and unseen power that directs human lives. It is believed to permeate everything, especially animal life. Langdon Gilkey described the human situation in the face of it:

> Men are also deeply troubled by anxious fears arising from their weakness as creatures. The feeling of dependence and contingency, of being subject to uncontrollable forces, forms the content of one of these anxieties. The experience of temporality and mortality, of an approaching "deadline to one's powers and life," forms the frightening content of the other. These experiences of our "creaturehood" foster an undertone of anxiety in our lives; from this dread, too, we need rescue if we would be whole.[1]

In the face of these anxieties, traditional Africans seek mystical means of communicating with and controlling the spirit world. The more life force a human being can acquire, the greater his or her strength, power and success. Those with an abundant supply of life force or spirit-power can rise above the ordinary and will be able to do extraordinary things. They will also receive

---

1. Gilkey, *Maker of Heaven and Earth*, 6.

more protection or guidance than others. Clearly, added spirit-power brings a sense of security and will allay fears and anxieties.

Methods of Acquiring Power

Traditional Africans believe in luck or chance. They accept that luck may bring the needed power. One may be fortunate and obtain it through birth or heredity, but this means of acquiring life force or spirit-power is very selective, leaving out many. Steyne suggested other ways that life force can be acquired.[2] The extent to which these means are used can vary from moderate to extreme, depending on the type of ritual practices being followed.

Through the Senses

For centuries, in Africa and around the world, drugs have been regarded as a means of increasing spiritual and mystical potency. Drugs such as marijuana, peyote, and LSD are still used by some contemporary religious groups to heighten their awareness of spiritual powers or to enhance the activities of the spiritual powers. Yet, where drug abuse has increased in the modern world, demonic activities and crime have also increased.

Life force and spiritual power can also be acquired through various forms of severe self-discipline, such as vision quests, night vigils, ritual self-emptying and purification, fasting, meditation and silence, postures, and ritual dances. Certain types of music are also thought to secure and enhance spiritual powers.

Some of these practices and rituals have been incorporated into certain African expressions of Christianity, Islam, and modernism. But it is important theologically to remember that they are fundamentally rooted in traditional African beliefs in spiritual and mystical powers. They reveal the interplay between the spiritual phenomenon and power phenomenon, the fusing of spiritualism and dynamism which forms the basis of traditional spirituality. These traditional practices are avenues for strong demonic activities.

Through One's Ancestors and Associates

Traditional Africans believe very strongly that maintaining good relations with the ancestors ensures the continuation of the life force and increases the vigour and potency of the spiritual and mystical powers. The association with

---

2. Steyne, *Gods of Power*.

the ancestors takes various forms, including continued respect for them as the revered guardians of the family and community, contact with and use of sacred objects known to have been used and kept by the ancestors, and consulting the spirits of the ancestors. But, although the ancestors or the living dead are by no means demons, association with them involves dealing with their spirits and this means one is in danger of playing with demonic powers.

It is believed that by keeping in close contact with great men or women (heroes, heroines, leaders, and warriors) one may be able to absorb a significant measure of the life force. Spirit-powers can also be transferred from parents to children or from leaders to their followers. As a result of this belief, men and women of stature, status, and power usually attract many disciples. This applies to religious leaders in modern Africa and is evident among certain Christian groups in their expressions of African Christianity. Followers are attracted by the unusual spiritual and mystical powers manifested by these religious leaders and so these leaders can wield tremendous influence, some even holding their followers captive by the use of spirit-powers. When spirit-powers are used to maintain a relationship, then demonic activity is involved.

Through Charms, Sacred Objects, Weapons and Other Paraphernalia

The belief that objects can possess life force leads to a pervasive belief that spiritual and mystical powers can be acquired through the use of charms and sacred objects. A vast variety of objects are considered to have varying degrees of potency. These include,

> objects formerly used by ritual and/or religious specialists, objects associated with sacred paraphernalia, parts of animals, or human beings, sacred cords, animal claws, precious and semiprecious stones, pieces of leather, special metal objects, religious symbols, sacred Scripture texts, ointment or salve.[3]

Objects can be carried about as charms, amulets and weapons; but they may be kept at home or buried in strategic places. These charms can be used to gain protection or to harm others or to cause calamity.

The essential thing to look for in all these items is their source, to discover what powers were imputed to them and by what ritual. If it was through anointing, we need to ask which power or name was invoked during the anointing. From the study of African pagan spirituality and traditional

---

3. Steyne, 115.

religion, it is clear that these rituals, ceremonies, festivals, and religion are not "neutral." Behind them is the reality of spirit beings and supernatural powers. Satan rules the fallen human culture. African Traditional Religion is part of the world, therefore Satan rules it too. However, it is also important to remember that only certain elements of African Traditional Religion have been strongly influenced by Satanic and demonic forces.

Through Sacrifices

Blood plays a significant symbolic role as ritual sacrifices and the use of blood are believed to empower those who perform them. The sacrificed meat or food is eaten in a prescribed manner and so is the blood. The potency of the sacrifice or of the blood depends on what is sacrificed. Some animals have a higher life force than others, but the life force of a human sacrifice is the most potent of all.

In modern Nigeria, certain politicians, military officers, and civil servants are said to have buried animals in order to increase their life force so that they can acquire political or public power. These animals are buried in strategic places and there are even rumours that human beings have been buried under buildings in order to enhance the spiritual power and life force there. Wealth, which is seen as a mark of power, may be acquired through the sacrifice of a whole human being or the use of certain potent parts of a human being. The drinking of blood or eating of human parts is also associated with witchcraft and sorcery as a means of acquiring spiritual and mystical powers.

This is not the place to go into detail about these ritual practices. What is important here is that these are significant and influential beliefs in African Traditional Religion.

Through Religious Rituals and Ceremonies

A ritual has been defined as,

> a formula for eliciting help from the spirit world and mastering nature to serve man's purposes. It is the means whereby the spirits may be manipulated. Underlying ritual is the conviction that such manipulation can secure control over events, circumstances, or people.[4]

---

4. Steyne, 93–94.

The rationale is:

> If I do this and this, the other source – be it spirit or god – must do that and that. In fact, the spirit is not merely obliged, but rather is coerced into responding according to the practitioner's desire. If the devotee or officiant of the ritual says the right chant or mantra, performs the right sacrifice, or goes through a liturgy in a particular order, then the god or spirit must do such and such ... The interrelationship between belief and ritual is so complete that the ritual act is also an act of worship – a recognition of a superior spiritual power available to man. The ritual act is sacred and efficacious. Regardless of who practices it, says it or uses it, it is in itself the key which unlocks the door to the desired goal.[5]

Besides their function of maintaining harmony and communication between humans and the spirit and mystical world, rituals and ceremonies are essential in order to transfer spiritual powers from the sources of power to the one seeking them. They are also a means by which African specialists acquire the knowledge, skills and powers which enable them to carry out their professional roles.

Rituals have more to do with emotions than with reason or clear thinking. Confidence in the ability to tap into a power source through ritual gives those performing the ritual a great sense of security. Their primary focus is on the end result and their sense of well-being, rather than on issues of morality and ethics. However, spiritual and mystical powers have a tendency to decrease or disappear if the one who holds them is not constantly in touch with their source. To maintain this contact and to enhance one's life force one must participate regularly in elaborate rituals and ceremonies to control and conciliate the spiritual and mystical powers.

These ritual contacts include the laying on of hands; contact with various parts of the body; anointing with sacred oils; painting, marking or tattooing the body; wearing sacred objects; drinking or eating blood, sacred drinks or foods; burying animals or sacred objects, incantations, recitations, and singing.

Traditional Africans may find that religions that do not address this area of their worldview are not relevant. For this reason, African independent churches and some new Christian groups have incorporated this worldview and its spirituality into their religious practices. The search for spiritual and mystical

---

5. Steyne, 93–94.

powers through religious celebrations, liturgies, and rituals is still prevalent in certain expressions of African Christianity.

Through Belonging to a Mystery or Secret Cult

Mystery means "that which is unknown or which was unknown prior to or apart from its disclosure in divine revelation."[6]

The awareness of the existence of mysteries and mystical powers in the traditional religions seems to dominate religious and social beliefs, practices, behaviours, and attitudes. The traditional religions produce and apply the presence of *mysterium tremendum* by creating the law of secrecy and secret cults or societies. This law of secrecy has an impact on African religion and magic; charms and medicine; witchcraft and sorcery; as well as rituals, rites, and ceremonies. It also impacts on the work of African specialists. Taboos and secret cults reinforce it.

Onaiyekan made the following observations:[7]

(1) At the level of doctrine, the

> *law of secrecy* is taken seriously by everyone . . . There are always some teachings and notions that are reserved to one segment or the other of the society. There are things which children should not be told, others are not to be divulged to women. Women on their part may have their own secrets, which they keep to themselves. Thus, knowledge of the deeper elements of the traditional religions often require as a condition an initiation into a secret group within which such knowledge is said to be reserved.

(2) At the practical level of worship

> the same phenomenon of secrecy [prevails.] Not everyone has access to every shrine and there are ceremonies which only initiates are allowed to take part in [and in almost all cases] children and women are strictly excluded.

(3) And finally,

> the secrecy-mystery attitude has been carried over into areas which though not strictly religious are religiously perceived, [such as] traditional medicine [which] is intricately mixed with religion

---

6. *Eerdmans Bible Dictionary*, s.v. "mystery."
7. Onaiyekan, "Divine Mysteries," 5.

and at times with magic [and traditional healers] who keep their knowledge and skill a secret.

In the traditional worldview, because the deeper things of life are best known and understood in secret, devotees are initiated into various secret cults or societies. "Secret knowledge" can be acquired through these cults so they are seen as a gateway to spiritual and mystical power. This accounts for the proliferation of these secret cults and societies.

Even when traditional Africans become Christians, there is a tendency to want to search for deeper and secret things. Christianity may sometimes be seen as just a first step or a gateway to "secret things" or mysteries.

This worldview has to be contrasted with that of Christianity. Onaiyekan pointed out that, "while mysteries are a common element of both Christianity and traditional religion, Christianity has no room for secret cults."[8] Jesus Christ is the final revelation of the *mysterium*. In him, the secret of life has been revealed.

---

8. Onaiyekan, 15.

17

The Exercise of Power

Once these mystical powers and life force have been obtained, they need to be used to ensure one's own safety and prosperity and to exercise control over the spirit world. A number of tools have been developed to make this possible and specialists have emerged who are experts in the use of these tools.

Tools for Exercising Power

According to Steyne, the most common means of exercising control are incantations, symbols, magic, charms, fetishes, witchcraft, and sorcery.

Incantations (Word Power)

Belief in the power of words is pervasive among Africans, whether they are traditionalists, Christians, or Muslims.

The power produced by uttering the right words may be impersonal or it may be associated with spirit-powers, as when formulas are used in exorcisms or to summon spirits. Steyne stressed that "there is a vital connection between life force, magic and words" and that words are powerful instruments that can be used for "protection against the contingencies of life brought about by the spirit world."[1]

Using words may involve "chants, repetitious singing, recitations or other special worship forms." These words will have the greatest effect if they are pronounced by a religious specialist. If the words are said correctly, the desired result will automatically follow. This is particularly the case with the magic formulas used when casting spells and curses, swearing oaths, and when attempting to control nature, people, and the spirit world.

---

1. Steyne, *Gods of Power*, 100.

However, words also have the power to kill and the unguarded use of words may be dangerous. A person can be harmed if the secret of his name is known so, to avoid this, euphemisms are sometimes substituted for powerful words. Sometimes protective or harmful words may be inscribed on objects or made into amulets and charms.

The traditional belief in the power of words has been reinforced by the theologies of some of the independent churches and the non-traditional Pentecostal and charismatic groups. The prosperity gospel has resonated with this belief. While the theological words are Christian, the beliefs are rooted in traditional African spirituality and power consciousness. Consequently, principles for life and living developed in this way may be contrary to Christian principles.

Symbols

Religious symbols can be seen in the use and sprinkling of blood, the use of colours, and of religious paraphernalia, clothing, objects, and shapes. Charms too are symbolic objects that possess mysterious power through their association with spirits or with someone of high status. Even gestures can constitute a symbolic language with specific meanings.

There is also power in symbols:

> Symbols serve to secure and protect places, people, and times from the attacks of evil spirits and to invite the benevolent spirits to exercise their good offices on behalf of the supplicants. Under the protection of the symbol, devotees feel secure, endued with power and confidence.[2]

Steyne pointed out that symbols "excite respect and fear" and "must be handled with great care and caution." They can be "used as charms to either ward off evil or invite good luck" or as "a sentry on guard in the interest of its owner, watching over the welfare of his goods."

Religious symbolism is very powerful in traditional religion, and even when Africans become Christians this religious worldview still persists. The independent churches exhibit a marked continuity between the pre-Christian religious and cultural heritage and Christianity. Theologically, however, it is important that symbolic language and meanings are properly defined in the context in which they are used. It is possible that some of the

---

2. Steyne, 106.

symbolism is rooted in traditional spirituality and power consciousness and not in Christianity.

Magic

Magic is similar to divination. However, it goes beyond it in that it does not merely seek to know what is going to happen in the future, but also attempts to use occult and supernatural powers to influence events.

Steyne identified the following different kinds of magic:

Divine magic: Divine magic occurs "when God himself enters the human context and permits a miracle."

Thaumaturgy (natural magic – conscious and unconscious): This involves the manipulation of impersonal forces to achieve desired results. Conscious natural magic involves rituals that generate psychic power to make the magic energy flow. Unconscious natural magic does not involve the use of psychic powers, and the mere performance of a ritual is sufficient to induce the flow of magic energy each time the ritual formula is repeated. This type of magic may be used to identify the perpetrators of crimes or offenses. The ritual may involve the use of holy books, the calling of special names, and prayers.

Black magic: "Black magic attempts to produce evil results through curses, spells and alliance with evil spirits."[3] Steyne stated that it is malevolent and antisocial and that it is usually motivated by self-interest. Those associated with this magic are "usually sorcerers, wizards or shamans" who use "magic words or objects to inflict suffering."

White magic (theurgy): "White magic tries to undo curses and spells and to use occult powers for the good of oneself or others." This practice involves invoking "good powers and/or spirits to accomplish good purposes."[4]

Homeopathic magic: This practice is based on the law of similarity, the idea that "like produces like."[5] It involves the use of effigies and objects that are similar to the object being targeted. If something evil is done to a simulacrum, there is a corresponding evil effect on the victim.

---

3. *New Concise Bible Dictionary*, s.v. "black magic," 328.
4. *New Concise Bible Dictionary*, s.v. "white magic," 328.
5. *New Concise Bible Dictionary*, s.v. "homeopathic magic," 328.

Magic by contagion: "Magic by contagion operates by the law of contact."[6] Steyne stated that: "Once things have been in contact (conjoined), they are forever thereafter conjoined" and "what is done to one must similarly affect the other."[7] Because of the nature of this magic power, people seek to ensure that they will not come into contact with it, personally or publicly. Public places, such as "houses, villages, towns, fields and other places and things" are usually protected against it.

Belief in and the use of magic has a profound influence on African expressions of Christianity but it is important to remember that similarity in forms of beliefs and practices may disguise differences in theological meaning.

Charms (Amulets and Talismans) and Fetishes

Belief in and the use of charms, amulets, and fetishes is pervasive among Africans.

A charm is "an object worn by some people to keep away evil or bring good luck" and is also "an object, act, or phrase believed to have supernatural powers."[8] Steyne described fetishes as objects that are believed to "exercise an occult influence according to the possessor's wishes."[9]

Some Africans see Missionary Christianity and Western rationalism as having stripped Christianity of all mystery, magic, and awe. For this reason, many Africans want to bring back these elements to invigorate Christianity.

Specialists in Exercising Power

Belief in witchcraft and sorcery is deeply embedded in African Traditional Religion. It may be best to start by clarifying the terms, distinguishing between witchcraft, sorcery, magic, and divination:

> Whereas the power of a sorcerer is embodied in the medicine he uses, the power of witchcraft, on the other hand, is a mystical and innate one even though witches also use medicine when the need arises. Divination is the ability to discover or explain mysterious causes of sickness, death or other misfortune, which cannot be unraveled by the ordinary observer. Magic is the art of

---

6. Steyne, *Gods of Power*, 113.
7. Steyne, 113.
8. *New Concise Bible Dictionary*, s.v. "charm," 98.
9. Steyne, *Gods of Power*, 116.

using spells to invoke supernatural powers to influence people or events. Sorcerers, witches and "witch doctors" can employ both means in their arts.[10]

Central to these concepts is the belief "that certain persons in a community will . . . bring harm to their fellows . . . by the use of nefarious supernatural means."[11] Witchcraft and sorcery therefore are still dreaded social practices which spread fear and panic in modern Africa. Use of them is rooted in selfish ambition, fear, and tyranny. Mysterious deaths (usually of young people), accidents, and incurable diseases are attributed to them.

Witchcraft can be used as a means of explaining the problem of evil. There are many reported cases of old people in modern Africa who are beaten to death after having been accused of being witches or sorcerers. Charges of witchcraft are common in African churches and among Christians. It has even been reported that urban residents will sneak away without bidding farewell to relations and kinsfolk after visiting their birthplaces or villages for fear of witchcraft and sorcery.

A weak biblical theology of the origin of evil and sin makes African Christians turn to the old beliefs of spirit-power.

Witches

According to Nyirongo, witches are said to inherit their powers from their parents or grandparents who were involved with witchcraft.[12] This inheritance may be either innate or passed on as a specific gift. Someone who wants to be a witch but has no family tradition to draw on may purchase these powers from a sorcerer who practices witchcraft as a commercial undertaking. Those who received their abilities directly from a god, however, are the most powerful.

In order to maintain their powers, rules and rituals must be observed. A witch must stay on good terms with other witches through blood sacrifices and through attending secret meetings at which they plan their activities. They attend these meetings as "personality souls," rather than in their bodies. Witches have a well-organized hierarchy and individual witches have specific responsibilities.

---

10. Nyirongo, *Gods of Africa*, 183.
11. Steyne, *Gods of Power*, 118.
12. Nyirongo, *Gods of Africa*, 188.

The tools of their trade include cultic objects such as calabashes or horns (which may contain curious substances), talismans, beads, rings, small pieces of cloth, a stick (which can act as a gun), masks, and statuettes. Each witch also has a totem, perhaps an animal (leopard, lion, hyena, elephant), a bird (owl, bat, vulture, parrot), a snake (python, puff-adder) or an insect (bee, firefly). By applying certain herbs to her cultic objects, a witch can transform herself into her totem animal, bird, or snake.

Witches can do more than merely harm their victims; they can even kill them. Such killing can be accomplished from a distance by casting spells or tampering with the victim's hair or nail clippings, or with articles worn by the victim. Witches are also skilled in the use of poisons.

Traditional Africans resort to witches for a variety of reasons: "to avoid failure or attain success, one is entitled to use a powerful charm. When one has become successful, one is also expected to shield oneself from one's relatives with a powerful charm. Indeed one is justified to kill those contemplating one's downfall."[13] Witches may also be consulted if there are poor relationships at home (e.g. between in-laws, co-wives, parents, and children) or in public life (e.g. between chiefs, *indunas*, and elders). People are also said to use witchcraft to invoke evil spirits or to cause deformity, sickness or insanity.

Given the range of motives for an interest in witchcraft, it is not surprising that almost anyone in a community can be suspected of making use of some kind of witchcraft or charm.[14]

Nyirongo pointed out that "witches believe that the ultimate source of all their powers is a great benevolent Being or God." Nevertheless he concludes his study of the African view of witchcraft with the following statement:

> There can be no "middle ground" regarding the Jew and the Christian's attitude to witchcraft. In whatever form, witchcraft is a violation of the first two commandments. Anything I depend on more than God – even if it promises success, riches, good health or protection – is an idol.[15]

---

13. Nyirongo, *Gods of Africa*, 188.
14. Nyirongo, 188.
15. Nyirongo, 188.

Sorcerers

Sorcerers differ from witches in that whereas "witchcraft is a mystical innate power used to bring about evil, sorcery is evil in which the practitioner deliberately resorts to maleficent substances or rituals to bring about deliberate harm." What motivates sorcery is basically "revenge in the face of injustices, inequalities, human interference, envy or downright malice."[16]

The Bible does not deny the spiritual reality behind the heathen practices of magic, sorcery, and witchcraft. It has an "extensive vocabulary for the various aspects of magic, their practitioners, and adherents"[17] and strongly prohibits their use.

Nyirongo presents several biblical examples to "illustrate the idolatrous nature of witchcraft" (e.g. Deut 18:10–13; Acts 8:9–24; 13:6–10). After a lengthy discussion of various issues he states:

> It is clear that no devout Jew resorted to magic or divination as pagans do. Any traces of witchcraft among the Israelites simply demonstrated a departure from true worship . . . In our discussion of the African's view of witchcraft we noted that it is not necessarily the witchcraft power itself which is evil, but the practitioner's motives. If a man uses witchcraft to protect himself or to get rich, his motives are good and he need not feel guilty. Similarly, if he uses witchcraft to revenge or eliminate his enemy he is doing a commendable thing. However, if he uses witchcraft to destroy innocent life, then his motives are bad. Is this what we expect from a Christian? Absolutely not. As far as God is concerned, witchcraft and whatever "good things" it promises all originate from sinful motives. This is because Satan – the power behind witchcraft – has no good sides to his character. He can project himself as an angel of light. He can pose as a miracle worker, as a giver of great wealth or as a concerned shepherd, but his aim is to destroy. He is the master imitator and deceiver . . . African witchdoctors, sorcerers, witches, diviners and magicians can also transform themselves into shepherds. They promise good health, riches and supernatural power only to deceive and enslave the community.[18]

---

16. Steyne, *Gods of Power*, 119.
17. *Eerdmans Bible Dictionary*, 679.
18. Nyirongo, *Gods of Africa*, 192–193.

Christians need not fear witchcraft. Not only are we promised full protection by God when we die (Matt 10:28), but we have more than enough weapons to fight and defeat witchcraft in this life. These weapons are: the knowledge of God's Word, the truth (Acts 8:9–24; 13:6–10); the power of the Holy Spirit (Acts 13:9); prayer (Col 4:2); and holy living (1 Cor 16:13; Eph 6:13).[19]

---

19. Nyirongo, 193–194.

18

Being Human

In the preceding chapters, the focus has fallen on the relationship between human beings and the cosmic spiritual and mystical forces. Now it is time to focus on the traditional African understanding of human nature as expressed in the question, "What does it mean to be human?"

This question is important because definitions of human nature inform many beliefs about how people should live and how they should relate to the world around them. Many scholars argue that the traditional religion of Africa is anthropocentric, that is it starts with a focus on what is important for humans and what is required by human nature, rather than with a focus on the divine.

Individual Human Nature

There have been numerous attempts to define the African understanding of human nature. All of them are in agreement that humans were created by God and that a distinction needs to be drawn between the physical body that decays in the grave and the human spirit that survives death.

In his works Emefie Ikenga-Metuh identified four life principles that link human nature to other aspects of reality (ontological orders).

Breath: A vivifying principle, a life force which links man with other life-forces in the universe and is in vital relationship with them.

The destiny soul: An emanation or spark of the Creator inside man.

The ancestral guardian spirit: Incarnate in man, linking him with the life-force of the clan, family and other human groups.

The human person: The unique individual person created by God.[1]

African societies differ in the way they see how these human principles operate in society alongside its life forces. It is easy to see how these principles relate to what has already been discussed: breath is equivalent to the impersonal forces in the universe; the destiny soul links to the discussion of destiny as a gift from the Supreme Being; the ancestral spirit links to the discussion of spirit beings; while the human being is the person who is in relationship to these spiritual forces.

Nyirongo's list of aspects of human nature is less philosophical. Rather than focusing on humanity's place in the universe, he focused on the elements that constitute an individual human being:[2]

Vital breath: Acts like a spirit. "Believed to have power to live on in the cosmos. Once it leaves the body it can animate into a new being, such as an animal, bird or snake." This is equivalent to reincarnation.

Shadow (or double): Acts like an enabling force residing in man. "Both the visible shadow cast by a man's body" and his physical energy or bodily strength. The shadow provides the "enabling force" and "at death the shadow and soul are transformed into a spirit."

Ghost: It is a "visible manifestation after death but exists only for a short time." A ghost emerges from a deceased person who did not receive proper burial, who lived a bad life, or who died a violent death. When seen by the living, a ghost is a bad omen and purification rites are required to ward off evil.

Destiny spirit: This "does not inhabit the person but influences his personality." Inherited at birth, it determines whether individuals will be poor or rich, good or bad, and whether they will bear many children or suffer infertility.

Name: "The name is a seal on a man's individuality or personality." A name has the capacity to influence the individual who bears it or his relatives. "It can promise or represent good or evil."

---

1. Ikenga-Metuh, *Towards an African Theology*.
2. Nyirongo, *Gods of Africa*, 100.

Human Nature in Community

In traditional African thought it is almost impossible to think of a human being in isolation. Humans are always conceived of in relationship: with those who are alive, with those who inhabit the spirit world, and with the mysterious powers of nature. As Steyne put it, an individual "relates not only to people, but to almost everything else."[3]

Ikenga-Metuh writes powerfully of the balance between the understanding that a human being is an individual in relation to the cosmos but that humans exist within communities.

> The African doctrine of man strikes a balance between the social and individual dimensions of man. Man is essentially seen as a member of a community of beings as well as a uniquely individual person. He is a force in a universe of living forces, a member of the community of men and at the same time a unique individual endowed with a unique destiny which only he himself can realize . . . Man is linked to the universe of forces by an ontological principle from inside man himself. Through his life-force . . . he can influence and be influenced by other forces outside himself. This life-force can be strengthened, weakened and may die. Man is integrated into his family, clan and other social groups through another potent principle – ancestral life-force . . . Through this, the life-force of the family flows in him. Man's individuality is assured by his personal destiny. This destiny received from the Creator . . . is uniquely his and each person has to work out its content by himself. He may count on the help of his ancestors, the deities, but he has also to contend with the snares of the countervailing forces like witches, sorcerers and evil spirits. How he steers his course successfully or unsuccessfully through this spiritual economy will determine his status in the after-life and the possibility of reincarnating in his descendants. In other words, through his destiny package, man makes his own personal contribution to the life-force of his family, clan and tribe and indeed to the whole universe. The supreme and ultimate goal of human life is the increase of his own life-force and the life-forces

---

3. Steyne, *Gods of Power*, 61.

of the family and other groups to which he belongs. The greatest evil is the weakening or extinction of his life-force.[4]

Nyirongo made a similar point:

> According to the African, man's individuality is fulfilled through his participation in the tribe. In other words, the individual is not a person until the community has accepted him. In traditional life, the individual does not and cannot exist alone except corporately . . . It is what the community does to the individual that matters most, not the individual's view of himself . . . It is the community that gives him identity [that] is gained step by step, through various rites.[5]

Steyne suggested the following implications of this deep-rooted sense of community:

> Man believes he is incomplete and inadequate without his fellows.
>
> Man needs the support of the community and only feels normal when he is in relationship with it.
>
> Man fears a broken relationship between persons of the same group. A broken relationship can be termed sin.
>
> Without ancestors and their influence in life, man loses both his focus and reason for being and life without ancestral focus is empty and meaningless.
>
> The belief in reincarnation provides communities with a link to the past through its ancestors and a link with the future through the unborn.
>
> The community sets parameters of the normative in life, because community is designed for harmony and for this reason, everything must be done to maintain this harmony.
>
> Idiosyncrasies, withdrawal or undue publicity are feared and man as a member of society conforms emotionally and intellectually to societal customs or pressures, which he accepts with little or no objection.

---

4. Ikenga-Metuh, *Towards an African Theology*, 6–7.
5. Nyirongo, *Gods of Africa*, 101–102.

Diversity or non-conformity is costly to the community and may signal the activity of evil spirits and there is overt and covert pressure to conform to community norms.[6]

Membership in a Community

A community consists of the living dead, the presently living, and the unborn. Although the spirit world plays a role in determining which community one is born into, merely being born into a community is not enough to establish full membership. Certain rites of passage are required. One who has not gone through these rites "remains a child, an outsider, a 'half' person or nobody."[7]

Community and Social Status

The traditional worldview is hierarchical. Just as divinities and spirit beings are part of a hierarchy, certain ethnic, racial, or tribal groups claim to rank higher than others on the basis of the destiny assigned to them at creation.

Within a particular community, the typical human hierarchy places the ancestors ("the living dead") at the top, followed by the aged, the elders, the headmen, and the leaders. These are followed by adult men, women, children, and the unborn.

Within this hierarchy, social status is further defined by age, birth order, social role, ritual status, and material possessions. "An African's worth and identity in the tribe depends on where his tribe places him. Consequently, his behavior and conduct are governed by what the tribe believes is right for him. The community makes the individual."[8]

One is expected to maintain close relationships with one's age mates. Respect for seniors is also deeply ingrained as old age bespeaks wisdom and respectability and elicits reverence. In many traditional African communities, political authority or power resided in the hands of the elders, and particularly in the council of elders. They acted as representatives of the corporate personality of the clan, lineage group, or tribe. In council, decisions on matters of public concern were usually taken in the name of the clan, lineage, or community. Only those who had attained mature status, that is a ripe old age, could represent people and act as titular heads. Thus power and authority rested in

---

6. Steyne, *Gods of Power*, 61–62.
7. Nyirongo, *Gods of Africa*, 101.
8. Nyirongo, 106.

the hands of the oldest men, who were normally the heads of families, clans, lineages, or communities. No absolute power rested in the hands of one man.[9]

Some communities had centralized authority, administrative machinery, and judicial institutions. These societies were differentiated internally on the grounds of wealth, privilege, and status corresponding to the distribution of power and authority. However, the type of decentralized system which lacked sharp divisions of rank, status or wealth was far more widespread.[10]

African leadership is rooted in these traditional forms. The transformations that have taken place in African societies have affected this form of kinship leadership and have resulted in complex political problems in modern African states.

Social Status and Ethics

One's position in the hierarchy has important implications in terms of what counts as moral and ethical behaviour. Those who hold a higher destiny or social status at creation or in society are not morally and ethically responsible to their juniors or subordinates.[11] This belief is reflected in the Hausa saying that "A superior does no wrong, he can only err." The reverse is true of juniors or subordinates.

Basing human relationships, morality, and ethics on the creation principle of destiny has had devastating consequences for African societies, as we have already discussed. It has led to the negative doctrines of inequality, superiority, and inferiority that have manifested themselves in ethnicity, racism, and tribalism. There is also no doubt that greedy and arrogant people can exploit the traditional worldview, twisting it to their advantage and, once corruption has become established, it is accepted as legitimate.

Change in the Community

The traditional concepts of destiny and hierarchy assign every human being a particular place in life. Everyone has to accept and live by whatever destiny or status the gods have bestowed upon them. Moreover, because they are products of a family, clan, tribe, and of what the spirits made them, they are under a moral obligation to be loyal, faithful, and committed to that community.

---

9. Okonjo, *British Administration*.
10. Turaki, *British Colonial Legacy*.
11. Ikenga-Metuh, *Comparative Studies*.

This includes abiding by the "do's and don'ts" of the community. There is thus a strong desire to maintain the traditions, conventions, and cultures as the ancestors handed them down. Social change is usually frowned on and is inhibited by religious, cultural and social norms.

This belief in maintaining the status quo conflicts with the human desire to pursue wealth and status. Even though some may seek personal advancement regardless of what it may do to the welfare of others, there is a fear that the desire "to be successful over and above one's fellow man opens the door to all kinds of exploitative, unjust, unethical and dehumanizing practices." Van der Walt points out that individual initiative is not appreciated or encouraged.[12] Good human relations are considered far more important. The character traits that are valued are modesty, compliance, pliability, and a willingness to compromise – all traits that lead to peaceful co-existence with one's fellows.

Yet even though the status quo is maintained at the societal level, there is usually scope for individual advancement in life. One's social status can be changed, and Africans do work to achieve this. African society is not a caste system. Those who work hard and bring fame to their communities are usually honoured. Personal achievements obtained within religious and cultural rules and norms are usually honoured and recognized.

It is also important to be aware of the tremendous security and the strong personal relationships that result from the traditional emphasis that one exists within both the human and the cosmic community.

---

12. Van der Walt, *Afrocentric or Eurocentric?*

19

The Meaning of Life

It is time to attempt to examine the answer that the traditional worldview gives to one of life's ultimate questions: What is the meaning of it all?

The Meaning of Life in the Cosmos

We have looked at length at the human quest for meaning through religion and have examined religious beliefs, practices, rituals, and ceremonies to ascertain what is being sought. We have considered how human beings relate to mysterious cosmic and spiritual forces. We have seen that the main aim of turning to the spirit world is to obtain power that can be used in the human community. There is no desire to escape from the community to the world of the spirit; rather the desire is to live a happy and fulfilled life in the community. There is no salvation in the spirit world, nor is there anyone there who is known intimately. Were it not for the need for power, humans would have nothing to do with spirits.

A human being cannot abandon fellowship and communion with the ancestors and go out to live among the gods or divinities. Because spirits need food to eat, beer to drink, and sacrifices and offerings, the gods and divinities come to dwell among humans and there is no need to seek for them out in the cosmos.

The Meaning of Life in the Community

In traditional Africa the meaning of life is understood in terms of the law of kinship. Life is oriented toward the community and not to the world outside. The community makes life and gives purpose and meaning to life. It is both the lawgiver and the judge. Outside of the community, there is no life, no hope, no peace, no identity, no destiny, and no existence, in short, no salvation.

The meaning of life in community revolves around the issues of birth and adulthood, marriage and family, health and wealth, sickness and death, and the ancestors. Birth, life, and death are not regarded merely as biological processes; they are thought to be initiated and controlled by the spirit beings that are intimately and actively involved in the affairs of the community. Life in the community is unthinkable without the presence of spirit beings, especially the ancestors. Their active presence and involvement in community life gives it meaning and destiny.

Life passages, such as birth, puberty, and death, are all gateways to community life. Accordingly, rites and rituals are required at every stage to ensure that the individual is properly integrated into the community. They bring the person into association with the human members of the community and with the physical and spiritual worlds. Rites of initiation bind the initiates to the family, clan, tribal gods and divinities that are the guardians of the community. These rites are actually covenants, bringing the initiate into covenant relationships with the living members of the community, the ancestors, and the gods and divinities. The communities to which these individuals belong live under covenants and bonds that have been entered into with certain deities or divinities. These deities or divinities therefore claim certain rights over the individuals and the communities. The breaking of these covenants or bonds is usually accompanied by curses, punishments or other calamities.

Many pioneering missionaries in Africa attested to the fact that there is spiritual warfare between Christianity and the spiritual and power phenomena of traditional religion. Turning to Christianity incurs wraths, curses and calamities. The old religious covenants are broken when the convert enters into new covenants with the Lord God Yahweh.

However, the first five books of the Old Testament developed a theological approach to living in a community while surrounded by the Canaanite religion and culture. Believers were instructed to serve only the Lord God Yahweh. They were told to sever links and relationships with things that were prohibited and that were declared to be abominations.

Now there is a need for a Christian theology of rites of passage to be developed that cements the relationship between an individual and the community, even though the person has abandoned the traditional religion. African Christians have to deal with their ancestral past and settle such matters concretely. Moreover a Christian theology of covenants has to be developed in order to address their role and function in traditional society. The nature of this relationship with the kinship community also requires us to think carefully about how we should address theological questions relating to sin, life passages, marriage and family, health and wealth, sickness, suffering and death, the ancestors, covenants, and the like.

Part III

Engagement and Interaction between Christianity and the African Traditional Religion and Worldview

20

Introduction

In an attempt to provide a comprehensive understanding of the religious worldview of African Traditional Religion, we sought to understand how the modern African mind has been shaped by African Traditional Religion and its worldview, as well as by Missionary Christianity, colonialism and modernity. We went on to examine each fundamental belief.

We now move on to the third section of this work where we consider how biblical and Christian theology can renew and transform the African mind. Our aim here is to develop a method of interaction and engagement between Christianity and African Traditional Religion. Biblical and Christian theology will be applied to the cardinal beliefs so that traditional religious beliefs and practices will be matched with biblical beliefs and practices and the biblical worldview. Clearly, however, we shall not be able to consider every theological issue which was mentioned in the first part of this book.

How are we to proceed? Any teachings and any presentation of the gospel of Christ to people in traditional Africa must bear in mind the great influence of these religious and social beliefs and practices. Christianity cannot provide less than traditional religion offered to Africa.

I suggest, therefore, that we ask the following questions:

- What do traditional Africans feel about particular religious beliefs, for example, the belief in spirit beings (the spiritual phenomenon) or the belief in mystical, mysterious, unseen and hidden powers and forces (power phenomenon)?
- What attitudes, behaviours, and practices accompany, support, and reinforce this belief?
- What religious and social feelings, attitudes, behaviour, understandings are affected when such a fundamental belief encounters Christianity, or Islam, or modernity?

- What is the impact of such a belief as it shapes and moulds the traditional African mind, or the Christian mind in Africa, or modernity in Africa?
- What religious and social practices, rituals, rites, and ceremonies of traditional Africa are rooted in beliefs that shape and mould the African response to Christianity and modernity?

Before moving on, however, we must remind ourselves of the theological position of each religion. African Traditional Religion is within general revelation and its theological discourse is that of creation theology. Like all other religions in the world, African Traditional Religion was created by humankind after the fall. All its theological discourse is therefore that of human revelation and is without God's specific self-disclosure. When we grasp this, we will realize that there is nothing wrong or primitive about the African views about the nature, character, and attributes of God.

Christianity and the Bible, on the other hand come within special revelation and their theological discourse is that of redemption theology. The theology of salvation and redemption is God's special revelation to humanity through Jesus Christ and it defines the means of salvation and redemption.

However, if we get our methods wrong, we will be liable to misunderstand, misinterpret, and misapply theological data. This is what happened in the past when those using the comparative and descriptive approaches spent their time looking for similarities or differences between Christianity and African Traditional Religion and when phenomenologists looked for religious meanings. Any theological discourse apart from God's special revelation in the Bible and in Jesus Christ would merely be an analysis of human theology.

Our approach must therefore be somewhat different. We shall tackle each traditional belief in turn. In each chapter we shall consider how that traditional belief and practice can be approached in the light of the special revelation in the Holy Scriptures and in Jesus Christ. This will allow us to present salvation and redemption to African Traditional Religion even though it is rooted in general revelation. God is seeking renewal and transformation for Africa in the light of his special revelation.

21

Engaging with the Traditional Belief in Impersonal (Mystical) Powers

This dynamic worldview is governed by the law of power and tries to define the meaning of life in terms of impersonal (mystical) powers. The pursuit of power and life force dominates the traditional mind which believes that whatever is needed by the individual or the community can be obtained through the use of power. This means that the people of traditional Africa will turn to mystical, unseen powers and forces for help, guidance, and protection against diseases, evil spells, calamities, sorcery and witchcraft. In most cases these dealings involve spirit powers and sometimes even demonic influence.

This traditional worldview has therefore led to the development of a system of beliefs and practices. It includes ceremonies, as well as various mystical means of exercising control over the supernatural world and of communicating with the supernatural world. Specialists are trained to formulate and conduct the necessary rituals and ceremonies so that these mystical powers and forces can be acquired, used, controlled, and conciliated.

When we see how the belief in impersonal (mystical) powers affects human beings, we see that there is gross misunderstanding of both the source and the use of supernatural powers. It is useless, then, to argue about whether these powers are real or not; whether they work in life situations or not. The fact is that mystical powers and forces are real to traditional Africans. They believe strongly in the potency of these mystical and mysterious powers and forces. This was one of the mistakes made during the era of Missionary Christianity, when some Western Christian theologians and scholars denied the existence of demons and interpreted such power phenomena as superstitions while others went to the extreme of labelling everything as demonic.

The traditional African dependence on mystical powers and forces stands in sharp contrast with the ultimate, universal power of Christ. Everything traditional Africa has been looking for has been provided in Jesus Christ, our only mediator. Through him, humankind's fear of spirit beings, especially the fear of their exercising of their limited powers, can be eradicated. Humankind's deep-seated needs for guidance and direction are answered by God's sovereignty, providence, and wisdom. God's sovereignty addresses questions about power and control in the universe. God's providence addresses questions about man's sustenance and provision, while God's wisdom addresses questions about man's understanding, interpretation, guidance and meaning of life in general.

When biblical and Christian theological categories are introduced into traditional Africa, however, the traditional African mind understands and interprets any presentation of the blood of Jesus Christ, of the person and work of God the Father, Jesus Christ the Son or the Holy Spirit, as well as many other related topics, in terms of this traditional power-consciousness and spirituality. This means that some African Christians may not grasp the nature and scope of Christ's power. Even though they believe in Jesus Christ, the Holy Spirit and God, they may sometimes still solicit or consult mystical or supernatural powers. They do not realize that because God is all sufficient, no one needs to go to the spirit beings or to other powers for help.

The task of biblical teaching and Christian theology is to make Africans understand and apply biblical and Christian truths so that they can see their belief and application of power-consciousness and spirituality in the light of this new truth. They need to realize that the power phenomenon and spirituality of power in traditional religion are not the same as that of Christianity; both come from different revelations. However, since they already have a rudimentary, comparable concept of power in their traditional religion, they will be able to build on this foundation and will be able to understand the deeper truths of power as manifested in the Bible and Christianity. This understanding, interpretation, and application will then be reflected in their expressions of Christianity.

Although this aspect has been ignored by some theologians and scholars, it is essential to identify the power which lies behind the power-phenomenon. We know that impersonal or supernatural powers are imbedded in nature or the cosmos (universe). The universe is pregnant with them. For example, we see the power of the sun, the seas or oceans, the mountains, the winds, the rain, and the thunder. Human beings respond to such powers with awe, anxiety, fear, worship, and reverence. It is a small step from there to thinking that the powers generate a call for worship and reverence, and so some of these natural and heavenly bodies or powers become deified or regarded as gods, divinities, or deities. Thus the emergence of divinities, deities, and gods in traditional religion is rooted in the source of these powers. If they had known more, people would not have turned them into divinities, deities and gods.

The power of God is misunderstood because there is a lack of understanding of his creative powers and creation. The creation story in the Bible holds the theological key which can answer these questions about the source of the power phenomenon. This power phenomenon is rooted in God who is the ultimate source of all the powers in the universe. We therefore need to develop and formulate a theology of God's creative powers that can address man's innate quest for power.

God and His Supernatural Powers

The Sovereign Lord cannot be proven or disproven by science or philosophy or by any human means. However, the Bible points out that "without faith it is impossible to please God, because anyone who comes to him must believe that he exists and that he rewards those who earnestly seek him (Heb 11:6). One must therefore simply believe that he exists. Faith is the starting point to knowing God.

> The greatest and the most profound idea the human mind can ever conceivably entertain concerns the possibility of the existence of a personal God. The sheer importance of man's response to this idea cannot be exaggerated, for it will not only govern his life down here but also determine his ultimate destiny. Unless one satisfactorily answers the who question, he cannot possibly solve the how, why, when and where problems of his own existence.[1]

As a result, we shall not seek philosophical proofs for the existence of a personal God. Many philosophers have done so in history, though not very effectively. The Bible itself does not present any arguments for the existence of God. It simply makes categorical statements about his existence: "The fool says in his heart, 'There is no God'" (Ps 14:1); "In the beginning, God created the heavens and the earth" (Gen 1:1). God is simply believed by faith (Heb 11:6). Willmington refers to Clark Pinnock who summarizes the Scriptures as follows:

> For the Scripture then, the existence of God is both a historical truth (God acted into history), and an existential truth (God

---
1. Willmington, *Willmington's Guide to the Bible*, 591.

reveals himself to every soul). His existence is both objectively and subjectively evident. It is necessary logically because our assumption order, design, and rationality rest upon it. It is necessary morally because there is no explanation for the shape of morality apart from it. It is necessary personally because the exhaustion of all material possibilities still cannot give satisfaction to the heart. The deepest proof for God's existence apart from history is just life itself. God has created man in his own image and man cannot elude the implications of this fact. Everywhere their identity pursues them.[2]

Our God is a person, not a power, or a force, or an influence, but a unique, distinct and transcendent person who is not a part of the created order or universe. Willmington, quoting Robert Lightner, points out that,

> personality involves existence with the power of self-consciousness and self-determination. To be self-conscious means to be able to be aware of one's self among others. [For one to be is to objectify oneself] . . . Self-determination has to do with the ability to look to the future and prepare an intelligent course of action. It also involves the power of choice . . . there are three elements of personality – intellect, emotion and will.[3]

The Bible further reveals that this one God, the Triune God, exists in three persons: God the Father, God the Son and God the Holy Spirit. God the Creator of the heavens and the earth is one: "Hear O Israel: The Lord our God, the Lord is one" (Deut 6:4). Willmington, quoting Charles C. Ryrie's definition of the Trinity, says the following: "There is only one God, but in the unity of the Godhead there are three eternal and co-equal Persons, the same in substance, but distinct in subsistence."[4] The Trinity is a mystery, but it can be summarized in three statements: "God is three persons. Each person is fully God. There is one God."[5] The Triune God has ultimate authority and power over the entire universe over everything (Ps 62:11).

The Bible makes specific reference to the power of each person in the Trinity. The power of God the Father is manifested in creation (Gen 1, 2; Ps 148:5; Jer 51:15); in sustaining the world and keeping watch over the nations (Ps

---

2. Willmington, 592.
3. Lightner quoted in Willmington, 594.
4. Ryrie quoted in Willmington, 595.
5. Grudem, *Systematic Theology*, 226.

65:5–11); in human affairs (Exod 15:6); in the virgin birth of Christ; in miracles, signs, and wonders; and in the resurrection of Christ.[6] The power of Christ is revealed in both the prophetic and apostolic teachings. God gave all authority to Christ (Matt 28:18). Christ's power manifests itself in creation (John 1:3, 10); in sustaining and upholding all things (Heb 1:3); in miracles (Luke 4:36); in regeneration (John 5:21–26); in salvation (Heb 7:25); in resurrecting believers (John 5:28–29); in his power to forgive sins (Matt 9:6, 8) and in his second coming (Matt 24:30). The power of the Holy Spirit is manifested in creation (Gen 1:2); in Christ's virgin birth, ministry, miracles, and resurrection; and in the believer's regeneration and effective ministry.[7]

Jesus Christ is the final revelation of God. Christianity is rooted in an understanding of God's revelation in Jesus Christ through the incarnation (John 1:1–14). This cannot be nullified by any revelation outside of God. The God who is the creator of the heavens and the earth is the same God who is the God of Abraham, the God of Isaac and the God of Jacob. He is also the same God who is the Father of our Lord Jesus Christ. Jesus is the Son of God and is co-eternal with God the Father (John 1:1–14; Col 1:15–20; Heb 1:1–3; Rev 1:8, 17–18).

We must therefore begin our study by considering the creative powers of God, which speak to the traditional belief in the power phenomenon.

The Creative Power of God

The first sentence of the Bible states: "In the beginning, God created the heavens and the earth" (Gen 1:1). This establishes God as the Creator, the maker of heaven and earth. The Bible confirms this over and over again (Pss 89:11–14; 90:1–2; 146:5–6; Isa 40:28; 43:1–13; 44:24–26; 45:11–12; John 1:1–5; Col 1:15–20; Heb 1:1–3).

Wayne Grudem defined the doctrine of creation as follows: "God created the entire universe out of nothing; it was originally very good; and he created it to glorify himself."[8] We need to remind ourselves that God alone existed from eternity. Nothing ever existed before him; nothing is presupposed. There was no material, no process of nature, not even chaos except by the word of his power (Heb 1:3). Absolutely everything that was created came into existence through the word of his power. God alone is the cause of the existence of all

---

6. Vine, *Expository Dictionary*; *Open Bible*; *New Concise Bible Dictionary*.
7. *Open Bible*, 281.
8. Grudem, *Systematic Theology*, 262.

creation and all creatures. God's act of creation brought the non-existent to the existent, from nothing into something (*creatio ex nihilo*).

Gilkey made a very powerful statement about this:

> As the source of all existence, He does not receive His being from elsewhere: no other factors have united in a happy harmony to produce and maintain Him. Since He is the source of existence, and not its recipient, He is not at all dependent upon other things to bring Him into being; and correspondingly He is not at all dependent upon outside things to maintain Him in being. If, then, He is in this sense "uncreated" by anything beyond Himself because He is the Creator of all else, His existence must be derived from Himself alone. Solely dependent upon Himself, God is unconditioned by, because He is independent of, any other being. He is self-sufficient in His being.[9]

God and his Christ have their own timetable and know the duration of all that they have created (Rev 21, 22). For this reason, everything created, including heaven and earth, has a beginning, a time and an end. Nothing is eternal. Nothing was created by any other god. Nothing in the universe simply evolved. There is nothing that exists which is not created by God.

Yet there are those who look at creation – the earth, the heaven, the stars, the moon, the mountains, the seas – and see divine attributes in them. They do not realize that the natural physical world has no innate power or glory but merely reveals God's creative powers and his glory. The physical nature of the universe blurs their spiritual vision, and they cannot differentiate between God and his creation. Others discover god(s) within the natural physical order through their own human wisdom, religion, and spirituality. They too cannot differentiate the creator God from that which he created. We cannot truly come to know the God who is the creator of the heavens and the earth through the study of his created order. We can only know God truly by his own self-disclosure. Unless God reveals himself to us, we have no valid way of knowing him. That is why those who have sought to know God through human self-intuition or insight, and not through his revelation, his revealed word or person, have met only a god of their self-consciousness. Their spirituality is not of the Holy Spirit but of human consciousness or natural spirituality (the worship of nature).

---

9. Gilkey, *Maker of Heaven*, 87.

Knowing that God is the only creator of the heavens and earth defines God's relationship to his creation and vice versa. The primary objective of the Bible account of the beginning is to stress the fact of creation and that, as a consequence, worshipping the creature rather than God the creator is idolatry (Rom 1:24–25). God as the moral creator demands that his creatures worship no other gods or creatures but him alone. God's created order is not independent of him, but depends on him for its existence and sustenance. No creature that has been created can claim independence from him. We should not offer our worship, praises, blessings, and thanksgiving to creation or to creatures whose function is only to display and reveal God's power and glory in creation.

Those who believe that the universe evolved through natural processes without any supernatural act of creation are making the mistake of looking into the natural physical world and searching for God imbedded within the power of the created order. When God cannot be found through their philosophic means or scientific experimentation, they declare in ignorance that God does not exist. Their fault lies in their physical tools and creaturely reasoning.

Misunderstanding creation

The ancient Greeks assumed two eternal principles: first, that the eternal pre-existing matter had no form or shape, but was formless and, second, that the eternal principle of organization gives form, structure or shape to things. When these two eternal principles of matter and form (ideas) unite, things are brought into being. Creation therefore required three eternal principles: (1) God; (2) matter; (3) form. Since only God is a rational (thinking) being, he acted as a craftsman putting the other two together. God took eternal matter and united it with an eternal form or shape and, as a result, something was created. God was simply an organiser, not the creator of matter or form. This view limits God as it suggests that God is not the Sovereign Lord of the universe.

In later Greek thought, the form or idea was thought to be divine and good, while matter or material was thought to be evil.

> The source of goodness and fulfilment lay in the formal order of life, and source of evil in the material, chaotic elements of reality. The world of space and time, of material changing things, of bodily desires and passions, and personal love, of death and decay, seemed therefore to the later Greek mind to be a world of evil. This evil is, moreover, necessary and unconquerable.[10]

---

10. Willmington, *Willmington's Guide to the Bible*, 48.

This was how the Greeks explained the existence of evil in material creation. Their faulty concept of God and creation led them to believe that evil is imbedded and cannot be eradicated. Christianity rejects this view of creation, believing that God created the universe and that it was good.

Eastern religions, pantheism or monism, believe that all is God and God is all. This means that God is not apart from creation, but one with it. "Creatures are made, not out of matter, but are out of God, for creaturely existence is a manifestation of the divine."[11] In this view the material world becomes a prison or hindrance to people who are intent on becoming divine. The material world is viewed as evil and should be shunned. In pantheism, creaturely (finite) existence was viewed as illusory (not real) and evil. "What is not God, then, is neither real nor good."[12] This often leads to the desire to escape from space-time existence.[13] Just like the Greeks, the Eastern religions see evil as an eternal principle imbedded in creation. They believe evil cannot be eradicated. Christianity rejects this view of God and creation also.

African religious beliefs lie somewhere between the Greeks and Eastern Religions and may reflect some of their features. We have many versions of the creation story across the continent of Africa providing various answers to the question, "How did God create?" In many of them, the Supreme Being (God) is said to have created the world and the lesser gods or spirit beings. Thereafter, both God and the lesser gods were all involved in acts of creation. God is assumed to be the Supreme Creator, but he works along with lesser creators or gods. According to some of these creation stories, God or the lesser beings are said to have used pre-existing matter to create humans, animals, birds, mountains, rivers, oceans, heaven, and earth. In many traditions, clay symbolizes the pre-existing matter which God was presumed to have used to do his work of creation. The lesser gods are said to have used the pre-existing matter to create both good and bad objects. This is why the lesser gods are reputed to have brought evil and unlovely creatures into the world. It was believed that in defiance of God, lesser gods took the pre-existing substance and made something else out of it, acting in the same way as a carpenter does when working with wood.

Other stories describe creation as the result of a divine command (by fiat). In some versions, the gods bring forth creatures through mating and birth, although this concept was more pronounced in ancient Greek mythologies. A

---

11. Gilkey, *Maker of Heaven*, 59.
12. Gilkey, 51.
13. Gilkey.

further view of creation, coming mainly from Eastern religions like Hinduism and Buddhism, was that of emanation or overflow whereby the world and created things emanate or flow from their source in God.[14]

Most traditions of creation or cosmogonies in Africa relate to the tribal ancestors, to the birth of a tribal-nation. Such stories always relate mysterious or miraculous exploits by their founding fathers. The pride and status of the tribes flows from these stories, which contrast with those of their rival tribal-nations. In doing this, African communities like to trace their origins in comparison to those of another rival tribal-nation or ethnic nationality. The concept of the God of the tribe or the lesser tribal gods is rooted in these tribal cosmogonies.

However, to the African the origin of creation is usually shrouded in mystery. One does not have to find answers. In African philosophy and religion, mystery is often assumed to be the starting point of knowing. For this reason, one does not dissect a mystery; it is a given reality. Although Africans accept the fact of God as Creator, they believe that there are mysteries in life that one dare not expose.

How does African Traditional Religion then explain evil? Was it created or is it regarded as an eternal principle? The answer is not clear. Africans tend to regard this as another mystery that is best left unquestioned because these lesser beings have powers to invoke evil upon humans and creation. They are feared as treacherous beings who work contrary to God and humanity.

The presence of evil and its personification in some of the lesser gods leads to fatalism, although fatalism is not well defined as it is in Islam. To the African, fatalism is also a personification of evil, one which is rooted to one's destiny. It leaves one hopeless as nothing can be done to change one's destiny.

African perceptions or concepts of God as creator of humanity and creation may be rudimentary, not very clear nor clearly articulated. Nonetheless they serve as a starting point to introducing God's special revelation in the Holy Scriptures and Jesus Christ.

Creation: The Christian answer
The Christian doctrine of creation refutes all other views of God and creation. The first essential difference between them and Christianity is that, as Langdon Gilkey said:

> Christianity teaches that God is the only Sovereign Lord and source of all existence. God was never just the organizer of

---

14. Gilkey.

creation nor did all things emanate or flow out of him. God is in himself a determined and definite moral being quite distinct and separate from all his creation. He does not share his nature and character with anything that he has created. He is holy, distinct, and transcendent. God is the cause of our existence but we are not his extension.[15]

Second, Christians believe that nothing that our holy and glorious God creates or brings into existence can be evil. This world is not therefore dominated by fatalism or evil, or meaninglessness or vanity. It is ruled by a loving Sovereign Lord whose solution to the problem of evil is very different to that of traditional religion. When lesser gods in African religion became the embodiment of evil and spread it in the world, the Supreme God seems not to be powerful enough to contain the evil or to rein in its perpetrators. Instead humans are left to fend for themselves, soliciting protection and preservation among the lesser gods.

In contrast, God's divine way of dealing with the problem of Satan, evil and sin is through redemption, African Traditional Religion addresses it through ritual and blood sacrifices and offerings. However the work of Christ on the cross, especially his resurrection and cosmic rule over the universe, provides us with new hope and transformation through redemption. The Christian conception of God is that of Creator and Redeemer.

God as Law-Giver

As the creator and owner of the universe, God did not need the counsel, help or services of any lesser beings. He, therefore, has supreme authority and power over the cosmos that was created through his good pleasure and purpose, and through the counsel of his will.

God maintains and sustains the universe by means of universal laws. The God who created the heavens and the earth is a God of order, purpose, and meaning. The universe is not governed by the law of chance or the law of evolution. It exists in harmony with itself and with the will of its creator. It was created out of the goodwill and pleasure of its creator. The psalmist echoes this when he states: "The heavens declare the glory of God, and the skies proclaim the work of his hands" (Ps 19:1).

---

15. Gilkey, 329.

God's eternal existence and being are governed by his moral nature and character. Everything that is done is centred in his good pleasure and the counsel of his will. His nature, together with his eternal purposes, upholds his determined and definite moral order.

The Westminster Confession of Faith sums this up as follows:

> There is but one only living and true God, who is infinite in being and perfection, a most pure spirit, invisible, without body, parts, or passions; immutable, immense, eternal, incomprehensible, almighty, most wise, most holy, most free, most absolute; working all things according to the counsel of His own immutable and most righteous will, for His own glory; most loving, gracious, merciful, long-suffering, abundant in goodness and truth, forgiving iniquity, transgression and sin; the rewarder of them that diligently seek him; and withal, most just, and terrible in His judgments; hating all sin, and who will by no means clear the guilty.[16]

Because he makes laws and issues commands based upon his moral nature, we can see that God is not just a creator; he is also a law-giver. His laws are not human inventions or imaginings, but are a revelation of his nature. God instituted both physical and moral laws to govern and sustain his creation.

Universal physical laws: Source of power phenomenon

God's universal physical laws are the source of the power phenomenon which we studied in the traditional religion.

These laws were created by God to uphold the physical and material order of creation. They proceeded from the word of God's power during the act of creation and they demonstrated God's creative powers. Thus it is God's spoken word which provides the physical order for all of creation. He established and sustains "all things by his powerful word" (Heb 1:3 NIV).

When we study the nature and the characteristics of the physical world, we discover the existence of these scientific laws of nature and these laws are what modern science seeks to understand. They include, for instance, the universal laws of gravity and motion which determine the forces at work on the sun, moon, stars and the earth.[17] They help us to glimpse nature's causes and interactions because they govern the physical nature, the interaction, and the structural and natural causes of all things created. Nonetheless, God has

---

16. The Westminster Confession of Faith, chapter 2.1.
17. Gilkey, *Maker of Heaven*, 121.

the power to change the course or principles of nature which he set in place. When he does this through the word of his power, we see his miraculous deeds.

These physical laws, however, are temporal, not eternal. They were created along with creation and, at the end of the age, will also be destroyed along with the created order. God works through the universal physical laws of nature to achieve his will and purpose. Yet there are those who glory in the power of the universal physical laws themselves. They become fascinated by the mysteries of the universe, the earth, the sun, the stars, the oceans, and the deeps. The hidden, mysterious powers and forces that lie behind all of these elements excite their curiosity and fears. In their quest to understand these mysteries and powers, they invent gods or supernatural powers which they have come to believe lie behind these elements in the universe. They believe that these gods will provide explanations and purpose. One can see this in the old Egyptian mysteries as well as in African traditional religions. Humankind becomes so captivated by the mysteries and the powers of the natural physical world that it forgets the creator who made the entire universe with all its wonders, mysteries, powers, forces and universal physical laws.

Universal moral laws

God's created order is not only governed by the universal physical laws, but also by universal moral laws.

God is a moral being. He is good and perfect. His moral nature and activities, purposes and intentions are governed by the counsel of his perfect will (Eph 1:6, 9, 11). God's perfect moral nature is revealed in his moral attributes and these attributes are codified in his universal moral laws. These universal laws reflect the universal rule and authority of God the Creator.

Unlike the physical laws, these moral laws are not rooted within the created order. They transcend creation. They are eternal because they are based upon the nature of God himself who is eternal. They are divinely given in order to govern and maintain the relationships and the activities of all moral creatures and of the created orders of the universe. We see in Genesis 2:15–17 that the moral order that exists between God the Creator and the moral human being is governed by this universal moral law.

The Bible in its entirety is a moral guide on how moral beings ought to live and behave in relationship to God the Creator, the natural world, and their fellow moral beings. The relationship which God ordained between human beings, the created order and other creatures is governed by these universal moral laws (Gen 1:28–30). The same is true of the relationship between fellow human beings (Gen 2:18–25; 3; 4). The God of order has organized his created universe into a perfect morality to generate and engender peace, harmony and blessings. Every created order made and instituted by God is accompanied by complementary moral laws that are to govern and maintain that created order.

As the supreme creator, God is therefore also the supreme law-giver, and, as the law-giver, God is also the supreme judge. When moral beings refuse to obey the universal moral laws of God, they do so at their peril for any violation of God's moral order is always accompanied by the consequences of God's judgment and punishment. The loss of morality affects the nature and well-being of the physical world, creation, nations, peoples, and institutions, just as sin and the fall of Adam and Eve in the garden of Eden (Gen 3) affected the natural physical world. Without law and order, we see only chaos, conflict, crisis, and curses.

Humankind's pursuit of supernatural powers is mainly due to a lack of understanding. It is easy to see only the created or surrogate powers within God's created orders and to ignore or neglect God who is ultimate power. Those powers that amaze and dazzle the mind of man are simply powers within God's universal physical laws of creation; they simply manifest the creative powers of God which control the whole universe and creation. They are subordinate to the sovereign power of God.

In the light of this revelation, African Christians need to address the questions of evil and sin which raise their heads in so many social, economic and political issues facing the continent. They should seek to create a just and sustainable society based on the Christian concept of good creation and God's moral laws. This should be our moral and ethical priority. This is the only way to eradicate poverty, hunger, disease, war and the many vices and sins we see in Africa.

22

The Power of God's Sovereignty

Underlying the discussion in the last chapter is the concept of God's sovereignty. This is the eternal and ultimate power that adequately addresses the power phenomenon encountered in traditional religion.

Sovereignty "is God's exercise of power over his creation . . . God's sovereignty is his exercise of rule (as 'sovereign' or 'king') over his creation."[1] This means that God has absolute and supreme authority and power as God the Creator, Redeemer, Ruler, Law-giver, Judge and Lord of the entire universe. He is not subject to any power, authority, rule, or law in the heavens above, on the earth, or under the earth. God as sovereign has absolute "freedom, power, knowledge, wisdom and determination to carry out his predetermined course of action."[2]

God delegates power and authority to lesser, created moral beings who exercise them on his behalf, but his sovereignty and lordship cannot ever be usurped by any being, power, or authority. His sovereignty is both universal and eternal.

The law of sovereignty forbids any form of recognition or worship of any person, object, or power other than the sovereign Lord (Matt 4:10). God alone is worthy of being worshipped. All angelic and all human beings must accept this moral law and obey it absolutely, even those in positions of authority or leadership. We are warned by the biblical account of how Nebuchadnezzar was severely punished when he did not obey this law (Dan 3, 4). The sovereign Lord himself says:

> You shall not make for yourself an image in the form of anything
> in heaven above, or on the earth beneath or in the waters below.

---

1. Grudem, *Systematic Theology*, 217.
2. Willmington, *Willmington's Guide to the Bible*, 600.

You shall not bow down to them or worship them, for I, the Lord your God, am a jealous God. (Exod 20:4–5)

This law speaks to the traditional concept of spirit-power. No one can worship God while holding on to any other power. Some Africans claim to worship God along with some elements of spirit-power, but they are committing spiritual idolatry. The quest for spirit-powers in traditional religion is a direct result of our rejection of God's sovereignty. Rebellion, disobedience, and sin broke humankind's relationship with their maker and creator. Therefore, since the fall, humankind has no longer been under God's law and protection. We must face fate, evil, curses, anxiety, and fear of all creatures, powers, and forces without God. Because the thought of this is so daunting, those whose lives have not been transformed through God's special revelation think they have no other option but to look to spirit beings and supernatural powers for help.

The Eternal Nature of God

"From everlasting to everlasting you are God" (Ps 90:2). With these words, the psalmist recognized the eternal truth that God is the only eternal living being. God is self-existing.

> This is simply to say . . . that God exists because he exists. He is not dependent upon anything or anyone for his thoughts (Rom 11:33–34), his will (Rom 9:19; Eph 1:5), his power (Ps 115:3), or his counsel (Ps 33:10–11).[3]

Buswell enlarges on this, saying: "The being of God is eternal, both as to the past and as to the future. God has always existed and always will exist; He never began to be. He never will cease to be."[4] God is his own life-source and existence. He does not derive his life from somewhere or from someone else; he derives his life from himself and within himself. By nature he is life; he is existence. Buswell uses the term *aseity* to define the being of God. This means that God's being is uncaused.[5]

Willmington explains that, as a result, "This means God is absolutely free from the tyranny of time. In him there is no past or future, but one always and never-ending present. He is neither conditioned by nor confined by time."[6]

---

3. Willmington, *Willmington's Guide to the Bible*, 597.
4. Buswell, *Systematic Theology*, 40.
5. Buswell, 40.
6. Willmington, *Willmington's Guide to the Bible*, 597.

Thus it is true as Grudem says, that "God has no beginning, end, or succession of moments in his own being, and he sees all time equally, yet God sees events in time and acts in time."[7] God is the Creator of time. He preserves and rules over history, although he is outside of time and history. We on the other hand will always exist in time.

We know that "through him all things were made; without him nothing was made that has been made" (John 1:3). Yet all creatures or created beings derive the gift of existence from God, but they are not extensions of God or properties of God. The eternal God has no substance and no properties. He is the eternal and self-existing Spirit, non-material, non-corporeal. By contrast, all creation, including all other gods, is temporal, dependent, transient, finite, and dead. All creatures are dependent upon God for their very existence. God alone is not a dependent being.

The power of God is rooted in this living-power, this self-existence. No spirit-power can compare. God alone can fulfil the African pursuit of life force.

The Word of God's Power

We only know God's nature, character, attributes and his will or mind through his revelation as Word. God is the Eternal Word (*logos*). The Word of God is his self-revelation. He speaks the truth from his inner being which is devoid of any impurity or uncleanness. Because God is always true and faithful, his word is also righteous and dependable. Because the power of the word is rooted in God's omnipotence and sovereignty, his words have ultimate power, authority and dominion.

God uses his attribute of being the Eternal Word to accomplish all his works of creation. The word of his power was the absolute origin and the beginning of all things. God did not have matter or any substance at hand to begin with; he relied on the power of his word to create out of nothing. The fact that creation exists is a clear demonstration of this power. All the powers of the universe are rooted in the power of God's eternal word. The Bible states: "And God said, 'Let there be light,' and there was light" (Gen 1:3). At the command of his word, his intentions and purposes are realized. He commanded the sky (1:6, 14, 20–21). He commanded the waters (1:9, 20). He commanded the land (1:11, 24). When the Bible states, "And God said," it is referring to both the creative and the sustaining power of God in his spoken word. "He upholds the universe by the word of his power" (Heb 1:3 ESV).

---

7. Grudem, *Systematic Theology*, 168.

The use of ritual incantations reveals that the traditional Africans also believe in the power of the spoken word. But those who speak these rituals are created beings and their power is limited as they must rely on powers outside of themselves. They do not have in themselves the eternal power of the spoken word. They must be given power in order to perform miracles. Clearly, the Eternal Word and the Eternal Spirit have dominion and power over all created beings.

Jesus Christ as the Eternal Word and Eternal Bread

In his divine plan for the salvation of the world, later in time God revealed himself as the Word (*logos*) through his incarnation as Jesus Christ (John 1:1–14). Jesus was not spoken into being, but is God Incarnate. He is not a spoken word of God, but the Word of God himself.

As the Word and Wisdom, he was active during creation. Then, during the incarnation, he revealed redemption and salvation to the whole world, offering transformation and eternal life to all who received him (Col 1:15–22; Heb 1:3). He himself said, "I am the way, and the truth, and the life. No one comes to the Father except through me" (John 14:6).

The Word of God was also revealed in him as the Eternal Bread. Whereas daily bread sustains mortal life temporarily, Eternal Bread provides eternal life. Jesus reminded Satan of this when he was being tempted in the wilderness: "Man shall not live on bread alone, but on every word that comes from the mouth of God" (Matt 4:4). Jesus explained to his followers that, as the Word of God, he has the power to give eternal life: "I am the bread of life. Whoever comes to me will never go hungry, and whoever believes in me will never be thirsty" (John 6:35). Jesus warned them not to "work for food that spoils, but for food that endures to eternal life, which the Son of Man will give to you" (John 6:27).

Thus, the Eternal Word not only creates – he also sustains and transforms creation. He not only creates mortal life – through his eternal love and mercy he transforms created life into eternal life. Through Jesus Christ the Eternal Word, we – who have a beginning, a duration and an end – are granted access to eternal life. In redemption, God reveals his eternal love in Jesus Christ as the Saviour and Lord of the fallen and sinful world.

But there is also a warning in this promise. Just as the Eternal Word has the power to bless and create, he also has the power of judgment, punishment, and destruction. When God speaks, his word is absolute and must be obeyed. Disobedience to the word of God invites judgment and punishment. His consuming wrath is the power of holiness and perfection that will finally destroy evil and sin.

God alone has the eternal power to address the supernatural powers in the universe and the powers that menace human life. The biblical and Christian theology of power which is rooted in the nature, attributes, and character of God addresses the belief in impersonal (mysterious) or supernatural powers which dominates in African Traditional Religion. It is a pity that the rationalistic Christianity of the missionary era did not realize the release that this knowledge of the power of God's word could bring. When African Christians understand this, they can begin to cast off the shackles by which these supernatural powers bind them.

23

Engaging with the Traditional Belief in Spirit Beings

The belief in spirit beings is rooted in the spirit phenomenon, and traditional spirituality must be understood from this perspective. We must recognize the religious and social role that this belief plays in shaping and moulding both the traditional and the modern African mind.

When biblical and Christian theological categories are introduced into traditional Africa, they are generally interpreted within the belief, spirituality, and worldview of spirit-consciousness. This means that the traditional African mind understands and interprets the presentation of Jesus Christ, the Holy Spirit, God, and other related categories (such as Satan, demons, and angels) in terms of traditional spirit-consciousness and spirituality. This will affect their expression of Christianity.

The fact that Africans already have a rudimentary and comparable concept of spirit in their traditional religion, however, also means that they have a starting point from which they can understand the deeper truths of spirit as manifested in the Bible and Christianity. The belief in the existence of spirit beings is basic to both African Traditional Religion and Christianity, although there are marked differences between the two religions.

To traditional Africans, these spirit beings are real, active and power. They believe that spirit beings abound in the universe: on land, in rivers, in lakes, in seas, in oceans, on mountains, in forests, in caves, everywhere. They respond to the existence of such spirit beings with anxiety and fear. And, because they think that spirit beings exercise spiritual powers over the universe, they believe that the spirit beings must be worshipped and revered. Some spiritual powers are therefore deified and are regarded as gods or divinities or deities.

We need to develop a theology of the Spirit and spirituality that adequately addresses humankind's innate desire to communicate with and have fellowship with these spirit beings.

The traditional belief in spirit beings generates its own worldview of spiritual consciousness. This spiritual worldview is based on the following beliefs: that spirituality is the very essence of life; that life is saturated with spiritual possibilities; that everything in life can be influenced by and responds to the world of spirits; and that all of life is to be understood spiritually. The pursuit of the spiritual meaning of life dominates the traditional mind of Africa as spirit power is seen as essential to understanding and interpreting the meaning and purpose of life. "Life's questions and answers revolve around the spiritual rather than the physical . . . Catastrophes, natural disasters, disease, untimely death and other exigencies of life are all evaluated spiritually."[1]

The traditional African is keen to discover what spirit beings are in control in the universe and what spirit beings sustain and maintain the universe. In this way the African hopes to discover spirit beings that can provide the protection, guidance, sustenance, comfort, and peace that are needed in this chaotic and confusing world.

From our discussion it is clear that these theological questions are addressed by God's sovereignty, providence and wisdom. God's sovereignty addresses the questions of spiritual power and control in the universe. God's spiritual power addresses the questions of meaning and purpose in life through the ministry of the Holy Spirit. The redemptive work of Christ on the cross establishes God's spiritual power over the whole world, over all principalities and powers, and over all spirit beings.

The Theological Concept of the Spirit

Let us begin by making sure that we understand the biblical meaning and usage of the word "spirit" in order to set apart the Spirit of God (Holy Spirit) from the spirit beings in traditional belief, as well as fallen angels, Satan and demons in the Bible. The Hebrew word for spirit is *ruach*; the Greek equivalent is *pneuma*. These words convey various meanings at different times in the Bible:[2]

> *Wind* (Exod 10:13; 1 Kgs 19:11)
> *Breath or spirit*, in the sense of the life and vitality of living creatures (Gen 6:17)

---

1. Steyne, *Gods of Power*, 37–38.
2. D. Fleming, *Bridge Bible Directory*.

Divine power (Judg 3:10; 1 Sam 10:6)
Human emotion (Gen 41:8; Num 5:14; John 13:21)
Human understanding (Isa 29:24; Mark 2:8)
Will-power (Jer 51:11; Acts 19:21)
Human life itself (Gen 45:27; Luke 8:55)
Evil beings of the unseen world (1 Sam 16:23; Mark 1:23)
God's Spirit, the living power of God at work (Judg 6:34; Acts 8:39)

The list reveals that the word "spirit" in the Bible is always associated with God and his activities which give life to all human beings and animals. The "life-force" or "breath of life" which God gives to all people and animals for the duration of their earthly existence, and which he takes back at death belongs to God (Num 16:22; Ps 104:29; Eccl 12:7; Heb 12:9; Jas 2:26).[3]

God as Eternal Spirit

The Christian law of the Spirit is rooted in the glorious eternal nature of who God is. God himself is Spirit and manifests himself as the Holy Spirit. The Holy Spirit is not a mysterious force or impersonal power, but is the third Person of the Trinity. Because the traditional spiritual worldview does not differentiate between the material and the spiritual world, this creates great problems for African Christians in their understanding of the person and work of the Holy Spirit.

As Spirit, God is infinite and without any limitations. As Spirit, he is immutable, unchanging, and constant, "the same yesterday, and today, and for ever" (Mal 3:6; Jas 1:17; Heb 13:8). As Spirit, God is all-knowing (omniscient), present everywhere (omnipresent) and all-powerful (omnipotent). God maintains and sustains the entire universe by his eternal life-giving Spirit. The eternal and holy nature of God as Spirit is the foundation of all life.

When God is defined as Spirit (John 4:24), this is a reference to his unseen reality. God is uncreated and for this reason he does not have mass or matter as creatures have. Emory Bancroft is cited as stating: "God as spirit is incorporeal, invisible, without material substance, without physical parts or passions and therefore free from all temporal limitations."[4] We could also express this as follows: "God's spirituality means that God exists as a being that is not made

---

3. D. Fleming.
4. Willmington, *Willmington's Guide to the Bible*, 594.

of any matter, has no parts or dimensions, is unable to be perceived by our bodily senses, and is more excellent than any kind of existence."[5]

In the Old Testament, however, God is said to have arms (Job 40:9); eyes (Ps 33:18); ears (2 Kgs 19:16); and mouth (Isa 58:14). Of course, God does not actually have a body or form or shape, nor does he have these bodily parts. These statements are anthropomorphic expressions used to "explain some function or characteristic of God by using words descriptive of human elements."[6] God "is capable of doing precisely the functions which are performed by these physical properties in man."[7] God warned the Israelites not to make any carved images of him. They were not to represent him falsely, nor to equate him with creaturely forms. God cannot be represented by any form or shape as he is not created matter.

The Holy Spirit is the supreme eternal Spirit through whom humankind's needs and purposes can be met. Dependable and reliable, he is known as Comforter, Guide, and Teacher and is the one who empowers, regenerates, and sustains. This reveals the uselessness of pursuing spiritual meaning and power in this life apart from the Holy Spirit.

By the word of his power God as the Eternal Spirit created moral beings: angels and human beings. Angels are immaterial and incorporeal spirit beings with a spiritual nature, while human beings have a spirit, soul, and body. Both are created beings and are limited in time and space, although angels have immortality and human beings are mortal. These spirit beings need the eternal Spirit to give them existence, life, meaning, and purpose. This means that they are subordinate to him and that they are limited in terms of power, knowledge, intelligence, and abode.

Besides the created spirit beings, God also created the impersonal, immaterial, and unseen powers. These are the supernatural powers and forces that pervade the universe. Created supernatural powers and forces may be felt and experienced, but are not visible. Although these created spirit beings operate in both physical and spiritual realms, they may, on occasion, act contrary to the physical and natural laws that make up the universe.

When human beings come into contact with all these powers, they sometimes mistake the activities and the phenomena of these spiritual forces and powers as being of God. Not every physical and spiritual phenomenon can

---

5. Grudem, *Systematic Theology*, 187–188.
6. Willmington, *Willmington's Guide to the Bible*, 594.
7. Lightner, cited in Willmington, 594.

be attributed to God or originates from God. Spiritual beings and impersonal forces in the universe can act independently of God, and sometimes act contrary to God's holy will. This calls for caution and discernment. John, the apostle, advised us to test every spirit to differentiate between true and holy spirits and the wicked and false spirits (1 John 4).

Contact with spirit beings, spiritual forces or supernatural powers that do not come from the true living God is dangerous. Satan and demons have spiritual and supernatural powers with which they deceive and attack nations and peoples. These have to be contrasted with God's holy Spirit and the supernatural powers that come from the word of his power. Self-reliance and ungodly immoral guidance will only lead to ruin and death and to the rejection of God and his moral laws. This is why the traditional dealings with spirit beings and demonic influence has been prohibited by the Bible (Exod 22:18; Lev 19:26; 20:6, 27; Deut 18:9–14; Ezek 21:21; Gal 5:20; Acts 8:9–24; 13:6–12; 19:18).

It is not enough for human beings to be guided only by physical laws or by human laws and wisdom. Human beings need the guiding light and power of the Holy Spirit. The work of the Holy Spirit is to transform, regenerate and sanctify moral and spiritual beings so that they can conform to the holy and righteous character of God. The Holy Spirit works to solve the problem of sin, of evil and of the spirit of rebellion which entered this universe as a result of the rebellion of Satan and his angels and humankind (Gen 3). Thus, the eternal Spirit offers a different kind of spirituality, one which is obedient and submissive to the holy and glorious will and purposes of God. Apart from the Holy Spirit, we are embarked on a sure way of error, ruin, and death. As Scripture says: "'Not by might, nor by power, but by my Spirit,' says the LORD Almighty" (Zech 4:6).

Only God the uncreated eternal Spirit is holy and pure. Satan and his demons are unholy, unrighteous, evil, wicked, unloving, unfaithful, unkind, unforgiving, covetous, vindictive, vengeful, and malicious. Their only purpose is to deceive, devour, and inflict suffering upon people. Those who follow in their footsteps take steps toward death and eternal separation from God. God alone is the uncreated Eternal Spirit that commands Worship.

The Creative Power of the Spirit

The second eternal and holy attribute of God the Holy Spirit is his creative power. Genesis 1:2 describes the earth as formless, empty and dark. There was only lifelessness. The Spirit of God hovered or brooded over this chaotic or shapeless creation and brought life out of death, light out of darkness, order out of chaos, and form out of formlessness.

That was the power of God at work in creation, and this creative power of the Spirit of God continues to govern the entire universe, maintaining life, light, form and order. This is reflected in Scriptures such as "When you send your Spirit, they are created: and you renew the face of the ground" (Ps 104:30), and "The Spirit of God has made me; the breath of the Almighty gives me life" (Job 33:4). This spiritual power of God is therefore above and beyond all universal physical laws within creation. The power of God himself maintains and sustains both creation and its universal physical laws.

Universal physical laws can only operate within creation where they may be regarded as mysteries, forces or powers, for example in astronomy, physics, chemistry, gravity, and thermodynamics. Unfortunately, natural science and philosophy see only the physical creation laws, not the invisible creative power of the Spirit at work above and within the created order. Scientists may not even be aware that there is a superior law that sustains everything: the law of the Spirit.

The law of the Spirit establishes God as the creator and "sustainer" of life, both within and outside of creation. The Spirit created and established creation laws to govern all physical nature and physical interactions, overseeing the causes and the links between all things. The spring of life, the Spirit regenerates and renews the original and the fallen creation (all that is aging, dying, barren, formless, and chaotic). He is the spring of life and the source of spiritual empowerment. He invigorates and brings hope and light to hopeless, dark situations. God rules providentially to maintain law and order, peace, and harmony. Therefore this law has implications for the entire universe.

The Spirit as the Author and Transmitter of Prophecy and the Word of God

The Spirit does this through revelation (the spoken word); inspiration (guiding the accuracy of the transmitted word); and illumination (enlightening the written or preached word so it can be understood).[8] The Spirit of God is the author of both the Old Testament and the New Testament.

> Knowing this first of all that no prophecy of Scripture comes from someone's own interpretation. For no prophecy was ever produced

---

8. Willmington, *Willmington's Guide to the Bible*, 645.

by the will of man, but men spoke from God as they were carried along by the Holy Spirit. (2 Pet 1:20–21 ESV)

All Scripture is breathed out by God and is profitable for teaching, for reproof, for correction, and for training in righteousness, that the man of God may be complete, equipped for every good work. (2 Tim 3:16–17 ESV)

The prophets also bore testimony to this work of the Spirit of God:

The Spirit of the LORD spoke through me; his word was on my tongue. (David in 2 Sam 23:2)

"As for me, this is my covenant with them," says the Lord. "My Spirit who is on you, will not depart from you, and my words that I have put in your mouth will always be on your lips, on the lips of your children and on the lips of their descendants – from this time on and forever" says the LORD. (Isa 59:21)

Then the LORD reached out his hand and touched my mouth, and said to me, "I have put my words into your mouth." (Jer 1:9)

Contrasting the Work of the Spirit in the Old and New Testaments

In the Old Testament dispensation, the Spirit of God came upon the Old Testament saints to enable them to accomplish specific tasks. We can think, for example, of Joseph (Gen 41:39); Moses (Num 11:17); Joshua (Num 27:18); Gideon (Judg 6:34); and Samson (Judg 14:6; 15:14). After they had accomplished his tasks, the Spirit usually withdrew. He did not indwell the Old Testament saints and they did not partake of his holy nature. He simply came upon them in power and strength and might, enabling them to do exploits, miracles, signs, and wonders that they could not have done as ordinary human beings.

In the New Testament, by contrast, the Holy Spirit does two things, both of which arise from the finished work of redemption (salvation) through Jesus Christ on the cross.

First, he indwells believers. This means that he lives inside them, enabling them to bear the inner fruit of the Spirit. The Holy Spirit gives the gifts of God's grace to the believers enabling them to live a life of godliness, holiness and righteousness. Thus believers will become Christ-like, showing love, joy, peace, patience (longsuffering), kindness, goodness, faithfulness, gentleness, and self-control (temperance) (Gal 5:22); righteousness (Phil 1:11) and truth (2 Cor 4:1–2).⁹

Second, he comes upon the believers with power, enabling them to accomplish specific tasks just as the Old Testament saints did. He gives them the power to evangelize boldly, to speak prophetic revelations and words of wisdom, and to perform miracles, signs and wonders, healings, and tongues. These creative and regenerative powers of the Holy Spirit are superior to all created spirit-powers, including those that menace human life. The Holy Spirit confronts the wicked and the evil works of Satan, demons, and all other principalities and powers. Our Lord Jesus Christ and the apostles lived through the power of the Holy Spirit. "From his bodily conception to his final ascension, the Lord Jesus Christ was led by the Holy Spirit."[10] The same power is available to believers today.

God has absolute, universal, and eternal power over the entire creation. Furthermore, the work of Jesus Christ on the cross and his resurrection from the dead reveal that the Spirit exercises his redemptive powers over all creation and all created moral beings, both human and angelic.

The law of the Spirit, as explained in this chapter, can be used to engage and address both the power phenomenon and spirit phenomenon, and their combined spirit-power in traditional religion.

---

9. Willmington.
10. Willmington, 648.

24

Engaging with the Traditional Belief about the Origin of Spirit Beings

In traditional religion, the origin of the spirit beings is not certain, although some African myths attempt to explain their existence. Because the Supreme Being is believed to have created all things, these spirit beings are said to have been created by him. However, some of the spirit beings are also believed to originate from the spirits of the dead while others are said to come from a non-human source.

Since the source of spirit beings is uncertain, the traditional African also believes it is not possible to know their full nature, form, status, control, and destiny. But, as can be seen when one examines the stories and legends relating to the founding of many of the African communities or nations, clearly there is no doubt as to their existence. The traditional religious beliefs and practices reflect the African uncertainties, fears, and ambivalence concerning spirit beings. This is why traditional Africa has elaborate means of communication with and from the spirit world.

But the Bible is clear about the origins of the spirit beings. They are all created by God and are all therefore under the sovereignty of God who controls all that he has created. Their activities in the universe should therefore be understood within the context of God's sovereignty and will. However, God granted spirit beings the freedom of choice. As free agents, they can therefore exercise their free-will against the will of God in their acts of evil and wickedness. Nonetheless, although the spirit beings may not obey him or do his will, God has ultimate authority and power over them all. This power was confirmed in the cross of Jesus Christ which is the symbol of Christ's victory over all evil and spiritual forces and powers (Phil 2:5–11; Heb 1:3–9).

In the Old Testament the Jews were taught to turn away completely from spirit beings or deities. The Bible states categorically that humans should not worship spirit beings nor have any direct dealings with them, and that to do so is an abomination to the Lord God. Instead people were told to put all their trust and confidence in the one sovereign God (Deut 6:4). The Jewish religion was centred in the worship of the one sovereign God, the Lord Yahweh. No other gods or divinities were to be worshipped (Exod 20:1–5). God himself proclaimed this monotheistic principle, which contrasted with the heathen religions which surrounded the Jews in Canaan, Egypt, and Mesopotamia. The heathen religions which were denounced by God himself were similar to African Traditional Religion.

The New Testament shows us that Christ is utterly victorious over all principalities and powers, including all spirit beings. At his name all must bow, those in heaven, on the earth and under the earth (Eph 1:17–23; Phil 2:9–11). The victory of Christ over evil, sin, Satan and all principalities is the greatest good news humankind can ever receive, especially for those bound by traditional religions. The presence of the church of Jesus Christ is the sign of this victory.

Traditional religion does not seem to have a strong theology of the sovereignty of God over all of his creation, including supernatural powers and creatures or spirit beings. As a result, the traditional African feels the need to search for a theology of power that can counteract the menacing and capricious powers of spirit beings and supernatural powers. This is why we have examined both the creative powers of God in nature and also God's attributes so closely.

Good and Evil Spirits

The bulk of African religious and social beliefs and practices relate to spirit beings. Some of the spirit beings have assumed the status of deities, divinities or gods, while others remain to help whenever their help is sought. It is believed that these spirit beings have a mind of their own and can act independently of God or human beings. The terror or the wickedness which spirit beings can unleash on humans causes fear and anxiety. The belief is that these beings have to be placated through sacrifices and offerings so that they will do what humans want.

The nature of spirit beings in the traditional religion is unclear, but it is accepted that there are good and evil spirit beings. African myths attempt to explain why this is so. Some spirit beings are wicked or evil in themselves, either because they were created like that or because they became evil on their own. There is also a traditional belief that bad spirits can emerge from acts of impropriety. Then there are evil spirits which are related to animal and bird species, such as wild cats, snakes, owls, as well as other mysterious animals and birds. Wicked and evil people or spirits can take on the form of these animals, birds, and mysterious objects when they attack people. Furthermore, it is believed that improper burial can turn the spirits of the dead human beings into wicked spirit beings. Those who died a violent death as a result of lightning, drowning or murder can also become evil spirits. This generates terror and fear in relation to the dead, especially as traditional belief asserts that the spirits of the dead do not die but instead become the "living dead." Yet, although spirit beings are classified into good and bad, there is no clear distinction between the good and the evil.

The Bible on the other hand teaches that spirit beings are "heavenly beings created by God" and that:

> Angels are God's servants and messengers in the heavenly and spiritual realm, where they find true satisfaction in the unceasing worship and service of God. They were created before man, they belong to a higher order than man does and their number is countless (Pss 103:20–21; 148:2; Isa 6:23; Dan 7:10; Luke 12:8–9; 15:10; Col 1:16; Heb 12:22; Rev 4:8; 5:11–12; 7:11).[1]

However the Bible tells us that some angels, along with their leader Satan, rebelled against God and lost their sinless state (2 Pet 2:4; Jude 6). As a result there are good angels and evil angels. The good ones are the servants and messengers of God and carry out some functions on behalf of God's servants, while the evil ones are the servants and messengers of Satan, commonly referred to as demons.

Evil spirits or demons who are in rebellion against God are variously known as demons, evil spirits, unclean spirits, familiar spirits, spiritual hosts of wickedness, principalities, powers, rulers, authorities, evil spiritual forces, cosmic powers of evil and angels of the devil. These are the spiritual force behind heathen religions and false gods (Deut 32:17; Ps 106:37; 1 Cor 10:19–20; Rev 9:20). This means that those who follow these religions fear demons and use magic and sorcery, cooperating with supernatural evil powers although God clearly forbids this (Lev 19:26; 20:6; Gal 5:20; Rev 9:20–21; 21:8).[2]

---

1. D. Fleming, *Bridge Bible Directory*, 17.
2. D. Fleming, 17.

Because of the relevance of angels to the traditional belief in spirit beings, it is important that we note the following:

> Both good and bad angels are under God's sovereign rule [and] Satan and the evil angels (demons) can do their evil work only within the limits that God allows (Job 1:12; 2:6).[3]

This theological fact helps us to address the traditional belief in and the fear of the menacing and capricious activities of the spirit beings. It is a great comfort to know that they are under the watching eye and the sovereign power of God, and that they pursue their evil activities only under his divine will even though these acts are not sanctioned by God. According to the books of Revelation and Jude their evil activities will be judged and punished by the sovereign God on the day of judgment.

From biblical records, it is also clear that angels have more to do with God their creator than with humans. The primary tasks of good angels are to serve God (Ps 103:21), to praise and glorify him (Ps 148:2), and to join battle on his behalf (Gen 19:1–29; 32:1–2; 2 Kgs 6:16–17; Ps 78:49).[4] They are primarily the servants and messengers of God who sends them to guide (Gen 24:7, 40; Exod 14:19; Acts 8:26; 27:23); to protect (Pss 34:7; 91:11; Dan 6:22; 10:13, 21; Matt 18:10); to deliver (Dan 3:28; Matt 26:53; Acts 5:19); to interpret visions (Dan 8:15–16; Zech 1:8–14; Rev 1:1; 22:6) and to help in various other circumstances (Mark 1:13; Luke 22:43; Heb 1:13–14). God also sends his angels as messengers of punishment to the ungodly (Matt 13:39, 41; 25:31; Acts 12:23; 2 Thess 1:7–8).[5]

In African Traditional Religion, it is the humans themselves, and not God, who employ the services of spirit beings both good and evil. These spirit beings can be made to serve through religious practices, rituals, and ceremonies. By contrast, the Bible expressly forbids the worship of angels, demons, and Satan (Exod 20:3–6). This means that there may be no ritual act of reverence, no prayer and no attempts to communicate by making offerings or sacrifice to solicit their help. God alone is to be worshipped and anyone who worships any other god, person, thing, divinity or spirit being is guilty of idolatry (Exod 20:4–5; 32:8; Deut 4:19; 8:19; Acts 10:25–26; 14:11–15; Rom 1:25; Rev 22:8–9).

We must recognize that demons are active in every sphere of human life and work through the normal activities of human nature and human society.

---

3. D. Fleming, 17.
4. *Eerdmans Bible Dictionary*, 56.
5. D. Fleming, *Bridge Bible Directory*, 17.

Although not all human activity or religion is demonic, anything done in opposition to God is inevitably done under the influence of the opposing spirit-power. This means that any religious beliefs and practices that are contrary to the teachings of the Bible must be rejected. The believer in Christ can claim victory over evil powers (Eph 1:18–21; Col 2:8–10, 15).

This traditional theology and worldview can be addressed by the Christian theology of the sovereignty of God (God's power), Christ's power and the power of the Holy Spirit as discussed in the previous chapters.

Spirits Inhabit or Possess Certain Objects

Traditional Africans believe that spirits inhabit certain rocks, trees, mountains, idols, shrines, geographical areas, and people, both alive and deceased. It is also believed that some objects may possess their own spirits, for example that there are river spirits, mountain spirits, or forest spirits. The belief in these manifestations of spirit power is pervasive. These beliefs cause great fear and anxiety, since contact with such objects or persons is all too possible. This is why elaborate practices, rituals and ceremonies have been developed as a means of protection from and security against such contacts and the harm that may ensue.

The Bible makes it clear that objects do not possess their own spirits, but that spirits inhabit objects. Thus, rivers, mountains or forests do not produce their own kinds of spirits, but they can become the abode of spirits. This means that these places can become the abode of supernatural powers generated by spirit beings and it is this power that makes people equate the objects with the spirits themselves.

Here we see the power phenomenon at work. Generated supernatural powers can be imputed to objects and can influence nature and humans as a physical force which produces tangible or visible results. So, supernatural powers are visible with tangible outcomes. But there is also the spiritual influence. Spiritual power can produce feelings, attitudes, behaviours, or social and religious practices. The presence of spirit-powers in objects or in nature leads to all kinds of religious practices in order to cleanse or ward off the spirits from these objects, places and strategic sites. Although the spiritual influence or power is not visible, its outcome is visible. We have to keep the two spiritual phenomena of the spirit distinct.

It is entirely possible for Christians to be attacked by demons, either through a non-physical spiritual influence which causes a person to degenerate or to become spiritually weak, or through a physical supernatural power. These influences cannot be dealt with by exorcism rituals. Instead, the demonic sources of the attacks must be challenged through the power of the cross and the power of the resurrection of Christ. The shed blood on the cross offers God's salvation and forgiveness for sin (Eph 1:7), while the resurrection is our victory over all principalities and powers (Eph 1:19–23). We have to believe in and claim the power of the blood of the Lamb over our life and the power of Christ's resurrection in us. This is how Christians can exorcise demons and break their spiritual and supernatural power over people's lives. This gets to the very centre of the spiritual worldview that is dominated by anxiety and fear. The sovereignty and power of God the Creator and the victory of Christ the Redeemer give the Christian the confidence to live boldly. No Christian need be anxious about or fear the menacing and capricious activities of spirit beings and supernatural powers.

"Protective" Spirits

Traditional Africans believe that there are also spirits that protect one. These are known as "spirit doubles" or guardian spirits.

> Responsibility for the fulfilment of the person's destiny is ascribed to his double, which has all the possibilities, liabilities and often faults that good or bad fortune has given to it. Sacrifices, offerings and prayers are made to this protecting spirit. In a very real sense man thus worships an extension of himself.[6]

In some societies, such beliefs are extended to include an animal or a totem. This means that whatever happens to the animal or totem also affects the person who keeps it.

Once again, this contradicts Scripture. The Bible teaches that God alone is the source of protection and security. God's creative powers and Christ's redemptive powers provide a powerful assurance of God's protection and security against the attacks of the evil one. We are not to seek protection from spirit beings, for the work of protection is ultimately God's. The cross of Christ has disarmed all principalities and powers (2 Cor 10:4–6; Col 2:15). The blood of the Lamb that was slain provides victory and protection for the believers in Christ Jesus (Rev 12:10–11).

---

6. Steyne, *Gods of Power*, 78.

Soliciting Help from the Spirits

Humankind's association with spirit beings and with supernatural powers reveals its desire to make these powers serve its needs. People want protection, security, prosperity, and health; they want to know and to preserve their destiny and future. Instead of turning to God, however, traditional people turn to lesser beings for help. This pursuit of power drives people to spirit beings and supernatural powers so that their needs can be met. It may be that people do not have the courage to ask God for what they want. Possibly what they are asking for is morally wrong. These traditional beliefs in spirit beings have led to the development of many religious and social practices.

In Christianity, although it is accepted that spirit beings exist, Christians are prohibited from developing any religious and social practices involving any kind of spirit beings. Dealings with spirit beings are forbidden. The Mosaic law set out in Exodus, Leviticus, Numbers and Deuteronomy prohibits us from turning to spirit beings, even angels, for help. God alone is our help, our refuge and our protector (Pss 46, 92). The sovereignty of God and his sustaining power forbid us to seek protection and security from lesser beings. Jesus Christ gave his Holy Spirit to the church as the comforter, helper and guide. Worship of the triune God is exclusive. No one who truly worships him can play the prostitute with another god.

25

Engaging with the Traditional Belief and Good and Evil

Closely related to the traditional belief in spirit beings and supernatural powers is the traditional belief in good and evil.

According to African Traditional Religion, there is no clear distinction between right and wrong. Even God is seen as both good and bad. He is blamed at times for evil and fate, for affliction and wickedness, as well as for disease and death. This is why the cry goes out: "How can God be good in the midst of these manifestations of evil?" Evil looks unconquerable and God doesn't seem to provide a solution. The belief is that humankind must find its own ways and means of dealing with evil.

As a result much of the traditional African's association with spirit beings and supernatural powers is a search for the good or for a way to avoid evil. Laurenti Magesa in his analysis of "life force" seems to suggest that anything that hinders a person from obtaining the "life force" can be labelled evil and wicked.[1] The belief that the end justifies the means creates a morality and ethics problem for Africa.

These beliefs result from serious misunderstandings about God's character.

God as Eternal Goodness

God is perfect and acts in terms of his goodness. This eternal goodness of God is not just evident in the redemption he offers; it is also seen in his moral excellence. All his acts and decrees, his will, his mind, and all his purposes and intentions are an absolute negation of sin and evil. God simply cannot even think evil; he cannot sin. When human beings associate God with evil

---

1. Magesa, *African Religion*, 1997.

or believe that God has not dealt justly with them, they are revealing a serious lack of understanding of the true and glorious character of God.

This goodness is not easy to explain, so let us consider what Grudem has said: "God's perfection means that God completely possesses all excellent qualities and lacks no part of any qualities that would be desirable for him";[2] "God's beauty is that attribute of God whereby he is the sum of all desirable qualities";[3] "The goodness of God means that God is the final standard of good, and that all that God is and does is worthy of approval."[4]

Others have also tried to define God's goodness. Willmington cites Strong who says, "Goodness is the eternal principle of God's nature which leads Him to communicate His own life and blessedness to those who are like Him in moral character."[5]

He also cites Tozer who said that:

> The goodness of God is that which disposes Him to be kind, cordial, benevolent, and full of good will toward men. He is tender-hearted and of quick sympathy and His unfailing attitude toward all moral beings is open, frank, and friendly. By His nature He is inclined to bestow blessedness and He takes holy pleasure in the happiness of His people.[6]

God inserted the law of goodness into the creative and free activities of all moral beings within his universal order. It is God's eternal universal moral law and it is binding on all moral beings in the universe, both angels and human beings. When moral beings imitate God in acts of creation, leadership, or governance, this universal and eternal moral principle of goodness or perfection becomes as primary for them as it is for God.

Because of the fall (Gen 3), and their separation from the living God, human beings in themselves do not have any goodness that is acceptable to God. Jesus said, "That which is born of the flesh is flesh; and that which is born of the Spirit is spirit" (John 3:6 NKJV). Nothing that comes out of humankind is good or acceptable to God, except that which is done in the Spirit. Romans 5:12–8:17 explains that all human beings inherit sin, wrath, punishment and death through Adam the first man, but that through Jesus Christ, the Second

---

2. Grudem, *Systematic Theology*, 218.
3. Grudem, 21.
4. Grudem, 197.
5. Strong cited in Willmington, *Willmington's Guide to the Bible*, 606.
6. Tozer cited in Willmington, 606.

Adam, we inherit grace, righteousness, and life eternal. All humans born of Adam (flesh) must be born of the Spirit through Jesus Christ before they are acceptable to God.

God as Eternal Wisdom

Closely related to God's attribute of goodness is God's attribute of wisdom. The Bible reminds us that God is wise (Ps 136:5; Prov 3:19). Wisdom is

> the infinite, perfect comprehension of all that is or might be (Rom 11:33–36). God is the source of wisdom as of power and wisdom is given to people through the fear of the Lord (Job 28:28; Ps 111:10). In man, wisdom is an eminently practical attribute, including technical skill (Exod 28:3; RSV "an able mind"), military prowess (Isa 10:13), and shrewdness for questionable ends (1 Kgs 2:6). Wisdom is shown in getting desired ends by effective means. People of the world are often wiser in their generation than the children of light (Luke 16:8). The wisdom of Solomon was far ranging in statesmanship (1 Kgs 10:23–24); in understanding of human nature (3:16–25); and in natural history, literature, and popular proverbs (4:29–34). Wisdom is personified (Prov 8) in terms related to the concept of the Word in John 1:1–18, and became one of the names of God the Father and the Son, the Holy Spirit being the Spirit of Wisdom.[7]

God's actions are rooted in his glorious nature and character of eternal wisdom. God's wisdom is infinite. This means that God is omniscient, all-knowing. God's wisdom is eternal: "God's omniscience has always been His and will always be His." God's wisdom is unchangeable: "God's wisdom can have no wisdom added to it or subtracted from it, and that what he knows, that is everything without exception, He knows truly and immutably from eternity to eternity."[8]

But how can God be wise when we see evil? Our experience of evil and fate, affliction and suffering, disease and death seems to contradict the assertion that "God is wise." To understand this more clearly, we need to see God's wisdom in the light of his knowledge.

Willmington suggests the following in his definition of God's wisdom:

---

7. *NIV Bible Dictionary*, s.v. "wisdom."
8. Buswell, *Systematic Theology*, 57.

> God's wisdom is based upon his intellect, knowledge, goodness and perfection. God is all-knowing (omniscient). God possesses (without prior discovery of facts) complete and universal knowledge of all things past, present, and future. This includes not only the actual, but also the possible. This total and immediate knowledge is based on his eternity (he has always, and will always exist), and his omnipresence (he has been, is, and will always be everywhere at the same time.[9]

Lightner expanded on this:

> Though closely related, knowledge and wisdom are not the same. Nor do they always accompany each other. No doubt we have all known those who had acquired a great deal of facts but who lacked the ability to use them wisely. Both knowledge and wisdom are imperfect in man but perfect in God. Only He knows how to use His infinite knowledge to the best possible end. Through His wisdom God applies His knowledge to the fulfilment of His own purposes in ways which will bring the most glory to Him.[10]

We can be sure that "God's wisdom means that God always chooses the best goals and the best means to those goals."[11] God who possesses untaught knowledge must be complete in wisdom. Just as his knowledge is untaught and unlearned, God's wisdom is also untaught and unlearned (Isa 40:13–14).

Jesus Christ is revealed as both God's Word and God's Wisdom. He is therefore the model and the example of God's revealed Word and Wisdom. As Paul said: "He is the source of your life in Christ Jesus, whom God made our wisdom and our righteousness and sanctification and redemption" (1 Cor 1:30 RSV).

What Is the Law of Wisdom?

From God's attribute of wisdom, God established the law of wisdom as a norm to guide the use of our intellect, knowledge and facts. He inserted principles of wisdom, understanding, discernment, prudence, and intelligence into his created order. It is not what or how much one knows, but how wise and

---

9. Willmington, *Willmington's Guide to the Bible*, 598.
10. Lightner as cited in Willmington, 599.
11. Grudem, *Systematic Theology*, 193.

understanding one is. The wisdom of God and his understanding must be our example, model, and pattern for life.

True wisdom comes from God alone. Reliance upon human wisdom or knowledge will lead only to folly and ruin. "Trust in the Lord with all your heart and lean not on your own understanding; in all your ways submit to him, and he will make your paths straight" (Prov 3:5–6 NIV).

This lesson becomes clear when we read the third chapter of Genesis. Satan tempted Eve and Adam with wisdom and knowledge: "For God knows that when you eat from it your eyes will be opened, and you will be like God, knowing good and evil" (Gen 3:5). The Bible states that "When the woman saw that the fruit of the tree was good for food and pleasing to the eye, and also desirable for gaining wisdom, she took some and ate it" (Gen 3:6). But the knowledge of good and evil that the Tempter offered was not of God. After eating the fruit, Adam and Eve did gain wisdom and knowledge of good and evil, but this was not God's wisdom. Such counterfeit wisdom and knowledge is the root of human rebellion, disobedience, self and pride. It leads to selfishness, self-centeredness, self-seeking, and pride.

The Problem of Evil

Both traditional religion and Christianity note God's tolerance in allowing sin and evil into his world, but they come up with different solutions to the problem this creates. To traditional Africans it seems as if God is not powerful enough to contain evil and its perpetrators and they seek to address wrong-doing, evil, affliction, and especially witchcraft through rituals, blood sacrifices, and offerings. Christians, on the other hand, believe that the doctrine of redemption reveals God's way of dealing with the problem of Satan, evil and sin.

The traditional African's lack of understanding of redemption and of God as Redeemer means that they personify evil in fatalism, believing that "events are fixed in advance for all time in such a manner that humans are powerless to change them."[12] Fatalism is the root of one's destiny and one is hopeless; nothing can be done to change things.

African children soon learn that God is not always trustworthy. Whenever calamity strikes, for instance in the death of a young man, the mourning mothers complain bitterly and angrily because God is treacherous and has not been merciful, kind or protective. They sing mourning songs to God and to other spirit beings, bewailing the death. If we lack a clear concept of God

---

12. *Webster's New Collegiate Dictionary*, s.v. "fatalism."

and his holiness and goodness, we may wrongly assume they are right to do so. During times of tragedy or of the death of a loved one, many have accused God of not being loving or caring. Neither Job, nor his four friends, could reconcile his innocence with his suffering. In their crude theology, they believed that only the wicked suffered and that the righteous should never suffer. This reveals a wrong view of God and evil because God is being defined in terms of human circumstances.

Much of the research into human religions and cultures, including research into the African Traditional Religion, has defined God in these terms. When this occurs, scholars end up further removed from God than when they started. Sadly even some African Christian theologians have become remote from God, Christ, the Holy Spirit and Christianity as a result of their studies in African Traditional Religion and cultures.

What, Then, Is Evil?

Evil is the principle that negates goodness. It is not in harmony with the divine order. It is a mystery in the use of freedom when it posits itself against all God's goodness. When God completed his work of creation, he pronounced it good. Evil devastated and ruined creation and life so evil cannot be the work of God. It was never part of God's original creation.

Langdon Gilkey puts it like this:

> By evil we mean that which thwarts continuously and seriously the potential goodness of creation, destroying alike its intelligibility and meaning and making life as we experience it so threatening, so full of sorrow, suffering and apparent pointlessness.[13]

St Augustine said, "Evil is not a substance; it is the perversion of a nature that is essentially good."[14] Evil then is seen as an intruder, a perversion, a distortion and not an essential or necessary part of God's creation. Originally creation was good without any trace of evil anywhere.

What Is the Origin of Evil?

African religious thought concerning the origin of evil and sin is somewhat similar to that of the Bible. It is thought that God did his work of creation and

---

13. Gilkey, *Maker of Heaven*, 209–210.
14. St Augustine cited in Gilkey, 49.

created some powerful lesser beings or gods. These became powerful and rebelled against him. Some did not follow God's instructions to the letter and consequently brought evil with its devastating consequences for humankind and creation into being. Some of the lesser gods then became the embodiment of evil and spread it in the world.

How Did Evil Enter the Good Creation?

We must understand this from the context of God's universal physical and moral laws. The appearance of evil reflects the presence of an opposite law that is contrary to God's law of goodness. Evil is rooted in moral perversion or disobedience or lack of conformity to God's moral norms.

In the beginning, God created the universe and instituted his universal physical laws (creation laws) to ensure the well-being of the universe. Evil arose with the rebellion of Satan against God his maker (Isa 14; Ezek 28). Through the serpent, Satan deceived Adam and Eve causing them to disobey God and to fall into sin although God had forewarned them (Gen 2:15–17) about the consequence of disobedience to his law. Their disobedience had universal implications for humanity and the entire creation as God pronounced both moral and physical punishment upon them (Gen 3). The physically good garden of Eden was cursed and thus, consequently, the entire creation.

The outcome of evil has devastating consequences for both the physical and moral realms because the law of evil and fate works against the universal physical laws. This means that when a natural evil like an earthquake occurs, it goes against the universal physical laws and causes devastation. Natural evil and fate are rooted therefore in the fall and are the consequence of humankind's sin.

Gilkey summed this up: "Evil is not an essential or necessary character of our existence, but [is] an 'intruder' into a world that is by nature good."[15] Christians regard "evil as a perversion rather than a necessity of our existence."[16] "Evil could arise only when these good things were misused, distorted, and perverted."[17]

The fact that God permitted evil must be understood within the context of freedom of choice. God endowed his creatures with freedom or freedom of choice, but evil used the free will of God's creatures to ensure an evil choice from that which was originally created good.

---

15. Gilkey, 121.
16. Gilkey, 215.
17. Gilkey, 218.

Evil, then, is a mystery associated with the moral choice or free will of all free moral agents (beings). As long as free moral agents choose the good in line with the eternal goodness or perfection of God, only what is good will result. A sinful choice always produces devastating consequences in both the physical realm of creation and in the moral life of the creatures. As a result of the fall, human beings are faced with the problems of evil, fate, sin, death, sorrow, and suffering.

Why, Then, Did God Create Some Creatures with Free Will?

God chose to create them that way in accordance with the counsel and good pleasure of his will. God created them that way to glorify his name. We humans cannot advise God on how he should do his work of creation. God who is all-knowing and infinite in wisdom knows better than we, his mere creatures, do. According to Gilkey:

> Freedom was the capability of man to turn from God to himself, to make his own pleasure and security rather than obedience to God his ultimate end, and so to come to hate his neighbor rather than to love him. Because of freedom, the essential goodness of creaturely life has a possibility of becoming evil. In good creation, however, it was seen that evil could arise only from human freedom.[18]

Gilkey continues: The seat of evil "is in freedom rather than essential structure, evil is historical rather than ontological in character."[19] Evil as "intruder," "perversion," and "aberration" rather than an essential part of creation make the "biblical presentation of weakness, suffering, and death as the results, not of our created finitude, but solely of the Fall."[20]

Why Does God not Eradicate Evil Once for All?

Theologians and philosophers are often puzzled by the presence and dominance of evil. Evil presents itself as a mystery defying human understanding. They see structural evil embedded within creation and its enduring power and dominance in the affairs of human beings throughout history and this raises serious questions about the goodness of God and his omnipotence for them.

---

18. Gilkey, 218–219.
19. Gilkey, 220.
20. Gilkey, 221.

Evil has been permitted by God in order that his justice might be manifested in its punishment and his grace in its forgiveness (Rom 9:22–23). Because evil is "a perversion of nature rather than a part of its essence, evil can be removed."[21]

God as eternal wisdom knows what to do with evil which he did not create. God's wisdom in dealing with both evil and sin is the solution through the cross of Christ, his work of redemption and salvation. Paul has this to say about the wisdom in the cross of Christ:

> For the message of the cross is foolishness to those who are perishing, but to us who are being saved it is the power of God. For it is written: "I will destroy the wisdom of the wise; the intelligence of the intelligent I will frustrate." Where is the wise person? Where is the teacher of the law? Where is the philosopher of this age? Has not God made foolish the wisdom of the world? For, since in the wisdom of God the world through its wisdom did not know him, God was pleased through the foolishness of what was preached to save those who believe. Jews demand signs and Greeks look for wisdom, but we preach Christ crucified: a stumbling block to Jews and foolishness to Gentiles, but to those whom God has called, both Jews and Greeks, Christ the power of God and the wisdom of God. For the foolishness of God is wiser than human wisdom, and the weakness of God is stronger than human strength. (1 Cor 1:18–25)

The gospel of Jesus Christ is the message of hope: God has overcome evil and fate and has dealt with them decisively on the cross of Christ. God has dealt a death blow to the law of sin, fate, and evil.

However, salvation and redemption through the cross of Jesus Christ looks foolish to many people who trust in the wisdom and the activities of spirit powers and supernatural powers. The people who are involved in these activities are pragmatists. They see the results which spirit-powers produce, and ignore the adverse consequences that follow.

Africans need to call each other to a biblical perspective on life whereby every action in families, business, education, politics, and community relations is viewed in the light of God's standard of perfect morality.

---

21. Gilkey, 221.

26

Engaging with the Traditional Belief in Gods and Divinities

The whole array of traditional practices reflecting the belief in many divinities and gods has been outlined already, as has the impact and influence of this belief. African Traditional Religion and Christianity differ fundamentally in this area.

In traditional religion, the Supreme Being is believed to be greater than the lesser beings, gods or divinities. Africans can look into their traditional theology and establish the place of each god in the theological pantheon and hierarchy of beings. This is a form of polytheism in which the Supreme Being tolerates and accommodates other gods or divinities and all their accompanying religious practices. Because gods or divinities are limited in terms of status, power, and territory it is necessary to have a plurality of gods or divinities who can complement and augment each other in meeting humankind's needs. Most traditional theology, worship, religious beliefs, rituals, practices, and ceremonies have to do with the lesser beings and not with the Supreme Being. The lesser gods have become a substitute for the Supreme Being, although he is supposed to be at the centre-stage of traditional African life and worship.

The Bible believes in the centrality of God and vehemently opposes any belief in many gods or divinities. As has already been indicated, it labels all worship of other gods as idolatry:

> For great is the LORD and most worthy of praise; he is to be feared above all gods. For all the gods of the nations are idols, but the LORD made the heavens. (Ps 96:4–5)
>
> I am the LORD and there is no other; apart from me there is no God. (Isa 45:5)

Christian ideas about the Trinity (Jesus Christ as God the Son, the Holy Spirit as the Spirit of God and God as God the Father) are, however, often understood or interpreted in terms of the traditional theological belief in the plurality of divinities and gods. Theological engagement and discourse must take place at this point.

The Hierarchy of Gods and Divinities

African divinities or gods are held to be "co-equal" in some respects, while in other respects they are part of a hierarchy of status or power. The concept of equality among gods or divinities allows for plurality, and consequently for accommodation, toleration, adaptation, and domestication of some divinities or gods. At the same time, the concept of a hierarchy of gods or divinities allows them to be treated according to their rank, status, territoriality, influence, or power. This means that the most powerful gods or divinities dominate and influence society more than the weaker ones do. Because no single god has a monopoly on spirit-power, people search out the most potent gods, approaching as many as are available to meet their needs.

African Divinities and Gods as Intermediaries

The all-powerful Christian triune God, on the other hand, rules without any intermediaries, mediators, or lesser gods or divinities.

Because of the hierarchy of spirit beings, traditional belief allows divinities and gods to be designated as intermediaries or mediators. This means that, as has already been discussed, some scholars have argued that traditional religion is not polytheistic or idolatrous. It has been suggested that their divinities are only God's intermediaries or channels of communication with God. We need to examine this concept further in the light of the fact that African Traditional Religion falls under general revelation and creation theology, while Christianity falls under special revelation and redemption theology.

First of all, the term "intermediary" needs to be defined. An intermediary is "a mediator; a go-between; a person who acts as a means of communication between two other persons, groups of people, etc., especially in order to bring them into agreement."[1] In some ways, he is an "umpire." In this sense, African divinities serve as the "go-betweens" or as channels of communication between the Supreme Being and the Africans.

---

1. Watkins, *Complete Christian Dictionary*, s.v. "intermediary."

Since African Traditional Religion is like the heathen religions described in the Bible, let us examine the use of the terms "mediator" and "intermediary" in its pages:

> In the Bible both priests and prophets were mediators in different ways. The priest acted on behalf of the people in the presence of God (Heb 5:1ff). They represented the people before God. The prophet acted for God in the presence of the people (Deut 18:18ff), delivering his messages to them.[2]

From this definition we can deduce that, while the prophet Moses was the greatest mediator between God and the people of Israel in the Old Testament, Jesus Christ is the greatest Mediator between God and humankind in the New Testament (1 Tim 2:5).

In African religious thought, however, the term "intermediary" has to be applied differently. The traditional belief in the Supreme Being does not draw a definite distinction between him and the lesser divinities in terms of worship, rituals, sacrifices, or ceremonies. A traditional worldview is dominated by philosophical ideas such as holism, spiritualism, dynamism, and communalism. These views do not allow for theological distinctions or for God's holiness or transcendence. Therefore the biblical theology of the holiness and transcendence of God is absent from the traditional religious worldview, beliefs, and practices. Some theologians and scholars would argue therefore that traditional spirit beings are not mediatory in a biblical sense. They explain that a divinity is one who is in the position to receive gifts, prayers, offerings and sacrifices, and even reverence and worship. When these are offered, the divinity is not regarded as a mediator or intermediary. Instead they are seen in terms of their positions, rank, or status and stand as surrogate gods or substitutes for the Supreme Being who appears to be remote or distant.

We must remember that the primary religious orientation of traditional Africans is not towards the spirit world, but towards the kinship community. Traditional Africans only turn to the cosmic spirit beings to search for powers and life force in order to improve their life in kinship community. The ancestors who give meaning to life and to the community are not outside of the community, but are bona fide members of the kinship community. Even the gods and divinities come down to dwell in the human community, participating in the eating and drinking and dancing with the humans. The

---

2. *New Concise Bible Dictionary*, 344–345.

secret of immortality lies in the interdependence between the ancestors and the living. Salvation is not found outside the kinship community, but within.

So when ancestors stand as intermediaries, it does not have the same meaning as Christ's mediation, Mosaic mediation or prophetic mediation. In traditional religion mediation is merely the respect that traditional Africans give to their elders and to people of high social status. It does not carry any salvific meaning as in the New Testament. It is used strictly in the traditional African sense of the spiritual economy of all spirit beings: help can be solicited from any spirit being that could help bring the good or the needed help.

An African may therefore approach the pantheon of ancestors and request them to take his prayers to his own ancestor, not to God. In this case, an ancestor is taking the place of God as he is offered prayers, although the distinction between God and an ancestor may not be clear. The ancestor may even be playing a double role, as intermediary and as god. As a young African, I heard some adults soliciting the help of their father or grandfather, who was now a living-dead, through the pantheon of ancestors. My own understanding is that it may be too much of a generalization to say that ancestors are intermediaries between God and people. However, more will be said about this later.

Thus it is clear that the gods and divinities assume a role and position as a result of their function of meeting the needs of life, and not necessarily in terms of being agents to be worshipped. While there are rituals and ceremonies that are indeed spiritual activities and can take the form of worship, observation suggests that most traditional activities involving divinities, gods, or spirit beings do not fit with the Christian concept of worship, but are rather solicitations or petitions. The goal is not God as the object of worship, but pursuit of life force or the good life. If worship means anything, it is not about those who are out there, but about the active and meaningful life of the community.

The spirit beings and spiritual powers or forces are not worshipped. The emphasis falls on communication. Traditional Africans have elaborate means of communicating with and of receiving communications from the spirit world. They also have elaborate means of acquiring and exercising powers from the mystical powers and spirit beings. But only ancestors may qualify to act as intermediaries for the traditional kinship community, not spirit beings.

The Christian doctrine of the trinity provides the best theological answer to the traditional concept of "intermediaries." Christian mediation takes place within the Godhead. The one who is the mediator is within the Godhead. The one who receives worship is within the Godhead. All other mediation is useless.

The Bible is quite clear about who qualifies to be a mediator: "For there is one God and one Mediator between God and mankind, the man Christ Jesus"

(1 Tim 2:5); "Salvation is in no one else, for there is no other name under heaven given to mankind by which we must be saved" (Acts 4:12); "Therefore God exalted him to the highest place and gave him the name that is above every name, that at the name of Jesus every knee should bow, in heaven and on earth and under the earth and every tongue acknowledge that Jesus Christ is Lord, to the glory of God the Father" (Phil 2:9–11).

27

Engaging with the Traditional Belief in Ancestors

There is a general agreement among scholars that African ancestors are revered, rather than worshipped as divinities. There is also general agreement among scholars that ancestors play the role of being intermediaries in the community.

It is clear that ancestral roots and lineage are very important to traditional Africa as they were to the Jews in the Bible. The Old Testament tells the story of God's dealings with one family called out of all humankind to be the avenue through which God would redeem humanity. God established a special relationship with this family, formalizing the relationship in the great Old Testament covenants. Membership in the covenant community, therefore, was a matter of physical descent from the family founders – Abraham, Isaac, and Jacob. The identity of the individual, and his claim to a special relationship with God, rested on ancestry.

> Genealogies, therefore, were essential. They alone could guarantee the right of Jewish individuals and families to membership in the community and in relationship with God.[1]
>
> It is clear, then, that ancestry is a basic and absolutely essential aspect of OT faith and life. God is the "God of Abraham, of Isaac, and of Jacob." Relationship of the OT believer to God was mediated by physical descent from these ancestors.[2]

However, the biblical understanding of the function of ancestors is different from that of traditional Africa. Traditional Africa battles to draw

---

1. *New International Encyclopedia of Bible Words*, s.v. "ancestors."
2. *New International Encyclopedia of Bible Words*, s.v. "ancestors."

a definite line of distinction between the religious and social practices, the rituals and ceremonies associated with the ancestors, and those associated with the worship of divinities or the Supreme Being. The difficulty arises from the African holistic and communal view of many gods or divinities and spirit beings.

What makes things more difficult is the fact that there are certain religious and social beliefs and practices associated with the ancestors that are condemned in the Bible. It is important to examine African beliefs and practices in the light of the Scriptures to see which ones are condemned and which can be upheld.

There are two aspects to the traditional belief concerning the ancestors.

First, the dead must be remembered through their names (memorial of the dead). As a result their descendants do many things in order to keep alive the memory of the dead. Some of these actions involve specific rites and rituals.

The second belief is that the spirits of the dead ancestors live on as ancestral spirits. There are also rites and rituals relating to these spirits of the dead. These include prayers or invocations to the ancestors or through the ancestors; food or drink offerings and sacrifices and libations to the ancestors; and communication with and by the spirits of the dead.

While ancestors can be remembered in memory by name through a memorial that does not take the place of Christ and that is not idolatrous,[3] the practices listed above are idolatrous and contrary to the teachings of the Bible. When the ancestors function as intermediaries in that they receive prayers, libations and invocations, then the ancestors are taking the place of Christ who is the only mediator, between God and men (1 Tim 2:5). Jesus Christ is the only one who can receive prayers.

If the ancestors are seen as having become spirits, then dealing with them falls under the condemnation of interacting with "familiar spirits." All beliefs and practices that seek to placate the spirits of the dead through elaborate burial ceremonies, prayers, offerings and sacrifices to the dead ancestors for help and protection, and speaking to or calling up the dead, are condemned in the Bible (Exod 22:18; Deut 18:9–12, 14; 1 Sam 28:3, 9–14).

Ancestors and Abrahamic Faith

There has been much debate among African theologians about how to relate the role and place of ancestors in traditional religion with Christianity. Some

---

[3]. Gehman, *African Traditional Religion*.

scholars have suggested that the ancestors be given some christological definition, in other words comparing the role of Christ to the intermediary role of the ancestors.[4] If that is accepted, then Christ could be called our ancestor.[5]

Bediako proposed that, through Christ, African believers become the "children of Abraham" and the inheritors of all the Old Testament promises and Jewish ancestors. In his opinion, this opens a scriptural way for African Christians to access the Old Testament: the African Christian gains Jewish ancestors first through Christ and then through the Abrahamic promise. As a result, African Christians stand in solidarity with the Old Testament ancestors. Similarly, through Christ, African Christians stand in solidarity with their African ancestors.

All other African theologians and scholars who have proposed ancestral Christology (such as Harry Sawyerr, John Pobee and Charles Nyamiti), have also based their analysis upon the concept of identity. Jesus was simply identified as an ancestor and his role and function as a mediator was seen as similar to those of the African ancestors. These proposals are the result of comparative or descriptive methods and, for this reason, the theological significance of this conclusion has been missed.

We need to examine the idea that we can equate ancestors with Old Testament and Christian saints. The spiritual link between the New and the Old Testament is fundamentally covenantal, as it spelled out the essential relationship between God and his covenant nation, Israel.

Abraham had two kinds of children, by the flesh and by faith. "Membership in the family of Abraham did not guarantee an individual a personal relationship with God. That was won by faith and was demonstrated in obedience to the Mosaic law."[6] As a result, not all Old Testament ancestors qualify as saints in terms of Hebrews 11. Those without faith cannot be included. The "Abrahamic Faith" is rooted and grounded eschatologically in the cross of Christ (Rom 4; Heb 11). Failure to adhere to Abraham's beliefs automatically excluded those ancestors from finding their fulfilment in Christ Jesus. The old "Abrahamic faith" is fulfilled in Christ, in accordance with Scripture (Rom 1; 1 Cor 15). Those who believe in Jesus the Messiah are linked to Abraham, not by biology, but by faith as Paul argues in Romans 4 and Galatians 3.

Given this biblical understanding, the question arises as to whether it is theologically appropriate for the African believer in Christ to bring his

---

4. Nyamiti, *Jesus Christ, the Ancestor of Humankind*.
5. Bediako, *Christianity in Africa*.
6. *New International Encyclopedia of Bible Words*, s.v. "ancestors."

ancestors into the "communion of saints" or to join them to the chain of Old Testament saints or ancestors? Can this be done "biologically" and not by faith or "according to Scripture?"

African ancestors, who had an Abrahamic Faith, are indeed children of Abraham. The basis of righteousness with God is still the same. Such ancestors are joint heirs with Abraham and with the saints of the Old and New Testament, even though they had never heard of the covenant and the law and the cross. They did not have to wait until their offspring became Christians before they could be counted as such. They are brought in, not as a result of their biological birth, but as a result of their spiritual birth into faith which pointed to the coming redemption of Christ (Acts 10:34–35; Rom 2:11–16). God alone can judge the worthiness of their faith; it has to be approved and accredited by God himself.

But if the theological assumption is that by virtue of their being the biological ancestors of African Christians, they automatically qualify to become Christian saints without any prior Abrahamic Faith, then we need to examine this teaching. They cannot become a community of saints without being part of the covenant people of God, without any messianic prophecies and without Christ. The saints of Hebrews 11 are with Christ in his kingdom because they have demonstrated their active faith. The criterion for becoming a member of the "body of Christ" is strictly applied to the "living," so it cannot be applied partially to the "dead spirits." Even in Israel, not all ancestors qualified and why should it be different in Africa? A communion of saints cannot be formed with "dead spirits" who did not believe in Christ, who had no "Abrahamic Faith" and who, consequently, had made no covenant with Christ. Without any Abrahamic faith and without Christ, there are no grounds by which African ancestors can become Christian saints.

Furthermore the induction of African ancestors into the Christian communion of saints violates the traditional religious beliefs and practices.

Ancestors and Christology

One must also take issue with the suggestion of a christological link with the African ancestors.

Charles Nyamiti developed "African Ancestral Christology" on the basis of five areas of comparison: kinship, superhuman sacred status, exemplary behaviour in the human community, mediation, and the right or title to hold regular sacred communication with earthly kin.⁷ He then proceeded to outline similarities and differences between the role and function of African ancestors and those of Jesus Christ. The outcome of his formulation was simply to Christianize the African concept of the ancestor.

There is nothing wrong with comparing the role and function of Jesus Christ with that of ancestors. The strength of Nyamiti's theological analysis lies in the way his comparative and descriptive approach delineated the roles and functions of both the African ancestors and Jesus Christ. Nyamiti designated God as an Ancestor and suggested that Jesus became an Ancestor on account of his role as a son.

However, the fact that Jesus Christ does what the ancestors did or even the fact that they had similar roles and functions does not mean this qualifies as Christology. Some scholars have no idea what is meant theologically by this term. They take Christology simply to mean the role and functions of Christ or what Jesus could do. They have a certain picture of Jesus: as a healer, as a warrior, or as an ancestor. But giving names to Jesus because of what people assume does not qualify as Christology; describing Jesus in terms of Africans conceptions does not qualify as Christology. For an attribute to qualify as having christological value, it must be rooted in an eschatological expectation based upon a prophecy, looking forward to its fulfilment in Jesus Christ in accordance with God's covenant promises and prophecies to the ancestors or fathers.

There are also some important biblical concepts that need to be defined in relationship to Christology. Let us use the description in the book of Hebrews where Melchizedek, the king of Salem, is presented as a type of Christ. As High Priest, Melchizedek took tithes from Abraham (Gen 14:17–20) and played the mediatory role of High Priest (Heb 7).

A "priest" is "one who offers sacrifice and has the charge of things pertaining thereto."⁸ The high (chief) priest represents the whole people before God. In the Old Testament, a priest had to be a son of the family of Aaron and had to be without physical blemish. Both the Aaronic and Melchizedek priesthood pointed to the priesthood of Christ.

The life, death, resurrection, and ascension of Jesus, therefore, signified the end of the old priestly structures. In the book of Hebrews, Christ is presented as the High Priest (4:15; 5:5, 10; 6:20; 7:26; 8:1, 3; 9:11) according to the order of Melchizedek (5:10; 6:20; 7). "One of the great objectives of this Epistle is

---

7. Nyamiti, *Jesus Christ, the Ancestor of Humankind.*
8. Vine, *Expository Dictionary*, 210.

to set forth the superiority of Christ's High Priesthood as being of an order different from and higher than the Aaronic, in that he is the Son of God, with a priesthood of Melchizedek order."[9] The writer to the Hebrews is therefore reminding us that Jesus is the new and true High Priest who alone can take away sin (Heb 5:5–10) because his priesthood attains the perfection the old one failed to reach (Heb 7) and will continue for all eternity (Heb 8). In Christ all Christians, not just the priestly order, have full and regular access to God (Heb 10:11–25).[10] In other words, Christ took the priestly role and fulfilled the covenant with Israel, according to the Scriptures. Jesus Christ came physically in the body and fulfilled the prophecy. We can see beyond the symbols of the body and cross of Christ to grasp their true spiritual meaning: ultimate redemption and salvation for humankind.

Jesus came as the Christ, the Anointed One. He was the one to whom the Old Testament referred, the anointed one who would come as saviour and redeemer. At this stage we must define "Christology" which is derived from the Greek word *chrio* which means "anointed." This word is linked with two offices, king and high priest. "It was prophesied that Jesus, from David's kingly line, would one day hold ultimate authority in our world. As high priest, Jesus offered himself up for us and lives today to make intercession for us."[11] The Christ that was to come "was thought of as Israel's deliverer. God's Anointed would redeem Israel, rule as king over the restored kingdom, and answer all mankind's questions about God's plans and purposes. And this Redeemer would be the very Son of the Blessed One."[12]

The concept of the Anointed One is rooted in God's covenant promise and prophecy to the Jewish ancestors, the patriarchs. They looked forward with expectation to the coming of the Anointed One. The Old Testament is full of types or symbols that point to his coming. These earthly representations are not only physically fulfilled by Christ's coming, they also express the eschatological spiritual reality of the work of Christ as Saviour and Redeemer. So, for example, the tabernacle and Old Testament sacrifices are physical, but prophetically they point to their fulfillment in Jesus Christ.

The promised Anointed One, the Messiah or the Christ, was expected to come and fulfill three important messianic offices: King, Priest, and Prophet.

---

9. Vine, 211.
10. *New Concise Bible Dictionary*.
11. *New International Encyclopedia of Bible Words*, s.v. "Christ."
12. *New International Encyclopedia of Bible Words*, s.v. "Christ."

This fulfilment has eternal consequences for all humankind. Christology in its biblical meaning and sense is therefore an eschatological expectation, a looking forward to the coming and the fulfillment of expectations, the promises and the prophecies concerning the Anointed One.

The New Testament revealed in a special way God's truth in Christ that had been previously hidden (Eph 3:1–12). In Christ, God's eternal plans, purposes, and love are shown with unmistakable clarity. Every aspect of God's eternal plan is brought into focus in Christ. He is the central figure, the focus of history, the climax of the sacred drama, the one through whom all things are at last explained (Col 1:15–20).

It is therefore theologically and christologically wrong to look back through history and to suggest that Jesus should be regarded merely a patriarch or ancestor. He did not come to fulfil the "ancestorship" of Abraham, Isaac, or Jacob, but to fulfil God's promises and prophecies that had been given to them. The patriarchs and their descendants looked forward eschatologically and christologically to the coming of the Messiah or Christ with all his christological attributes of king, prophet and priest.

Where is the christological link for the African ancestors? Is it based on the fact that grandchildren have embraced Christ? If it is, then the basis of this Christology is biological and kinship affinity. Scripture, however, makes it clear that flesh and blood cannot inherit the kingdom of God (1 Cor 15:50).

The Fatherhood of Ancestors

The ancestors were known more by their attribute of fatherhood rather than through their mediation. For instance, in the traditional religion of the Gong people in central Nigeria, the name for the ancestors is *Bogha* which simply means "the fathers." They held a kind of initiation during which the initiates were introduced to Gha (the Father). Seeing Gha was the highest pride of an initiate so the question, "Have you seen Gha?" suggested the highest form of knowledge and identity that one could ever reach.

Ancestors play the role of fathers in an African community. They are indeed called "the fathers" or "forefathers." In this role, their fatherhood relates to God, just as the patriarchs (ancestors) of Israel knew God as their father. God had revealed himself as the God of the patriarchs or ancestors, Abraham, Isaac, and Jacob. His fatherhood was not hidden, nor did it have to wait for Christ to be revealed at some time in the future. The suggestion that one should see Jesus in the light of the ancestors and impute to him the attributes of fatherhood is to strip him of the christological attribute of Sonship. The Father made a promise to the fathers or patriarchs of a Son who would come as King, Priest, and Prophet, as well as Saviour, Redeemer, and Lord. The patriarchs or ancestors were expecting this Messiah or Christ.

Fatherhood or "ancestorship" is not an eschatological promise or prophecy that was awaiting fulfilment in Jesus Christ. The ancestors had already earned the title as fathers on account of their faith in God. It was on the basis of this faith that God made a covenant with them and gave an eschatological and christological hope.

Christ does not look backwards, desiring to be like the ancestors! Looking back would empty the promise of the Son of its eschatological and christological prophecy and meaning.

Ancestors as Priests

In the Old Testament, after the period of the patriarchs and under Mosaic law, the religious institution of the priesthood carried the role of mediator. No dead ancestor in Israel was ever accorded any role as a mediator, not even a patriarch. The patriarchs or the ancestors in Israel did not stand between God and the people. The patriarchs were highly respected, but they were not treated as Africans treat their ancestors.

In most African situations, the ancestors were the recipients of prayers, sacrifices, and offerings from their children, the living. Some theologians believe that the ancestors acted at times as the messengers of the living in that they received the offerings from the African priests or the living and then passed on whatever they had received to the gods and divinities or the Supreme Being. Even if this aspect did exist in traditional religion, there was another practice: the ancestors were also revered or worshipped in themselves.

It is worth noting that in traditional Africa, Africans do not look for salvation or immortality, but for mystical and spiritual powers and forces that can be used to enhance the well-being of the community of the living and the ancestors. In the strange world of the spirits and cosmic powers, if there was any mediator role for the ancestors, it was for the well-being of the living in their community.

The traditional cult of ancestors demands that anyone who wants to belong must be initiated through rite and ritual. Membership is not automatic. It is based upon a covenant and blood relationship. Similarly, Christianity is based upon a new covenant with Christ. It too is not automatic; a covenant has to be made. A traditional African has to break his covenant with the cult of ancestors in order to become a Christian and a follower of Christ (2 Cor 6:14–18). This severing of the links suggests that it is impossible for African ancestors who belonged to the cult of ancestors to become members of the body of Christ. Spiritually and biologically, they do not qualify in the light of covenant theology and Christology. Even on traditional grounds, they could not become members of Christ. Their covenant makes that impossible.

What is more, it is the children of African communities, the new descendants, that are inducted into communion with their ancestors through rites of passage and covenants. Ancestors are never inducted into the communion of the living. Their presence is recognized and invoked through rites and rituals. It is the memory of the ancestors that should be emphasized. They can be remembered for who they were. It is not necessary to invoke their spirits into communion with the Christian saints through prayers, libations, offerings, and sacrifices.

The traditional theological issues of the intermediaries, mediators, ancestors, gods and divinities can be addressed by a Christian theology of trinity, a theology of covenant, a theology of worship and a theology of redemption. The dominant role and function of ancestors in traditional religion requires that we examine the theology of the intermediary or mediator role of Jesus Christ. We need to establish the full christological meaning of the work of Jesus Christ as the mediator between God and mankind.

Ancestors and Jesus Christ

To the Gentiles Jesus was introduced as the Son of the God who had created the heavens and the earth and the God of our ancestors (Acts 17:16–31). Since all ancestors know the one who is the Creator of heaven and earth, the apostles were careful to show his link with Jesus Christ. The God whom the ancestors call the Creator is indeed the Father of the Lord Jesus Christ. Therefore, while the patriarchs of the Israelites were given the christological promise and prophecy about Jesus Christ, the ancestors of the Gentiles were given God's grace through the cross of Jesus Christ. This is how the apostle Paul describes the plan of God for the Gentiles:

> Therefore, remember that formerly you who are Gentiles by birth and called "uncircumcised" by those who call themselves "the circumcision" (which is done in the body by human hands) – remember that at that time you were separate from Christ,

excluded from citizenship in Israel and foreigners to the covenants of the promise, without hope and without God in the world. But now in Christ Jesus you who once were far away have been brought near by the blood of Christ. (Eph 2:11–13)

The Gentiles did not come through the Mosaic law, but by grace through the cross. The apostle Paul describes how:

> For he himself is our peace, who has made the two groups one and has destroyed the barrier, the dividing wall of hostility, by setting aside in his flesh the law with its commands and regulations. His purpose was to create in himself one new humanity out of the two, thus making peace, and in this one body to reconcile both of them to God through the cross, by which he put to death their hostility. He came and preached peace to you who were far away and peace to those who were near. For through him we both have access to the Father by one Spirit. Consequently, you are no longer foreigners and strangers, but fellow citizens with God's people and also members of his household, built on the foundation of the apostles and prophets, with Christ Jesus himself as the chief cornerstone. (Eph 2:14–20)

If the patriarchs of Israel sat in wait for the coming Christ, they could not theologically assume the attributes of that Christ. They themselves stood in need of Christ through the Abrahamic covenant. In like manner, the African ancestors stood in need of Christ through grace in the cross of Christ.

28

The Mediator: Jesus the Messiah

We live in a world where there are many prophets and gods who make wild claims about being intermediaries or mediators between God and man. The primary objective of this chapter is to contrast these claims with the biblical, prophetic, apostolic, and the historical record of the work of Jesus the Messiah. Christ's mediatorial and redemptive work on the cross challenges all such beliefs and practices, just as it did in Judaism. Christ is the answer to all the intermediaries that play a part in African Traditional Religion.

A mediator is one who stands between God and man in order to reconcile them. A mediator acts "as an intermediary agent in bringing, effecting, or communicating" between God and man.[1] The primary task of a mediator is that of reconciliation.

Our African ancestors, just like the Jewish patriarchs, awaited the coming Messiah (Christ). Jesus Christ could not be the same as the ancestors otherwise his coming to them would have lacked any messianic value. All human beings who live under the jurisdiction of general revelation and creation theology lack God's special revelation in Jesus Christ. Their ancestors, therefore, stand eschatologically in need of the christological benefits of salvation and redemption.

Although African ancestors were not party to the messianic promises and prophecies made to the Jews, they too could receive Christ as their Mediator, Saviour and Lord. Clearly, a person who needs a mediator cannot be that mediator. Jesus Christ is not offering himself to them as their equal.

Another reason why we cannot compare the role and function of an ancestor with that of christological mediation is that there is no ultimate sacrifice of the mediator. Without this, there can be no reconciliation. That is why Jesus Christ gave himself for us. His work as mediator and reconciler

---

1. *Webster's Collegiate Dictionary*, s.v. "mediator."

includes sacrifice, propitiation, and redemption. In Mark 10:45, Jesus himself explains: "For even the Son of Man did not come to be served, but to serve, and to give his life as a ransom for many."

The apostle Paul confirms that this is indeed what happened: "For there is one God and one Mediator between God and mankind, the Man Christ Jesus, who gave Himself as ransom for all people. This has now been witnessed to at the proper time" (1 Tim 2:5–6). The writer of the book of Hebrews adds a graphic description of how Jesus the Messiah acted in mercy and reconciliation:

> Since, therefore, the children share flesh and blood, he himself likewise shared the same things, so that through death he might destroy the one who has the power of death, that is, the devil, and free those who all their lives were held in slavery by the fear of death. For it is clear that he did not come to help angels, but the descendants of Abraham. Therefore, he had to become like his brothers and sisters in every respect, so that he might be a merciful and faithful high priest in the service of God, to make a sacrifice of atonement for the sins of the people. Because he himself was tested by what he suffered, he is able to help those who are being tested. (Heb 2:14–18 NRSV)

All this was in fulfilment of the prophecy that Jesus was to be the Suffering Messiah, intent on the work of reconciliation:

> He was despised and rejected by mankind, a man of suffering, and familiar with pain . . . Surely he took up our pain and bore our suffering; yet we considered him punished by God, stricken by him and afflicted. But He was pierced for our transgressions, he was crushed for our iniquities; the punishment that brought us peace was on him, and by his wounds we are healed . . . and the Lord has laid on him the iniquity of us all. He was oppressed and afflicted, yet he did not open his mouth; he was led like a lamb to the slaughter, and as a sheep before its shearers is dumb, so he did not open his mouth . . . for the transgression of my people he was punished . . . yet it was the Lord's will to crush him and cause him to suffer, and though the Lord makes his life an offering for sin, . . . he will see the light of life and be satisfied; by his knowledge my righteous servant will justify many, and he will bear their iniquities . . . because He poured out his life unto death, and was numbered with the transgressors. For he bore the sins of many and made intercession for the transgressors. (Isa 53:3–12)

But none of this would have been of any value if Christ had not been worthy of serving as the mediator between God and man. In his prophetic vision, Daniel conveys his wonder at this:

> In my vision at night I looked, and there before me was one like a son of man, coming with the clouds of heaven! He approached the Ancient of Days and was led into his presence. He was given authority, glory and sovereign power; all nations and peoples of every language worshipped him. His dominion is an everlasting dominion that will not pass away and his kingdom is one that will never be destroyed. (Dan 7:13–14)

Daniel's prophecy is reflected on several occasions in Revelation. Revelation 11:15, for instance, states: "And there were loud voices in heaven, which said: 'The kingdom of the world has become the kingdom of our Lord and of his Messiah and he will reign forever and ever!'" In his interpretation of the prophet, Daniel, John describes Jesus the Messiah as the one who was found to be worthy by God and, on this account, was given the right to mediate between God and man. In dramatic and pictorial language, the apostle John states (Rev 5):

> Then I saw in the right hand of him who sat on the throne a scroll with writing on both sides and sealed with seven seals. And I saw a mighty angel proclaiming in a loud voice, "Who is worthy to break the seals and open the scroll?" But no one in heaven or on earth or under the earth could open the scroll, or even look inside it. I wept and wept because no one was found who was worthy to open the scroll or look inside. Then one of the elders said to me, "Do not weep. See, the Lion of the tribe of Judah, the Root of David, has triumphed. He is able to open the scroll and its seven seals."
>
> Then I saw a Lamb, looking as if it had been slain, standing at the centre of the throne, encircled by the four living creatures and the elders . . . He went and took the scroll from the right hand of him who sat on the throne. And when He had taken it, the four living creatures and the twenty-four elders fell down before the Lamb . . . And they sang a new song, saying: "You are worthy to take the scroll and to open its seals; because you were slain, and with your blood you purchased for God persons from every tribe and language and people and nation. You have made them to be a kingdom and priests to serve our God and they will reign on the earth" . . . "Worthy is the Lamb who was slain to receive power and wealth and wisdom and strength and honor and glory and

praise!" ... "To him who sits on the throne and to the Lamb be praise and honor and glory and power for ever and ever!"

Paul sums up Jesus's attitude in the following passage:

> Have the same mindset as Christ Jesus: Who, being in very nature God, did not consider equality with God something to be used to his own advantage; rather, he made himself nothing by taking the very nature of a servant, being made in human likeness. And being found in appearance as a man, he humbled himself by becoming obedient to death – even death on a cross! Therefore God exalted him to the highest place and gave him the name that is above every name, that at the name of Jesus every knee should bow, in heaven and on earth and under the earth and every tongue acknowledge that Jesus Christ is Lord, to the glory of God the Father. (Phil 2:5–11)

The Holy Scriptures provide many more testimonies that Jesus the Messiah is the only mediator between God and men. There are many more passages that we could quote. The humility of Christ was made effectual on the cross, which was the ultimate sacrifice, and also in the resurrection, which showed the ultimate power of God towards sinful humanity.

Jesus explains that he alone is the mediator between God and humankind when he says: "I am the way, the truth and the life. No one comes to the Father except through me" (John 14:6). Pluralism vehemently rejects this, teaching that there are many paths that lead to God. Yet Scripture proclaims the uniqueness of Jesus the Messiah as the only way to God.

Similarly, other religions also offer eternal life, but there is only one who conquered death and so can offer life to others. Jesus our Lord and Messiah says: "I have come that they may have life and have it to the full" (John 10:10b). He goes on to say: "I am the resurrection and the life. The one who believes in me will live, even though they die; and whoever lives by believing in me will never die" (John 11:25–26).

The New Testament clearly presents Jesus the Messiah as the only Mediator, the only channel and the only means of obtaining God's salvation, life eternal, truth, righteousness, forgiveness of sins, love, and peace (John 3:16, 36; Rom 3:21–26; 5:1–2, 8). He is indeed the mediator between God and humankind. And the signs of his work of mediation and redemption are the cross, the resurrection, the ascension and the promised second coming. This has been attested to by God himself, by his prophets, by his apostles and finally by his Holy Spirit and his church.

29

Engaging with the Traditional Belief in the Supreme Being

The difference between the traditional beliefs in the Supreme Being and the biblical teachings on God lies in the theological content and meaning ascribed to each.

We have already observed that in the hierarchy of beings the Supreme Being (God) stands higher than the lesser beings or divinities; that the Supreme Being is not actively or intimately involved with or concerned about humankind and the world; that humankind seeks out the lesser powers to meet its desires; and that the divinities stand as surrogate gods or substitutes for the Supreme Being. These traditional beliefs make the Supreme Being appear diffuse and indistinguishable from lesser beings. For this reason many Christians in Africa who come from a traditional background do not seem to have a clear understanding of who God is.

The nature and character of God stand in clear contrast to those of the Supreme Being in African Traditional Religion. The Christian God cannot be kept in the background, as is the case with the Supreme Being in traditional religion. Christians are privileged to have a far deeper knowledge of God.

God's Self-Disclosure through Scripture

The fact that Christianity is rooted in special revelation means that God has revealed himself through his powerful word:

> I am the LORD and there is no other; there is no God besides Me. (Isa 45:5 NKJV)

> I am the First and I am the Last; besides Me there is no God. (Isa 44:6 NKJV)

> Before Me there was no God formed, nor shall there be after Me. (Isa 43:10 NKJV)

> Hear, O Israel: The LORD our God, the LORD is one! You shall love the LORD your God with all your heart, with all your soul and with all your strength. (Deut 6:4–5 NKJV)

The Bible is God's special revelation and describes the attributes, nature and character of God. Even before the coming of Jesus Christ, many truths about God had already been revealed to his people.

The book of Genesis describes God as the Creator, sovereign over everything. The relationships between God and nature as well as between God and humankind are well defined. God initiated and made covenants with his chosen people, Israel. He is revealed as the God of Abraham, Isaac, and Jacob, but he is also the God of our African ancestors and of all peoples of the world.

The NIV Study Bible states that Exodus "lays a foundational theology in which God reveals his Name, his attributes, his redemption, his law and how he is to be worshipped."[1] Exodus is rich in the theology of worship, revealing that God is with the Israelites through the physical presence of the tabernacle in their midst, through Moses the prophet, and through Aaron the priest:

> By means of the tabernacle, the omnipotent, unchanging and transcendent God of the universe came to "dwell" or "tabernacle" with his people, thereby revealing his gracious nearness as well. God is not only mighty in Israel's behalf; He is also present in their midst.[2]

There is no parallel in traditional religion where the Supreme Being is remote, and only the lesser divinities and ancestors are part of the kinship community.

Leviticus teaches about the absolute transcendence and holiness of God and demands that "man must revere God in holiness." God, the King and Lord of Israel establishes "his administration over all of Israel's life,"[3] ensuring that holiness and purity become the basis of all aspects of religious life. There is no suggestion that the Supreme Being is transcendent or holy in traditional religious beliefs or practices.

---

1. *NIV Study Bible*, "Introduction to the Book of Exodus."
2. *NIV Study Bible*, 84.
3. *NIV Study Bible*, "Introduction to the Book of Leviticus."

God chose "to establish his kingdom in the Promised Land in the midst of the nations." The book of Numbers "portrays Israel's identity as the Lord's redeemed covenant people and her vocation as the servant people of God, charged with establishing his kingdom on earth."[4] Deuteronomy makes it clear that the relationship between God and Israel is based on his love for his chosen people. This contrasts strongly with the remoteness of the Supreme Being in traditional religion.

The Psalms are full of worship, prayer, and praise for God. Those who worship God do so "in professions of faith and trust."

> At the core of the theology of the Psalter is the conviction that not only the gravitational centre of life (of right human understanding, trust, hope, service, morality, adoration), but also of history and of the whole creation (heaven and earth), is God (Yahweh, "the Lord"). He is the Great King over all, the One to whom all things are subject. He created all things and preserves them; they are the robe of glory with which He has clothed Himself. Because He ordered them, they have a well-defined and "true" identity (no chaos there). Because He maintains them, they are sustained and kept secure from disruption, confusion or annihilation. Because He alone is the sovereign God, they are governed by one hand and held in the service of one divine purpose. Under God creation is a cosmos – orderly and systematic.[5]

---

4. *NIV Study Bible*, 183.
5. *NIV Study Bible*, 776.

30

The Doctrine of God

We have already spent time reminding ourselves that God is above all gods, that he is Sovereign; Eternal; the Eternal Word; the Eternal Spirit; Good and Wise. A loving, gracious God who is willing to forgive, he is nonetheless utterly holy, unique and distinct.

In order to understand the vast difference between the Supreme Being and God, we need to ensure that we have an even clearer picture of his nature and attributes.

God Is Holy

We shall consider this statement in the light of three quotations:

Tozer reminds us that:

> Holy is the way God is. To be holy He does not conform to a standard. He is that standard. He is absolutely holy with an infinite, incomprehensible fullness of purity that is incapable of being other than it is. Because He is holy, all His attributes are holy; that is, whatever we think of as belonging to God must be thought of as holy ... God is holy and He has made holiness the moral condition necessary to the health of His universe ... The holiness of God, the wrath of God, and the health of the creation are inseparably united.[1]

Grudem adds a further dimension: "God's holiness means that he is separated from sin and devoted to seeking his own honor."[2]

---

1. Tozer cited in Willmington, *Willmington's Guide to the Bible*, 601.
2. Grudem, *Systematic Theology*, 201.

Buswell reminds us that, "Holiness is the center and essence of His moral character . . . the ethical character of God. God's holy will expresses his holy character" and it is also "perfectly holy . . . God's holiness is the source of moral standards . . . God is infinite, eternal and unchangeable in His holiness."[3]

We see from these comments that there are two aspects to God's holiness. The first reflects his moral attribute: his perfect goodness, purity and sinlessness. God's holiness hates sin, iniquity and transgression, and his holy anger burns against it. In order to preserve a holy relationship with his creatures, God provided moral, spiritual and ceremonial laws for the Israelites (Exod 10:10–25; 20:1–17, 35–40; Lev 1–7; 11–15; 23).

The second aspect of God's holiness is that God is absolutely different, distinct and separate from all that is created. He is not like any of his creatures and cannot be compared with them. "Who is like you, O LORD, among the gods? Who is like you, majestic in holiness, awesome in glorious deeds, doing wonders?" (Exod 15:11 ESV). "Before me no god was formed, nor shall there be any after me. I, I am the LORD, and besides me there is no saviour" (Isa 43:10–11 ESV). "I am the first and I am the last; besides me there is no god" (Isa 44:6 ESV).

The Hebrew word used for holiness, *qadash*, means to be consecrated, to be dedicated, or to be set apart. When something is declared holy, then it is no longer common, but sacred and must be treated as such. Yet our focus here is not on things, places or objects that have been set apart as holy, but on God himself who is absolutely holy, pure and sinless.

God is often referred to as "the Holy One (of Israel)" (2 Kgs 19:22; Job 6:10; Pss 22:3; 89:18; Isa 40:25; 41:14, 16, 20; 43:3, 14, 15; 45:11; Jer 50:29; 51:5). In his nature, character and deeds, God is holy. Thus "God's goodness is holy, His being is holy, His anger is holy, His love is holy."[4] His sovereignty, majesty, power, and glory all display his holiness and all creatures stand in awe, in reverence and in worship. The moral holiness and purity of God himself are our examples for life, hence the necessity of the law of holiness.

> I am the LORD your God; consecrate yourselves and be holy, because I am holy. Do not make yourselves unclean by any creature that moves along the ground. I am the LORD, who brought you up out of Egypt to be your God; therefore be holy, because I am holy. (Lev 11:44–45)

---

3. Buswell, *Systematic Theology*, 64–65.
4. Gilkey, *Maker of Heaven*, 98.

> Speak to the entire assembly of Israel and say to them: "Be holy because I, the LORD your God, am holy." (Lev 19:2)

The law of holiness makes the absolute holiness of God a standard for all moral beings to emulate. In Leviticus God repeatedly told his people to "Be holy because I, the LORD your God, am holy" (Lev 11:44–45; 19:2; 20:26). The moral holiness and purity of God himself are to be our pattern for life. This means that all who are placed in positions of leadership or power should organize human beings in such a way as to preserve their moral health and purity. Sadly, this law of holiness has yet to become the norm and pattern of human societies.

There are several concepts which flow from God's holiness:

Purity

The Old Testament teaches us that nothing which was unclean, impure, defiled, or ceremonially polluted was allowed to be part of the worship of the holy God. If people had come into contact with anything designated as unclean, they needed to be purified or cleansed before they could worship him.

However, worship of God does not just demand ceremonial or ritual cleanness, the inner motive or disposition of a person is more important than ceremonial or ritual purity. This is why Jesus told the Samaritan woman:

> Yet a time is coming and has now come when the true worshipers will worship the Father in the Spirit and in truth, for they are the kind of worshipers the Father seeks. God is spirit, and his worshipers must worship in the Spirit and in truth. (John 4:23–24)

This is why Jesus reprimanded the Pharisees. They were meticulous about outer righteousness, but neglected inner righteousness. Inner motives are the best judge of outer acts; actions which appear righteous may be motivated by selfishness and corruption.

> But the LORD said to Samuel, "Do not consider his appearance or his height, for I have rejected him. The LORD does not look at the things people look at. People look at the outward appearance, but the LORD looks at the heart." (1 Sam 16:7)

Godliness

All persons who emulate God and live under his moral guidance and laws are described as "godly." A godly person is one who has received God's grace and who demonstrates this by living a life devoted to God. God looks for leaders like Israel's King David who fear him and obey his moral laws.

Righteousness

Moses made this statement about God: "All his ways are just. A faithful God who does no wrong, upright and just is he" (Deut 32:4). Abraham had this to say about God: "Will not the Judge of all the earth do right?" (Gen 18:25). God speaks of himself: "I, the LORD, speak the truth, I declare what is right" (Isa 45:19).

God's righteousness is rooted in his nature as Eternal Righteousness. When God acts, there is no contradiction between his visible action and his inward motives. God is morally perfect and sinless, so he can never be influenced by sin or evil. Therefore, when God acts, he does so in righteousness and perfection (Ps 89:14; Jer 9:24).

God righteousness is infinite, eternal and unchangeable. "God's righteousness means that God always acts in accordance with what is right and is himself the final standard of what is right."[5] This means that God always "has a right relationship with people, and his action is to maintain that relationship . . . both in judgment (chastisement) and in deliverance (Pss 68; 103:6; Lam 1:18)."[6]

His attitudes and acts are never arbitrary, but are guided by the whole counsel of his will (Isa 40:12–14). Because he is perfect, God does not make mistakes and cannot be accused of being ignorant, imperfect, partial, or unjust. He is the righteous judge.

God sets up moral standards to guide both the inner and outward righteousness of humankind. Because God is righteous, when he makes laws they are indeed perfect, righteous and just. In retrospect, we acknowledge that the written law of Moses could not bring life because of sin but "through Jesus Christ the law of the Spirit who gives life has set you free from the law of sin and death" (Rom 8:2). Human beings can become righteous after God.

The law of righteousness must govern all human leadership and the organization of society. It has instituted principles of moral equity, justice, impartiality, and fairness. The law of righteousness gives one access to God (Ps 31:19–20), fellowship with God (Gen 5:22, 24; 6:9), and joy in God (Pss 9:2; 104:34; Isa 9:3; 29:19; Luke 1:47; Rom 5:11).

---

5. Grudem, *Systematic Theology*, 203.
6. *Zondervan Bible Dictionary*, s.v. "Righteousness."

God Is Just

The biblical terms "justice" and "righteousness" are very similar and are often used interchangeably. This is how Willmington distinguishes between them:

> God is righteous and just. Righteousness can be defined as moral equity. Justice is the illustration of this moral equity. In righteousness God reveals his love for holiness. In justice God reveals his hatred for sin.[7]

Willmington goes on to differentiate between God's intrinsic righteousness and his justice (Exod 9:27; Ezra 9:15; Neh 9:8). Righteousness is imputed to God (Rom 4:3, 6–8; Phil 3:7–9; 1 Pet 2:24), whereas God's legislative righteousness and justice (Ps 96:10) rewards the good (2 Tim 4:8); and punishes evil (2 Tim 4:14; Rev 16:5–7).

Buswell defines God's justice as follows:

> Justice is the outgoing of God's holiness with reference to moral (or immoral) creatures . . . Since the creature is unholy and unjust, it follows that God in His justice must vindicate His holy character and maintain His creation as an expression of that holy character. A holy God, if he maintains a creation, must maintain a holy creation, and must be hostile to all things in it which are in violation of his own holiness. If there is any difference between right and wrong, God in His righteousness must be hostile to the wrong.[8]

Hugh Wetmore suggests that justice implies the following: impartiality; equal access to the law courts; the rule of law; the rights of victims taking precedence over the rights of criminals; and balancing retribution, reparation, and deterrent.[9]

> Justice in the OT is both a personal and a societal issue. Law not only shows individuals how to act toward each other but also lays the foundation for a moral society. Thus the OT law contains developed legal justice and social justice mechanisms.[10]

This is a concern for both individual justice and social justice.

---

7. Willmington, *Willmington's Guide to the Bible*, 602.
8. Buswell, *Systematic Theology*, 67.
9. Wetmore cited in Adeyemo, *Is Africa Cursed?*, 10–12.
10. *New International Encyclopedia of Bible Words*, s.v. "justice."

> The spirit of justice continues to be that of concern for one's neighbor, and God shows his deep concern by designing a social system within which justice can be done ... Justice is a concept that calls us to loving concern for those who are weak and oppressed, not simply to moral action in our interpersonal dealings.[11]

We live in a sinful and fallen world. Things are not perfect. Although God's law of justice should govern all human leadership and all organizations, there are many examples of imbalance, the denial of rights and freedoms, injustice, and oppression in human society. The cry for God's justice, righteousness and truth resounds more than ever in our modern world. God has instituted the principles of moral equity, impartiality, and fairness. Our works, deeds, leadership, governance, and organizing should be characterized by these (Prov 24:23; 28:21).

> Ultimately our understanding of justice has its source in the person of the one who gave mankind his law. . . . Doing justice has to do with how human beings treat one another, individually and in society. The norm or standard that defines just behavior is a moral and ethical one. It is derived from God's character and is expressed in those commands of the law and exhortations of the prophets that reveal how God expects his people to relate lovingly to those around them.[12]

Once again there are related concepts which we need to note:

Injustice and the Unjust

> Justice and injustice are mirror images of each other. Honesty in business practices is just; dishonest practices are unjust. Impartial courts are just; courts that show partiality to any individual or social group are unjust (Lev 19:15; cf. Hab 1:4). Oppression of others is also injustice (1 Chr 17:9; cf. Hab 2:12).[13]

Injustice is an abomination to God (Prov 17:15), and to the righteous (Prov 29:27). God calls on civil administration to abhor it (Ps 82:2; Lam 3:34–36).

Supreme Law-Giver

This has already been discussed, so it is included here simply for completeness.

---

11. *New International Encyclopedia of Bible Words*, s.v. "justice."
12. *New International Encyclopedia of Bible Words*, s.v. "justice."
13. *New International Encyclopedia of Bible Words*, s.v. "justice/injustice."

God is the only Law-giver. The Bible is full of instances where God gave commands and laws. These commands established the authority of God in his relationship with various people and set boundaries for the ultimate good of all his moral creatures who need to recognize and admit their position as mere creatures.

Jesus Christ, whose work of redemption on the cross fulfilled the prophecy concerning the Law in Jeremiah 31:31, said: "Do not think that I have come to abolish the Law or the Prophets; I have not come to abolish them but to fulfil them" (Matt 5:17).

God qualifies as the only Supreme Law-giver because of his perfect moral nature. In contrast, the laws made by human beings often simply reflect their inner corruption, selfishness, greed, and lust.

Supreme Judge

God is also the only righteous Judge because of his perfect moral nature and character. His nature does not reflect impartiality or corruption, but holiness, righteousness and truth. As the law-giver, he is the only one above the law. All moral beings and human beings with their rulers, magistrates and judges live under God's law but cannot judge perfectly or righteously. God is the sovereign Lord of the universe from whom all authority is derived.

> Say among the nations, "The LORD reigns." The world is firmly established, it cannot be moved; he will judge the peoples with equity. Let the heavens rejoice, let the earth be glad; let the sea resound, and all that is in it; let the fields be jubilant, and everything in them; let all the trees of the forest sing for joy. Let all creation rejoice before the LORD, for he comes, he comes to judge the earth. He will judge the world in righteousness and the peoples in his faithfulness. (Ps 96:10–13)

There are many other references which support the statement that God is the Judge of all the earth (Pss 82:8; 94:2; 96:13; 110:6). All will have to "give account to him who is ready to judge the living and the dead" (1 Pet 4:5; cf. 2 Tim 4:1, 8; Heb 10:30; 12:23; 13:4).

> God's judicial acts are but one aspect of his rule. To affirm God as judge is to assert that he is governor of all, not only with every right to command but also with responsibility to vindicate and to condemn.[14]

---

14. *New International Encyclopedia of Bible Words*, s.v. "judge/judging."

God has given all authority and power to Jesus to judge the world (Matt 28:18; John 5:19–47). The book of Revelation records the demonstration of his power (Rev 20:11–15).

The law of sovereignty and lordship has power and authority over all moral beings, whether angelic or human. Nonetheless we all know of the rebellion of Lucifer (Satan) and his fallen angels and the Bible is full of similar accounts of human beings rebelling against the sovereignty of God.

God Is True

In Hebrew, the word "true" means "established, certain, or faithful."[15] Strong states: "By truth we mean that attribute of the divine nature in virtue of which God's being and God's knowledge eternally conform to each other."[16] "God is the ultimate and only source and standard of truth."[17] His nature reflects truth, integrity, certainty, reliability, and faithfulness. God cannot lie and indeed there are no traces of falsehood, deception, or lies in his character (Titus 1:2). This is unchanging and eternal.

> God never differs from himself. He may on occasion alter his dealings with men in a dispensational sense, but his divine character remains constant.[18]

Because God is immutable, one can count on God and on his word (Heb 1:10–12; 13:8; Jas 1:17). God's word is the truth and is completely trustworthy, exposing lies, falsehood, inconsistency and deception. The light of God's truth dispels the darkness. Jesus Christ personified truth when he stated: "I am the way and the truth, and the life. No one comes to the Father except through me" (John 14:6).

God is the ultimate and only source of truth. He establishes his word and law to enforce and reflect his truth and his standards. The law of truth is meant to be the pattern for all forms of leadership and governance. Based upon this law of truth, God has instituted the principles of integrity, transparency, honesty, sincerity and faithfulness which should govern all actions in society.

---

15. Renn, *Expository Dictionary of Bible Words*, s.v. "true."
16. Strong cited in Willmington, *Willmington's Guide to the Bible*, 603.
17. Willmington, 603.
18. Willmington, 599.

God Is Faithful

The faithfulness of God is often commented on in the Scriptures (Deut 7:9; Pss 36:5; 119:90). "God's faithfulness refers to his self-loyalty and to that of his entire creation. He will not (indeed, cannot) change his character nor fail to perform all he has promised."[19]

In Hebrew, the word "faithfulness" means "firmness, steadiness, and fidelity." These words "express the total dependability of his [God's] character or promises."[20] God's faithfulness is rooted in his unchanging and immutable nature and character. We can put our hope in him because he is faithful, upright and just.

God establishes himself as the Faithful One. All human leadership and governance should reflect this and be based upon God's principles of faithfulness: loyalty, fidelity, steadfastness, reliability, and dependability.

God Is Love

The Christian faith differs from all other religions when it proclaims the amazing truth that God is love. In fact, love is God's primary attribute and his eternal virtue (1 John 4:7–12).

John took time to define what love is: "This is how we know what love is: Jesus Christ laid down his life for us" (1 John 3:16). "This is how God showed his love among us: He sent his one and only Son into the world that we might live through him. This is love, not that we loved God, but that he loved us and sent his Son as an atoning sacrifice for our sins" (1 John 4:9–10). These verses reveal the dimension of God's love. Jesus is the revelation of God's love. It is only when we understand the implications of the cross of Christ that we may begin to understand what God's love is all about (John 3:16). Through the cross Jesus Christ brings reconciliation with God (Eph 2:14).

Paul explains the theological basis of God's divine love in the following words: "in accordance with his pleasure and will"; "in accordance with the riches of God's grace"; "according to his good pleasure which he purposed in Christ"; "according to the plan of him who works out everything in conformity with the purpose of his will" (Eph 1:5, 7, 9, 11). From this we can see very clearly that God's love is motivated, not by anything outside of himself, but by his own nature of grace. God does not love out of pity, but out of the abundance of his grace and the good pleasure of his will.

---

19. Willmington, 604.
20. Renn, *Expository Dictionary of Bible Words*, s.v. "faithfulness."

The biblical concept of love, especially in the New Testament, is not a human quality. Love in its essence is divine in nature and is a manifestation of God's truthfulness, faithfulness, goodness, and sincerity.

The cross of Christ reveals that redemptive love means sacrifice, giving, and dying for others. Jesus Christ said: "Greater love has no one than this: to lay down one's life for one's friends" (John 15:13). He also makes several references to the fact that the good shepherd lays down his life for the sheep. God's love on the cross has become a divine norm, an example and a model for us. A Christian who is born of God through faith in the finished work of Christ on the cross should be in a position to love, for the seed and the gift of God, which is love, resides in him. "Everyone who loves has been born of God and knows God. Whoever does not love does not know God, because God is love" (1 John 4:7–8).

Love, then, is the fruit and manifestation of our salvation. In 1 Corinthians 12 and 13 Paul clearly indicates the supremacy of love in his description of spiritual gifts and of the fruit of the Spirit. The list of spiritual gifts indicates that they go far beyond any human quality or attribute. Love enables one to use the spiritual gifts and to measure the motive behind their use. Spiritual gifts used without God's love have no power. The Holy Spirit who indwells believers enables them to reflect this love and to live out what God has given them and to love as God loves.

Paul encourages every Christian to grow the fruit of the Spirit. Divine love should be the foundation of all relationships, just as it is the basis of God's relationship with redeemed humanity in Christ. Our Lord Jesus Christ pointed this out to the young Jewish lawyer when he told him to: "Love the Lord your God with all your heart and with all your soul and with all your mind . . . Love your neighbor as yourself" (Matt 22:37–40). The apostle John also picks up on this in his first letter, pointing out that one's love for one's fellow human beings is inseparable from one's love for God.

Divisions, quarrels, wars, prejudices, discrimination, selfishness and greed result from our lack of knowledge of who God is and of his love. Yet we pursue human transactions and peace treaties which lack this principle of love. Our response to the revelation of love in the cross of Christ should be evident in our love for humankind.

Despite the sinful nature and the wickedness of humanity and the world, God's love is undeterred and steadfast. Paul states: "But God demonstrates his own love for us in this: while we were still sinners, Christ died for us" (Rom 5:8). This should be the norm for all leaders. All human leadership and governance must be based upon God's principles of sacrificial love.

God Is Gracious

Because of our sins, we do not deserve God's love and forgiveness; we deserve his wrath and judgment. The fall, sin and rebellion against our Creator, altered our relationship with him. If God were to deal with us according to his holiness and justice, we would fall under his severe wrath and judgment. But the cross of Christ reveals to us that he is also our Redeemer. What we lost at the fall is redeemed and regained through Christ, thanks to God's grace.

The apostle Paul recognizes that grace springs from the same fountain as God's love (Eph 1:5, 7, 9, 11). We are granted God's unmerited favour, favour that we do not deserve. We have done nothing and added nothing to make salvation possible. Paul explains that works and the law cannot earn salvation: "For it is by grace you have been saved, through faith – and this is not from yourselves, it is the gift of God – not by works, so that no one can boast" (Eph 2:8–9). From start to finish, salvation is God's work.

It is through the cross that we are reconciled with God. It is the cross that enables us to receive his forgiveness and all his spiritual blessings. God's acts of love, peace, redemption and reconciliation in the cross of Christ are signs of his grace. We who were once enemies of God have been forgiven and reconciled. He loves us unconditionally despite our sins. "While we were still sinners, Christ died for us" (Rom 5:8). God's grace toward us is unfathomable. No matter what we do in response to God's grace, we cannot outdo what God has already done for us in Christ.

The unregenerate person who lives in sin cannot live a Christian life because God's divine qualities have not been bestowed on him. It is only God's power through his indwelling Spirit that enables us to live out his divine character. How Paul longed that the early church should receive this gift: "Grace to you and peace from God our Father and the Lord Jesus Christ." God's grace to us is manifested in his spiritual blessings which are indeed God's gracious gifts to us (Rom 12; 1 Cor 12; Gal 5:22–26; Eph 4).

Clearly, God's grace is the opposite of the sin that is at work in us. By nature we are born sinners. Through sin, we fulfil all the lusts of our nature. Through God's grace, we are able to fulfil the desires of the Spirit of God. "But where sin increased, grace increased all the more, so that, just as sin reigned in death, so also grace might reign through righteousness to bring eternal life through Jesus Christ our Lord" (Rom 5:20b–21).

God's grace must become the motivating factor behind every Christian social action and responsibility and ultimately behind our spiritual service to God and humanity. The law of grace becomes the basis of Christian involvement

God Is Merciful and Kind

What makes God withhold his anger and punishment from sinners? The psalmist provides the clue: "Have mercy on me, O God, according to your unfailing love" (Ps 51:1). God's mercy is founded on his abounding, steadfast love for his creation (Ps 103:8).

"God's mercy allows him to withhold merited punishment. God's grace allows him to freely bestow unmerited favour."[21] Strong states that, "Mercy is that eternal principle of God's nature which leads Him to seek the temporal good and eternal salvation of those who have opposed themselves to His will, even at the cost of infinite self-sacrifice."[22] "Mercy is condescending love, reaching out to meet a need without considering the merit of the person who receives the aid."[23] Based on his holiness and justice, God would be right and just to punish sinners and evil doers. But God's mercy makes him choose to save sinners, to forgive, and to show kindness.

God's acts of mercy, kindness, and compassion are deeply rooted in his nature of love and grace. He forgives freely without any compulsion. Only God knows the deepest needs of human beings in this sinful, fallen and imperfect world, and moves to meet those needs. But God cannot simply exercise mercy. If he did, then he would cease to be holy and just. This is why the cross of Jesus Christ stands at the centre of mercy.

We too must be merciful. Jesus taught: "Be merciful, just as your Father is merciful" (Luke 6:36). "Blessed are the merciful, for they will be shown mercy" (Matt 5:7). All those who lead and govern human societies must do so in light of God's moral laws of kindness, love, justice and righteousness.

God Is Forgiving

God graciously forgives (1 John 1:9; Ps 103:10–12; Isa 55:6–7). In forgiveness, God's divine favour is restored, God's wrath is removed and God removes the barriers between himself and us. Forgiveness therefore restores fellowship between God and humankind.

---

21. Willmington, *Willmington's Guide to the Bible*, 606.
22. Strong cited in Willmington, 606.
23. Renn, *Expository Dictionary of Bible Words*, s.v. "mercy."

God cannot forgive, however, unless his holiness and justice have been fulfilled. God would be untrue to his holy nature if he simply forgave out of sheer benevolence. Forgiveness came through the atoning sacrifice in the old dispensation (Lev 1–7) and comes through the cross of Christ in the new covenant.

The writer of the book of Hebrews is at pains to explain that the cross is a fulfilment of the Law's requirements. When they were enslaved in Egypt, the Israelites were delivered from the hand of Pharaoh through the redemptive value of the Passover which required that the Israelites mark their doors with the blood of a lamb. In the time of Moses, the principle was established that: "the law requires that nearly everything be cleansed with blood, and without the shedding of blood there is no forgiveness" (Heb 9:22). The supreme sacrifice ("once and for all") of Christ fulfilled and so supplanted the entire Jewish sacrificial system. "How much more, then, will the blood of Christ, who through the eternal Spirit offered himself unblemished to God, cleanse our consciences from acts that lead to death, so that we may serve the living God!" (Heb 9:14).

This explains why Jesus established the new covenant in these words, "This is my blood of the new covenant, which is poured out for many for the forgiveness of sins" (Matt 26:28). The Lord's Supper (Holy Communion) was the messianic fulfilment of the Jewish Passover.

The issues of *sin* (nature) and *sins* (acts) are dealt with on the cross of Christ. He who knew no sin was made sin for us (2 Cor 5:21; Isa 53). By taking humanity's sins in his body on the cross and by dying for our sake, Jesus Christ became our substitute and paid in full the wages of our sins. He laid the eternal foundation for God's gracious forgiveness and the removal of his wrath and punishment from us. God's offer of forgiveness, then, is his way of dealing with the problem of sin, rebellion and alienation.

Repentance, however, is strictly our affair. It is we who turn away from God our Creator in sin and rebellion. If we are to have fellowship with a holy God, the barrier of sin that separates us from God must be removed. Feelings of guilt and sin or of remorse as a result of wrongdoing are not the basis of repentance. Repentance, like forgiveness, is based on the finished work of redemption on the cross. We have nothing to offer God except what Christ effected on our behalf on the cross. The cross of Christ stands as God's offer to humankind and repentance is the response to God's offer. Forgiveness and repentance are received because God's holiness and justice have been satisfied in the atoning sacrifice.

The teachings of Jesus remind us that we must forgive our neighbour as God forgives us. Forgiveness receives divine value because it comes from God. All those who lead and govern human societies must exercise God's moral law for the healing of human societies through forgiveness and repentance.

31

Engaging with the Traditional Roots of Spiritual Idolatry

In their comparative studies of traditional religion and Christianity, many scholars have ignored the significance of the spirit-powers and forces in traditional religion and culture.

A study of the non-Jewish religions referred to in Scripture reveals striking similarities between them and African Traditional Religion, especially with regard to their religious and social practices. Many of the abominations of the Canaanite and other non-Jewish religions are also found in African Traditional Religion. This is why it is important to examine how the Israelites were told to handle these religions and cultures.

The Pentateuch and the books of Joshua and Judges in the Old Testament established a theological model for them. There were generally two aspects to this model: religious and social practices were prescribed for the Israelites while, on the other hand, prohibitions, abominations and taboos were codified.

As we proceed, it is important to bear in mind that worshipping the holy God meant excluding all other spirit beings and divinities. The Bible states:

> When you enter the land the LORD your God is giving you, do not learn to imitate the detestable ways of the nations there. Let no one be found among you who sacrifices their son or daughter in the fire, who practices divination or sorcery, interprets omens, engages in witchcraft, or casts spells, or who is a medium or spiritist, or one who consults the dead. Anyone who does these things is detestable to the LORD; because of these same detestable practices the LORD your God will drive out those nations before you. (Deut 18:9–12)

In contrast, the basic religious practices of the other religions were geared at building relationships with the mysterious, mystical spirit powers and forces.

In order to establish communication with the spirit world, they had built up an array of rituals (sacrifices and offerings), and ceremonies which were practised by various traditional specialists. The same is true of African Traditional Religion.

The Bible prohibits these religious practices because they violate the nature and character of God. Rituals and ceremonies directed to spirits or mystical powers undercut humankind's complete dependence on him who alone is able to help.

It is important to realize that in modern Africa such practices have not disappeared. Spiritual idolatry is rampant in modern Africa. It has simply resurfaced under new guises with the rise of neo-pagan religions, cults and syncretism. In order to identify religious practices and beliefs that reflect genuine spirituality, but which may not necessarily be Christian or biblical, we must make sure we understand the nature of spirituality in modern Africa. Many of the characteristics which communities, societies, tribes, and nations display are rooted in the phenomenon of spirit-power.

Even many who regard themselves as Christians are being drawn into cults or sects that have an outward form of Christian spirituality, but which are founded on a bed-rock of pagan spirituality. Because the manifestations of pagan spirituality (such as tongues, miracles, and healings) are so similar to the manifestations of Christian spirituality, many fall prey to counterfeit spirituality.

African Christians therefore need guidance so that they can identify spiritual idolatry. If they are not deeply rooted and grounded in the Word of God and in the teachings of the Bible, they may find themselves caught up in practises which are forbidden to Christians. Furthermore, Christian theology, rituals, and practices must be vetted by the Christian community. Experimenting with rituals and practices may lead to the adoption of religious beliefs and practices that fall short of biblical teachings and doctrines. Some Christians get involved in these spiritual activities out of ignorance or lack of spiritual discernment, whereas others have not been renewed or transformed by the Word of God and the gospel of Christ.

It is important to note, however, that not every traditional social or religious practice implies spiritual idolatry. Some of these practices are excellent. For our purposes here, however, we shall focus on those that contradict the teachings of the Bible and Christian theology.

The Quest for Spiritual and Mystical Powers

African spirituality has always included a deep desire for spiritual and mystical powers. The quest for this has not diminished in twenty-first century Africa as a result of modernity; rather it has increased in popularity. Because traditionalists, Christians, and modernists all exhibit some forms of spirituality or religion, Christianity has to define its distinctive nature of spirituality, showing how it differs from other forms of spirituality.

Let us consider the following questions:

May a Christian seek to control, conciliate, acquire and use spiritual and mystical powers and forces to meet his personal or communal needs and purposes?

One must ascertain whether there is evidence that the spirit-powers involved are not sanctioned by God or the Bible. If not, this is an example of spiritual idolatry. John states:

> Dear friends, do not believe every spirit, but test the spirits to see whether they are from God, because many false prophets have gone out into the world. This is how you can recognize the Spirit of God: Every spirit that acknowledges that Jesus Christ has come in the flesh is from God, but every spirit that does not acknowledge Jesus is not from God. This is the spirit of the antichrist, which you have heard is coming and even now is already in the world. (1 John 4:1–4)

May a Christian develop rituals and ceremonies as means of controlling, conciliating, and acquiring spiritual and mystical powers and forces?

People may be asked to perform rituals or ceremonies which involve spirit-powers that are not sanctioned by God or the Bible, such as consulting the spirits of the dead for guidance or divination. Be on your guard! Since spirits can imitate Christ-power or the Holy Spirit, this practice requires spiritual discernment. One has to be very careful of not playing into the hands of some strange spirit-powers that are contrary to those of Christ or the Holy Spirit.

May a Christian develop spiritual or mystical means of exercising control over the spirit world or the supernatural world?

Some people seek mystical, psychic or spiritual powers that will give them control over certain things. These include visions, revelations, performing healings, miracles, speaking in tongues. Some think that if one is able to do wonders and miraculous signs, then one must be a very good Christian. However, this is not a criterion for determining who is a Christian. Spirits are able to imitate and can actually perform miracles, signs and wonders similar to those of the Holy Spirit. In Genesis and Daniel, magicians, astrologers, enchanters, and diviners performed the same signs and wonders that Moses and Daniel did in Egypt and Babylonia, respectively. These signs and wonders were, however, clearly not sanctioned by God. In order to discriminate one must look at the source of the powers. Does the power come from God and his Holy Spirit or from other spirit beings?

Jesus warns:

> Not everyone who says to me, "Lord, Lord," will enter the kingdom of heaven, but only the one who does the will of my Father who is in heaven. Many will say to me on that day, "Lord, Lord, did we not prophesy in your name and in your name drive out demons and perform many miracles?" Then I will tell them plainly, "I never knew you. Away from me, you evildoers!" (Matt 7:21–23)

May a Christian develop mystical or spiritual means of communicating with the spirit world?

Many people desire communication with the spirits of their ancestors, with demons and with other spirits. Some want to know what is going to happen in the future. Seeking spiritual guidance is a good thing; knowing whether something is right or wrong, wise or foolish, honours God. But the books of Exodus, Leviticus, Numbers and Deuteronomy repeatedly prohibit any communication with spirit beings. Guidance should be sought through prayer and fasting, or by seeking counsel and guidance from mature Christians.

Once again, we need to be sure we identify all sources of spiritual communication and guidance. Many people talk about communicating with God, Jesus, and the Holy Spirit, but this is not proof that such communications come from God. Spirit beings can imitate God, Jesus, or the Holy Spirit. Just as in the Old Testament when the priests, prophets, kings, and judges represented people before God and represented God before the people, priests, pastors, bishops, presbyters, elders, deacons, and deaconesses are to carry out their responsibilities according to the Bible and the laws of the church.

May a Christian consult specialists in various fields on how to do the above?

Since many people think that they are limited when it comes to spiritual and supernatural matters, they rely on spiritual specialists whom they believe possess spirit-powers that are beyond the ordinary. This may involve visiting prayer houses, shrines, caves, covens, mountains, rivers, forests, graveyards, or other important locations. By seeking the help of those who are not Christians, however, many are misled into demonic practices and spiritism. Many spiritual specialists add to the teachings of the Word of God and adopt elaborate rituals which are contrary to the Bible. Once again, we need to identify the source of the powers that a spiritual specialist has. Not everyone who begins with God, Jesus Christ, the Holy Spirit or the Word of God, is a follower of God. Many end up providing teachings or practices that are not biblical.

If an African Christian is keen to take part in any of the above practices, it is very possible that such a person has strong traditional beliefs which have led them into neo-pagan practices, into a cult, or into negative religious syncretism. Because not every expression of Christianity in Africa is true to biblical and Christian theology, we need spiritual discernment and theological guidance. It is very possible that, through these practitioners Africans may be consulting lesser beings, gods or divinities, or even mystical powers and forces. If an African Christian turns to any of the above for help, it is probable that the Christian is engaging traditional beliefs, even if God is also being consulted.

The key question which must be asked is, "Who answers the prayers or rituals or ceremonies?" If someone is regarded as being in a position to grant prayers, then that ancestor, spirit or saint has usurped God because they have become the objects of the supplicant's worship. They have become centres of spiritual powers for prayers are said in their names. This is spiritual idolatry.

Roman Catholicism would argue that the saints are not worshipped, but that they are seen as intermediaries who will take the prayers to God. The same mediatorial role and reverence is accorded to Mary as the Mother of God. The problem, as we argued in an earlier chapter, is that Scripture declares that Christ is the only mediator between God and humanity (1 Tim 2:5). One can see the confusion which this Roman Catholic practice creates when some Africans argue that, if saints perform this role in Christianity, the ancestors should also be allowed to mediate.

The Acquisition of Life Force and Spirit-Powers

As already described, traditional Africans believe that the acquisition or possession of life force or spirit-power adds strength, power, or success to one's life. This added spirit-power provides security and allays fears and anxieties.

The Desire to Maintain Harmony with the Spirit World

Traditional Africans are fully aware that they cannot have their needs met by the gods and spirits unless they are on good terms with them. The law of harmony proclaims that each person must therefore maintain a good relationship with the gods and spirits so that there can be a spiritual equilibrium or balance between the two worlds. However, the human world is unstable; it is chaotic, vulnerable, fragile and subject to invasion and caprice by the more powerful gods and spirits and, therefore, the harmony or the balance is constantly under siege.

Reciprocal communication with the spirit world needs to be maintained by means of fellowship or communion. Humans respond to the spirit world by whatever means the gods and spirits demand. Generally it is believed that they must make sacrifices and offerings to the gods and divinities. Sometimes the methods are prescribed by the gods and spirits themselves, and sometimes humans just assume that this is what is expected of them.

Spirit-power has a tendency to decrease if one is not in constant touch with its sources. It is believed therefore that one must enhance or maintain spirit-power through regular participation in traditional religious celebrations, liturgies, and rituals. Some of these practices may appear to be harmless but, when they are contrary to biblical teachings, they are forms of spiritual idolatry. For example, some Christians think that pouring libations onto the ground for the ancestors is not wrong, or that praying in the name of ancestors is not wrong. Yet the Bible enjoins all Christians to pray only in the name of Jesus (John 14:13).

This desire for harmony is a constant source of temptation for Christians. They feel under pressure to make these sacrifices, offerings, or gifts to appease the gods or ancestors so that they can avert evil or calamity.

Ceremonies and Rituals

The traditional African life revolves around ceremonies and rituals, and Africans attach a very high social and religious value to these. For this reason, it is very important that Christians have a clear biblical guideline to follow as they view these matters.

Divination

There are many reasons why Africans resort to divination. It may be that they want to find out about their own future, destiny, and well-being. It may be that they are concerned about the well-being of their family, clan, tribe or even humanity in general. It may be that they want to tap into the mystical and spiritual powers to meet specific needs, such as how to protect and secure themselves against the evil activities of witches, wizards, mediums, and the wicked, dreadful, unseen, and unpredictable mystical and spirit powers. It may be that they want to gain power or confidence so that they can face the challenges of life triumphantly and overcome their human limitations. Finally it may that they simply desire to maintain harmony between humans and the spirits or gods.

Divination can take many forms, such as:

Rhabdomancy: throwing sticks in the air and examining their position when they fall;

Hepatoscopy: examining the entrails of an animal;

Teraphim: consulting the teraphim which were the images of dead ancestors and suggests spiritualism (Ezek 21:21);

Necromancy: consulting the dead (Lev 19:31);

Astrology: drawing conclusions from the relative positions of planets (Isa 47:13);

Hydromancy: observing pictures in water (Gen 44:5).

The Bible has much to say about the various forms of divination and those who practice it: Astrologers (Isa 47:13), Diviners (Deut 18:14), False Prophets (Jer 14:14), Magicians (Gen 41:8), Mediums, Necromancers and Spiritists (Deut 18:11); Sorcerers (Exod 22:18; Acts 13:6).

The Bible describes divination as: a "a system of fraud" (Ezek 13:6-7); "lucrative employment" (Acts 16:16); "abomination" (Deut 18:11-12) and "punishable by death" (Lev 20:6-27).[1] It manifests a stern attitude towards divination, and its judgment on magic, sorcery, witchcraft, divination, and a variety of occult practices is fierce (Exod 22:18; Lev 19:26; 20:27; Deut 18:10-14; Rev 21:8). *The Complete Christian Dictionary* states that: "Divination is a pagan counterpart of prophecy. Divination is by demonic power, whereas genuine prophecy is by the Spirit of God. God, therefore, detests divination of any kind."[2] Similarly, Fleming both warns and admonishes:

Divination, witchcraft and all these associated practices are contrary to the ways of God, not only because they depend on

---

1. *Open Bible*, 112.
2. Watkins, *Complete Christian Dictionary*, 189-190.

evil spirit-powers for their operation, but also they are a denial of faith. True believers walk humbly with their God, accepting that, no matter what the circumstances, God is still in control of their affairs. Having been saved by faith, they now live by faith (Gal 2:20; Eph 4:17–24; Col 1:11–13; Heb 11:6). Jesus Christ has triumphed over all the unseen powers of evil and through him believers too can triumph (Eph 1:19–21; 2:6; Col 2:8–10; 3:1–3).[3]

If an African Christian practices any of the above divinations or sorceries, it is probable that such a person is practising traditional beliefs, or is engaging in neo-pagan practices, cultism or negative religious syncretism.

Taboos

These are social norms and practices based upon certain beliefs. Taboos in African tradition govern numerous aspects of social, cultural, and religious life because they function as sacred moral codes that prescribe the social, customary, and religious behaviour required to maintain cosmic or communal harmony. They are tools for socio-cultural and religious conditioning, maintaining the social order.

This is why it is important that Christians in Africa identify the sources of their moral, ethical and social behaviours and practice. Christians need to be clear about which practises are based upon beliefs that are contrary to biblical teachings and Christian theology. It is very possible that taboos are rooted in a concept of spirit-power contrary to that of the biblical worldview.

Sacred objects

We have seen that the cult of ancestors plays a very significant part in man's search for spirit-powers. Although association with these ancestors takes various forms, in some instances it becomes evident through contact with or the use of sacred objects known to have been used and kept by the ancestors.

Through rituals, certain objects can be "imputed" with spirit-powers and can be carried about as charms, amulets, sacred objects, or weapons. In certain rare cases, this might pass as a Christian ritual, but such practices have to be thoroughly examined in the light of Scripture and sanctioned by the believing Christian community.

---

3. D. Fleming, *Bridge Bible Directory*, 271.

Sacrifices and offerings

There is a firm belief in the potency of sacrifices and offerings in traditional religion. These serve many purposes, meet many needs and cement cordial relationships, fellowship, and communion between the gods and their devotees.

Sacrifices also featured strongly in the religious life of the Jews, so certain parallels can be drawn. The instructions presented in the Pentateuch were meant to serve as a substitute for the forms of sacrifices, ceremonies, feasts, festivals, and worship the Jews would observe among the Canaanites and the surrounding religions and which the children of Israel were forbidden to copy.

It is very important that Christians study the Old Testament sacrifices, festivals and ceremonies so that they can determine which of them can be preserved and practiced. Christians must recognize that they cannot be involved in any blood sacrifices or in offerings to solicit spirit-power.

Clearly, the Jewish sacrifices related only to the worship of God and that anything else was an abomination in the eyes of the Lord God Yahweh. The Jewish sacrifices, however, were largely abrogated by the sacrifice of Jesus on the cross which laid aside the old covenant and its sacrificial system (Heb 8:13). According to the *New Concise Bible Dictionary*, the sacrifice of Jesus can be described as follows:

> Jesus is the sacrificial lamb of God who takes away sin (John 1:29, 36; 1 Pet 1:18ff); "the true Passover lamb" (1 Cor 5:6ff); "He is a sin offering" (Rom 8:3); and He is the guilt-offering suffering Servant of Isaiah 53 (cf. 1 John 1:7ff).[4]

Christ's one sacrifice has already brought complete release from sin's penalty (Heb 10:17–18). The only sacrifices which Christians can subscribe to are spiritual sacrifices offered through Jesus Christ. These are sacrifices of worship, praise and service (Heb 13:15). "They will, however, be able to present such sacrifices properly only when they have first given themselves to God as living sacrifices (Rom 12:1; 2 Cor 8:5)."[5]

Festivals

In addition to sacrifices, there was also an elaborate system of festivals, holy feasts and sacred days in the Old Testament. Traditional Africa also had a sacred calendar with sacred feasts and festivals for its religious and social life.

---

4. *New Concise Bible Dictionary*, 488.
5. Fleming, *Bridge Bible Directory*, 385.

They celebrated the new moon, the beginning of the rainy season or planting season, the harvest season, the new yams, and the hunting season.

Some of these religious festivals, rituals, and ceremonies may be acceptable as Christian festivals, rituals and ceremonies, but even these must be developed and sanctioned by the Christian community. The believing community must act as a hermeneutical body to determine and ascertain under the Spirit and wisdom of God what rulings should be made with regard to all festivals, ceremonies, rituals, and sacral days and also what food, drink, sacrifices and offerings should be avoided.

Some traditional religious festivals are clearly not acceptable in Christianity, such as the days of the new moons, and days and seasons set aside for the worship of deities, divinities, or gods, or certain holy places. These days do not honour God.

African Specialists (Professionals)

The complex nature and variety of African traditional beliefs and practices, especially in relationship to the spirit world, have produced what we may call African specialists or professionals that people can turn to for professional help. These specialists stand between the ordinary people and the gods or spirit-powers. They are believed to have "extraordinary skills" and powers to deal with problems and are believed to know the secrets and mysteries of the gods, spirits, powers and humankind. The most common specialists are the priests, medicine men and women, mediums and "workers of evil" (sorcerers, witches and wizards).

Some scholars, ignorant of the traditional conception and use of spirit-power, describe these specialists as manipulators. To an outsider, their work may well seem like manipulation. But in actual fact, it is a prescribed act of soliciting spirit-powers, following a ritualistic formula so that the outcome can be realized.

African spirituality regards religious professionals highly so the "man of God" is consequently also highly regarded and revered. If an African Christian goes to any of these specialists contrary to what is expected of a Christian, for a cause or reason that is contrary or unacceptable to biblical teaching or practice, it is possible that such a person still has traditional beliefs, or is involved with a religious cult or some negative religious syncretism.

Mystery and Secret Cults

In African Traditional Religions, "the sense of the sacred and the mysterious is deeply felt" and acknowledged. Mystery is a term which means "that which is unknown or which was unknown prior to or apart from its disclosure in divine revelation."[6]

Secret cults often have an important role in traditional religions. Religious cults and occultic groups believe that there are mysteries in religion and life, far beyond common sense. They suggest that only initiates will have access to these. In his comparative study on this subject, John Onaiyekan states:

> While mysteries are a common element of both, Christianity has no room for secret cults. Jesus Christ is the revelation of God. In Him all mysteries have been revealed. There remains no hidden secret with Jesus Christ. As we have already observed, the sense of the mysterious and the mythical abound everywhere in African life.[7]

When such groups offer a deeper knowledge of Jesus Christ or the Bible beyond what is common knowledge, they are actually just appealing to human curiosity. All that we need to know about Jesus Christ is presented in Scripture. Anything beyond God's revelation in the Bible is really a quest for spirit-power.

---

6. *Eerdmans Bible Dictionary*, s.v. "mystery."
7. Onaiyekan, "Divine Mysteries," 1.

32

Engaging with the African Holistic Worldview

The traditional philosophical foundations can be broken down into the following components: holistic, spiritual, dynamic, communal, and fatalistic. These beliefs and worldviews influence how traditional and modern Africans understand life. Christian theology must therefore address these fundamental philosophical beliefs and worldviews.

The Influence of the Traditional Holistic Worldview

We have already observed that the holistic worldview holds to the following: that the sky, the spirits, the earth, the physical world, the living and the deceased all act, interact, and react in consort; that the universe, the spirit world and humans are all part of the same fabric; that there are no distinctions between the physical, material or the spiritual, between the sacred and the profane, or between the religious and the secular.

We have learned that this holistic worldview is governed by the law of cosmic harmony. Humankind seeks to maintain peaceful relationships, communion and fellowship with all spirit beings and also to maintain harmony, balance or equilibrium with the entire spirit world. Fellowship and harmony are maintained through sacrifices and offerings and the observance of taboos and prohibitions.

This raises serious theological questions for Christianity. We need to know what the theological basis is for maintaining fellowship, communion, peace, and cosmic harmony, as well as for restoring breached relationships. We must develop a biblical worldview and theology that can address this traditional philosophical belief and worldview.

The Theology of Redemption and Reconciliation

Christians believe that the whole universe is in a state of disarray or chaos as a result of the fall and sin described in the first chapters of Genesis. We are a fallen humanity living in a fallen universe. The universe stands in need of law and order, regeneration, restoration, recreation, renewal, reformation, reconciliation, harmony, balance, unity, peace, justice, love, and forgiveness.

The Cross of Christ

Central to the theology of redemption and reconciliation is the cross of Christ. It is essential that we understand how the effects and the benefits of this historic act serve as the foundation and basis for cosmic harmony, unity, world peace, forgiveness, repentance, justice and reconciliation (Eph 1:10).

Isaiah 53 and John 1:29 both point to Jesus as the one who takes away the sin of the world. He is "our righteousness, holiness and redemption" (1 Cor 1:30). "God made him who had no sin to be sin for us, so that in him we might become the righteousness of God" (2 Cor 5:21). God put away sin by the sacrifice of Jesus on the cross (Heb 9:26) and brought grace through Jesus Christ (Rom 5:12–21).

Salvation from sin and human ruin involves the love of God, the giving of his Son, and the sending of his Holy Spirit. God's grace, love, justice, forgiveness and peace are manifest in the cross. "God was reconciling the world to himself in Christ" (2 Cor 5:19).

This Christian theology of reconciliation and restoration contrasts with the traditional religious concepts of the restoration of harmony through sacrifices, rituals and ceremonies. The involvement of spirit beings and divinities in the restoration of spiritual and cosmic harmony in traditional religion can be contrasted with the redemptive work of Christ on the cross.

Reconciliation in Christ

Let us consider three of the aspects of reconciliation which are rooted in the cross of Christ:

God and humankind

Whereas God's wrath and judgment fell on humankind as a result of the fall, we have access to God and to peace and forgiveness by the cross (Rom 5:1, 2, 8–11; 8:1). Jesus took our sins into his body when he died on the cross, thus taking away God's wrath and judgment. He paid the penalty for the sins of every man, woman and child who has ever lived or ever will live.

Christ's atoning work on the cross is the basis through which God makes peace with rebellious humanity, restoring fellowship with humankind, and also restoring his fallen creation. The cross of Christ, therefore, is the starting point of man's search for God's peace and fellowship through repentance and forgiveness.

Unless a person is at peace with the Creator, there can be no real and lasting peace on earth and no benefits of salvation can be experienced. God's peace, grace, forgiveness and love are the benefits of his act of salvation in Jesus Christ. We are reconciled to God not by what we do, nor by the works of a great prophet, but by what God has done through the cross of Jesus the Messiah (Eph 2:8–9).

We are restored and reinstated into a relationship with our Creator in and through Christ's work on the cross.

Person to person

The second aspect of reconciliation is found in Ephesians 2:11–22 where the apostle Paul states that Christ in his body on the cross destroyed the enmity which existed between Jews and Gentiles. The wall of division and enmity, which had existed between them, was destroyed and abolished by Christ on the cross. On the cross Christ reconciled them, making Jews and Gentiles one in him.

Similarly, when we are made anew in Christ, there can be no walls of division and no enmity or hatred, prejudice, stereotyping, discrimination, and bias. Those who are born again in Christ are born into this new humanity and new creation which transcends the old human divisions and enmity (Gal 3:28). People are called out of their different backgrounds into a new fellowship, the messianic community, and the church which is the body of Christ.

The new humanity in Christ is characterized by a new unity, oneness, and love. These are the qualities of peace, and the new humanity has peace in the sense that it is no longer judged by anyone or threatened by anyone or is at war with someone. In place of war, chaos, disunity, and factions, "There is one body and one Spirit, just as also you were called to one hope, when you were called; one Lord, one faith, one baptism, one God and Father of all, who is over all and through all and in all" (Eph 4:4–6).

This is good news for all humanity. If humanity can come to a position of oneness and unity, there will be the opportunity and the capacity to love again and to live in peace. However, to become a member of Christ's new community, one must leave behind all tribal gods or divinities and turn to Christ who is the Head of this new humanity. The rules of membership are clear.

> If anyone comes to me and does not hate father and mother, wife and children, brothers and sisters – yes, even their own life – such a person cannot be my disciple. And whoever does not carry their cross and follow me cannot be my disciple. (Luke 14:26–27)

> Whoever wants to be my disciple must deny themselves and take up their cross daily and follow me. For whoever wants to save their life will lose it, but whoever loses their life for me will save it. What good is it for someone to gain the whole world and yet lose or forfeit their very self? (Luke 9:23–25)

One cannot join this messianic community without having one's background radically transformed by the new values of this new humanity in Christ. Painful as it may be to get rid of the old, no one who is still bound by the tribal or racial gods can experience the reconciliation and forgiveness which is the expression of God's peace for humanity. Christ's peace and justice and reconciliation must first be internalized through faith before we can live out the implications of this reconciliation.

True salvation and lasting peace and justice for all humanity must issue from the cross of Christ otherwise our placards urging peace and justice are meaningless. Only in Christ Jesus do we have a way to destroy selfishness and greed and enmity. Only in Christ Jesus do we have the chance to abolish and destroy the divisions, racism, tribalism, ethnicity, and nationalism that threaten world peace and justice. Humanity searches for peace in vain apart from Christ, the Prince of Peace (Isa 9:6). The foundation for unity, oneness, and love in humanity has been laid in the cross of Christ; this is what salvation is all about.

Only in Christ Jesus, we can become the carriers of peace, justice, and reconciliation to the whole world. Only through the work of reconciliation, which was wrought in the cross of Christ will Christianity have the capacity to offer salvation to communities and to the world and to bring principles of peace and justice to the fore. Only through him shall we have the basis for a Christian response to Islam, secularism, and other faiths. We can reach them through Christian peace, justice, and reconciliation. Sadly, these fundamental Christian values have often been lacking in the Christian response to the challenge of world religions and cultures.

God and fallen creation (cosmic restoration)

Even the fallen creation has been reconciled in the cross of Jesus Christ. Isaiah looks forward to this state of reconciliation in which humanity and the rest of creation will live in peace and harmony in the messianic kingdom (Isa 11:6–9). In Revelation the apostle John sees a vision of the destruction of the fallen creation to make way for the new earth and new heaven. He looks forward into the future (eschatologically) to the coming final day of redemption, to the consummation of our divine salvation. The chief actor in this work of re-creation will be our Lord himself, the Prince of Peace and the righteous judge who earned these responsibilities as a result of his victory on the cross (Rev 5).

The cross of Christ judges the fallen world and nature and will restore them to harmony with God the Creator and with humankind. Thus, the final consummation of our salvation and the restoration of the new created order took effect eschatologically on the cross of Christ (Rom 8:18–25; Rev 20–21).

33

The Power and Authority of Jesus the Messiah

In the face of the spirit-powers that dominate African traditional life, Jesus Christ needs to be presented and proclaimed in Africa as the One who has supreme power and authority over all principalities and powers, indeed over the whole world. To do this, we need to grasp the christological meaning of Jesus Christ as the Saviour, Redeemer and Lord of the entire universe through the cross.

Messiah is derived from a Hebrew word *mashiah* that means the "anointed one," the expected king and deliverer of the Jews. In Greek, *Christos* also means the "anointed one." This is the christological meaning of Jesus Christ. The title *Messiah* or *Christ* was conferred upon Jesus of Nazareth in the light of his redemptive work on the cross. His death and resurrection, which accomplished God's work of salvation, were indeed the fulfilment of the Old Testament prophecies concerning the coming Messiah. Peter refers to this prophetic fulfilment when he states, "Therefore let all Israel be assured of this: God has made this Jesus, whom you crucified, both Lord and Messiah" (Acts 2:36).

Jesus of Nazareth is, indeed, the anointed one who will sit on the throne of authority in power over the whole world. He is heir to the throne of David (Isa 9:1–7; 11:1–16; Luke 1:32; Heb 1:5–9). He is the Son of God (Ps 2:7). The kingdoms of this world have been handed over to him (Ps 2; Dan 7:13–14; Rev 5:6–14; 11:15).

Lordship, authority, power and supremacy are all christological attributes that set Jesus apart and make him unique. Our Messiah is not only the Lord and Saviour of the church and individual believers, but also of the whole world. He is the Lord of the universe, the Saviour of the world, the Prince of Peace and the Righteous Judge as foretold by the prophets in the Old Testament and the apostles of the New. The apostles fearlessly proclaimed the universal lordship, authority, power and supremacy of Christ over the whole world and his victory over evil, the world, death, sin and Satan, and the demonic powers.

Closely associated with these major christological themes are the biblical and apostolic teachings on the death, resurrection and exaltation of Jesus the Messiah. That is the basis of his universal lordship.

Let us consider the major christological attributes of Christ:

The Saviour of the World

The Gospels present Jesus the Messiah as God the Son, the Son of Man and the Saviour of the world. Matthew states that Jesus "will save his people from their sins" (Matt 1:21), while Mark emphasizes the fact that "the Son of Man has authority on earth to forgive sins" (Mark 2:10). Luke, meanwhile, highlights the fact that Jesus is the Saviour of the world who has been born of human flesh, the God-Man and who has been sent to humankind as the fulfilment of God's messianic prophecies. He is the hope and expectation of humanity. John makes reference to Jesus as the "Lamb of God who takes away the sin of the world" (John 1:29). John sums up his testimony in the words, "But these are written that you may believe that Jesus is the Messiah, the Son of God and that believing you may have life in his name" (John 20:31). Christ's saving power springs from his deity (John 1:1–18), from God's approval (Matt 3:17; Luke 9:35; John 12:23–30), and from his cross (John 3:14–21; 19:21).

This theme of Christ's universal salvation is also the central focus in the apostolic teachings, writings and proclamations. Acts reinforces these messages, stating that: Salvation is found in no one else; for there is no other name under heaven, given to mankind by which we must be saved" (Acts 4:12).

Thus, Jesus the Messiah is established by the New Testament as the saviour of the whole world. This witness goes out to all world religions and cultures for the Christian and biblical concept of salvation is always universal in scope and application. It is not limited to Christians or the church. The gospel of Christ is good news to those who have not heard it, nor believed it. Jesus the Messiah still invites the whole world of religions and cultures to accept him as Lord and Saviour. No one is excluded from this invitation. It is valid for everyone, including adherents of the African Traditional Religion. The Messiah came so that they, too, could have new life in him.

The Lord of the World

The apostle Peter outlined the basis of Christ's authority on the Day of Pentecost in Jerusalem:

> [Jesus the Messiah] was handed over to you by God's deliberate plan and foreknowledge and you, with the help of wicked men, put him to death by nailing him on the cross. But God raised him from the dead, freeing him from the agony of death because it was impossible for death to keep its hold on him. (Acts 2:23–24)

From this it is clear that Christ's lordship and his Messiahship, his exaltation and glorification, spring from his death and resurrection (Acts 2:32–33; 3:13; 4:27). "God has made this Jesus, whom you have crucified, both Lord and Messiah" (Acts 2:36). After his death on the cross, Jesus the Messiah became, indeed, both Lord and Saviour. The Easter experience crowned him and his apostles all realized he was indeed Lord and God (John 20:28).

This theme continues to emerge strongly throughout the New Testament. Paul in his writings (1 Cor 15; Phil 2:1–11; Col 1:15–23) argues in very clear terms that Jesus the Messiah is the Lord and Saviour of the whole world and that this came about through his death and resurrection.

> Therefore, God exalted him to the highest place and gave him the name that is above every name, that at the name of Jesus every knee should bow, in heaven and on earth and under the earth and every tongue acknowledge that Jesus Christ is Lord, to the glory of God the Father. (Phil 2:9–11)

The name of Jesus is the name above all names. Homage and worship are to be offered to him as the Lord of the whole world. This lordship is an historic event. It does not rest on the outcome of a debate or a decision by the religions and cultures of the world.

His Supremacy

Christ is supreme over the whole of creation. John presents Jesus the Messiah as the Creator in the following verse: "Through him all things were made; without him nothing was made that has been made" (John 1:3). Paul makes a similar statement:

> The Son is the image of the invisible God, the firstborn over all creation. For in him all things were created; things in heaven and

on earth, visible and invisible, whether thrones or powers, or rulers or authorities; all things have been created through him and for him. He is before all things and in him all things hold together. (Col 1:15–17)

The same truth emerges in the book of Hebrews where Jesus is presented as the heir of all things. His supremacy over the whole of creation means that he is supreme over all angels, all prophets, all priests, all leaders, all principalities and all powers. Throughout the New Testament and in the Book of Hebrews especially, Jesus the Messiah is presented as the only one approved, appointed, anointed, and exalted by God. This establishes Christ's supremacy over all of creation, principalities, and powers.

For this reason, he exercises authority over all human affairs, including religions and cultures. But Christ is not supreme simply on account of his creative powers (as the Creator); he is also supreme by virtue of his redemptive powers (as the Redeemer). This eternal principle was confirmed, consolidated, and established by his death and resurrection and by his ascension into heaven.

His Authority and Power

Christ is not just supreme over the whole world; he also has universal authority over the whole world. This was foretold by the prophet Daniel:

> In my vision at night I looked, and there before me was one like a son of man, coming with the clouds of heaven. He approached the Ancient of Days and was led into his presence. He was given authority, glory and sovereign power; all nations and people of every language worshipped him. His dominion is an everlasting dominion, that will not pass away and his kingdom is one that will never be destroyed. (Dan 7:13–14)

And by the psalmist:

> "I have installed my king on Zion, my holy mountain." I will proclaim my LORD's decree: He said to me, "You are my Son; today I have become your father. Ask me, and I will make the nations your inheritance, the ends of the earth your possession." (Ps 2:6–8)

Our Lord himself confirmed that he had been given this authority:

> All authority in heaven and on earth has been given to me. Therefore go and make disciples of all nations, baptizing them

in the name of the Father and of the Son and of the Holy Spirit,
and teaching them to obey everything I have commanded you.
And surely I am with you always, even to the very end of the age.
(Matt 28:18–20)

In the book of Revelation, the Messiah's universal authority is lauded in the worship and praise of the angelic host in heaven.

> You are worthy to take the scroll and to open its seals, because you were slain and with your blood you purchased for God persons from every tribe and language and people and nation. (Rev 5:9)

> Worthy is the Lamb who was slain to receive power and wealth and wisdom and strength and honor and glory and praise. (Rev 5:12)

> To him who sits on the throne and to the Lamb be praise and honor and glory and power, for ever and ever. (Rev 5:13)

> The kingdom of this world has become the kingdom of our Lord and of his Messiah, and he will reign for ever and ever. (Rev 11:15b)

The gospel accounts of the miracles of Jesus record the power he had over nature, disease, death, principalities, and powers, including those of Satan and the demonic powers. This power is derived from his deity. Jesus was the God-Man and these accounts show his creative power in action through his created order, the world.

However, Christ also has another kind of power through his death and resurrection. He has the power to break and dethrone the evil power of Satan and all demonic powers. Satan holds humanity in death, but Jesus has broken that hold:

> That by his death he might break the power of him who holds the power of death – that is, the devil – and free those who all their lives were held in slavery by their fear of death. (Heb 2:14–15)

> Do not be afraid. I am the First and the Last: I am the Living One; I was dead and, now look, I am alive for ever and ever! And I hold the keys of death and Hades. (Rev 1:17b–18)

In his death and resurrection, "having disarmed the powers and authorities, he made a public spectacle of them, triumphing over them by the cross" (Col 2:15). The cross of Christ has dealt a death blow to Satan, to all his demonic powers and to death itself, the last enemy of humankind. This resurrection power has placed Christ above all other powers, as Paul explains:

> And his incomparably great power for us who believe. That power is the same as the mighty strength he exerted when he raised Christ from the dead and seated him at his right hand in the heavenly realms, far above all rule and authority, power and dominion and every name that is invoked, not only in the present age but also in the one to come. (Eph 1:19–21)

Christ's authority over the whole world is therefore both creative and redemptive. Prior to his incarnation by virtue of his deity and his divine authority as Creator, the Messiah has authority over all creation (John 1:3). After his resurrection, his messianic authority as redeemer is derived from his victory over the cross. This is the authority that the apostles proclaimed (Eph 1:3–10, 19–23).

Although his power is proclaimed to the whole world, there is a sense in which the resurrection power of Christ is effectual only within the church and individual believers.

It is true that the name of Jesus exercises tremendous power and authority over the entire universe; that it is a mighty tower where people can shelter and obtain salvation; and that miracles, signs and wonders can take place through faith in his name. But this is the power of salvation to everyone who believes: baptism, in Jesus's name; forgiveness of sins in Jesus's name; effectual prayers in Jesus's name; faith in Jesus's name; and works of miracles in Jesus's name. "By faith in the name of Jesus, this man whom you see and know was made strong. It is Jesus's name and the faith which comes through him that has completely healed him, as you can all see" (Acts 3:16). The use of his name demonstrates faith in him. "And I will do whatever you ask in my name, so that the Father may be glorified in the Son. You may ask me for anything in my name, and I will do it" (John 14:13–14).

The universal application of Christ's lordship, authority, power, and supremacy becomes effectual only when there is faith in Jesus the Messiah. Salvation occurs only when one believes in his name. The use of the power in Jesus's name is limited to his church and believers. Let us not forget Paul's powerful statement:

> For I am not ashamed of the gospel, because it is the power of God that brings salvation for everyone who believes . . . For in the gospel the righteousness of God is revealed – a righteousness that is by faith from first to last, just as it is written: "The righteous will live by faith." (Rom 1:16–17)

On the last day, Christ will use the power that he has been given when he sits on his judgment seat to judge the whole world. There he will judge all angels, all spirit beings, Satan and all his demons, and all humanity. The spirit-powers will come under his judgment for Christ-power is supreme, above any spirit-power.

The cross of Christ is a particular historical event, but with powerful universal implications for the whole world. It stands at the centre of all human religiousness and all human religions and cultures. It fulfils and supplants human religiousness and religions. Jesus the Messiah cannot be domesticated, accommodated, or even enthroned as one of the "ancestors" in any religious pantheon. Any such act negates his uniqueness as Lord and Saviour.

34

Engaging with the Traditional Communal Worldview

Modern Africans have many social and religious questions relating to sin, life passages, marriage and family, health and wealth, sickness and death, affliction and suffering, evil, fate and witchcraft, ancestors and divinities, and covenants, blessings and curses. The value and strength of a religion are seen in its ability to provide answers to these issues of life. Christianity in Africa is very poor in this area as it does not seem to have a well-developed theology that addresses the traditional meaning of existence in a kinship community. It has not been able to develop the theology of the messianic community in Africa. This chapter will attempt to show how that can be done in African Christianity.

The traditional worldview that influences how traditional and modern Africans understand life in general is governed by the law of kinship.

The Meaning of Life in Community

The reason for existence is defined in terms of community life and the meaning of life in community is rooted in the law of kinship. Outside of the community, there is no life, no hope, no peace, no identity, no destiny, and no existence, and no salvation. The community is both the lawgiver and the judge. Life is oriented towards the community and not outside the community.

Certain aspects of community life define the meaning of life in community. These include life passages: birth, adulthood, death; marriage and family; the pursuit of life or health and wealth; sickness and death and the ancestors. Birth, life and death are not regarded as mere biological or physiological processes; they are seen as being initiated and controlled by the ancestors who interact with the human community. The ancestors are therefore intimately and actively involved in the activities of the community. Life in the community cannot exist without the presence of the ancestors and the divinities whose active presence and involvement give it its meaning and destiny.

Many of the good traditional values and social and religious institutions in Africa have been lost to history because colonialism, Western education and Missionary Christianity destroyed them without replacing them. Consider the initiation rites for both boys and girls which prepared them for various aspects of adult life. These traditional ways of training, nurturing and cultivating values, morality, and discipline could have been adapted and modified by Christianity instead of being thrown away. Sadly, within the context of hostile modernity in Africa, it is very difficult for Christianity to forge and institute new values and institutions. The power of neo-colonialism and the globalizing civilizing forces militate against any meaningful development of Christian values and institutions now.

Nonetheless, Christianity needs to study and understand the African religious practices, rituals and ceremonies that relate to life passages so that Christian rituals can be developed to enrich what Africans believe and practice in these areas. The Roman Catholic priests of the school of inculturation attempted to provide an example of this, developing Christian rituals using traditional materials.[1] If Christianity as a whole is seen to be lacking meaningful teachings, practices, festivals, rituals and ceremonies in this area, Africans may revert to traditional ways which do not fit in with biblical and Christian beliefs and practices.

The first five books of the Old Testament present a theological model for life in community. This model shows how the covenant with Israel dictated how they must react to the Canaanite religion and culture. In order to serve the Lord God Yahweh, people had to sever all links with the prohibited covenants of the Canaanite religion. These were labelled as abominations in the sight of the Lord, even though they linked the traditional individual to the traditional community. Similarly therefore, becoming a Christian requires that the African covenants with the traditional society and its divinities and ancestors have to be broken before a new covenant can be made with the Lord God and Jesus Christ.

Only then can one enter the new community of believers. The traditional concept of the kinship community has been renewed and transformed through Christ's redemption and reconciliation. He has created a new messianic community of believers.

---

1. See various books published by the Pauline Press (Nairobi, Kenya) on inculturation.

The Meaning of Life in the Cosmos

The meaning of life in the cosmos (universe) relates to both the spirit phenomenon and power phenomenon or, in short, spirit-power. The meaning that humankind seeks is portrayed in its religious beliefs, practices, rituals, and ceremonies. We have noted that in traditional Africa humankind's orientation to the spirit and supernatural world is primarily to obtain help from spirit-power so that they can live a meaningful and fulfilled life in a kinship community. People are not looking for escape from the community to the abode of the spirit and supernatural world, but for that which can help them to live happy, fulfilled and meaningful lives in their kinship community.

Given this orientation and the nature of man's relationship with the cosmos, how do we approach questions about good and evil, or heaven and hell in traditional Africa? The theological basis of our discussion has already been established: the cross of Christ brought about cosmic restoration. Let us use that fact to address the issue of the cosmic community and the meaning of life.

Christ's power and authority has been established over the entire cosmos. Life has meaning and purpose because Christ rules supremely over the entire universe. The cross of Christ judges the fallen world and nature (cosmos), but it also restores them also to harmony with God the Creator and with humankind. This means that the traditional pursuit of cosmic harmony, unity, or balance can find its fulfilment in Christ's work of reconciliation, re-creation and regeneration. Fallen humanity and the fallen creation (cosmos) can be restored to live in harmony. Thus, questions about good and evil, heaven and hell, and Satan and demonic powers are answered in Jesus Christ's work of reconciliation on the cross.

The cross of Christ established a messianic community that has new values that transcend those of the traditional kinship and communal values. These messianic communal values have the power to transform the parochial and relative morality and ethics of the traditional African. They have the power to address tribalism, sectionalism, racism, and religious bigotry in Africa. The ultimate goal of the messianic community is to reach out to all human communities, and Christians should engage and interact with all human communities in terms of the communal messianic values of love, peace, grace, justice, and reconciliation.

Sadly, neither Missionary Christianity nor post-Missionary Christianity have succeeded in developing a relevant Christian theology of community. Christianity in Africa has tended to follow either what Western colonialism and education created or what evolved from its contacts with African societies. The Western philosophies of secularism, religious pluralism, cultural relativism, modernism, humanism, and individualism have profoundly influenced Christianity in Africa. Western colonialism and education and Christianity have broken down the religious and social structures of the traditional African societies without offering any adequate replacement.

However, all is not lost. African Christianity has the opportunity to create its own unique and distinctive Christian communitarian values and ethics by developing a new theology of community. The communitarian values of the messianic community can be used to renew and transform traditional communal values and institutions.

There are, however, certain aspects of the Christian community which we must consider. We know that the traditional community is founded upon certain covenants, rites, ceremonies, and festivals that bind all members of the community together, but what binds the messianic or Christian community?

The new covenant of Christ through the Holy Spirit

A messianic or Christian community is founded upon a covenant with its Lord, Jesus Christ. The promise of this new covenant is recorded in Jeremiah:

> "The days are coming," declares the LORD, "when I will make a new covenant with the people of Israel and with the people of Judah. It will not be like the covenant I made with their ancestors when I took them by the hand to lead them out of Egypt, because they broke my covenant, though I was a husband to them," declares the LORD. "This is the covenant I will make with the people of Israel after that time," declares the LORD. "I will put my law in their minds and write it on their hearts. I will be their God and they will be my people. No longer will they teach their neighbour, or say to one another, 'Know the LORD,' because they will all know me, from the least of them to the greatest," declares the LORD. "For I will forgive their wickedness and will remember their sins no more." (Jer 31:31–34)

Four provisions are made in this covenant. These are: regeneration – God will put his law in their inward parts and write it in their hearts; a national restoration – Jehovah will be their God and the nation will be his people; the personal ministry of the Holy Spirit – they will all be taught individually by God; and, finally, full justification – their sins will be forgiven and completely removed.

The new covenant contrasts with the "old" covenant which was made with Israel (Jer 31:32; Heb 8:6–13). It accomplishes what the Mosaic covenant could only point to, that is, the child of God living in a manner that is consistent with the character of God.[2]

At the appointed time in history, God revealed himself to humanity in Jesus the Messiah. The blood of Jesus Christ, the Lamb of God, sealed the new covenant between God and his people. That blood which secured the new covenant for Israel also provides for the believers who comprise the church. The new covenant and the new law are implemented by the ministry of the Holy Spirit. This is in fulfilment of the prophecy of Joel: "And afterward, I will pour out my Spirit on all people . . . Even on my servants, both men and women, I will pour out my Spirit in those days" (Joel 2:28–29).

The fact that Jesus himself inaugurated the new covenant is essential to our understanding of what is involved in relating the gospel of Christ to world religions and cultures. Jesus the Messiah is not an accident of history, but the prophetic and messianic fulfilment of God's promises and covenants with Israel.

However, it goes further than that. In this new covenant Jesus relates to the whole world, to all religions and cultures. Paul's theological analysis in Romans 9–11 explains how Jesus relates both to Israel and to the Gentiles; both relationships are in God's eternal plan of salvation. The salvific work of Christ on the cross destroyed the wall of division between the Jew and the Gentile (Eph 2). The Jew was separated from the Gentile by the law, but in Christ Jesus, this law has been laid aside to clear the way for a new humanity and a new relationship.[3]

Let us consider the covenants of the traditional community with this new covenant in Christ Jesus. A traditional community makes sense of its existence through its covenants with ancestors, divinities, or spirit-powers. However, because traditional religion operates under a different set of covenants, these have to be laid aside if one is to become a disciple and follower of Christ. The messianic community has the covenant of Christ as its foundation, not the covenants of traditional religion. Faith in the Lord Jesus Christ is the passport to the new community. Just as in traditional communities, there is no "free" association where people simply live and do what they want. Life in the messianic community means submission to God, to the work of Jesus Christ on the cross and to the ministry of regeneration and sanctification of the

---

2. *Open Bible*, 777.
3. Turaki, *Tribal Gods of Africa*.

Holy Spirit. This covenant theology must be dominant in the life of messianic or Christian communities.

Baptism, unity and the body of Christ

The messianic community requires a ritual which seals one's faith and belief in Jesus Christ. Baptism replaces the initiation rituals of traditional religion. Water baptism initiates new believers into the messianic community or the church. This is the physical and social manifestation of what the Holy Spirit effected at conversion and of one's faith in Jesus Christ (Rom 6:1–11).

> There is one body and one Spirit, just as you were called to one hope when you were called; one Lord, one faith, one baptism; one God and Father of all, who is over all and through all and in all. (Eph 4:4–6)

> For we were all baptized by one Spirit so as to form one body – whether Jews or Gentiles, slave or free – and we were all given the one Spirit to drink. (1 Cor 12:13)

In this new community, believers are no longer strangers or aliens from different backgrounds, but brothers and sisters in Christ, united by one Lord, one faith, one baptism, one Father and one Spirit. This transcends any human classification, race, tribe, and nationality. Believers cannot live in this new messianic community with their old ethnic, racial, or tribal values, attitudes, and practices that exclude others. Their inward baptism by the Holy Spirit and their outward water baptism have sealed their new identity. From now on, they are to live in love and unity. They must live in terms of the new: "Therefore, if anyone is in Christ, the new creation has come: the old has gone, the new is here!" (2 Cor 5:17).

This inward transformation has huge social implications. The new messianic covenant defines how they ought to live among themselves and with outsiders. They live under the rule of God (theonomy) and under Christ's law. Just as the Mosaic law governed the social and spiritual life of the Israelites and just as the traditional moral and ethical laws and taboos governed the social and moral life of traditional Africans, so the law of Christ governs the life of all believers.

The gospel of Christ and the law of kinship and strangers

It is necessary to re-examine how the gospel of Christ addresses the traditional law of kinship with regard to strangers or outsiders.

The life and character of Jesus and his teachings become the norm for the new community. Biblical Christianity transforms the law of kinship by making the Lord Jesus Christ the head of a new humanity (Col 1:15–18), the church (Eph 4–5).

> Anyone who loves their father or mother more than me is not worthy of me; anyone who loves their son or daughter more than me is not worthy of me. (Matt 10:37)

The messianic community is a representation of a new humanity, which has been re-created in Christ Jesus. Kinship and tribal values have been transformed by the cross of Christ. In Christ, ethnic groups, races and tribes are no longer strangers to one another, but brothers and sisters. The walls of hostility and enmity have been broken down to make way for a new relationship and brotherhood in Christ. These are the new communal values.

Humanity is given a new definition through Christ's work on the cross. Ethnic or tribal identity is transformed into the image of Christ and it can therefore become an instrument of blessings to others. The new communal values of the messianic community address the excesses and vices of the traditional communal and kinship values that breed the tribalism, ethnicity, and racism that are destroying African nations. This is the gospel ethic that should become the norm.

35

Engaging with Traditional Moral and Ethical Beliefs

All human societies are built upon particular moral and ethical foundations. The motivations behind ethical and moral actions in traditional Africa are quite different from biblical principles of ethics and morality. We need to examine the differences.

The cross of Christ generates benefits or blessings which have strong communal values and which therefore address the traditional moral and ethical values, namely the pursuit of cosmic harmony, spiritual meaning, mystical and spirit powers, kinship community and human destiny. However, these moral and ethical pursuits take on new spiritual meanings when we apply the biblical concepts and principles of salvation, reconciliation, peace, grace, love, justice, forgiveness, and repentance to them. The spiritual and social impact of Christianity upon human societies is felt most powerfully when Christ's death and resurrection power and authority over evil, sin, death, Satan, and all principalities and powers is seen as applicable to the society.[1]

God as the Foundation of Morality and Ethics

The nature, character, and attributes of God reveal him to be a moral and ethical personality. These moral attributes of God, which we have discussed in previous chapters, can be summarized as universal moral laws: (1) the law of Sovereignty (power and authority); (2) the law of the Spirit; (3) the law of eternity (life); (4) the law of God's spoken Word; (5) the law of light; (6) the law of goodness; (7) the law of wisdom; (8) the law of truth; (9) the law of justice; (10) the law of holiness; (11) the law of righteousness; (12) the law

---

1. Turaki, *Tribal Gods of Africa*.

of faithfulness; (13) the law of love; (14) the law of grace (kindness, mercy, compassion); and (15) the laws of the God-human relationship: humility and pride, repentance and forgiveness, stewardship and sloth, blessings and curses, rewards and punishments.

But what is a moral law? The Westminster Larger Catechism provides the following answer:

> The moral law is the declaration of the will of God to mankind, directing and binding everyone to personal, perfect, and perpetual conformity and obedience thereunto, in the frame and disposition of the whole man, soul and body, and in performance of all those duties of holiness and righteousness which he oweth to God and man.[2]

This definition prompts another question: "What is the nature of this moral law?" William O. Einwechter gives an answer:

> The moral law is based on God's own holy nature (1 Pet 1:15–16), and it establishes the righteousness of God that men are to emulate in their own lives (Matt 5:48; Eph 5:1) . . . Since the moral law is a reflection of the holy nature of the sovereign God of creation, it must be universal (binding upon all men everywhere) and unchanging (binding upon all dispensations) because God himself cannot change (Matt 3:6; Jas 1:17; Ps 102:25–27), and as Creator he is King over all the earth (Gen 1:1; Ps 47:2). The moral law is therefore the one unchanging rule of right conduct for all men and for all time. It will be on the basis of this moral law that God will judge all peoples and nations (Pss 9:7–8, 16–20; 96:10, 13; 98:2, 9; Acts 17:31; Rom 2:5–12; 3:19).[3]

From this we see that God's moral law is rooted in his nature, character, and attributes. It is also eternal and universal.

The Hebrew word translated as law is *torah*. It means "teaching" or "instruction." A law then is a teaching or instruction on how one should live. For example, "My son do not forget my teaching [*torah*], but keep my commands in your heart, for they will prolong your life many years and bring you peace and prosperity" (Prov 3:1). However, Moses clearly had a fuller understanding of the law and so we conclude that "the law consists of all the

---

2. Westminster Larger Catechism, answer #93, http://www.apuritansmind.com/westminster-standards/larger-catechism/.

3. Einwechter, *Ethics and God's Law*, 11–12.

statutes, ordinances, precepts, commandments, and testimonies given by God to guide his people."[4]

God alone is the true law-giver as he is the creator. He gives his moral law to his moral creatures as moral instructions and guides for life and conduct. This law is rooted in his nature and character and expresses his attributes. The best example of this moral law is that between God and his covenant people, the Israelites.

> The law was given to Israel in order to strengthen God's covenant with Israel. Law was introduced to meet a need that existed within the context of the covenant. God acted in covenant faithfulness to bring Israel out of Egypt. But Israel's unresponsiveness to God demonstrated that this people needed guidance and structure. At Sinai, God provided the needed structure. He established guidelines for Israel for living with him and with others, as individuals and in community. God also made clear the consequences of obedience and disobedience. The individual or generation that lived in harmony with the divine teaching would receive blessing. The individual or generation that wandered away from the path marked out by law would be disciplined.[5]

Moses explained why Israel must keep God's laws:

> See, I have taught you decrees and laws as the LORD my God commanded me, so that you may follow them in the land you are entering to take possession of it. Observe them carefully, for this will show your wisdom and understanding to the nations, who will hear about all these decrees and say, "Surely this great nation is a wise and understanding people." What other nation is so great as to have their gods near them the way the LORD our God is near us whenever we pray to him? And what other nation is so great as to have such righteous decrees and laws as this body of laws I am setting before you today? (Deut 4:5–8)

> Then the LORD your God will make you prosperous . . . if you obey the LORD your God and keep his commands and decrees that are written in this Book of the Law and turn to the LORD your God with all your heart and with all your soul. (Deut 30:9–10)

---

4. *New International Encyclopedia of Bible Words*, s.v. "law."
5. *New International Encyclopedia of Bible Words*, s.v. "law."

From these quotations we can see the significance of God's moral laws as instructions or as a moral guide for life and conduct. All moral creatures, whether human or angelic, must submit to and obey all God's moral laws. This is essential in order to maintain God's determined and definite moral order, purpose, peace, and harmony. His laws are the divine means of ordering of human life and creation.

God's universal moral laws are:

> revealed by Moses and the Prophets and by Jesus and the Apostles... The law of God sets the standard for personal, family, church, and societal ethics. According to Deuteronomy 6:8–9, the law of God is to guide all our deliberations, all our actions, all that takes place in our homes, and all that transpires outside of our homes. The moral law is a comprehensive ethical blueprint which is to direct the individual, the parent, the elder, and the civil magistrate.[6]

While God's nature, character and attributes form the foundation of all moral laws, Christian morality and ethics were expressed in the teachings of Jesus and the apostles. These teachings form the basis of Christian morality and ethics.

The Moral and Spiritual Teachings of Christ and the Apostles

Whereas taboos and customs in African traditions govern numerous aspects of social, cultural, ethical, and religious life, African Christians need to develop a moral and social ethic that reflects biblical and Christian teachings. We have discussed this already so what follows will simply pick up on that discussion.

The Beatitudes (Matt 5–7) stress the fact that "happiness" or "blessings" are rooted in moral and spiritual principles. They set high moral and spiritual standards, indicating that morality and ethics should not be judged at the level of "acts" or "deeds," but ultimately at the level of "motives." The motive or reason for any moral, ethical, or spiritual act must be right, pure, and rooted in God's consciousness. This means that morality and ethics are to be built from the inside first at the level of motives and disposition. Then morality and ethics from the outside, at the level of acts, will be authentic and true.

Motives are rooted in God as the highest moral and spiritual principle and not in men or material things (to be seen by men). God judges and sees the

---

6. Einwechter, *Ethics and God's Law*, 13–14.

heart beyond mere religiosity or hypocrisy. One's motives should arise from one's personal relationship with him (Matt 23). The inner being, the habits of the heart and motives must be built upon the foundation of God's word and his moral laws. The universal standard for morality and ethics is God himself. In short, morality or ethics means imitating God.

The principles of humility and selfless service (sacrifice) form the basic moral and spiritual norm for attitude and behaviour. These principles are reflected in moral maxims, such as:

> Love your neighbour as yourself.
>
> Do unto others as you want them to do to you.
>
> Judge not so that you may not be judged.
>
> The measure that you measure unto others, the same will be measured to you.
>
> The first shall be last, and the last shall be first.
>
> He who exalts himself shall be abased, but he who humbles himself shall be exalted.
>
> He who wishes to be great must be a servant.
>
> He who wishes to be first must be a slave of all.
>
> Thus, humility and meekness form the basic moral and spiritual principles of service and sacrifice.[7]

These moral maxims are universal and are not limited by communitarian or kinship values as in traditional societies.

Godliness as seen in the moral nature and the character of God is a very strong antidote to any form of corruption. There is a great need to develop a biblical and Christian theology of leadership and governance in response to the weakness of African theology when it addressed questions of development, transformation, good leadership, and governance in Africa in the 1960s soon after independence.

The Moral Lifestyle of Jesus and the Apostles

But how do we develop godly morality and ethics? A godly character can only be sustained by a disciplined, moral lifestyle. A moral and disciplined

---

7. Turaki, *Tribal Gods of Africa*, 144–145.

lifestyle is produced by training in righteousness. The teachings of Jesus and his apostles were modelled in a definite and disciplined moral lifestyle. We need therefore to examine that.

I have deliberately selected some of the more difficult and extreme teachings of Jesus and the apostles to show the significance of a disciplined moral lifestyle for Christians. Here are some examples from their teachings on violence and persecution:

> Blessed are the peacemakers for they will be called children of God. (Matt 5:9)

> If you love those who love you, what reward will you get? . . . And if you greet only your own people, what are you doing more than others? . . . Be perfect, therefore, as your heavenly Father is perfect. (Matt 5:46–48)

> For all who draw the sword will die by the sword. (Matt 26:52)

> Love your enemies, do good to those who hate you, bless those who curse you, pray for those who mistreat you. If someone slaps you on one cheek, turn to them the other also. If someone takes your cloak, do not withhold your shirt from them. Give to everyone who asks you, and if anyone takes what belongs to you, do not demand it back. Do to others as you would have them do to you. (Luke 6:27–31)

> Do not repay anyone evil for evil. Be careful to do what is right in the eyes of everyone. If it is possible, as far as it depends on you, live at peace with everyone. Do not take revenge, my dear friends, but leave room for God's wrath, for it is written: "It is mine to avenge; I will repay," says the Lord. On the contrary: "If your enemy is hungry, feed him; if he is thirsty, give him something to drink. In doing this, you will heap burning coals on his head." Do not be overcome by evil, but overcome evil with good. (Rom 12:17–21)

> Brothers and sisters, as an example of patience in the face of suffering, take the prophets who spoke in the name of the Lord. As you know, we count as blessed those who have persevered. (Jas 5:10–11)

> But if you suffer for doing good and you endure it, this is commendable before God. To this you were called, because Christ suffered for you, leaving you an example that you should follow

in his steps. "He committed no sin, and no deceit was found in his mouth." When they hurled insults at him, he did not retaliate; when he suffered, he made no threats. Instead, he entrusted himself to him who judges justly. "He himself bore our sins" in his body on the tree, so that we might die to sins and live for righteousness; "by his wounds you have been healed." (1 Pet 2:20–24)

Nobody can possibly practice these ethical maxims without a sustained disciplined moral lifestyle. This lifestyle is quite different from mere human virtue. In fact, the teachings are contrary to human wisdom. Jesus and the apostles teach that this lifestyle requires a deeper spiritual discipline in order to produce a strong inner character that can resist or stand up to the worst of human character or conditions. Patience and perseverance can only arise out of a firm belief in the sovereignty of God and his coming kingdom. Faith in God and what he can do in humanity unleashes tremendous spiritual and moral power in the face of suffering or persecution. Despite Jesus's meekness and humility, this disciplined lifestyle is neither weakness nor submission, but rather the demonstration of the power of God over human weaknesses or human circumstances.

Our Lord Jesus Christ and the apostles are role models in both word and deed, as well as in moral character. Their example of meekness, humility, peace, love, sacrifice, suffering, perseverance, and unshakable faith in God and his kingdom are the sources of their inner strength and power, hence the quality of their moral life. Moral character like this can only be formed or forged out of discipline. The apostle Paul states:

> Not only so, but we also glory in our sufferings, because we know that suffering produces perseverance; perseverance character; and character hope. And hope does not put us to shame, because God's love has been poured into our hearts through the Holy Spirit who has been given to us. (Rom 5:3–5)

The apostle Peter made similar remarks about moral discipline, stressing goodness, knowledge, self-control, steadfastness (perseverance), godliness, mutual affection and love (2 Pet 1:5–8).

The character of a person is moulded, conditioned and defined by God's moral laws. We emulate God by cultivating a moral character and lifestyle that takes after God's nature, character, and attributes. There is no doubt that our nations, peoples, institutions, and social orders need godly men and women who fear God and are humble enough to serve both God and the people faithfully and fearfully.

36

Engaging with the Traditional Concept of Leadership

In traditional African society, the elders are the recognized leaders. An elder is a product of the community who works for the community. The elder's meaning and function are rooted in kinship communal values. The elder therefore accepts the communal principles of morality and ethics.

Leadership and Communitarian Values

The biblical concept of elder is closely related to this concept of a ruling elder in African traditional society. However, the values that define, shape and mould an elder are not those of kinship or blood-relationship but those of the messianic community. Elders are no longer governed by tribalism, sectionalism, racism, or nationalism. Instead, God's universal moral laws and Christ's law apply.

In Hebrew, the word *zaqen* means an elder or someone advanced in age. As such, an elder deserves respect and is usually valued as a counsellor.[1] In Israel, elders formed local or national ruling bodies, quite similar to the African council of elders. These elders also had judicial and governing roles.

> The supervision of the life of the community was placed in the hands of a group of elders, not in the hands of a single elder. The wisdom of several rather than of one was considered necessary for those matters that an elder team had to deal with ... The elder system settled matters within the community. The elders were members of the community; their judgments would flow not only from knowledge of law and custom but also from intimate

---

1. Renn, *Expository Dictionary of Bible Words*.

knowledge of the persons who might stand before them. This community aspect of the elder system stands in contrast to modern bureaucracy, which tends to create increasing distance between individuals and those who decide civil or criminal issues that might affect them.[2]

The Greek word *presbyteros* also describes an older person or persons.

> "Elder" came to indicate the rank and importance typically gained by older persons . . . These men were spiritual leaders of a congregation and of the wider community. They functioned in teams rather than individually in directing the affairs of a local community. They were carefully selected to meet specific moral and personal criteria (1 Tim 3; Titus 1) . . . Spiritual leaders are to provide living examples of the truths they teach. Leaders are to be models of that Christlikeness to which all believers are called.[3]

Elders were usually appointed on the grounds of their spiritual qualifications and were given tasks to do for the Christian community. The following quotation offers some valuable insights:

> Mature members of the local community, whose age and character have won respect, were recognized as elders . . . Elder-style leadership was not exercised by individuals but entrusted to groups of men who served as a team in overseeing community life . . . Elders of the church were drawn from the local community and were required to have a character that merited respect. Elders in the church also functioned in teams: one-man oversight is not biblical, though gifted individuals may make significant contributions to the life of a local congregation . . . While the specific tasks entrusted to elders remain undefined, the Bible's teaching on the function of leadership within the body of Christ provides clues not only to the elder role but also to the gifts required for effective team leadership."[4]

Christian communities need to establish biblical principles of good leadership and governance which are rooted in the messianic communal

---

2. *New International Encyclopedia of Bible Words*, s.v. "elders."
3. *New International Encyclopedia of Bible Words*, s.v. "elders."
4. *New International Encyclopedia of Bible Words*, s.v. "elders."

values. For a Christian elder to be effective in his community, he must cultivate morality in his private life and in the public social order of the community.

Leadership in Modern Africa

Modern society has developed forms of democratic leadership and governance that are very different from those of ancient times. African nation-states generally have a constituted authority or government which has defined powers. When this "constituted authority" is conferred on a "constituted body," leadership comes alive. This is legitimate leadership and it has authority.

This contrasts with Old Testament times when leadership was personalized. Leaders were usually designated as elders, judges or kings and all governmental functions resided in that particular person who played a critical role in all human affairs. Today, leadership is institutionalized and governed by a constitution or set rules. The three arms of governance – executive, legislative and judiciary – provide checks and balances on the authority and power of leaders.

Nonetheless there is considerable emphasis on influence and power. Some even define leadership as "the ability to influence others to do what you want, regardless of the consequence." The focus of this type of leadership is on ensuring a lasting, powerful influence over the followers. The subordinates exist under the guiding influence of their elders, leaders, or rulers. These leaders may not have the skill to bring peace and harmony to the people or institutions; they simply rely on the power which their authority gives them and on the power of their influence over people and institutions. Good leaders are distinguished from bad solely by the results or consequences of their leadership. The morality and ethic behind their influence or power is not important, and the leader can influence people to achieve good or bad ends.

As we commented in Part I, the African elders who started the movements of "African identity" and "African freedom" did not have a concept of how to develop and transform Africa after independence. The issues of leadership and good governance were also ignored because of the overemphasis on this quest. At that time Africa did not have elders who had a broad enough view (a communal understanding) of their role as an elder of African communities and peoples. They simply did not understand the needs of the hour.

This is why it is important that questions be raised about the moral nature of influence and power. The use of power must be judged in terms of what it does for the good or benefit of the ruled or the governed. When the community is neglected and the leaders benefit, then power or influence must be labelled as selfish or corrupt or immoral. Eldership, leadership and governance are simply morality and ethics in action.

The misuse of influence or power stands condemned by God's justice, righteousness, kindness, and humility. God's moral laws continue to apply, both to persons and to institutions. It makes no difference whether they lead in a monarchy, a democracy, a socialist state or in any other form of government. God is aware of the needs and the aspirations of the ordinary people or citizens and holds all elders, leaders, and rulers accountable to them. This is why the prophets of the Old Testament challenged those who were leading his people about their injustice towards the poor, the widows, and the orphans. The prophetic books of the Old Testament are full of God's injunctions to the elders, leaders, and rulers, urging them to rule and judge the people in righteousness, justice, kindness, and humility (Jer 9:23–24; Amos 5; Obad 1–14; Hab 1).

The prophet Jeremiah says:

> Among my people are the wicked men who lie in wait like men who snare birds and like those who set traps to catch people. Like cages full of birds, their houses are full of deceit; they have become rich and powerful and have grown fat and sleek. Their evil deeds have no limit; they do not seek justice. They do not promote the case of the fatherless; they do not defend the just cause of the poor. (Jer 5:26–28)

Elders, leaders or rulers are called to lead their people in justice, righteousness, and in kindness and humility.[5]

Leadership as Constituted Moral Authority

But leadership can also be stolen. It can be illegitimate, taken by force. In a power conflict, for example, soldiers take power by force and impose their leadership upon the people. However, this does not exempt such leaders or rulers from the need to exercise moral leadership or governance.

Although those who see only worldly sources of authority or leadership do not realize this, every authority in human society is rooted in God's creative authority. The biblical concept of leadership asserts that the source and origin of constituted authority or leadership is God himself, the maker of heaven and earth. The entire book of Daniel and some of the writings of the apostles, Paul and Peter, indicate that God is the ultimate source and origin of authority

---

5. Wetmore cited in Adeyemo, *Making a Difference*, 5–15.

and power (Rom 13:1-7; 1 Pet 2:13-25). As its creator, God owns the entire universe and every human society, but God delegated his authority and power to humankind in the garden of Eden. Humankind was given the mandate to rule God's creation, the animal world, the human world, and nature. This means that it was through God's creative powers that human social orders were instituted. As a result human authority is rooted in God's moral nature and character.

The prophet Daniel made this abundantly clear to the rulers of Babylon and, by extension, to all rulers of human kingdoms throughout all ages. The entire book of Daniel is, in fact, a definition of how humankind's delegated authority or leadership relates to God's sovereignty. God alone is the Supreme and Sovereign Ruler of all kingdoms. When the book of Revelation records that all the kingdoms of the earth will come under the rule of the Messiah (Rev 11:15), this is a fulfilment of the prophecy of Daniel (Dan 7:13-14). When Jesus the Messiah sets up his universal rule and kingdom, the supreme rule of God will finally be established throughout the entire universe.

Clearly then, all leaders fall under the supreme sovereignty, authority, power, and rule of God (Rom 13:1-4). God administers or rules the universe, first through his nature and character, and then through his delegated elders, leaders, rulers, and principalities. As the Sovereign Lord, he rules his creation in holiness, righteousness, justice, and truth. The same moral standards are also required of all elders, leaders, rulers, and principalities, without exception.

The proper role and function of elders, leaders, rulers, or social orders therefore is to recognize, to submit to, to mediate, and to reflect God's holiness, righteousness, justice, and truth. Leadership must reflect, promote, and defend God's universal moral laws so that the governed will experience stability, peace, and unity. These universal moral principles and standards are binding upon all who possess authority or power, whether they are godly or ungodly, whether they acquired their power legitimately or illegitimately. God demands the same from all leaders.

If God is the final ruler and the final judge, it means that all those exercising eldership or authority are doing so under his rule and judgment. No human leader can misbehave without incurring God's wrath and judgment. If God's moral laws are not applied, leaders invite chaos, crisis, conflict, and even death for their peoples, communities, societies, or social orders. If one wishes to bring peace, harmony, blessing, and prosperity through one's jurisdiction of eldership, leadership, or rule, there is no other way except through the Sovereign Lord and ruler of the universe. The Bible records that nations or peoples were blessed because of their godly leaders or rulers. By contrast, nations or peoples were judged and punished by God when their leaders, elders and rulers were ungodly and wicked. The biblical accounts in 1 and 2 Samuel, 1 and 2 Kings, and 1 and 2 Chronicles reveal many such instances. God's attitude has not changed. He still rewards nations and peoples whose rulers and leaders are godly. God still judges and punishes nations whose rulers and leaders are ungodly and wicked.

This means that those in authority must approach their task reverently and fearfully. Their power is merely delegated authority; no one is supreme or pre-eminent. They hold their positions in trust. If the primary objective of eldership, leadership, or rule is to establish God's reign and rule on earth, then everything must be designed to achieve that moral purpose and obligation. Being an elder, leader or ruler is a serious business; a task in which God has revealed his deep interest.

If they do not focus on these universal moral laws, they can invent new socio-political and economic institutions in vain. When a nation, a people, a society, or a social order fails, it is very likely because their leaders have failed to implement God's moral laws. This has been true throughout history.

The Spiritual Qualities of Eldership and Leadership

Although the modern world emphasizes human and social knowledge and skills, these make very little contribution to change or progress. More Africans are educated today than in yesteryear, but no tangible development or progress has been made. In fact conditions in Africa today are far worse than they were when independence came in the 1960s. People often say that the reason for this has been the lack of good leadership and governance. This is true, but they have missed a key issue. If Africa is to thrive, our elders, leaders, and rulers must cultivate the moral and spiritual qualities of good leadership and governance. This is how Christianity can help to bring about renewal and transformation in Africa.

We have seen that moral laws are derived from the nature, character and the attributes of God who is a moral and ethical personality. Those who emulate God are described in the Bible as godly. These are those who fear him and worship him, those who have received God's moral character or grace and who demonstrate this by living a life totally devoted to God. This will be evident in their deep faith, reverential awe, and obedience to God.[6]

---

6. Renn, *Expository Dictionary of Bible Words*.

This is the first step towards biblical eldership, leadership or rule or governance. All who want to be effective elders, leaders or rulers must nurture this attitude in their private lives. The inner being, the habits of the heart, must be built on the foundation of God's word and his moral laws. Morality and ethics must be built from the inside, at the level of motives and disposition. Otherwise, leadership stands on quicksand.

But what is Godliness? In Hebrew "godly" refers to "one who exercises loving-kindness toward others," and who "demonstrates faithfulness to God." In the New Testament, the meaning of the Greek word connotes piety and devoutness. A devout life is always contrasted with that of heretics – unbelievers who oppose God's truth – and libertines who live a carefree life, unconcerned about correct morals (1 Tim 2:2; 4:7–8; 6:3; Titus 1:1; 2 Pet 1:6–7; 3:11). There are far fewer godly people than ungodly people.

Godliness therefore is the foundation of character and the root of self-understanding and motivation. Godly qualities make a good elder, leader, ruler, administrator, or governor. God does not look for influential and powerful people to serve in these roles; he looks at the heart, the seat of all motives and dispositions. It is the moral quality that satisfies God and not the external qualities. "The LORD does not look at the things people look at. People look at the outward appearance, but the LORD looks at the heart" (1 Sam 16:7).

The prophet Isaiah explained that the messianic ruler will have these inner qualities:

> The Spirit of the LORD will rest on him –
> > the Spirit of wisdom and of understanding,
> > the Spirit of counsel and of might,
> > the Spirit of the knowledge and fear of the LORD –
> and he will delight in the fear of the LORD.
> He will not judge by what he sees with his eyes,
> > or decide by what he hears with his ears;
> but with righteousness he will judge the needy,
> > with justice he will give decisions for the poor of the earth.
> He will strike the earth with the rod of his mouth;
> > with the breath of his lips he will slay the wicked.
> Righteousness will be his belt
> > and faithfulness the sash around his waist. (Isa 11:2–5)

A godly leader is one after the pattern of the Messiah. He or she must not be influenced by human considerations. Instead a godly leader must be empowered by the Spirit of God to do extraordinary things. Godly leaders must be guided by the moral standards; by the Spirit in the wisdom, understanding, fear, and knowledge of God; by God's principles of righteousness, equity, justice and faithfulness; and by God's word of truth and judgment. A godly leader will be protected, guarded and strengthened by God's righteousness, integrity, and uprightness.

The Bible also makes it very clear that the fear of the Lord is the basis of godliness. Godly people tremble at God's word. When they observe the glory, power, majesty, and holiness of God, they fear him.[7]

Godliness then is a very strong antidote to any form of corruption among our leaders. It is not enough to have power and influence over people, to have social and human skills, or even managerial and administrative skills. These skills must be rooted in a godly character and in total obedience to the divine moral laws. Without a doubt, our nations, peoples, institutions, and social orders need godly men and women who are humble enough to serve both God and the people faithfully and fearfully.

Cultivating Godly Leadership Skills

Spiritual qualities must be cultivated so that the inner person will be able to stand on solid moral and spiritual grounds while discharging their role. Let us consider some of the principles suggested in the *Leadership Bible*.

An Elder or Leader Must Have a Good Moral Character

In 1992 a friend and I reviewed our curriculum and identified an important aspect that had not been a priority in our pastoral and ministerial training. We had not paid sufficient attention to cultivating the moral and spiritual character of our young pastors in training.

In the New Testament, the Greek word for character is *dokime* which means, "testing as a means of determining genuineness and thus as grounds for giving approval."[8] The *Leadership Bible* states: "Character is not a matter of outward technique but of inner reality . . . Leaders cultivate character by acquiring wisdom and understanding."[9] Elders or leaders must have "a value

---

7. Edwards, *Religious Affections*.
8. Renn, *Expository Dictionary of Bible Words*.
9. *Leadership Bible*, 730.

system that encompasses an attitude of service, personal integrity, dedication to task and to family and a clear sense of purpose."[10]

> Character isn't shaped by intellectual comprehension of truth. It's forged by biblical truth that penetrates to the depth of the human heart. That only occurs as a man or woman grapples with God's Word and contemplates its meaning and application.[11]

The apostle Peter lists some characteristics that Christians, especially Christians in leadership, should display:

> For this very reason, make every effort to add to your faith goodness; and to goodness, knowledge; and to knowledge, self-control; and to self-control, perseverance; and to perseverance, godliness; and to godliness, mutual affection; and to mutual affection, love. For, if you possess these qualities in increasing measure, they will keep you from being ineffective and unproductive in your knowledge of Jesus Christ. (2 Pet 1:5–8)

The apostle Paul makes similar remarks in Romans 5:3–5, and in Galatians 5:22 he lists the qualities as: "love, joy, peace, forbearance, kindness, goodness, faithfulness, gentleness and self-control." Paul, in fact, emphasizes the significance of moral character as a quality of spiritual leadership more than any other New Testament writer. He lists the qualifications for eldership in 1 Timothy 3:1–13 and Titus 1:6–9.

If we followed worldly standards, we would look to people who have great influence and power for leadership, but God looks at leadership differently. In 1 Samuel 16:1–7, the people whom God "chooses to do great things for him are called on the basis of inward character, not on the basis of outward impressiveness . . . God looks at the leader's heart."[12]

An elder or leader without a moral and spiritual character is already a failure.

An Elder or Leader Must Be Committed

> Effective leadership flows from commitment to the right things. As followers of Christ, the single most important commitment of

---

10. *Leadership Bible*, 1412.
11. *Leadership Bible*, 206.
12. *Leadership Bible*, 329.

our lives is to God. Any true (and eternal) success we experience will flow from that commitment . . . God calls us to be a people of commitment, first to him and then to others.[13]

Joshua was committed to serving God faithfully and so was able to challenge the people of Israel whom he was leading to dedicate themselves to the Lord also (Josh 24:14–27). Later Jesus emphasized commitment when he said: "Whoever wants to be my disciple must deny themselves and take up their cross and follow me. For whoever wants to save their life will lose it, but whoever loses their life for me will find it" (Matt 16:24–25; see also Matt 10:37–39).

Godly elders, leaders, rulers, and administrators should be committed to the primary cause of keeping and obeying all of God's universal moral laws.

An Elder or Leader Must Be Courageous

> Leaders need courage to make the tough decisions they're faced with every day.[14]

God requires that leaders put their trust and faith in him, as Joshua and Caleb did when they stood firm in faith unlike the other ten spies (Num 13:26–14:10). Later we read how God encouraged Joshua as he faced the military challenge of the Canaanites. "Have I not commanded you? Be strong and courageous. Do not be afraid; do not be discouraged, for the LORD your God will be with you wherever you go" (Josh 1:9). The courage to stand up for God at all costs was what made the prophet Daniel unique in Babylon, where he lived in very difficult political and administrative circumstances in a foreign land. Daniel's faith was rooted in his fear of the God of Israel and he was determined to keep God's moral laws faithfully. This is the type of courage that modern leaders and rulers need if they are to tackle the endemic vices and the corruption that plague Africa.

An Elder or Leader Must Be Dependent on God

> As leaders who want to impact our generation for Christ, we need to lead in a way that allows others to see our faith in God. One

---

13. *Leadership Bible*, 1334.
14. *Leadership Bible*, 242.

way we can do that is by depending on God in the face of our daily pressures.[15]

Let us take our cue from the psalmist who says: "The LORD is with me; I will not be afraid. What can mere mortals do to me? . . . It is better to take refuge in the LORD than to trust in humans. It is better to take refuge in the LORD than to trust in princes" (Ps 118:6, 8–9).

Young Joseph in Egypt, Joshua and Caleb in the wilderness, king David and young Daniel and his friends in Babylon provide examples of lives lived in complete dependence upon God. Leaning upon God and his spiritual resources is the only way to success in leadership. As the writer said: "Trust in the LORD with all your heart and lean not on your own understanding; in all your ways submit to him, and he will make your paths straight. Do not be wise in your own eyes; fear the LORD and shun evil" (Prov 3:5–7).

An Elder or Leader Must Be Humble

> The main goal for godly leaders – and Christians in general – is to reflect the life of Christ in their own lives. And the character trait that best enables us to do that is humility . . . humility is not a matter of weakness or passivity; from a biblical point of view, it is disciplined strength and other-centered power. In his earthly life, Christ himself was the perfect example of true humility.[16]

Jesus reminds us of the need for humility when he says: "Take my yoke upon you and learn from me, for I am gentle and humble in heart, and you will find rest for your souls. For my yoke is easy and my burden is light" (Matt 11:29–30). Paul commented on how Jesus himself had laid aside his divine and heavenly glory, power, and dominion, humbling himself to take on our sin-nature of slavery and being willing to go to the cross (Phil 2:1–11). Christ's humility paid the redemption price for the entire world.

While it seems that humility places leaders in positions of weakness, the apostle Paul demonstrated the power of humility and weakness in these words:

> My grace is sufficient for you, for my power is made perfect in weakness. Therefore I will boast all the more gladly of my weaknesses, so that Christ's power may rest upon me. That is why,

---

15. *Leadership Bible*, 1122.
16. *Leadership Bible*, 1389.

for Christ's sake, I delight in weaknesses, in insults, in hardships, in persecutions, and in difficulties. For when I am weak, then I am strong. (2 Cor 12:9–10)

This Scripture indicts many leaders whose priority is to seek power, influence, rewards, status, and glory for themselves, often at the expense of those whom they lead. Elders, leaders and rulers must cultivate the habit of walking humbly with God (Mic 6:8) and must not exhibit the characteristics of pride and arrogance. Proverbs 25:27 suggests that it is not "honourable" to seek one's own honour.

Jesus said, "instead, whoever wants to become great among you must be your servant and whoever wants to be first must be slave of all. For even the Son of Man did not come to be served, but to serve, and to give his life as a ransom for many" (Mark 10:43–45). He also said, "You know that those who are regarded as rulers of the Gentiles lord it over them, and their high officials exercise authority over them. Not so with you" (Mark 10:42–43).

This wisdom of God runs counter to the worldly concept of leadership where one must present oneself as the first, the most influential and the most powerful.

An Elder or Leader Must Be a Person of Integrity

If people are going to follow someone, whether into battle or in business or ministry, they want assurance that their leader can be trusted. They want to know that he or she will keep promises and follow through with commitments . . . The biblical virtue of integrity points to a consistency between what is inside and what is outside, between belief and behavior, our words and our ways, our attitudes and our actions, our values and our practice.[17]

The prophet Samuel is a very good example of this kind of integrity and honesty:

I have been your leader from my youth until this day. Here I stand. Testify against me in the presence of the LORD and his anointed. Whose ox have I taken? Whose donkey have I taken? Whom have I cheated? Whom have I oppressed? From whose hand have I accepted a bribe to make me shut my eyes? If I have done any of these, I will make it right. (1 Sam 12:2–3)

---

17. *Leadership Bible*, 320.

There are many other similar examples: Abraham, in instructing his family (Gen 18:19); Joseph, in resisting Potiphar's wife (Gen 39:8–12; 40:15); Moses, in taking nothing from the Israelites for his services (Num 16:15); Nehemiah, in his decision to accept no compensation for his services (Neh 5:14–19); and Job (Job 1:8; 10:7; 13:15; 16:17; 27:4–6). The psalmist also often wrote of the need for personal integrity and honesty (Pss 7:3–5, 8; 17:3; 26:1–3; 69:4; 73:15; 119:121).

Elders and leaders must be able to be trusted. We need upright leaders who shun every form of evil. Psalm 15 gives a lengthy description of those who have integrity. Psalm 26 lists the following characteristics. Men and women of integrity trust God without wavering; call upon God to test their hearts and minds; are always mindful of God's steadfast love; and walk in reliance upon God's faithfulness. They do not associate with people who are false; do not consult hypocrites; hate the assembly of evil doers; and refuse to sit with the wicked. Instead, they wash their hands in innocence and praise the wondrous deeds of God with thanksgiving. Psalm 1 picks up on this description, stating that men or women of integrity "do not walk in step with the wicked or stand in the way that sinners take or sit in the company of mockers." Their "delight is in the law of the Lord" and they "meditate on his law day and night."

When we consider leadership, both in the secular world and in the church, we see that men and women of integrity are very few in number.

An Elder or Leader Must Be Obedient to God

> A godly leader's commitment to God should be such that he or she will obey him no matter what he or she is offered to compromise ... A brief overview of Israel's history shows that the fundamental problem of God's covenant people was their repeated failure to obey God's commands, habitual disobedience.[18]

Although Saul was the king of Israel, he did not obey the word of the Lord and God cut him off (1 Sam 15:1–24). The primary duty of elders, leaders, rulers and administrators is to obey God at all times. John the apostle reminds us that "love for God [is] to keep his commands. And his commands are not burdensome" (1 John 5:3). Jesus himself summarized the prophets and the law saying: "'Love the Lord your God with all your heart and with all your soul and with all your mind' ... And the second is like it: 'Love your neighbor as

---

18. *Leadership Bible*, 327.

yourself.' All the Law and the Prophets hang on these two commandments" (Matt 22:37–40).

The test of leaders' love for God is measured by their obedience to his moral laws. The prophet Daniel and his friends in Babylon showed this in their public life and administration. The early apostles in Jerusalem told the Jewish religious and political leaders: "Which is right in God's eyes: to listen to you, or to him? You be the judges! As for us, we cannot help speaking about what we have seen and heard" (Acts 4:20).

Obedience to God and to his moral laws requires boldness. Elders and leaders must defend the truth, speaking boldly and fearlessly.

An Elder or Leader Must Prioritize

> Effective leaders have the ability to discern not only the difference between the good and the bad, but also the difference between the good and the best... We have to decide what matters most or we become victims of the loudest or latest demands.[19]

We need wisdom as we evaluate our lives and arrange our priorities. Our focus should be on "knowing and understanding God and pleasing him."[20] "Our perspective should determine our priorities, and our priorities should determine our practice... anything that keeps us away from the love of the Father is idolatrous, no matter how 'good' it appears."[21] The apostle John gives us both the perspective and the warning:

> Do not love the world or anything in the world. If anyone loves the world, love for the Father is not in him. For everything in the world – the lust of the flesh, the lust of the eyes and the pride of life – comes not from the Father but from the world. The world and its desires pass away, but whoever does the will of God lives forever. (1 John 2:15–17)

Elders and leaders must be focused and must not be side-tracked by trivial things. Paul addresses this important subject when he states: "But one thing I do: Forgetting what is behind and straining towards what is ahead, I press on

---

19. *Leadership Bible*, 1218.
20. *Leadership Bible*, 884.
21. *Leadership Bible*, 1467.

toward the goal to win the prize for which God has called me heavenward in Christ Jesus" (Phil 3:13–14).

When politicians or religious leaders seek positions of leadership, they often make glowing promises of what they will do. Unfortunately, they often do not do what they promised and end up achieving nothing. Jesus warned his disciples and followers: "No one who puts his hand to the plow and looks back is fit for service in the kingdom of God" (Luke 9:62).

An Elder or Leader Must Be Purposeful and Passionate

> Effective leaders . . . are those who have figured out what they stand for. They have identified their purpose and pursue it with a passion.[22]

In Joshua 14:6–14, Caleb demonstrated that he was a man of purpose, passion, enthusiasm, faith, and commitment to the Lord. Paul does the same in Philippians 3:7–14. Leaders usually have an agenda, a programme of action, something definite which they want to achieve. But sadly good programmes and good intentions are often never realized. Perhaps this is because the leaders are not propelled by the desire to accomplish something to the praise and glory of God.

An Elder or Leader Must Be Self-disciplined

> Self-discipline may be defined simply as that quality that allows a person to do what needs to be done when he or she does not feel like doing it . . . Self-discipline is a character trait that helps leaders evaluate what they're doing, stop doing what is harmful, and start doing what's constructive . . . If you want to be an effective leader, identify the habits you need to build into your life so you can lead with diligence – habits such as physical fitness, balance between work and home, financial and personal accountability, proactivity in the work-place, and the like . . . Composure, presence of mind, cool-headedness, patience, self-possession, restraint – only a few people display these qualities, and those who do usually make effective leaders.[23]

---

22. *Leadership Bible*, 1392.
23. *Leadership Bible*, 745, 1348.

Self-discipline is a very important quality. Many leaders, both in the secular world and in the church, have fallen victim to immorality and corruption simply because they lacked a disciplined moral lifestyle. Shame, disgrace and dishonour are usually the lot of undisciplined leaders. A leader cannot be successful if self-discipline is lacking.

An Elder or Leader Must Have Core Spiritual Values

> Values drive behavior; a person will pursue what that person loves . . . Values run far deeper and are far more important to a leader's effectiveness than any other single factor.[24]

Study and meditation on the word of God are the only ways of building up spiritual core values. Elders, leaders, and rulers must build a reservoir in their hearts so that they can store up spiritual values to guide their life and conduct.

David underscores this point, saying "I have hidden your word in my heart that I might not sin against you . . . I meditate on your precepts and consider your ways. I delight in your decrees; I will not neglect your word" (Ps 119:11, 15–16). He makes a similar statement in Psalm 19:7–11 where he says:

> The law of the LORD is perfect, refreshing the soul. The statutes of the LORD are trustworthy, making wise the simple. The precepts of the LORD are right, giving joy to the heart. The commands of the LORD are radiant, giving light to the eyes. The fear of the LORD is pure, enduring forever. The decrees of the LORD are firm, and all of them are righteous.

David goes on to say that these spiritual values are more to be desired than gold and are sweeter than honey.

Leaders without a spiritual core will not exhibit a moral and spiritual character or discipline in their leadership.

An Elder or Leader Must Have a Vision

> Good leaders foresee something out there, vague as it might appear from the distance, that others don't see. Godly leaders . . . must first have a vision of who God is and the future he holds for them. They must also have a sense of what God has called them to do.[25]

---

24. *Leadership Bible*, 635.
25. *Leadership Bible*, 1368.

Joseph the interpreter of dreams in Egypt was a man of vision and insight. After interpreting the dreams of Pharaoh, he advised as follows: "And now let Pharaoh look for a discerning and wise man and put him in charge of the land of Egypt. Let Pharaoh appoint commissioners over the land to take a fifth of the harvest of Egypt during the seven years of abundance" (Gen 41:33–34). Nehemiah also was a man of vision and insight and he used that to overcome the threats and the deceit of his opponents, Sanballat, Tobiah, and Geshem (Neh 6:1–14). Mordecai, through his vision and insight, was able to save the Jews in Persia with the help of Queen Esther. The apostle Paul was also a man of vision (2 Cor 4:16–18; 12:1–6).

An Elder or Leader Must Have Wisdom

> Wisdom is the ability to use the best means at the best time to accomplish the best ends. It is not merely a matter of information or knowledge, but of skilful and practical application of the truth to the ordinary facets of life.[26]

Wisdom comes through receiving and treasuring God's commandments (Prov 2:1–11). James reminds us: "If any of you lacks wisdom, you should ask God, who gives generously to all without finding fault, and it will be given to you" (Jas 1:5). The young King Solomon chose wisdom above all else: "Give your servant a discerning heart to govern your people and to distinguish between right and wrong. For who is able to govern this great people of yours?" (1 Kgs 3:9).

An Elder or Leader Must Have Human and Social Skills

An elder or leader in society needs to have social, relational and people skills. Without these skills, knowledge cannot be put to good use and people, communities, societies, institutions, and nation-states cannot be developed. The *Leadership Bible* lists the following as important for building effective human relationships: encouragement (Acts 9:27); exhortation (2 Tim 2:14–21); healthy alliances (1 Sam 22:1–5); interpersonal relationships (Hos 2:1–23); power and influence (Ps 82:1–8); and servant leadership (John 13:1–17). An elder or leader who uses these skills can transform the lives of the people he serves.

---

26. *Leadership Bible*, 739.

37

Engaging with Governance, Management and Administration

Modern African is lost in an urban public setting that is devoid of traditional communal values. The communal concept is being replaced by the word "public." People are regarded as individuals without a community and are no longer governed by communal values, but by municipal or nation-state laws. This means that leadership, management, or administration has to take place in public within a social order or within an institution. The challenge for Christian leaders, managers, and administrators is to bring their private spiritual qualities and moral lifestyle into the open so that they can make a godly and moral difference in their nations, and among their peoples in the institutions, organizations, and social orders where they serve.

It is necessary that those who govern, manage, or administer do so effectively. At the time of independence African nationalists and politicians were mainly elders and leaders who had no training and so were not skilled in governance, management or administration of the institutions of government.

Principles of Governance, Management, or Administration

Good governance, management or administration is the ability to mobilize the needed human and material resources to achieve the goals and objectives of the organization. A good manager must be skilled in sourcing and mobilizing human and material resources; in identifying and prioritizing goals and objectives; and in implementing programmes and projects to achieve the desired ends, results, and outcomes.

However, those who are involved with governing, managing and administering need more than just skills and knowledge. They also need the guidance of the Holy Spirit and the wisdom of God. Moses needed men who were skilled in their arts, but they needed the anointing of the Holy Spirit to accomplish their work on the tabernacle:

> Then the LORD said to Moses, "See, I have chosen Bezalel son of Uri, the son of Hur, of the tribe of Judah, and I have filled him with the Spirit of God, with wisdom, with understanding, with knowledge and with all kinds of skills – to make artistic designs for work in gold, silver and bronze, to cut and set stones, to work in wood and to engage in all kinds of crafts." (Exod 31:1–5)

The apostles recognized this important principle when they said: "Brothers and sisters, choose seven men from among you who are known to be full of the Spirit and wisdom. We will turn this responsibility over to them" (Acts 6:3).

Moral and spiritual values will primarily determine whether the chosen are going to be good or bad leaders, strong or weak leaders, sectional or national leaders; self-less or self-serving leaders; morally upright or corrupt leaders. Whether we are leading or ruling people, or whether we are governing, managing, or administering institutions, organizations, or social orders, the moral nature and character of God must be our model. The primary objective of Christian leadership and governance is to transform and change human societies, institutions, and social orders for the glory of God.

The Bible nonetheless provides examples of many of the skills that Christians need to develop to ensure effective governance, management, and administration: accountability (Gen 43:8–9); the ability to handle change (Mark 2:18–22); communication skills (1 Chr 28:1–21; Prov 18:2); the ability to manage conflict (Matt 5:23–24; 18:15–17); the ability to make decisions (Esth 4:12–16); the ability to empower others (Acts 1:8); the ability to develop leadership skills in others (Luke 10:1–24); organizational skills (Exod 18:13–26); the ability to plan (Gen 3:15); the ability to develop and manage human resources (Eph 4:11–16); problem-solving skills (Neh 6:1–14); the ability to hold people accountable through quality controls (Col 3:23–24); good stewardship (Matt 25:14–30); team building skills (2 Sam 23:8–17); time management skills (Ps 90:12); and the ability to analyze systems (1 Cor 12:12–29).[1]

---

1. *Leadership Bible*, home page contents.

Social Variables, Social Factors and Social Orders
Society Is a Public Domain

Margaret Peil defined society "as a group of people with shared values, beliefs, symbols, patterns of behavior and territory."[2] This means a society consists of the following three broad components: (1) social structures or institutions; (2) social values, beliefs or cultures; and (3) people. The interaction between these variables generates public processes that affect the social structures or institutions; the social values, cultures, beliefs, meanings; and also the persons in society or people group.

Christian elders, leaders, managers and administrators have to deal with all these components of society. These will include unjust and corrupt institutions, social values, cultures, beliefs, social practices, as well as people who make life very difficult for others. Herein lies the challenge for Christian elders, leaders, managers, and administrators. They are required to be both salt and light in their societies, among their peoples, and in their social institutions (Matt 5:13–16). God's universal moral laws and biblical principles have to be publicly demonstrated by Christian elders, leaders, managers, and administrators.

Culture as a Public Social Tool

Culture is a public social tool and can never be private. The most relevant definition of culture for our use is that of Clifford Geertz:

> Culture denotes an historically transmitted pattern of meanings embodied in symbols, a system of inherited conceptions expressed in symbolic forms by means of which men communicate, perpetuate, and develop their knowledge about and attitude toward life.[3]

Three important components emerge from this definition: culture is an ordered system of meaning, of symbols, and of conceptions. These will influence public social interactions and behaviour in society and in so doing will affect the public social system or structure. Later Geertz expanded on the above definition, "Culture is an ordered system of meaning and of symbols, in terms of which social interaction takes place, while the social system is the pattern of social interaction itself."[4] This suggests that culture is the public framework

---

2. Peil, *Consensus and Conflict*, 16.
3. Geertz, *Interpretations of Cultures*, 89.
4. Geertz, 89, 144.

of beliefs, expressive symbols and values in terms of which individuals define their world, express their feelings and make their judgments.

The area of culture will be the greatest challenge for Christian elders, leaders, managers and administrators. These components exert a very powerful and pervasive influence over people and can hold them in captivity and servitude. All aspects of culture must therefore be evaluated, assessed, and addressed in the light of God's universal moral laws and biblical principles. In this way Christian leaders can be powerful moral agents for social change and social transformation.

Persons as Moral Agents in Society

People are the moral agents in society as they determine the morals and ethics. Peil observed that a people have "shared values, beliefs, symbols, patterns of behaviour and territory" while Geertz stated that people "communicate, perpetuate, and develop their knowledge about and attitude toward life." Thus, in the words of David Bidney, "man is the measure of culture and society."[5] Humans therefore have the power to transform and influence their societies. However, this role will be of limited value if it is subject to conditioning by the society in which the leader exists.

Geertz uses two concepts to further define the meaning of culture; namely "ethos" and "worldview."

> A people's ethos is the tone, character, quality of their life, its moral and aesthetic style and mood; it is the underlying attitude toward themselves and world that life reflects, [while] their worldview is their picture of the way things in sheer actuality are, their concept of nature, of self, of society. It contains their most comprehensive ideas of order.[6]

These two factors are very important as we seek to understand how people see and view themselves as humans and also how they see and view society and the world in which they live in relationship with others. People usually justify corrupt and immoral public practices by referring to their history and contemporary society. Many people practice corruption and immorality, either privately or publicly, because of social pressure, influence, and conditioning

---

5. Bidney, *Theoretical Anthropology*, xxx.
6. Geertz, *Interpretations of Cultures*, 127.

which have been generated by their traditions, cultures, and worldviews. This is what the apostle Paul calls "the world" or "worldliness" (Rom 12:2).

However human beings cannot use these pressures as an excuse. They are moral beings, responsible agents, standing before their creator and must therefore be accountable for their corrupt and immoral practices. If Christian leaders are to transform these corrupt practices, they must set a public example of a godly lifestyle patterned after the moral character of God, Jesus Christ and the apostles, and the teachings of the Bible.

The behaviour of people in society depends on what values they draw from and what values they have decided are desirable. Values are therefore also a public social tool as they reflect how people view themselves and their world. The most relevant definition of "value" is that of Clyde Kluckhohn. He defined a value as "a conception explicit or implicit, distinctive of an individual or characteristic of a group, of the desirable which influences the selection from available modes, means and ends of actions."[7] Undesirable values can lead to corruption and immorality, but when people draw from the storehouse of Christian and biblical values this leads to godliness and integrity. Christians must advocate values which reflect God's universal moral values as well as biblical moral and ethical principles.

> Values are uncompromisable, undebatable truths that drive and direct behaviour. They are motivational – they give us reasons why we do things; and they are restrictive – they place boundaries around behaviour . . . If we look at the world for our moral values, we will be confused by self-interest, social conditioning and situational ethics. The values of our cultures are shallow and subjective, but the moral standards of Scripture reflect God's absolute and unchanging character.[8]

The selection of desirable values is a social behaviour that has a profound influence on others. Since human beings are moral agents, social values inform their behaviour. This means that the human factor in society is affected by culture (values), on the one hand, and by social structure (order), on the other. But people have the capacity to transform and modify cultural values and social structures or institutions. Good leadership and governance, then, comes from men and women who have been morally and spiritually transformed by the word of God. Their godly lives, spiritual qualities and character, disciplined

---

7. Kluckhohn, "Values and Values-Orientation," 395.
8. *Leadership Bible*, 634.

lifestyle, and human and social skills can be put to good use transforming human societies and institutions for the glory of God. God has called Christian elders and leaders, not just to practice their Christianity privately, but to practise it publicly in building human societies, institutions, governments and social orders. They are called upon to make a difference in leadership and governance. They are to ensure the implementation of godly norms of justice, equality, equity, freedom, and rights in human societies and institutions by godly elders, leaders, rulers, managers, and administrators in the public eye.

The rise and fall of nations in history is rooted in God's universal moral order. Even secular history testifies to the fact that the reason for the fall of great empires in history was their moral indiscipline, decadence and decay. The only moral values that can sustain and uphold the stability of nations or peoples in history are God's universal moral laws.

When these are applied, human social orders will attain stability, peace, harmony, unity, progress, and prosperity. God created and instituted moral order, and all human social orders must be managed in accordance with the moral prescription of their Creator. Just as the physical world functions best within the norms of the universal physical laws, so the human social orders and institutions function best under the universal moral laws and biblical principles.

38

Engaging with the Need to Create a Responsible and Just Society

Let us now turn our attention to the ethics of communities, societies and nation-states in modern Africa. Both the church and governments have overemphasized an individualistic approach to social and communal problems of Africa and have neglected the communal approach.

The title of Reinhold Niebuhr's book *Moral Man and Immoral Society* highlights the problem. The solution cannot just depend on one individual or "moral man." Individual ethics and morality cannot create a sound environment or community. They must be augmented by social and communal ethics and morality. We need a moral society, a moral institution, and a moral nation-state.

Given the crisis-ridden and chaotic African states and the lack of human rights, peace, justice, and equality in Africa, it is essential that we develop moral concepts that can address Africa's communal and social problems.

A Responsible Society

The idea of the "responsible society" was developed after the Second World War by the World Council of Churches (WCC). The organization sought to deal with social problems such as disorder in society, the problems of economic and political organizations, and the problems arising from communism and capitalism. It also sought ways in which the church could become more effectively involved.

The norms which the WCC developed for a responsible society were used to evaluate economic, political and social relations domestically and internationally. Walter Muelder's book *Foundations of the Responsible Society* developed the idea of a responsible society still further. He developed norms and goals such as freedom, justice, equality, and respect for persons, and went on to discuss how these norms could be used. He has shaped my own thinking. Muelder listed eight areas which need to be explored if one wishes to establish a responsible society:

> (1) the role of religious norms in a just and free society;
>
> (2) the conception of man, his dignity, rights and self-realization in community with others;
>
> (3) the nature, authority, and scope of the modern state and its functions in relation to the community;
>
> (4) the interpretation of political, economic and social spheres of society;
>
> (5) the tensions of such ideals as equality, freedom, and justice within the general idea of responsible living;
>
> (6) the responsibility of persons to domestic and international orders of freedom and justice;
>
> (7) the accountability of power groups within nations;
>
> (8) the responsibilities of nations to one another and to the future of responsible international order.[1]

The theological basis of the responsible society rests on the belief that: "Man is created and called to be a free being, responsible to God and his neighbour."[2] This was expanded as follows:

> Moral advice and proclamation of moral ideals are insufficient. Only that which transcends morals, namely, the knowledge of the ultimate accountability of man and society to God and of the Grace of God by which men, being forgiven, forgive one another, can be the foundation of personal responsibility and responsible society.[3]

The "responsible society" was not seen as an alternative socio-political system. Instead it was a criterion by which all existing social orders could be judged and a standard which could guide societies when they had to make

---

1. Muelder, *Foundations of the Responsible Society*, 214.
2. World Council of Churches, *Statements of the WCC on Social Questions*, 19.
3. World Council of Churches, 26.

choices. "Christians are called to live responsibly, to live in response to God's act of redemption in Christ, in any society, even within the most unfavorable social structures."[4]

Thus the idea of the responsible society was a normative concept concerned with social justice and the development of social conditions in which human dignity and freedom could find their expression as befits the nature and destiny of man as a child of God.[5]

African elders, leaders, and rulers should hold on to this moral and ethical norm, ensuring that it is instituted within African communities, societies, institutions, and nation-states.

A Just, Participatory and Sustainable Society

The main focus of the ecumenical social thought and action of WCC was the struggle for a more just and socially responsible society. This included the more equitable distribution of wealth and income, and the transformation of political and economic institutions which caused injustice. The values of a "responsible society," which include justice, equality, freedom, respect for personality, and responsibility to God and the people, need to be sustained through justice and participation. These are the principles, norms, and goals through which we can address social and communal problems.

According to Muelder, the concept presupposes the acceptance of five theological concepts which involve both personal ethical principles and social and communal ethics:

> (1) Moral accountability to God and neighbor; (2) the solidarity of the human family; (3) the sacred worth of each person and, hence, the primacy of equality over inequality; (4) historical freedom as a precondition of effective participation; and (5) the reality of sin and, therefore, the need to control (limit) economic and political power.[6]

The struggle for a just, participatory and sustainable society is part of a broader context: the relation between God, humanity and nature.[7] Humanity and nature are part of God's history with his creation in which justice and

---

4. World Council of Churches, 49.
5. World Council of Churches.
6. Muelder, "Just, Participatory and Sustainable World," 19.
7. Albrecht, *Faith, Science and Future*, 29.

injustice, and even life and death, are in conflict as a result of the fall. Modern Africa, together with the rest of the world, risks destruction as a result of this broken relationship between God, humanity and nature. In order to save the depleted resources of the earth, we must develop an ethical and moral approach to our society and to the world. Albert uses two theological concepts to show the relationship between God, humanity, and nature: *imago Dei* (image of God) and dominium.[8]

Imago Dei is the biblical concept which indicates humanity's relation to God and the relationship of humanity with the non-human creation. Because we are created in God's image, human beings should live in community as men and women, brothers and sisters, in families, "tribes" and peoples.

> As God's image, humanity is to rule with care over the non-human creation and in this way share in the preservation of earthly creation and further its development. Humankind as a whole has been created in God's image without distinction of sex, class or race.[9]

The concept of *dominium* speaks of the responsibility of humanity towards the non-human creation. It covers two areas: first, where humanity is the maker (*homo faber*), and second, where humanity is the cultivator. These two concepts must be integrated so that limits are set for the maker, although there is opportunity for creative imagination. This means that the reshaping of nature involves cooperation with nature[10] and calls for the careful use of nature, creation and the environment. Issues of deforestation, depletion of natural resources, endangered species, pollution and degradation of the environment must be addressed by this theology of environment or ecology. The relationships between God, humanity and nature show that society (human relations) and ecosystems (non-human creation as humanity's home) are intimately interconnected. Similarly, justice and the sustainability of creation are also inter-connected.[11] This holistic view of life reflects the traditional African worldview.

The biblical mandate for humanity is that there must be responsible dominion over the earth. There must be worldwide responsibility and stewardship in the face of the blatant misuse and exploitation of the world, its

---

8. Albrecht.
9. Albrecht, 30.
10. Albrecht.
11. Albrecht.

people, and its resources. This includes the struggle for "a just, participatory and sustainable society" through expressing solidarity with others and recognising neighbours as people.[12]

We need to develop some theological norms and principles for addressing the problems of human societies and communities.

Sustainability

Albrecht defines a sustainable society as:

> One in which people live with each other and the physical environment in ways that lead to continuing life rather than destruction. In recent years much of the world has discovered that its present habits of consumption threatens the physical environment and the resources by which people themselves live. Humanity is one member of the ecosystem (also part of God's creation) and has to live in continuing interaction with it. Practices destructive of the ecosystem will also destroy human society. In this respect, justice characterized a human relationship with the whole ecosystem as well as the relationship with other human persons and groups.[13]

Traditional African societies before colonialism were self-sustaining and viable. After the colonial encounter with the West, African societies were left dependent and unsustainable. As a result, traditional communal or kinship values are no longer adequate for modern African societies. Many African peoples and nation-states depend on handouts, aid, and rely on having their budgets balanced by contributions from rich countries. There is also anxiety with regard to global warming because of irresponsible stewardship of God's creation. African nations are in danger of depleting their resources and damaging their environment as they search for wealth, food, and security. Professor Charles Birch states:

> A prior requirement of any global society is that it be so organized that the life of man and other living creatures on which his life depends can be sustained indefinitely within the limits of the earth. A second requirement is that it be sustained at a quality that makes possible fulfilment of human life for all people. A

---

12. Albrecht.
13. Albrecht, 92.

society so organized to achieve both these ends can be called a sustainable global society in contrast to the present unsustainable global society.[14]

Humanity's responsibility, therefore, is:

> To make a deliberate transition to a sustainable global society in which science and technology will be mobilized to meet the basic physical and spiritual needs of people, to minimize human suffering and to create an environment which can sustain a decent quality of life for all.[15]

Sustainability emphasizes social responsibility in the current technical age and must be taken very seriously. "A society which is sustainable and considerate of the future must resolutely combat the wastage of the earth's riches and make the development of renewable energy a top priority."[16]

The need for sustainability affects areas such as energy, food, and other resources. It also includes limiting the use of political, economic, or technological power. This means the moral values of responsibility, justice, and participation should guide the use of creative and natural resources in Africa.

Walter Muelder points out that sustainability emphasizes the unity and the limits of the earth's resources, the interdependence of human beings, and their dependence on nature. It lifts ecology to the level of an applied ethical principle. It does not only look back at wasteful failures in incoherent policies of growth, but looks forward to responsibility out of respect for coming generations because people are the stewards of posterity. Sustainability demands attention to small ecosystems as well as to the whole biosphere and evokes a new understanding of nature as having history.[17] Paulos Gregorios reminds us that sustainability creates a new humanity with a new ethical reflection on human presence that mediates between God and nature.[18]

Clearly, dealing with human social problems involves more than simply dealing with moral or immoral individuals. The social and communal problems that affect human societies must be handled, as must nature (ecology).

---

14. Birch cited in Albrecht, 4.
15. Albrecht, 4.
16. Albrecht, 4.
17. Muelder, "Just, Participatory and Sustainable World," 21.
18. Gregorios, *Human Presence*.

Justice

Traditional kinship and communal values are also unable to deal effectively with issues of social justice. A just society is defined in the following words:

> A just society is the kind of society heralded by the prophets and Jesus in the words translated as "justice" and "righteousness." "Let justice roll down as waters" (Amos 5:24). "Seek first his kingdom and his justice (or righteousness)" (Matt 5:33). In a just society persons and groups (family, occupational, social, ethnic, national) relate to one another for the benefit of all. Persons and groups have the opportunity to become human in freedom and responsibility. We can give no single universal description of what truly human life is, for that is in part a function of cultural and social institutions. Yet we recognize a common humanity among all created "in the image of God."[19]

The prophets of the Old Testament challenged the injustice of a society in which the poor went hungry and were exploited by the rich. This was picked up in the gospel of Christ which leads Christians to a commitment to an equitable society in which every human being has significance and dignity and where none is oppressed.

> Justice is inseparable from the Christian concept of love or agape, which means, among other things, creative sympathy for the suffering and the oppressed, siding with them and furthering the interests of others even at the expense of one's own.[20]

According to Muelder, justice seeks a responsible society and "embraces the drive to correct mal-distribution of scarce resources and the products of earth and labor and to reduce radically and persistently the gap between rich and poor countries and classes."[21] Philip Potter of the World Council of Churches defined justice in the following words:

> It is interesting to note that the Hebrew word for righteousness, justice, *sedeq*, means the ability to maintain oneself, to act according to one's nature, to have firmness and strength, integrity of character. In its social application, it means mutual acknowledgement of persons, mutual maintenance of each other's

---

19. Albrecht, "Faith and Science in an Unjust World," vol. 2, 148.
20. Albrecht, 148.
21. Muelder, "A Just, Participatory and Sustainable World," 20.

> honour and integrity, enabling one another to maintain themselves and to play their full part in love of the covenant community. Truth and justice are therefore closely related... Sustainability depends on truth and justice and the gift of what is good. It has been rightly said that "the good" is that which increases communication and multiplies responsibility.[22]

It is clear that these definitions of justice mean there must be social equity and social responsibility through social participation, and not only through social distribution. Most of the social crises plaguing Africa are caused by a lack of participation by all ethnic groups in the politics of the nation-states. In most cases Africans define themselves simply by their ethnic nationalities or by tribes and so a lack of social equity or social responsibility affects not only individuals, but also these ethnic nationalities.

Participation

> A participatory society includes in the process of decision-making all those whom any decision affects. Decisions are thus made by people, with people, for people. The modes of participation are likely to vary in different societies and in different decisions within societies. But everywhere participation is concerned not merely with the making of decisions but also with the sharing of resources, both material and spiritual, and the sharing of the suffering and the benefits... Justice and participation must characterize the relationship between societies as well as the relationships between individuals in society.[23]

The pursuit of justice involves participation. Potter stated:

> Participation calls for a recognition of everybody's right to be consulted, to be heard and understood, whatever their political, economic or social status may be in society. Everyone must be involved in planning and action, giving as well as receiving. Participation means that each one takes initiative in formulating

---

22. Potter cited in Shinn, "Faith and Science in an Unjust World," vol. 1, 26.
23. Albrecht, "Faith and Science in an Unjust World," vol. 2, 148.

or changing policies and becoming involved in directing their implementation.[24]

As people become involved in making decisions in a society, they see the need for structural change at every level, especially when questions of development are involved.[25] According to Muelder, the normative characteristics of "participation": imply development from below rather than from top down; include the motif of freedom central to the idea of the "responsible society" and self-determination; challenge both capitalistic elites and socialist elites; challenge the style and structure of elitism often found in science and technology; challenge all decision-making that bypasses the oppressed, the underprivileged, the marginalized and ordinary people; and it clarifies the meaning of social justice.[26]

Although the goals and norms which have arisen out of the concepts of a "responsible" and "just, participatory and sustainable society," were developed from global perspectives, they are relevant to modern Africa. We can use these norms to address, and evaluate the communal and social problems of justice, equality, freedom, participation, and sustainability.

The social and communal problems that haunt modern Africa need to be examined in the light of history. The freedom of many ethnic groups or races was denied under colonialism when they came under the political control of other extremely powerful ethnic groups. For this reason, they were denied any political participation. Thus, the primary basis of the colonial socio-political structure was inequality, rather than equality, and the social orders created by colonial administrations in Africa were far from just, participatory and sustainable. Instead, they were characterized by differential treatment of ethnic groups or persons; by the denying of political participation to some groups; by stratified inequality between ethnic groups, tribes, races, and regions; and by institutionalized socio-political, economic and religious structures of inequality.

Justice, participation and sustainability must become the vision for a new social order in Africa.

The continuing consequences of these injustices must be addressed from the perspective of the norms and goals of Christian social thought. The church is the new humanity, the messianic community, which is governed

---

24. Potter cited in Shinn, "Faith and Science in an Unjust World," vol. 1, 27.
25. Arruda, *Ecumenism and a New World Order*.
26. Muelder, "Just, Participatory and Sustainable World."

by Christ's new communitarian ethics and morality. These ethics should also address the structural problems of the nation-states. Injustices, oppression, discrimination, bias, prejudice, corruption, conflict and violence should not just be "confessed," but must be seen to be redressed and eradicated. This means there must be social and communal implementation of structures and institutions of peace and harmony, as well as spiritual confessions, repentance, forgiveness, and reconciliation.

Moral engineering (through moral values and religion) though useful is not enough. Moralists have failed to impact and transform African societies permanently. Social engineering (through politics, economics and technology) though useful is not enough. Social engineers have failed to impact and transform African societies permanently.

The dominant spirit-powers that lie behind them can only be dealt with through the power of the Spirit of God and the sacred Scriptures. Christian morality cannot simply be an attitude of mind; the Christianity of good, moral individual Christians does not last beyond their generation. Christian morality needs social institutions to strengthen and sustain it. Christians do not operate in a vacuum; they are in the world with all its dominant spirit-powers and values. A Christianity that lasts is the one that renews and transforms humans, societies, communities, tribes, races and nations.

39

Engaging with Traditional Human Values

Given the degradation of human values and personality in modern Africa, it is important that we develop a biblical view of humankind that enhances the value, dignity, rights, sanctity, and sacredness of human life. We need to emphasize the divine basis of human dignity and human rights. Furthermore, given the over-glorification of humankind and the social and spiritual needs in traditional Africa, the true nature of humankind as sinners before God needs to be understood. There are great mysteries beyond our understanding which have been solved in Jesus the Messiah, rather than through the spirit beings and the "fake" offers of prophets, philosophers and religious people.

Divine Basis of Human Dignity: *"Imago Dei"*

Human dignity cannot just be rooted in the historical consciousness of humans or in some sort of value forged by humans. Human dignity needs a criterion or a grounding that gives us a better definition and deeper understanding of humankind beyond the realm of the nature, beyond social sciences, beyond philosophies and beyond tribal, ethnic, or racial values and interpretations. In order to find this unique foundation of human dignity, we need to turn to the biblical creation narratives.

The biblical creation narratives have accorded humans the highest value in God's creation. They are the only creature created in God's image and also the only creature appointed to rule God's creation (Gen 1:27–28). Roland B. Allen states:

> Man's dignity rests in God who assigns an inestimable worth to every person. Man's origin is not an accident, but a profoundly

> intelligent act by One who has eternal value, by One who stamps his image on each person. God created men and moves heaven and earth to redeem them when they fall. Our origin is in creation and our destiny is for redemption. Between these points every human heartbeat has value.[1]

Allen further explains the moral basis of human dignity:

> To man, a creation of seeming insignificance, God has given great dignity. To man, little and lost in the vastness of space, God has given sovereignty. To man, puny and restless and weak, God has given part of himself. Of all God's creatures, only man is made in his image. Man is the crown of the cosmos, the measure of creation. Man, as male and female, is God's finest work.[2]

The fact that humankind was created in God's image and that it received God's divine command form the basis and foundation of human dignity, worth, sacredness, and dominion. "Man in the image of God is a majestic creature; he has great dignity in the eyes of the Maker."[3] Humankind is the apex or crown of God's creation.

The "image of God" marks humankind out from the rest of the created things and provides the reason for the sanctity of human life. God makes humankind unique and distinct from the rest of creation, and humankind has the right to be recognized as such.

Humankind's dignity, worth, sacredness, and dominion therefore are universal moral principles and values. These are inherent, emanating from humankind's very being, and are not conferred upon humankind by any other means. Humankind must recognize these universal and divine moral principles and values and must accept the responsibility for protecting, affirming, and defending them. The demands that people make of others and of social institutions must be noted, as human dignity cannot be subordinated to any unjust social, political or economic arrangements. Human dignity is described in the following words: "Dignity is a characteristic of all persons – the ground from which emerge all moral claims, all rights, all duties. The preservation and promotion of human dignity is the sum and substance of all such claims, rights and duties."[4]

---

1. Allen, *Majesty of Man*, 73.
2. Allen, 73.
3. Allen, 113.
4. Hollenbach, "Development of Catholic," 60.

> Human persons have dignity. They are sacred and precious. In its most basic meaning dignity is not granted to persons by the ethical activity of others. The family, society or the state does not bestow dignity on persons. Rather the reality of human dignity makes claims on others that it be recognized and respected . . . Human dignity, however, is more fundamental than any moral principle itself . . . Secondly, human dignity, again in its primary meaning, is not a concept which derives its meaning from a particular class or genius of human action. It has reality in all situations, independent of the kinds of actions, which give them structure. Dignity is thus a transcendental characteristic of persons. Human persons have a worth, which claims respect in every situation and in every type of activity. Dignity is a norm by which all forms of human behaviour and all the moral principles, which are formulated to guide behaviour, are judged. Human dignity is therefore . . . a concrete reality which exists wherever persons exist.[5]

Human dignity, therefore, gives humankind the primary position in creation, above all social institutions. It also defines man as "the foundation, cause and end of all social institutions." Only if social institutions "are in service of all persons, are they properly ordered."[6]

This biblical theology of man is a serious indictment of the way people have been treated in Africa since the colonial days.

Human Nature and the Fall

Although traditional Africa has much to say about human nature, one question was never dealt with: How did humankind fall into sin and evil? African traditional theology did not develop any understanding of the sinful nature of humankind or the problem of sin and evil. Sin, evil and the fall of humankind must consequently be a major focus of the Christian contribution towards defining humankind in Africa.

Humankind's historical consciousness, self-awareness and enlightenment coupled with its search for dignity, rights, identity, and meaning have created values and ideals which have in turn become the enemies of humanity. No one can ignore the fact that human nature is not consistent. Sometimes, we

---

5. Hollenbach, 60.
6. Hollenbach, 3–4.

act like angels and, at other times, we act like beasts. No wonder it is possible to create false identities and gods. No wonder wickedness thrives.

Human nature has been perverse and corrupt throughout history. This inner corruption reveals the monstrous complexity of human nature. And this is where the biblical account of the fall of humankind and the world (or cosmos) in Genesis 3 comes in. It is sin that has perverted and corrupted human nature. The effect of sin is a reality that must be taken seriously. If we do not do so, the analysis and prognosis arising from human and social sciences, religions and philosophies will be grossly defective.

The sinfulness of humankind taints the state, ethnic group, race, and tribe. These social differences can become false gods and instruments of wickedness and oppression. When we are faced with human persecution, discrimination and other issues of human liberty, we must return to this biblical basic understanding of the fall of man. Issues of human dignity, rights, identity and meaning are indeed basically moral and spiritual. A good resource in considering the moral consequences of our sinful treatment of our fellow humans and the created order is the book by Bruce Milne, *Know the Truth: A Handbook of Christian Belief*.

Langdon Gilkey also addressed the complexity of the human nature:

> Man's existence is perverted by sin because his creaturely powers that could be creative if his spirit were rooted in God became destructive and disrupted when he is centred in himself . . . Man without God becomes prey to all the terrors of non-being: of the ultimate loss of existence, of significance, of purpose and of loss of existence, of significance, of purpose and of eternal life . . . His essential temporality and weakness come now to threaten the meaning of his life and he . . . seeks too desperately to achieve meaning and significance at the expense of others.[7]

Humankind's sin against God, the Creator, has created a state of disunion and chaos; we do not live in harmony with our Creator, or with the world of creation, or with our fellow humans, or even with ourselves. Our sin and our fall from our original state lie at the root of our identity crisis and our need to search for meaning. The chaos of sin and the anxiety of human selfishness and greed allow no room for peace and justice; hence humanity is in a state of incessant conflict with itself, with others, and with God. World religions and

---

7. Gilkey, *Maker of Heaven*, 232.

cultures have sought to find solutions, but have been ineffective, providing no eternal values or solutions to the chaos.

Christianity and Human Mystery

In African Traditional Religions, as we have already learned, humans undertake intense quests to plumb the depths of mysteries through mystical arts and occult powers. There humanity and the spirit beings, divinities, gods, ancestors, and specialists take centre stage and God, who is the author of mysteries, has been left out.

However, this stands in sharp contrast to biblical understanding. In both the Old and the New Testament, the concept of mystery places God at its theological centre. God is at the centre of mysteries, unfolding and revealing his eternal plans in and through his Son Jesus Christ; Jesus Christ is at the centre of mysteries, unfolding and revealing the nature of Godhead, the Triune God; the Holy Spirit is at the centre of mysteries, unfolding and revealing the spiritual work of regeneration by God the Father and God the Son and through the formation of the church.

Onaiyekan puts it well when he says that Christianity and the Bible accept that mysteries exist and that they play an important part in the life of the Christian, but that they are "mysteries without secrets. . . . Christianity has no room for secret cults."[8] Jesus Christ, who is the climax of God's mystery, has been revealed as the Saviour, the Mediator, the Lord, and the Light of the world. It is through this revelation of God in Christ Jesus that we examine the concept of mysteries and mystical powers in African Traditional Religions. Jesus Christ is the eternal solution to humanity's quest for spirit-powers and their supernatural and mysterious manifestations in the cosmos (universe).

The term mystery is derived from the Greek (*musterion*) which originally referred to "that which is known to the 'initiated' (*mustes*)."[9] This Greek concept seems to be foreign to the Old Testament. The prophet Daniel used a cognate Aramaic term *raz* (Dan 2:29) which meant "that which is hidden and needs to be made known . . . The mysteries of which Daniel speaks are contained within God's eternal plan."[10] John Onaiyekan stated that "the concept of divine

---

8. Onaiyekan, "Divine Mysteries," 5.
9. Vine, *Expository Dictionary*, 97.
10. *New Concise Bible Dictionary*, 366.

mystery however, is very much present in the Old Testament"[11] (e.g. Isa 55:8–9; Job 42:1–3; Ps 139:17–18).

> It is left to God to decide whether and when to reveal his secrets and mysteries to men. While he does this at times through his prophets (Amos 3:7) he normally demands faith from his chosen people so that they can see his hand working in the facts of nature and the events of their history. The practice of divination and magic is condemned (Exod 22:18; Lev 19:26, 31; Deut 18:10–12; 2 Kgs 17:17) because it shows man's reluctance to rely on God's provident and merciful care.[12]

All hidden secrets or mysteries have been revealed by God. There is therefore no room for secret cults in Christianity, for there are no deeper secrets yet to be revealed. Christianity has no hidden secret that has not been revealed in Jesus Christ who is the beginning and the end of all secrets, as the Bible and the Holy Spirit testify. Any secret knowledge or mystery apart from Christ is demonic in origin. Christianity is not a secret religion; it has no secrets and there are no deeper secrets anywhere in the universe beyond Christ, the Bible and the Holy Spirit.

D. Fleming defined the New Testament usage of mystery not as a puzzle or a secret that leaves a person in ignorance, but as a truth that God reveals to man. It usually refers to something that man normally would not know, but which God in his grace makes known to him (Eph 3:4–5; Col 1:26; Rev 17:7).[13] The truths concerning salvation through Jesus Christ are mysteries in this sense. Man could not work them out by himself, but God who planned salvation from eternity reveals them to him (Rom 16:25–26; 1 Tim 3:9, 16).

Onaiyekan stated that the two greatest mysteries revealed in the New Testament are the mystery of Jesus Christ and the mystery of the kingdom of God (Matt 13:11; Mark 4:11; Luke 8:10). The mystery of Christ "is the plan of God from all eternity for the salvation of the world as it unravels itself in the life and teaching of Christ."[14]

> The climax of this mystery is Christ on the Cross, "to the Jews an obstacle that they cannot get over, to the pagans madness" (1 Cor 1:22). This mystery is, however, an "open secret" meant to

---

11. Onaiyekan, "Divine Mysteries," 13.
12. Onaiyekan, 13.
13. D. Fleming, *Bridge Bible Dictionary*, s.v. "mystery."
14. Onaiyekan, "Divine Mysteries," 15.

be proclaimed to all men (Rom 16:25; Acts 15:14) and the very fact "that pagans now share the same inheritance" as Jews is itself part of this mystery.[15]

The Four Great Mysteries

Gilkey suggested that traditional people face four great mysteries in life: the mystery of creation and life; the mystery of evil and fate; the mystery of sin; and the mystery of death.[16] Traditional religion has come up with its own answers and solutions to these mysteries, which contrast with those of Christianity.

The Mystery of Creation and Life

The desire to solve this mystery has led humankind to postulate all kinds of theories about creation, life, and the Creator. We have already noted that traditional Africans have many myths and legends about creation and the origin of life. In most traditional African societies, however, the origin of creation and life remains a mystery. This mystery is compounded by the presence of the many gods, divinities and spirit beings.

The Apostles' Creed states: "I believe in God the Father Almighty, creator of heaven and earth." Creation is "a divine act in which God called into being 'heaven and earth' – or all of reality – out of 'nothing' or without resorting to any pre-existing matter."[17]

Langdon Gilkey stressed that this Christian doctrine of creation is the basis of other Christian beliefs:

> The idea that God is the Creator of all things is the indispensable foundation on which the other beliefs of the Christian faith are based. It affirms what the Christian believes about the status of God in the whole realm of reality: He is the Creator of everything else. On this affirmation logically depends all that Christians say about God, about the world they live in and about their own history, destiny and hope.[18]

---

15. Onaiyekan, 15.
16. Gilkey, *Maker of Heaven and Earth*.
17. *Eerdmans Bible Dictionary*, s.v. "creation."
18. Gilkey, *Maker of Heaven and Earth*, 4.

God is the author and originator of creation and life, but the mystery of creation and life has been revealed in and through Jesus Christ (Col 1:15–18; Heb 1:1–3). Jesus Christ reveals who God is and God cannot be known apart from him (John 1:1–14, 18). Pascal make the following important statements:

> Jesus Christ is the only proof of the living God. We only know God through Jesus Christ. Without his mediation there is no communication with God. But through Jesus Christ we know God. All those who have claimed to know God and to prove his existence without Jesus Christ have done so ineffectively . . . Not only is it impossible to know God without Christ, but it is useless also . . . To know God without knowing our own wretchedness only makes for pride. Knowing our own wretchedness without knowing God makes for only despair. . . . Without Christ man can only be sinful and wretched. With Christ man is freed from sin and wretchedness.[19]

Pascal is talking in terms of special revelation here. He is not referring to general revelation so this statement does not mean that people in history did not have any concept or notion about God. However, the trinity could not be revealed by general revelation.

Religions claim to know God, but there are two ways of knowing God. There is the knowledge of God which leads to eternal life. "Now this is eternal life: that they know you, the only true God, and Jesus Christ, whom you have sent" (John 17:3). There is also the knowledge of God which leads to eternal death. Religions that claim to know God, but which do not acknowledge Jesus Christ, the Messiah and Saviour, are rooted in general revelation and cannot offer salvation and eternal life, which come through God's special revelation in Jesus Christ.

The secret of all creation and life have been entrusted to Jesus Christ (John 1:1–5; Col 1:15–20; Heb 1:1–4, 10–13). He is therefore the Lord of life and the answer to the human quest for spirit-powers.

The Mystery of Evil and Fate

We have recognized that, in traditional Africa, fatalism is rooted in the law of destiny, and one's destiny lies in the mystery of the unforeseen and unpredictable forces of evil and wickedness which dominate the world. The

---

19. Pascal, *Mind on Fire*, 147, 151, 153.

traditional view of life is shaped by these vast forces and spirit beings and, as a result, humans search for knowledge, security, power, and control. They live in fear and helplessness, seeing only the spirit-powers of evil. God's sovereignty and providence are often not regarded as potent enough to conquer these evil forces.

In the Gospels, we see how Jesus Christ demonstrates his power and authority. This world is not chaotic, but is ordered by God's divine power (Matt 28:18; Col 1:15–18; Eph 1:19–23; Heb 1:1–3). The death, resurrection, ascension, and return of Christ are the signs of Christ's victory over death, sin, Satan and demonic powers, principalities, and powers. The apostles proclaimed this Christ-power to the whole world. The book of Revelation describes the final destruction of evil, fate, Satan, and all his fallen angels (demons) by the world leader and king, Jesus Christ. Jesus Christ has control over the secrets of evil and fate in the cosmos (universe). The destiny of humanity and of the entire universe is in his hands.

The Mystery of Sin

Traditional Africans define sin as wrong-doing. Their moral codes, taboos, and customs regulate both moral actions and moral attitudes. Sin or wrong-doing, however, is always defined within the communal context and little emphasis is placed on personal understanding, consideration and interpretation of sin. This communal definition of sin tends to make Africans pay less attention to the issue of personal sins against God or against the community.

On the other hand, African Christians, in line with the Western emphasis on individualism, have tended to overemphasize personal sin and have neglected the communal and social means of dealing with sins. The African church must recover this lost communal value. The church of Jesus Christ as a new community has profound communal values that can be used to strengthen the moral social behaviour of Christians.

The root of evil or sin is not as clearly defined in African Traditional Religion as in the Bible. The African conception is that it is those who are inherently evil who normally reveal it through wrong actions and attitudes. However, not all people are inherently evil or are born evil; evil is not human, but it can enter into, or co-habit with, humans. This is why it is very important for African Christians to understand the origin, nature, and power of sin.

It is very important to state right at the beginning that our definition of sin must be derived from God's moral character and moral law. We cannot begin to understand sin unless we sit it in the light of the holy and glorious nature and character of God. Sin is: "In essence, the failure or refusal of human beings to live the life intended for them by God their Creator." It is, therefore, more than just the "violation of moral standards of society . . . rather, sin in its basic sense is always ultimately against God himself rather than against mankind or any human person."[20] Sin could also be defined as "any attitude of indifference, unbelief, or disobedience to the will of God revealed in conscience, law, or gospel – whether this attitude expresses itself in thought, word, deed, or settled disposition and conduct."[21]

In the light of these definitions, it is clear that all humans are sinners, fallen from a higher moral and spiritual status. The Bible says that "all have sinned and fall short of the glory of God" (Rom 3:23) and that "everyone who sins breaks the law; in fact, sin is lawlessness" (1 John 3:4). The Westminster Shorter Catechism question 14 states: "Sin is any want of conformity unto, or transgression of the law of God." Sin is committed when a person deliberately or accidentally steps over the line of the law of God. Missing the mark is breaking the law.

This definition is perhaps broadened when we refer to the words translated as "sin" or "to sin," first in the Old Testament and then in the New.

The Old Testament words are: *hata* meaning "to miss the mark, to fail"; *abar* meaning "to pass beyond or transgress"; *awon* meaning "an iniquity or perversion"; *pasa* meaning "to revolt, to transgress"; *sagag* or *saga* meaning "to err, to go astray"; *ta'a* meaning "to err, to wander"; *ra* meaning "evil"; *rasa* meaning "wicked."[22]

The following Greek words define the biblical concept of sin in the New Testament word: *hamartia* meaning "to miss the mark"; *parabasis* meaning "a transgression"; *adikia* meaning "unrighteousness"; *asebeia* meaning "impiety"; *anomia* meaning "contempt for and violation of law"; *poneria* meaning "depravity"; *eepithumia* meaning "the desire for what is forbidden."[23]

In traditional religion and in the Old Testament sin was removed by blood sacrifices. The blood symbolically cleansed, washed and purified the sinner. "But those sacrifices are an annual reminder of sins. It is impossible for the blood of bulls and goats to take away sins" (Heb 10:3–4). The various sacrifices described in the book of Leviticus find their fulfilment in the cross of Christ.

---

20. *Eerdmans Bible Dictionary*, 951.
21. *International Standard Bible Encyclopedia*, vol. 4, 2798.
22. *Eerdmans Bible Dictionary*.
23. *International Standard Bible Encyclopaedia*, vol. 4, 2798.

The blood of Jesus was offered in place of the blood of animals, and Christ was sacrificed once and for all.

Jesus Christ through the cross provides the solution to the mystery of sin. On the cross, Christ defeated the power of sin and opened a new pathway to reconciliation, repentance and forgiveness for humankind. The mystery and power of sin has been removed.

The Mystery of Death

Humankind's search for knowledge, for the secret of the good life, for security, for power, for happiness, for satisfaction, for riches, and for immortality are all threatened by the mystery of death. Death is beyond our control. Even though we know that we are mortal, we fight against mortality. We want to live, if possible, forever.

The Bible provides the answers to every question about death. Genesis explains that death came about as a result of man's disobedience to God's command in Genesis 2:15–17. Death was the punishment. "The dust returns to the ground it came from, while the spirit returns to God who gave it" (Eccl 12:7). Jesus Christ demonstrated his power over death by raising Lazarus and a widow's son from the dead. 1 Corinthians 15 and Romans 5 deal at length with the mystery of death and Christ's victory over it, showing how on the cross Christ defeated and destroyed the power of death. The entire book of Revelation is a description of Christ's victory over death and its power. "I am the Living One; I was dead, and now look, I am alive for ever and ever! And I hold the keys of death and Hades" (Rev 1:18). Jesus Christ has power over the mystery of death.

40

Engaging with the Doctrine of Man

We have already discussed what it means to be human in terms of traditional African understanding. In this chapter, let us seek to define human beings in biblical terms as the Bible definition has implications for our theological understanding of humankind in Africa. Although these definitions have some elements of similarity, there are also huge differences between traditional religion and Christianity.

It is impossible to separate the basic teaching of the Old Testament from the concepts of the New Testament entirely, as they are intertwined. So although we may miss some nuances, we shall look at both testaments at the same time.

The Biblical Definition of Humankind

The Old Testament defines a human being as a complete whole and does not separate the spiritual and the physical as Greek dualism or African tradition do. Even though African anthropology is generally similar to that of the Old Testament, human beings in African tradition are defined in terms of their composite "parts."

The biblical creation narratives accord human beings the highest value in God's creation. God's act of creation crowns all human beings with universality, commonality, equality, and unity of nature and identity. The psalmist expresses his wonder like this:

> When I consider your heavens, the work of your fingers, the moon and the stars, which you have set in place, what is mankind that you are mindful of them, human beings that you care for them? . . .

You have made them rulers over the works of your hands; you put everything under their feet. (Ps 8:3–6)

This verse reveals that human nature and life in all its dimensions is God's gift to us. Human beings therefore have God as their origin and central focus. They are created to worship, to serve and to live in obedience to their Maker.

This truth is amplified in certain key words used in Scripture in relation to humankind.

"Ruach" and "Pneuma"

These words mean "spirit" in Hebrew and Greek respectively. Generally the word is associated with God "who gives life to all human beings and animals."

The Old Testament sees human beings as both breath and spirit. The "life-force" or "breath of life" which God creates belongs to him and he "gives it to all people and animals for the time of their earthly existence and he takes it back at death" (Num 16:22; Ps 104:29; Eccl 12:7; Heb 12:9; Jas 2:26).[1] Because this is so, life should never be taken for granted or misused.

In the New Testament the apostle Paul likes to use the word, *pneuma*, to describe the human spirit after conversion when it has come under the powerful influence of the Spirit of God. Thus it describes a new creation, a person's Christian *pneuma* (Rom 8:16; 2 Cor 5:17). It is also used of the Holy Spirit, the Spirit of God or the Spirit of Christ.[2]

Even though Africans believe in the Supreme Being as the Creator, traditional religion seems to suggest that the lesser beings have the monopoly over issues of life. This is why Africans solicit the help of the ancestors, divinities, gods, specialists, and spirit beings to ensure their survival and well-being in the community, in the world of nature and in the spirit world. But these efforts cannot change their natural spirit or *pneuma* which is doomed to death and damnation.

However, while lesser beings, gods, or divinities may have the power to kill, the Bible reassures us that they are not the origin or source of life. Only the Spirit of God can give it life; only the Spirit of God can quicken it into new life. This is the offer Christ makes (1 Cor 2:6–16). At conversion, the Holy Spirit gives the uncreated Spirit of God to the dead spirit of humankind and makes it alive to eternal life.

---

1. Fleming, *Bridge Bible Directory*, 418.
2. Guthrie, *New Testament Theology*, 165–167.

"Nepesh" and "Psyche"

These parallel words are usually translated as "soul" or "breath of life." Genesis 2:7 states: "Then the LORD God formed a man from the dust of the ground and breathed into his nostrils the breath of life, and the man became a living being." The sense here is that humans do not have being; they are beings. Humans also do not *have* souls; they *are* souls. This speaks of the whole person, the totality of one's existence.[3] The emphasis of the word is on living, being alive, or existing.

The Greek term *psyche* usually refers to life in general and reflects normal earthly life. However, the New Testament makes it clear that this normal and ordinary life is not "earth bound," but somehow "transcends" this "earthly life" (Matt 10:28; 11:29; Luke 16:25). Life, therefore, should not be lived as if it has no purpose or meaning. There is more to it than it seems. Life is not an end in itself; instead it gives us hope for a better one. We can even lay aside this ordinary life so that we may gain a better life (Matt 20:28; Luke 9:23–26; John 10:11, 15, 17; 12:24–25).

The word *nepes* also suggests one who thirsts, hungers, and who expresses and experiences desires and appetites.[4] In other words, one who is in a state of need. This reflects that we are totally dependent on God for sustenance and provision. We receive life from God, but are not to live independently. We live in relationship with others: with God; with the human and animal worlds and with the world in general. However, the highest and the most valuable relationship is that between the creature and the Creator so that in the Old Testament the covenant relationship between God and Israel takes precedence over all other human relationships (Exod 32:29; Deut 13:1–18).[5]

Traditional Africans understand the concept that a covenant with God makes one totally dependent on him. In traditional Africa covenants and the practice of a covenant relationship are highly revered. Many covenants are made, and the covenant makers are bound in a relationship.

Nonetheless the African view of humankind does not accord completely with the biblical view. Traditional religion assumes that each person, each living being, has additional life parts or distinct qualities, such as a shadow or double, a ghost, vital breath and an ancestral guardian spirit. It is believed that some of these additional life parts have not come from the Creator, but from other sources such as parents or ancestors. Traditionally it is believed that at death, the shadow leaves the "tangible body" and the different parts go off to

---

3. Nelson, "Class Notes TH 842 Medical Ethics."
4. *Eerdmans Bible Dictionary*, 964.
5. Nelson, "Class Notes TH 842 Medical Ethics."

different destinations. Dismembered at death, therefore, human beings can become ghosts, spirits, or reincarnations or living-dead. There is no certainty with regard to eternal identity.

Christianity also does not see the soul as a deposit or entity of life which is carried about, as in African thought. The Bible teaches that this earthly life is temporary and will perish. It teaches that preoccupation with the things of this life means impending doom and damnation. Yet Africans continue to be preoccupied with this ordinary, earthly life. They spend much time, energy, and resources consulting with the lesser beings, gods, and divinities in order to prolong this life and to improve their lot in a world dominated by the mysterious, mystical, and spirit powers. Although they believe that some aspects of human nature do not die out, although they believe in reincarnation, in ancestral guardian spirits, in vital breath, in destiny spirits, ghosts and shadows, they see that this earthly life carries the stamp of death. The offer Christ makes enables this earth-bound life-chain to be broken.

Christianity accepts that the spirit of the person leaves the decaying body at death, but asserts that both body and spirit await the Second Coming (Advent) of Christ. Then the decayed body, along with the human spirit (whether in heaven or hades), will be resurrected into newness of life (1 Cor 15:12–57; 1 Thess 4:13–17; 2 Thess 2:1). The resurrected Christ has become the life-giving Spirit, the firstborn from the dead, and the one who gives eternal life to all who believe in him.

On the other hand, Africans may be closer to the Bible than those from the west when they define humans as a "spark," for the Hebrew word *naphach* means, among other things, to puff, to kindle, a blow, a breath. God uses his breath of power to animate dead things and to grant the gift of life. God uses his breath of power to give a different spirit, one apart from his being. The transcendent Spirit of God is holy and is not the same as the spirit of man. God simply used his breath of power to animate and to give the gift of life. The breath of life becomes the principle of life (John 6:63). Thus the Genesis passage is also the basis of our understanding of God's offer of the gift of eternal life through Christ.

"Basar" and "Sarx"

The Hebrew word *basar* is usually translated as flesh, as is the Greek term *sarx*. The term can refer to the human body or to those with whom one shares "the circumstances of life" (Isa 58:7) or to "people in general."[6]

---

6. *Eerdmans Bible Dictionary*, 385.

When humankind is called *basar*, this describes both physical and spiritual states. Physically, a human being is nothing but a creature. Human beings are finite and mortal, limited in many ways. Humankind also operates under the law of sin, which dominates all life (Ps 78:39; Isa 10:18; 40:6–7; Jer 31:13). Our very nature is intrinsically sinful and we are incapable of pleasing our maker, showing rebelliousness instead (Rom 7:7–25; 8:1–11; 2 Cor 4:16; 10:3; Gal 5:6, 19). Through Adam, we inherit sin, God's wrath, judgment, and death, and we need liberation and redemption.

African liberators or intermediaries are all caught up in this Adamic condition, the corruption of the human flesh. A person steeped in the flesh cannot please God, nor become a worthy intermediary. What is more, even some of the spirit beings that Africans associate with are fallen angels who fell along with Satan. They cannot serve as gods, divinities or intermediaries or as God's messengers. They are awaiting God's final judgment in the last days.

The only external principle that is powerful enough to break the power of sin and its law is Christ from whom we inherit God's grace, righteousness and life eternal (Rom 5:12–21). However, because of the powerful influence of the law of the flesh or the principle of sin and because of the influence of demonic forces, humankind in Africa does not serve or worship God directly. We might feel that there is wisdom in not worshipping God directly, but this wisdom is foolishness before God (1 Cor 2:6–16).

"Leb," "Lebab" and "Kardia"

The Hebrew words *leb* and *lebab* are usually translated "heart," as is the Greek term *kardia*. In general usage, the words refer to the core of a person, although they can also refer to "physical being, personality, emotions, intellect, will and relationship with God" and "volition and morality."[7] In some cases the terms are translated as mind or understanding (Job 12:3; Prov 16:9; Jer 7:31). The term is also used within the context of humankind's relationship with God as it reflects both the turning to God and the turning away from him (Deut 8:14, 17; 9:4; 2 Chr 26:16).

The power house of the heart controls and affects the totality of the human being (Rom 10:10; 2 Cor 1:22; 4:6; Eph 1:18). Yet the heart is inherently corrupt (Rom 1:24; 2:5; 6:17; Jer 17:9) and has been captured by sin and the invader holds sway over the person's will or volition, intellect or mind, and affections or desires.

---

7. *Eerdmans Bible Dictionary*, 471.

Jesus Christ explains this:

> For it is from within, out of a person's heart, that evil thoughts come – sexual immorality, theft, murder, adultery, greed, malice, deceit, lewdness, envy, slander, arrogance and folly. All these evils come from inside and defile a person. (Mark 7:21–23)

God's work of grace through Jesus Christ wages war against the enemy who has captured the stronghold of the person's being, the heart. The heart can then receive redemption, cleansing, regeneration, and sanctification. When we turn our heart to God, the qualities of faith, commitment, devotion, loyalty, obligation, affection, and affinity will become evident. But when we turn away from God, the opposite qualities will dominate (Mark 7:21–23).

When traditional Africans turn their hearts away from their Maker, this creates deceit and wickedness in their hearts. They can use this deceitfulness and wickedness to rationalize their sinful and rebellious actions, saying for example: "I am not worshipping any gods, or idols, or spirits. I know my Creator lives and I worship him through these noble divinities who are his very intermediaries." Or "My religion is not idolatry, as some would call it due to ignorance and bias, but it is 'pure' and 'holy,' reflecting our own uniqueness and our own understanding of God through his self-disclosure to our forefathers and ancestors." Yet, when we examine this in the light of the Bible, we see that they have stopped "on the doorstep" of the intermediaries who have captured their devotion and worship. True worship of God has been replaced with something other than God, even though it has the "form of godliness."

"Dam" and "Haima"

The Hebrew word *dam* is usually translated "blood"; in Greek this is *haima*. Blood is the essential fluid of human, animal, and, in the form of sap, even of plant life. In Old Testament usage, it is the equivalent of life itself. As a result, humans were forbidden to eat blood, in other words, flesh "with its life"; humans were forbidden to eat animal flesh from which the blood had not been drained; human bloodshed was forbidden; the blood and the fat of animals belonged to God and, as symbols of atonement, must not be eaten, but must be offered on the altar (Lev 3:16–17; 16:14–15; 17:10–13). Animal blood atoned for real life; a life offered for the sins of the person making the sacrifice.[8]

---

8. *Eerdmans Bible Dictionary*, 164.

The concept of the use of blood plays a dominant role in traditional African society. Most religious and social rites, rituals and ceremonies are accompanied by sacrifices involving the shedding of animal blood. But human blood is seldom used as it is regarded as very precious. Only rituals of secret societies, the practices of witchcraft and sorcery, may use human blood or human parts. This relates to the belief which attaches mystical, mysterious or magical powers to human blood. M. Y. Nabofa states:

> In the thinking of the Africans, when blood is shed a mysterious super-power or force will be let loose and it could destabilize the murderer and the society to which he belongs. Many Africans avoid unnecessary shedding of blood because of the mysterious power in it and its connection with the soul. They also guard against coming in contact with various types of blood that defile man.[9]

Because there is no forgiveness without the shedding of blood (Heb 9:22), Christ's own blood was offered once for the sins of many. The blood of Jesus, God's Son, cleanses us from all sin (1 John 1:7). The eternal covenant required the death of the mediator in order to become effective.[10]

"Hayyim"

Hayyim refers to the relatively short life span that humans have. They are mortal and will soon fade away (Pss 39; 90). Human life is on loan as a gift from the Creator. This makes them dependent before their Maker.

"Soma"

Soma is the Greek word for the body. It is described as mortal (Rom 8:10–11), but God can give life to it through his Spirit.

1 Corinthians 6 makes it clear that the body is not meant for immorality. Indeed those who commit immorality sin against their own body. The real purpose of the body is to be a temple of the Holy Spirit. Because of this, God can be glorified in the body.[11]

---

9. Nabofa, "Significance of Blood," 2–3, 7.
10. *Eerdmans Bible Dictionary*, 164.
11. Guthrie, *New Testament Theology*, 175.

Africans are far more likely to give their bodies to the spirits, divinities, and gods and to allow these to indwell them, rather than giving themselves to the Supreme Being. In fact, Africans regard gods and spirits as God-sent and even elevate them to the role of intermediaries. The preponderance of religious and social rites, rituals, and offerings allow the gods, divinities and spirits to dominate the body, for example, by spirit, ancestral or demonic possession of the African body. There are very few instances where the *soma* is given in total devotion and commitment to God.

The Bible condemns this involvement with unclean spirits and demonic activities (Exod 22:18; Deut 18:10). We are to give our bodies to the worship and service of God alone.

"Nous"

The Greek term *nous* is usually translated as mind and it refers to "the whole thinking man, man as a creature capable of understanding." The mind is also conceived of as "a universal aspect" of humankind and can be dominated by "either the Spirit of God or the flesh." "When the mind does not acknowledge God, it becomes base" (Rom 1:28). The "mind of God" must be seen in contrast to the "mind of man" which is able to be influenced by evil (Isa 40:13–31; Rom 12:2; 1 Cor 2:16).[12]

The traditional African mind, as we have already observed, has been given over to the influence of mystical, mysterious, and spirit powers. If the mind is dominated by the spirits and by the mystical or occult powers, such powers will exert a powerful and pervasive influence over it. In traditional Africa, God the Creator is regarded as kind and generous because he sends these myriads of spirits to take possession of the mind. The Bible, however, tells us that God shares his glory with no one. "I am the LORD; that is my name! I will not yield my glory to another or my praise to idols" (Isa 42:8; see also 48:11). The intermediaries who seem to act for and on behalf of God are, therefore, without God. God seeks to deal with us directly, through his Spirit without any intermediary.

The battle for the African mind is fierce. Africans need the Spirit of God alone, not those of the lesser spirits that pollute and confuse the mind.

---

12. Guthrie, 534.

"Syneidesis"

This Greek term *syneidesis* is usually translated as conscience which refers to being aware of oneself as a rational being.

The word is often used by Paul. In Romans 2:15 he implies that conscience is "universal" and that all people have the capacity to determine what is right. In Romans 9:1 and 2 Corinthians 1:12 the conscience is referred to as "a witness," able to accuse one but not to clear itself, for "it is the Lord who judges" (see 1 Cor 4:4). Conscience can become hardened, if disobeyed (1 Tim 4:2) or quickened by "the indwelling Spirit." The conscience of the Christian should be "more perceptive than the conscience of the natural man."[13]

The moral capacity of the traditional African reveals that conscience is indeed universal, but there is a real possibility that it will become hardened or "seared" as the "voice" of conscience is disobeyed. Although conscience is always subject to the social conditioning of the world, Paul argues that it is based upon the "eternal law" of God, whether this law is known or not. Our conscience therefore will ultimately be judged by the gospel of Christ (Rom 2:16). For this reason, the conscience cannot be appeased through rites, rituals, ceremonies, sacrifices, and offerings, but can only be cleansed by the power of the blood of Christ (Heb 9, 10), his Holy Spirit and word.

"Bios"

This Greek word is usually translated as a natural quality of life.

One cannot get much out of this natural life so, if this is all that there is to live for, there is much to be desired. However, people become so entangled with this life and all that it offers that they forget that it has a sad end. Such people "are choked by life's worries, riches and pleasures, and they do not mature" (Luke 8:14).

A preoccupation with *bios*, therefore, causes one to lose sight of God who offers a better and more satisfying life than this world can offer. We saw earlier that in traditional Africa much energy is expended on the pursuit of well-being through acquiring life-force and mystical and spirit powers. The life that God offers is far superior to the natural and perishing life-force.

---

13. Guthrie, 170–171.

"Zoe"

The last term we shall consider is the Greek term *zoe* which is usually translated as a quality of life that is above the ordinary, that is, eternal life. *Zoe* suggests a creative life from God, mediated through Jesus Christ. At the resurrection, God gives the eternal life which is far superior to this ordinary one (John 3:14–16; 5:21; 6:35, 51; 10:10; 11:25; 12:25; 14:6).

The life that we inherit from Adam is that of a living soul with a life-span. This life culminates in death, in hopelessness and futility. However, when Jesus Christ, the second Adam, brought redemption, he brought hope through his promise of eternal life (*zoe*). Jesus Christ is the origin and source of eternal life both now and in the future (John 1:1–4; 3:14–16). The hope of living beyond the *bios* becomes certain through the *zoe* offered by Jesus Christ.

African beliefs teach that witches kill the soul and leave the body. This is exactly the opposite of what Jesus our Lord teaches. The mortal body can be killed but only God can destroy the soul or life.

Jesus Christ deals with this when he states:

> I tell you, my friends, do not be afraid of those who kill the body and after that can do no more. But I will show you whom you should fear: Fear him who, after your body has been killed, has authority to throw you into hell. Yes, I tell you, fear him. (Luke 12:4–5)
>
> Do not be afraid of those who kill the body but cannot kill the soul. Rather be afraid of the One who can destroy both soul and body in hell. (Matt 10:28)

Humankind as Created Beings

The concept of "being" refers to existence, as opposed to nonexistence. We derive our being or existence from God who created us. This is not something that we can make or determine; it transcends our nature, character, and attributes. So, although we may be assessed in terms of the quality of our lives, we are what we are in terms of our being and not what people say about us.

Nelson suggested that human beings typically classify other human beings in three broad categories based upon their quality of life.[14] This status is then used to determine how such a person should be treated: some live a substandard life. This includes those who are deformed or disabled or poor. When

---

14. Nelson, "Class Notes TH 842 Medical Ethics."

they are judged in terms of their quality of life, they are usually accorded a status lower than that of others. Most of us live a normal life that measures up to the standards we set. We are ordinary people who are living an average life as complete human beings. Our status is higher and better than the first group. Finally there are those who live an extraordinary life. These are the geniuses – super-human beings who exhibit some human qualities that are above the ordinary.

However, the "being" of a person transcends such classification or treatment. All groups are equal in terms of creation and being; none is superior to the other. They are all human beings created by God. The sacredness, worth, and dignity of a human being is not rooted in quality or status. Thus a foetus at any stage of development is not less of a human being than a genius. Both a foetus and a genius are equally human beings. This is their theological and spiritual position before God, their maker. The sociological, psychological, economic, and social definitions of humankind all fall short of God's definition: that we are *beings*.

We can see that biblical anthropology gives us a different definition of humankind and its place, purpose, and meaning in life from that of African anthropology. In the Bible, we are defined in terms of our maker "for in him we live and move and have our being" (Acts 17:28). God takes centre stage in our lives, not secondary. Our religious and social activities all relate directly to God and not with the lesser beings. In all pursuits of life we should depend on God who is the source and giver of all life. God who is the maker of heaven and earth gives life purpose.

41

Engaging with the Doctrine of Sin

Most discussions by scholars about traditional Africa portray Africans as being very religious but they fail to see the power of sin at work in the lives of traditional Africans. Sin's power needs to be fully understood. The Bible and Christian teachings explain that traditional religious practices, rituals, festivals, and ceremonies do not deal with the power of sin in human life. In this chapter we consider the Christian concept of sin.

The Origin of Sin

Traditional Africans have no clear or definite concept of original sin, although there are legends about the origins of things, like the earth, the heavens, and many others.

It is only when evil or calamities come, that the question of sin or wrong doing arises. Offences committed against other people or spirit beings are regarded as sins because they violate the harmony or break the taboos and customs, perhaps by touching the forbidden things. But there is no clear teaching on the origin of sin or on how sin dominates life.

Africans value genealogy, lineage, or heritage very highly. In traditional society the characteristics and qualities of being human are believed to be passed down from parents to children through the ages, as are character traits or behaviours. All persons who are the descendants of one ancestor are brothers and sisters, united and linked together by one common ancestral blood. Behind biology or natural phenomena lie the spiritual and power phenomena. This means that even the power to practise things such as witchcraft and divination or to possess mysterious knowledge can be hereditary. For this reason, it is not difficult for Africans to believe that all humans inherit their sin nature from

Adam. They believe in kinship values and blood-group heritage. Traditional African reality lies in the spirit realm and the spirit-power of the ancestors has a profound influence upon their descendants. Thus, original sin is understood in terms of its spiritual or mysterious nature and is understood in terms of the spiritual dynamism or power. This is an area where classical theology and philosophy wrestle with rationalism and scepticism but the traditional African can understand the concepts.

Before the fall, the spirit ruled and kept one in subjection to God. In God's original creation the spirit, soul and body were to exist harmoniously, cooperating with each other to maintain the unity and wholeness of the person in worship, service and communion with God. The spirit was to transmit the divine communications from God to the soul and the soul was to command the body. There was therefore no conflict between the spirit, the soul and the body.

But at the fall, the spirit lost its supremacy. It could no longer control the soul and the body. And, because the Holy Spirit imparts himself and communicates with us through our spirit, it lost its connection with God too. Our fall into sin infected us at our roots like a deadly virus or poison. God's primary purpose in creating humans as spirit, soul, and body was disrupted. Sin got hold, not only of the external physical body, but also of humankind's spirit and soul. Sin now resides in human nature.

A Definition of Sin

The soul, the body and all sorts of spiritual surrogates and spirit-powers have usurped the place of God in human life. The spirit of humankind is now ruled by many forces and powers.

African traditionalists seem to have a deeper spiritual understanding of how this affects the total life of a human being than the average Christian does, despite all that the Bible teaches in this area. The fall brought humankind under the *spirit-power* of Satan and evil. The new master of our life, that is sin, reconstitutes our nature, affecting our essential relationships. What was originally created to worship and serve God with loyalty and dedication has been reorganized to serve our new master, Satan. Our original *imago Dei*, the spiritual power of God that clothed us, has now been removed. We now live dominated by Satan, evil and sin. The members of our bodies that were instruments of righteousness have become instruments of unrighteousness in our body of sin. We have been spiritually re-aligned.

However, it is important to recognize that what humanity inherited was the sin nature and the guilt before God, not the acts and deeds of the transgression and law-breaking. All humanity stands guilty before God on the basis of our fallen, inherited sin nature from Adam. Although our inherited sin nature gives each human being the disposition to sin, each human being must still make his or her own choices and these determine acts of sin. Each human being is judged by these acts of transgression or law-breaking.

It is through our consciences that the Spirit urges us to discern what is right and what is wrong. Nonetheless because of the fall, even the use of this faculty too has been marred by sin. Although when we do wrong our conscience accuses us immediately, we make a habit of silencing our conscience! The apostle Paul talks of those whose "consciences have been seared" (1 Tim 4:2) and whose "minds and consciences are corrupted" (Titus 1:15). He also talks of the blood of Christ which will "cleanse our consciences from acts that lead to death" (Heb 9:14).

Once again, rationalists or scientists look for rational and scientific proof or verification of something which is deeply spiritual. However, traditional Africans know that discernment is a spiritual activity, not a rational or scientific activity. This is why when they are faced with difficulties, or incurable sicknesses, or unimaginable circumstances, or calamities, traditional Africans do not appeal to reason or to science. Instead they seek deeper truths in the spirit realm. They call on diviners for spiritual discernment with regard to the causes of the problems. Sadly, Missionary Christianity failed to use this insight in speaking to Africans about spiritual discernment and simply presented a rational and scientific worldview. This matter needs to be addressed afresh in the light of biblical theology (1 Cor 2).

The Impact of the Fall

God's tolerance of evil must be understood within the context of free will and freedom of choice. Always at the back of their minds, people have the idea of a benevolent God, full of love, mercy, forgiveness, and kindness. People hate to think of a God who judges and punishes wrong-doing. Christianity sees God differently. We know that he is both loving and just.

In Genesis 3, after the sin and fall of Adam and Eve, God pronounced judgments upon them. African Traditional Religion knows the power or potency of curses. A curse is an invocation through a word of power that brings evil upon the one who is cursed. The words spoken carry such spirit-power that they affect not only the person, but even the environment and associates. Their impact is both spiritual and physical.

However, the faculty of the spirit to sense non-human communication or knowledge intuitively has been impaired. God and the Holy Spirit communicate with us by means of revelation and intuition, not through our physical senses or even the senses of our souls. Yet since the fall, our spirit is dulled by sin and can hardly hear or sense the Holy Spirit in our lives. "The natural man receives not the things of the Spirit of God" (1 Cor 2:14 NKJV).

Christians do not sufficiently exercise the faculty of intuition; we do not sufficiently cultivate the habit of sensing the Holy Spirit and God. The power and influence of sin in our spirit does not allow for that. Prayer and meditation, the exercises of the spirit, have been seriously weakened by the power of sin in our daily lives. Sensations and perception and revelation through the spirit have been dulled by rationalism and science. Modern Africa, dominated by Western principles of rationalism and science, has very little time for intuition and revelation. This drives Africans further away from the biblical worldview and, as a result, does not adequately address the inner longings of Africans. But Africans understand the reality of this way of knowing, even though their communication with God in the spirit realm has been cut off by surrogate spirit-powers and spirit beings.

The fall also affected the body. At times the body in rebellion overpowers the soul and the spirit and dominates them through its sinful desires, passions and earthy sensuality. We are aware that body worship takes many forms, for example idolatry, appetites, sensuality, sex and sexual perversion, as well as all bodily sins of uncleanness, impurity, and defilement (Rom 1). Many of the rituals, blood sacrifices, ceremonies and festivals in African Traditional Religion involve the giving over of one's body to causes that are opposed to God. The body needs to be delivered from these sinful works of the flesh. "Put to death [mortify], therefore, whatever belongs to your earthly nature" (Col 3:5). The good news is that the cross of Christ brings deliverance even to our physical bodies. "Don't you know that you yourselves are God's temple and that God's Spirit lives in you?" (1 Cor 3:16 GWT).

But God's curse on the primary actors in the garden of Eden also affected all that belonged to them: their environment, their possessions, and their inheritance. This meant that the physically perfect garden of Eden was cursed, as was the entire creation.

Even today, the sin and wickedness of moral beings impacts the normal "good" functioning of creation. God's curse on creation pervades the physical order of the universe and is the root cause of the disorder, chaos, conflict, and lack of harmony within creation. By their nature, all physical laws are constant in all their causal relationships, disorder or conflict crept in. The apostle Paul describes this phenomenon in the following words:

> For the creation waits in eager expectation . . . For [it] was subjected to frustration, not by its own choice, but by the will of the one who subjected it, in hope that the creation itself will be liberated from its bondage to decay and brought into the freedom and glory of the children of God. (Rom 8:19–21)

Dealing with Sin

Even today God's curse is always pronounced on evil and sin. The knowledge of God's judgment and punishment has increased humankind's anxiety and fear. Humankind knows that it is weak, that it must face and suffer death. Anxiety and fear are rooted in the act of transgression or disobedience and arouse shame and guilt.

How can one escape God's judgment? How can one be made righteous before God? Only by faith in Jesus the Messiah who is the revealed righteousness of God for all ages:

> God presented Christ as a sacrifice of atonement, through the shedding of his blood – to be received by faith. He did this to demonstrate his righteousness, because in his forbearance he had left the sins committed beforehand unpunished – he did it to demonstrate his righteousness at the present time, so as to be just and the one who justifies those who have faith in Jesus. (Rom 3:25–26)

The cross of Christ has eternal efficacy and is not limited by historical time. "But when the set time had fully come, God sent his Son, born of a woman, born under the law, to redeem those under the law, that we might receive adoption to sonship" (Gal 4:4–5).

The cross of Christ does not annul God's eternal and universal criteria for judgment and for righteousness. No human being can meet God's standards. No religion, law, or conscience has the capacity to do so.

> For what the law was powerless to do because it was weakened by the flesh, God did by sending his own Son in the likeness of sinful flesh . . . he condemned sin in the flesh, in order that the righteous requirement of the law might be fully met in us, who do not live according to the flesh but according to the Spirit. (Rom 8:3–4)

The cross of Christ was instituted in order to reveal God's grace, righteousness, and justice. There is no basis for our justification, except the cross of Christ. The apostle Paul says emphatically:

> No one will be declared righteous in God's sight by the works of the law . . . for all have sinned and fall short of the glory of God . . . We maintain that a person is justified by faith apart from the works of the law. (Rom 3:20–31)

> For it is by grace you have been saved through faith – and this is not from yourselves, it is a gift of God – not by works, so that no one can boast. (Eph 2:8)

It is the object of our faith that justifies or condemns. Jesus the Messiah and his finished work of redemption on the cross has from eternity been that object of faith. Even before God's revelation in Jesus Christ, God made faith the only means of man finding God's grace. Throughout history God who is a Trinity has been the ultimate object of faith and reveals himself at his appointed times. God's special revelation in Jesus the Messiah gives both the fuller meaning and the content of this faith. It is a redemptive faith, which reveals its full meaning in what Jesus did on the cross. It is also a saving faith in the person of Jesus the Messiah who saves us from our sins.

It is clear then that there are two dominant principles that can rule human life. Either one chooses the godly principle under God, that is life ruled by the Spirit of God or one chooses the ungodly principle under sin, that is life ruled by the spirit-power of Satan, evil and sin.

42

Engaging with the Concept of Covenants

Covenants make and sustain religions. They abound in traditional religion and those who study traditional religion must be aware of the role of covenants and of their spiritual and social implications and significance for their devotees. The theological issues of whether African ancestors should be incorporated into the messianic community, the church, are answered by covenant theology. The debate on continuity and discontinuity of traditional religion in Christianity is also settled by covenant theology. Covenants therefore have a vital role to play in the development of Christian theology in Africa.

Human beings cannot sit back and claim, on their own terms, that they have a God. Rather, it is God who makes claims on his creatures, through his laws, commandments and covenants. This is why the knowledge of the biblical history of humanity and of how God has dealt with each generation and each people is essential to the study of traditional religion and culture. Through Scripture we discover the general condition and the state of humanity in the sight of God after the fall (Rom 1–3). Through Scripture we come to understand how God addressed all humanity, religions, cultures, nations, and peoples in preparation for his coming kingdom. We learn how God used covenants and election, as well as prophetic and messianic promises to prepare for his kingdom. It is this covenant nature of the Old Testament Jewish religion and of New Testament Christianity that sets them apart from all other religions.

Covenant theology gives a deeper understanding of God's dealings with the peoples of the world and this should serve as a model for the Christian approach to traditional religion in Africa. A lack of knowledge of these covenants and of how they apply to a study of religions and cultures has resulted in a "Christianizing" of the African religious past, without any real biblical understanding.

Some people groups are indeed outside of God's covenants but that does not mean that all these people groups make no claim to a covenant relationship with God. These claims must be understood within general revelation and creation theology as they reveal human perceptions or notions about God and about his relationship with them. These people groups have not received any special revelation from God.

To understand what this means, let us consider the more important covenants in the Bible as outlined in the *Open Bible*.

The Edenic Covenant (Gen 2:15–17)

> The covenant in Eden is the first of the general or universal covenants. In it, Adam is charged to: (1) populate the earth (Gen 1:28); (2) subdue the earth (Gen 1:28); (3) exercise dominion over the animal creation (Gen 1:28); (4) care for the garden of Eden and enjoy its fruit (Gen 1:29; 2:15) and (5) refrain from eating the fruit of the tree of the knowledge of good and evil, under penalty of death (Gen 2:16–17). The Edenic Covenant was terminated by man's disobedience, when Adam and Eve ate of the fruit of the tree of the knowledge of good and evil, resulting in their spiritual and physical deaths. This failure necessitated the establishment of the covenant with Adam (Gen 3:14–21).[1]

The Adamic Covenant (Gen 3:14–21)

This covenant is universal in nature, affecting all peoples of the earth. It is still at work in humanity. The covenant with Adam is the second general or universal covenant. It could be called the covenant with mankind, for it sets forth the conditions which will hold sway until the curse of sin is lifted (Isa 11:6–10; Rom 8:18–23). According to the covenant, the conditions which will prevail are:

- The serpent, the instrument used by Satan to effect the fall of man, is cursed. The curse affects the serpent, but also the indwelling energizer, Satan. Great physical changes took place in the serpent. Apparently it was upright; now it will go on its belly (v. 14). It was the most desirable animal of the animal creation; now it is the most

---

1. *Open Bible*, 8.

loathsome. The sight or thought of a snake should be an effective reminder of the devastating effects of sin;
- Satan is judged – he will enjoy limited success ("you shall bruise his heel," v. 15), but ultimately he will be judged ("he shall bruise your head," v. 15);
- The first prophecy of the coming of Messiah is given (v. 15);
- There will be a multiplication of conception, necessitated by the introduction of death into the human race (v. 16);
- There will be pain in childbirth (v. 16);
- The woman is made subject to her husband (v. 16);
- The ground is cursed and will bring forth weeds among the food which man must eat for his existence (vv. 17–19);
- Physical change takes place in man; he will perspire when he works. He will have to work all his life long (v. 19);
- In sinning, man dies spiritually and ultimately physically. His flesh will decay until it returns to dust from which it was originally taken (v. 19).[2]

The Noahic Covenant (Gen 9:1–19)

The covenant with Noah is the third general or universal covenant. God gives the Noahic covenant so that Noah and all human race to follow might know that the provisions made in the Adamic covenant remain in effect with one notable addition: the principle of human government which includes the responsibility of suppressing the outbreak of sin and violence, so that it will not be necessary to destroy the earth again by a flood. After the Tower of Babel, God changed his strategy: instead of dealing with a composite "one people" (universal), God selected or elected persons, nations, events, and institutions to reveal his universal message to all humanity, to his entire creation. The provisions of the covenant are as follows:

- The responsibility to populate the earth is reaffirmed (v. 1);
- The subjection of the animal kingdom to humanity is reaffirmed (v. 2);
- Humans are permitted to eat the flesh of animals. However, they are to refrain from eating blood (vv. 3–4);

---

2. *Open Bible*, 10.

- The sacredness of human life is established. Whatever sheds a human's blood, whether man or beast, must be put to death (vv. 5–6);
- This covenant is confirmed to Noah, all humanity, and every living creature on the face of the earth (vv. 9–10);
- The promise is given never to destroy the earth again by a universal flood (v. 11). The next time God destroys the earth, it will be by fire (2 Pet 3:10);
- The rainbow is designated as a testimony of the existence of this covenant and the promise never to destroy the earth again by flood. As long as we can see the rainbow we will know that the Noahic covenant is in existence (vv. 12–17).[3]

After the tower of Babel, God changed his strategy of dealing with humanity, from a composite "one people" (universal) to selecting or electing persons, nations, events and institutions to reveal his universal message to humanity. However, God continues to deal with his entire creation as he deems fit.

The Abrahamic Covenant (Gen 12:1–3)

God called out and chose Abraham as his means of establishing a true religion and a true vehicle for saving mankind.

The Abrahamic covenant is the basis of all the other theocratic covenants and provides for blessings in three areas: (1) national, "I will make you a great nation"; (2) personal, "I will bless you and make your name great and you shall be a blessing"; and (3) universal, "In you all families of the earth will be blessed." The Abrahamic covenant constitutes an important link in all that God began to do, has done throughout history and will continue to do until the consummation of history. It is the one purpose of God for humans into which all of God's programs and works fit . . . The universal aspects of the covenant are threefold:

- blessings for those people and nations which bless Abraham and the nation which comes from him;
- cursing upon those people and nations which curse Abraham and Israel;

---

3. *Open Bible*, 17.

- blessings upon all the families of the earth through the Messiah, who, according to the flesh, is Abraham's son and provides salvation for the entire world.[4]

We can see that, even though God made this covenant with Abraham and his seed only, this covenant has universal significance and has implications for all of humanity. Other nations, religions and cultures are to be beneficiaries of this Abrahamic covenant.

Even though God made this covenant only with Abraham and his seed, in God's divine plan, this covenant, has universal significance and implications for the entire humanity. This covenant laid a solid foundation for the Coming Messiah. Other nations, religions and cultures become beneficiaries of this Abrahamic Covenant.

The Mosaic Covenant (Exod 19:3–8)

> Then Moses went up to God, and the LORD called to him from the mountain and said, "This is what you are to say to the descendants of Jacob and what you are to tell the people of Israel: 'You yourselves have seen what I did to Egypt and how I carried you on eagles' wings and brought you to myself. Now if you obey me fully and keep my covenant, then out of all nations you will be my treasured possession. Although the whole earth is mine, you will be for me a kingdom of priests and a holy nation.' These are the words you are to speak to the Israelites." (Exod 19:3–6)

The Mosaic covenant is conditional: "If you obey me fully ... then ... you will be my treasured possession."

> This covenant was given to the nation of Israel so that those who believed God's promise given to Abraham in the Abrahamic covenant (Gen 12:1–3) would know how they should conduct themselves. . . . The Mosaic covenant in no way replaced or set aside the Abrahamic covenant. Its function is clearly set out by Paul (Gal 3:17–19), who points out that the law, the Mosaic covenant, came 430 years after the Abrahamic covenant. . . . The Mosaic covenant was not given so that by keeping it people could be saved, but so that they might realize that they could not do

---

4. *Open Bible*, 22.

what God wanted them to do even when God wrote it down on tablets of stone. The law was given that humankind might realize that they are helpless and hopeless when left to themselves and realize that their only hope is to receive the righteousness of God by faith in Jesus (Gal 3:22–24).[5]

The Mosaic covenant addresses, in the main, the questions of other religions and cultures. All religions, according to the book of Hebrews, were preparatory to the cross of Christ. Jesus said: "Do not think that I came to abolish the Law or the Prophets; I have not come to abolish them but to fulfil them" (Matt 5:17).

The book of Hebrews explains how the cross of Christ fulfilled the messianic promises and prophecies of Judaism – and this same theological model applies to all world religions and cultures. The cross of Christ fulfilled and supplanted all traditional sacrifices and offerings, and all rituals, ceremonies, and festivals that go along with them. The believing messianic community knows what specific areas of traditional religion must be abolished in the light of the work of redemption through the cross of Christ.

Palestinian Covenant (Deut 29:10–15; 30:11–20)

The Palestinian covenant has two aspects: the legal aspects which are immediate and conditional (Deut 27–29) and also the grace aspects which are future and unconditional (Deut 30:1–9). The enjoyment of the immediate blessings is introduced by the conditional formula: "If you fully obey the voice of the LORD your God . . . the LORD your God will set you high above all the nations on earth" (Deut 28:1). Sadly, Israel did not meet the condition of obedience and is still experiencing God's curses and punishment for their disobedience (Deut 28:15–68). The unconditional grace aspects of the Palestinian covenant have yet to be realized. God will re-gather the scattered people of Israel and establish them in the land he has promised unconditionally to give them. The Palestinian covenant concludes with a final warning and a challenge to obey (Deut 30:1–20).[6]

---

5. *Open Bible*, 108.
6. *Open Bible*, 291.

The Palestinian covenant generally reflects how God deals with humanity in a state of rebellion against him. When humanity refuses to worship God on his terms, humanity suffers. Yet, in spite of human sin, God still works to fulfil his purposes according to the good pleasure of his will.

The Davidic Covenant (2 Sam 7:4–17)

In this covenant David is promised three things:

> a land forever (2 Sam 7:10); an unending dynasty (2 Sam 7:11, 16); and an everlasting kingdom. The birth of Solomon, David's son who is to succeed him, is predicted (2 Sam 7:12). His particular role is to establish the throne of the Davidic kingdom forever (7:13). His throne continues, though his seed is cursed in the person of Jeconiah (Coniah or Jehoiakim), who was the king under whom the nation was carried captive to Babylon. Jeremiah prophesies that no one whose genealogical descent could be traced back to David through Jeconiah and Solomon would ever sit on David's throne (Jer 22:24–30). Joseph, the legal, but not physical, father of Jesus traces his lineage to David through Jeconiah (Matt 1:1–17). David, however, had another son, Nathan. His line was not cursed. Mary, the physical mother of Jesus, traces her lineage back to David through Nathan (Luke 3:23–38). Notice the care and the extent to which God goes to keep his word and to preserve its truthfulness. The virgin birth was absolutely essential not only to assure the sinless character of Jesus but also to fulfil the Davidic covenant. Jesus receives his "blood right" to David's throne through his earthly mother, Mary and his "legal right" to David's throne through his adoptive earthly father, Joseph. The virgin birth guarantees that one of David's line will sit on David's throne and rule forever, while at the same time preserving intact the curse and restriction on the line of descent through Jeconiah.[7]

The dramatic fulfilment of the Davidic covenant is described by the apostle John in Revelation: the Messiah, who is the King of kings and the Lord of lords will establish his rule and the kingdom at the end of the Age.

---

7. *Open Bible*, 443.

The New Covenant (Jer 31:31–34)

> "The days are coming," declares the LORD, "when I will make a new covenant with the people of Israel and with the people of Judah. It will not be like the covenant that I made with their ancestors when I took them by the hand to lead them out of Egypt, because they broke my covenant, though I was a husband to them," declares the LORD. "This is the covenant I will make with the people of Israel after that time," declares the LORD. "I will put my law in their minds, and write it on their hearts. I will be their God and they will be my people. No longer will they teach their neighbour, or say to one another, 'Know the LORD,' because they will all know me, from the least of them to the greatest," declares the LORD. "For I will forgive their wickedness and will remember their sins no more." (Jer 31:31–34)

Four provisions are made in this covenant:

> (1) regeneration – God will put his law in their inward parts and write it in their hearts (Jer 31:33); (2) a national restoration – Jehovah will be their God and the nation will be his people (Jer 31:33); (3) personal ministry of the Holy Spirit – they will all be taught individually by God (Jer 31:34); and (4) full justification – their sins will be forgiven and completely removed (Jer 31:34). The new covenant is made sure by the blood of Jesus shed on Calvary's cross. That blood which guarantees to Israel its new covenant also provides for the forgiveness of sins for all the believers who comprise the church. Jesus's payment for sins is more than adequate to pay for the sins of all who will believe in Him. The new covenant is called "new" in contrast to the covenant with Moses which is called "old" (Jer 31:32; Heb 8:6–13) because it actually accomplishes what the Mosaic covenant could only point to, that is, the child of God living in a manner that is consistent with the character of God.[8]

At the appointed time in history, God spoke to humanity through Jesus the Messiah. The blood of the Lamb sealed the new covenant between God and his people. This paved the way for the new covenant and the new law, which are being implemented by the ministry of the Holy Spirit. Joel promised that

---

8. *Open Bible*, 1083.

it would be so: "And afterward, I will pour out My Spirit on all people . . . Even on my servants, both men and women, I will pour out my Spirit in those days" (Joel 2:28–29).

Jesus the Messiah himself instituted this new covenant at the right time in history:

> While they were eating, Jesus took bread, and when he had given thanks, he broke it and gave it to the disciples, saying, "Take and eat; this is my body."
>
> Then He took a cup and when he had given thanks, he gave it to them, saying, "Drink from it, all of you. This is my blood of the new covenant, which is poured out for many for the forgiveness of sins. I tell you, I will not drink from this fruit of the vine from now on until that day when I drink it new with you in my Father's kingdom." (Matt 26:26–29)

These covenants are essential to our understanding of the gospel of Christ in relation to world religions and cultures. Jesus Christ is not an historical accident, but a unique prophetic and messianic fulfilment of God's covenants with Israel and, indeed, with the whole world. Jesus relates to the Old Testament, both prophetically and covenantally. But he also relates to the whole world, including all religions and cultures through these covenants.

Paul's theological analysis in Romans 9–11 explains how Jesus relates to both Israel and the Gentiles, and how both relationships are in God's eternal plan of salvation. The salvific work of Christ on the cross destroyed the wall of division between the Jew and the Gentile (Eph 2). They were separated by the law but, in Christ Jesus, the law has been laid aside to clear the way for a new humanity and a new relationship.[9]

There was no need for prophetic covenants like these to be given to other religions and cultures. Instead, other religions and cultures are directed to Jesus the Messiah. God is building a kingdom and is calling all human beings to become a part of it.

This is why, when Africans become Christians, they must renounce any ancestral covenants and any alternate beliefs and subscribe to the covenant of Jesus Christ and his church. There can be no carryover from any other religious system into Christ; there must be a renunciation, a confession and a new faith

---

9. Turaki, *Tribal Gods of Africa*, 140–144.

and commitment to Jesus Christ. The new covenant of Christ and our new faith in him supplants all that was prior to Christ and his redemption in the cross. All our past has to be transformed.

Christians who want to carry their past into Christianity do not understand the covenant relationship between Christ and his followers. But they have also misunderstood their religious past. No one can carry one covenant over into another. The rules of initiation and the qualifications are different. This controlling spirit-power of traditional religion cannot be taken into the new covenant with Christ. It has to be broken and renounced. The way we used to understand and live in the old covenant must be transformed into a new worldview that is biblical and Christ-like.

Paul explains this as follows:

> Do not be yoked together with unbelievers. For what do righteousness and wickedness have in common? Or what fellowship can light have with darkness? What harmony is there between Christ and Belial? Or what does a believer have in common with an unbeliever? What agreement is there between the temple of God and idols? For we are the temple of the living God. As God has said: "I will live with them and walk among them, and I will be their God, and they will be my people." Therefore, "Come out from them and be separate," says the Lord. "Touch no unclean thing, and I will receive you." (2 Cor 6:14–17)

The God of the Bible and Christianity will not accept any covenant with a rival god or divinity. All other covenants must be renounced and forsaken. This is what is signified by confession of faith in Jesus Christ; in water baptism (which is a sign of inner baptism of the Holy Spirit) and in eating the bread and wine in Holy Communion.

43

Biblical Theology

I stated at the outset that the Bible was to be our primary theological tool in engaging with traditional religion. As we come to the end of this study, it is good to remind ourselves why we can use this approach with confidence.

The Bible is God's special revelation to man, making known God's nature, mind, will, and decrees in creation. It reveals humankind in terms of itself and also in terms of its relationship to God, to fellow human beings and to creation. It reveals God's intentions and dealings with humankind and with creation, as well as God's intervention and redemptive action in human history. It reveals the nature, the state, and the condition of humanity in nations, religions and cultures. Thus, the Holy Bible is the foundation of Christian beliefs, practices and theology.

As a result it provides a normative frame of reference from which one can address and study the religious and theological issues raised by African Traditional Religion. We call this biblical theology; the method is therefore bibliocentric.

A Bibliocentric Methodology

Biblical theology does not reject the use of any scientific, anthropological, sociological, or philosophical studies of religions and cultures. These can be used to throw light on and to provide insight, leading to a fuller understanding of the subject.[1]

Biblical theology is not just a phenomenological study of traditional religion, but the presentation of God's special revelation in both the Bible and Jesus Christ to the religions and cultures of the world.

---

1. Turaki, "Human Dignity and Identity."

Biblical theology is not just a comparative study of religions or cultures, but it is how biblical Christianity sees, understands, interprets and applies African Traditional Religion and culture in light of God's special revelation.

Biblical theology is not just a search for continuity or discontinuity between Christianity and the African pre-Christian religious heritage. However, it does involve identifying areas of human and religious commonality which can serve as points of contact or bridges to facilitate effective gospel communication and Christian witness and evangelism. Biblical theology therefore involves ascertaining truth and error in the African pre-Christian religious heritage in terms of the biblical revelation and God's revelation in Jesus Christ.

Biblical theology is not just a cultural or traditional agenda. Instead, it is a search for a genuine Christian understanding of the spiritual and social needs of African Traditional. Religion and culture can pave the way so that the presentation of the gospel and biblical teachings can be effective in addressing these needs.

Biblical theology is not just a quest for indigenization or Africanization of Christianity. However, it is a quest for biblical incarnation or inculturation of both the message (gospel) and the messenger (Christian) in the African context.

Biblical theology is not a glorification, rehabilitation, or integration of the African religious past. Instead, it is concerned with the glorification, proclamation and the promotion of the gospel of Christ and the Bible within the African Christian context so that the African mind can be renewed and transformed.

Biblical theology is not a Christianization of the African religious past. It aims to transform and redeem the African religious past in the light of God's special revelation in the Bible and Jesus Christ.

Biblical theology therefore is a search for an authentic Christian theology and expression with firm biblical and Christian foundations within the African context.

Biblical theology takes traditional religion from within its context of general revelation and creational theology and subjects it to the searchlight of God's special revelation in Jesus Christ. This redemption theology challenges all religions and cultures of the world to embrace its message of salvation and redemption in Jesus Christ.

A Particular but Universal Revelation

Our commonality means that every human being falls under the rule of God. God acts universally in creating and redeeming all of creation. Nonetheless he uses particular events, people, and institutions to convey his universal message to the whole world. God does not have to speak to each and every segment of humanity through its own particular or specific revelation. The particulars do not have to be made available to each separate segment of humanity; they are universal. Nonetheless, religious pluralism and cultural relativism have forced a paradigm shift in the Christian evangelization of cultures and religions.

There are some theologians and scholars who no longer regard the uniqueness of Jesus Christ and the teachings of Christianity, the Bible, the prophets, the apostles, and the Christian tradition as valid for other religions and cultures. Such theologians and scholars teach only creation theology and general revelation, without redemption theology and special revelation. As a result their message is defective.

These modern philosophies accept the plurality of religions and cultures and do not see the need for cross-cultural and cross-religious evangelization or for the presentation of the gospel of Christ. They argue that because traditional religion has its own intermediaries, salvation history, religious beliefs, rituals, and practices, it is unnecessary to present the gospel of Christ to its followers. Such pluralist and relativist arguments are contrary to the spirit of Christianity that is called to be both salt and light amongst world religions and cultures.

It is clear that all humankind, because it is created in the image of God, has some knowledge of its Maker. Throughout the ages, God has revealed himself through creation and history. This is what we call natural revelation or creation theology; God revealing himself through his created order. These communications play a very important role in traditional religion. We see an awareness of them among traditional Africans who long for communication with and from spirit beings or mystical powers and forces.

But what we can glean about God in this way is limited and could even be defective and inaccurate as it is subject to the corrupting influence of sin and of spirit beings. The created order and humanity have fallen into sin and are therefore no longer normative. Humankind needs a special revelation.

God therefore chose specific events, persons and institutions to reveal his universal message and will to the whole world. He chose to reveal his plans for humanity through Abraham and his seed, the nation of Israel. They were to be the covenant people through whom all the families of the earth would be blessed. This everlasting covenant and the giving of the Mosaic law were preparatory to the coming of the promised Messiah.

God repeated his promise of the coming Messiah again and again, through Abraham, Israel and David (Gen 12:1–3; Deut 18:15; 2 Sam 7:12–16; Luke

1:26–38, 40–56, 76–79). Thus in his eternal plan of salvation, God chose an individual (Abraham) and a nation (Israel). God's plan also included a covenant (with Israel), a law (the Mosaic), the promise of a coming Messiah (repeated through David and the prophets), redemption and salvation through the cross of Christ, and the establishment of the kingdom of God by the coming King of kings and Lord of lords, Jesus the Messiah.

These specific individuals, people, events and institutions were carefully chosen to convey God's intention of saving all creation and all humanity. God made deliberate and specific choices which, although in themselves "particular," have universal consequences and implications. God did not need to duplicate his particulars of salvation to every religion, culture, or people; any suggestion of duplication is merely the invention of human beings. The claims of religions and cultures that God has also spoken through them do not in any way negate God's eternal plan of using the specific and the particular to convey his message of salvation to all creation and humanity.

Comparative studies of traditional religion and of the Jewish Old Testament seem to overlook God's specific revelations. This has meant that there is little conception of fallen creation or of the sinfulness of humanity. As a result, there is a lack of understanding about the need for an intermediary who can satisfy the requirements of God's holiness. The Bible states:

> In the past God spoke to our ancestors through the prophets at many times and in various ways, but in these last days he has spoken to us by his Son, whom He appointed heir of all things and through whom also He made the universe. The Son is the radiance of God's glory and the exact representation of his being, sustaining all things by his powerful word. After he had provided purification for sins, he sat down at the right hand of the Majesty in heaven. (Heb 1:1–3)

This statement underlines the finality of God's special revelation in Jesus the Messiah as the unique Saviour of the world. The special revelation of Jesus the Messiah crowns all God's revelations to humanity. This revealed knowledge is therefore both distinct from and superior to other religions.

Comparisons must also take cognisance of the perfect universal moral law which is revealed in the sacred Scriptures. God's moral law is the apex of all the moral laws that govern the created universe, moral agents, and human beings. Its authority is not rooted in the philosophies, theologies, ethics or natural sciences of human traditions, but in the nature and attributes of God who created and rules over all that exists.

An understanding of these issues means that, although we can study the religions and ethics produced by human cultures as they observe creation, we must recognize that there are "deficiencies [that] must be overcome by the superior wisdom that comes only with faith" in the sacred Scripture.[2] Whatever we obtain from philosophy, natural science, or religion is "not enough for Christian life, either in this world or for salvation in the next."[3]

Oswald Chambers puts it as follows:

> We live in two universes: the universe of common-sense in which we come in contact with things by our senses, and the universe of revelation with which we come in contact by faith. The wisdom of God fits the two universes exactly; the one interprets the other. Jesus Christ is the expression of the wisdom of God.[4]

The final and highest form of revelation in the sacred Scriptures is the revelation of God in Jesus Christ. And it is this that distinguishes Christian and biblical revelation, theology, and ethics from that of other religions and traditions. Oswald Chambers commented on this:

> In the universe of common-sense, the faculty required is intellectual curiosity, but when we enter into the domain from which Jesus Christ talks, intellectual curiosity is ruled out, moral obedience takes the absolute place . . . [With the universe of revelation] our ordinary common-sense faculties are of no use. We cannot see God or taste God; we can dispute with him, but we cannot get at him by our senses at all, and common-sense is apt to say there is nothing other than this universe . . . we come in contact with the revelation facts of God's universe by faith wrought in us by the Spirit of God.[5]

The foundations of theology are clearly not based or rooted in the universe of common-sense or observation, but in the universe of revelation through faith in the Scriptures.

This is why the major thesis of this book is that theology is rooted ultimately in the nature, character, attributes, and being of God as revealed in the sacred Scripture. This must be the basis of theology for all human beings, regardless of race, creed, or faith. Unlike in traditional religion where the pursuit of

---

2. Adler, *Guidebook to Learning*, 49.
3. Adler, 49.
4. Chambers, *Studies in the Sermon on the Mount*, 52.
5. Chambers, 52–53.

spiritual meaning and power occurs by means of dreams, divination, sorcery, witchcraft, and spirit possession, in Christianity, God's dealings with creation are revealed through the Holy Spirit, the word of God, and the wisdom of God.

Translating the Scriptures

This means that a good knowledge of African languages is also essential when one wishes to communicate God's word to Africa. Biblical words, ideas, and concepts must be translated into African languages. Principles of language hermeneutics must be adhered to, while words, ideas, and concepts must be accurately translated.

However, an overemphasis on accuracy in translation and on hermeneutics, as well as on biblical criticism, often results in the Bible's symbolic language and symbols being overlooked. One cannot only be interested in the accuracy of or the hermeneutics of words, ideas, and concepts, one must also take note of how they are used symbolically throughout the Scriptures. For instance if we take a word like "holiness," we should study its meanings from the book of Genesis all the way to the book of Revelation, noting its historical development, its variations and progressions, book by book. We need to consider not only meanings but also how to interpret symbols.

A thematic study of biblical words, ideas, and concepts like this enriches the understanding of any theologian or biblical scholar. African theologians and scholars who use this method, however, will not only enrich their own scholarship but will also contribute biblical knowledge to world Christianity in a fresh and innovative way.

44

A Theological Framework of Religions and Cultures

This methodology proposes that we must research and study traditional religion and culture carefully. The primary objective is to gather accurate knowledge about the traditional religious system and its structures, beliefs, practices, and religious behaviour and attitudes. Accurate understanding, interpretation and application are essential if the presentation and proclamation of the gospel is to be relevant.

On one hand, this is not a new idea. Students of religions and cultures have long searched for the fundamental unity that brings all religions or cultures under one "overarching universal principle."[1] Similarities and commonalities among world religions and cultures reflect the fact that humankind is essentially religious and that, wherever they are found, people exhibit religious characteristics. Ken Gnanakan states:

> There is within them (humankind) the pressure of the ultimate, the direction towards God, a compulsion to get back to their Creator . . . But there is a direction towards God within every human being and God Himself is actively drawing all men and women to Himself.[2]

The human quest for God that Gnanakan calls "religionness" or even "Godness" is a genuine part of every human being. People have always at all times searched for their Maker in some form of religion. Although Satan can corrupt this genuine quest, "We must be careful not to ascribe this desire to Satan.

---

1. Gnanakan, *Pluralistic Predicament*, 203.
2. Gnanakan, 216–217.

Satan definitely deceives humankind taking desire for God and diverting it towards himself."[3]

This means that the desire for religion must not be viewed entirely negatively. The Bible reveals that, in spite of the fall and sin, God still operates universally within his creation. Moreover, the fact that God created human commonality must be recognized in all our dealings with human beings. Commonality comes from God; it is not a result of continuity or discontinuity.

A study of African Traditional Religion must identify these areas of commonality or similarity but must refrain from drawing conclusions that distort either the biblical meaning or the understanding of the nature and context of traditional religions. Gnanakan states: "We need to be clear that in developing our implications of the universality of the redemptive activity of Jesus Christ we do not justify the existence of sinful structures, even though sincerely made by men and women but hindered by sin and Satanic deception."[4]

In developing their African Theology, some African theologians and scholars have tended to water down the biblical affirmation of the finality of God's revelation in Jesus the Messiah. They have also tended to ignore or excuse the moral and ethical questions which exist in African Traditional Religion. Instead, their preoccupation with religious and cultural issues, on the one hand, and with ideological and political agendas, on the other, has tended to limit any serious biblical examination of the spirituality, morality, ethics, and salvation in the African Traditional Religion.

This problem arises from the theological presuppositions and beliefs of these scholars. The claims of a special revelation in the Bible and in Jesus Christ challenge their thinking. Even those who hold to the inerrant inspiration and authority of the Bible have largely failed to apply special revelation and redemption theology in their theological discourse. As a result their theological output may be scholarly and erudite, but it misses the truth of Christianity.

African concepts, views, and thoughts about God, supernatural beings, and worship are very important to our understanding of African religions and cultures, but these must come under the scrutiny of the Bible. Furthermore, African understanding of biblical ideas – the interpretation and application of biblical facts – must be scrutinized in the light of biblical knowledge by the community of believers.

The fact that sin has corrupted all human religions and cultures must be paramount in our discussion of religions and cultures. Philip Steyne in

---

3. Gnanakan, 216.
4. Gnanakan, 216.

his book *In Step with the God of the Nations: A Biblical Theology of Missions* (1992) focuses on the impact of the fall on religions and cultures. F. N. Lee made similar remarks concerning the fallen human culture in his book, *The Central Significance of Culture* (1976).

The religious and cultural ideas of African Traditional Religion, like those of all other human religions in the world, arose out of general or natural revelation. The biblical status of all these religions and cultures was clearly defined by the apostle Paul in Romans 1–5 and Acts 17:17–29:

> The wrath of God is being revealed from heaven against all the ungodliness and wickedness of people, who suppress the truth by their wickedness, since what may be known about God is plain to them, because God has made it plain to them. For since the creation of the world God's invisible qualities – his eternal power and divine nature – have been clearly seen, being understood from what has been made, so that people are without excuse.
>
> For although they knew God, they neither glorified him as God nor gave thanks to him, but their thinking became futile and their foolish hearts were darkened. Although they claimed to be wise, they became fools and exchanged the glory of the immortal God for images made to look like mortal human beings and birds and animals and reptiles. (Rom 1:18–23)

In his first commandment God, who revealed himself in creation, humanity, and history, indicates the difference between humankind's religions and true faith:

> You shall have no other gods before me. You shall not make for yourself an image in the form of anything in heaven above or on the earth beneath or in the water below. You shall not bow down to them or worship them; for I, the LORD your God, am a jealous God, punishing the children for the sin of the parents to the third and fourth generations of those who hate me, but showing love to a thousand generations of those who love me and keep my commandments. (Exod 20:3–6)

From this description it is clear that African Traditional Religion was self-made. After the attempted building of the tower of Babel (Gen 11), God rejected all such self-made religions, and all humanity languished under God's universal wrath, judgment, and curse. Thereafter God's strategy for dealing with rebellious humanity necessitated God's final and special revelation in Jesus Christ that brings salvation and redemption for the whole world.

Cultural and Religious People Prior to the Cross of Christ

African students of theology love to ask questions about the fate of their ancestors who lived before the arrival of the gospel of Christ in their areas. If one says that these ancestors are lost, they believe that this reveals the "hidden cruelty of God" and the destruction of their ancestral destiny and identity. They argue that if God is merciful, he cannot condemn the ancestors to eternal damnation. These ancestors were ignorant of the gospel of Christ which, through no fault of theirs, did not reach them. To provide answers, it is useful to quote Romans 2:11–16:

> For God does not show favouritism. All who sin apart from the law will also perish apart from the law, and all who sin under the law will be judged by the law. For it is not those who hear the law who are righteous in God's sight, but it is those who obey the law who will be declared righteous. (Indeed, when Gentiles, who do not have the law, do by nature things required by the law, they are a law for themselves, even though they do not have the law. They show that the requirements of the law are written on their hearts, their consciences also bearing witness and their thoughts sometimes accusing and at other times even defending them.) This will take place on the day when God judges people's secrets through Jesus Christ, as my gospel declares. (Rom 2:11–16)

Here the apostle Paul lays down some basic principles: human beings are judged by God according to God's truth (Rom 2:1–5); according to their works or deeds (Rom 2:6–10); and on how they apply the law and their consciences (Rom 2:11–16). Africans who died prior to receiving the gospel will be judged in the light of these three principles and their consciences. Although the final judge of all human beings is Jesus the Messiah (Rom 2:16), the judgment here is not by "profession of faith in Jesus" nor by "the hearing of the Gospel of Christ." Thus, professing Christ is not the final issue, but God's impartial judgment. Everyone will be judged equally, whether they are Jews, Gentiles, believers in Christ or non-believers. They will all come under the same divine standards of law and conscience.

But Paul goes further: he also presents the universal criteria for righteousness. Righteousness is not earned by works but by a personal belief or faith in God. "Abraham believed God and it was credited to him as righteousness" (Rom 4:3b). In other words, Abraham's righteousness was not earned through circumcision or through the law, because the commands concerning those two acts were given after his faith in God (Rom 4:9–15). The criterion is not religion, nor even culture, but faith.

This principle which applies to all humanity has not changed throughout history (Rom 9). Just as Paul points to Jesus the Messiah as the ultimate judge of all human beings, he also points to Jesus the Messiah as the ultimate one through whom, by faith, we can obtain righteousness. Even though Abraham lived many centuries before the cross and the gospel of Christ, by faith he believed the promises of God which pointed prophetically to Jesus the Messiah (Rom 4:16–22).

God's universal criteria for judgment and for righteousness apply to all human beings throughout history. One can only escape God's judgment and stand righteous before God by faith in Jesus the Messiah who is the revealed righteousness of God for all ages.

> God presented Christ as a sacrifice of atonement, through the shedding of his blood – to be received by faith. He did this to demonstrate his righteousness, because in his forbearance he had left the sins committed beforehand unpunished – he did it to demonstrate his righteousness at the present time, so as to be just and the one who justifies those who have faith in Jesus. (Rom 3:25–26)

The cross of Christ has eternal efficacy and is not limited by historical time. "But when the set time had fully come, God sent his Son, born of a woman, born under the law, to redeem those under the law, that we might receive adoption to sonship" (Gal 4:4–5). The Abrahamic faith and that of all saints prior to the cross was indeed eschatological, awaiting its fulfilment in the cross of Christ. This faith was also christological, an anticipation of the coming of Christ, his death and resurrection (Rom 4).

The cross of Christ does not annul God's eternal and universal criteria of judgment and righteousness. Both principles point to the fact that no human being is able to pass the test. There is no religion and no law that can enable one to pass God's test.

> For what the law was powerless to do because it was weakened by the flesh, God did by sending his own Son in the likeness of sinful flesh . . . he condemned sin in the flesh, in order that the righteous requirement of the law might be fully met in us, who do not live according to the flesh but according to the Spirit. (Rom 8:3–4)

There is no basis for our justification, except the cross of Christ. The cross of Christ was instituted in order to reveal God's grace, righteousness, and justice. And this is where the principle of God's grace comes in. "For it is by grace you have been saved through faith – and this is not from yourselves, it is a gift of God – not by works, so that no one can boast" (Eph 2:8). Salvation is the work of God's grace.

The apostle Paul says emphatically:

> No one will be declared righteous in God's sight by the works of the law . . . for all have sinned and fall short of the glory of God . . . We maintain that a person is justified by faith apart from the works of the law. (Rom 3:20–31)

Humankind has nothing that can save it; not religion, not law, not even conscience. We are left with God's grace and with faith. But it is the object of that faith that will justify or condemn. Jesus the Messiah and his finished work of redemption on the cross has from eternity been that object of faith. Throughout history, God who is a Trinity has been the ultimate object of faith and reveals himself at his appointed times. God's special revelation in Jesus the Messiah provides the fuller meaning and content of this faith. It is a redemptive and a saving faith in the person of Jesus the Messiah who saves us from our sins.

Prior to the gospel of Christ, men and women of God throughout history and all over the world and in all human societies have demonstrated their redemptive and saving faith in God. And throughout history God has demonstrated his grace to all those who trusted and believed him. "I now realize how true it is that God does not show favouritism but accepts from every nation the one who fears him and does what is right" (Acts 10:34–35). This statement applies to all human beings.

The Scriptures are clear on how God deals with all human beings, both before and after the cross of Christ. All human beings will be judged in terms of whether they had "the Abrahamic Faith" which pointed towards Jesus the Messiah, the seed of Abraham, or whether they had "faith in Jesus the Messiah" himself.

> So also Abraham believed God and it was credited to him for righteousness. Understand, then, that those who have faith are children of Abraham. Scripture foresaw that God would justify the Gentiles by faith and announced the gospel in advance to Abraham beforehand, "All nations will be blessed through you." So those who rely on faith are blessed along with Abraham, the man of faith. (Gal 3:6–9)

The principles of God's judgment and faith cannot be ignored. These are the eternal principles, which bring every religion, culture, and human being under the eternal rule of God.

45

To Sum Up

Christian theologians and scholars from different Christian traditions and backgrounds have propounded many methods, theories, hypotheses, and made many assumptions have addressed the subject of this book, seeking answers to the question: "How should Christianity approach the study of African Traditional Religion, worldview, and thought?"

> There are two extremes amongst Christians in their approach to the study of African Traditional Religion and culture. On the one hand, we find the random use of Bible texts and Christian doctrines of Western theological origin to address traditional beliefs, practices and behaviour. Such an approach is not systematic, coherent and comprehensive. More importantly: it does not take the traditional culture (including its religion and worldview) seriously. Sometimes it fails at addressing the traditional mind in terms of how it thinks and does both social and religious things. It produces a strong, but irrelevant theology that fails at addressing the African mind . . . On the other hand, we have those who use the Bible very sparingly in their study of African Traditional Religion. God's revelation in the Bible is not their primary starting point, but traditional culture which has to guide, elucidate and influence their theology. In this case we may have a more "relevant" approach, but at the same time the result is a weak, not very Christian, biblical theology and worldview.[1]

As a result of these shortcomings, the Word of God has failed to engage, challenge, and transform the mind of Africans. In fact, some African scholars

---

1. Van der Walt in Bower, *Embracing Christian Intellectual Responsibilities*, preface.

and theologians have succeeded only in producing a theology of conformity, an affirmation of African Traditional Religion and culture.

This book is an addition to the ongoing debate and suggests a third way. I have not ignored or degraded African Traditional Religion, culture and worldview, but have taken them very seriously, accepting that they must be thoroughly researched and understood. However, I have not overemphasized or glorified Africa's traditional heritage, defending its values in the face of Christianity or modernity.

The focus of this book has therefore not been on how the African understands and applies the Bible or Christianity, but rather, on how the Bible defines African Traditional Religion and culture. The starting point has been Jesus Christ and the Trinity, the inerrancy and authority of the Bible, and the authority of the church. A Christian scholar or theologian must be faithful to these Christian foundations or the developed theology will simply enable non-Christians to use it to argue against Christianity.

I have taken careful note of the fact that Christianity does not meet an empty traditional African mind, but one which is already preoccupied with traditional religious thought. When it receives Christianity, this mind has the ability to recast and transform it into its own categories of thought. This means that it can have a profound and dominant influence on African Christians.

With the introduction of Western colonialism and Missionary Christianity to Africa, certain valuable social, religious, and cultural values and institutions were replaced by Western ones, which have failed to meet Africa's social and religious needs. African social and religious values and institutions such as those of marriage, education, law, rites of passage, as well as age groups and guilds were discarded. This has created a crisis of meaning and structures that can only be adequately addressed by going back to the roots of the African understanding of such values and institutions.

There were therefore a number of components to this study:

A Definition of African Traditional Religion and Worldview
The first task was to develop a working definition of African Traditional Religion as a theological frame of reference.

The nature and the theological basis of traditional beliefs in gods, divinities and spirits were examined. Traditional beliefs in the spirit phenomenon were defined and interpreted, as was the power phenomenon that dominates African pagan spirituality.

The centrality of humankind in the traditional religious worldview was also addressed. This allowed us to examine the relevance of the traditional theological, philosophical, and ethical foundations. My primary objective was to understand the inner logic and workings of the traditional religious mind and thought.

Developing an Understanding of Traditional Religious Beliefs and Practices
It was essential that the role of religion in an African society should also be discussed as the role, function, and power accorded to a religion determine the strength of the adherents' commitment to such a religion. Religion in an African society provides solutions to problems encountered in life and seeks to answer the great mysteries of life.

Christianity must be in a position to meet the needs and expectations of traditional Africans, just as African Traditional Religion has over the centuries. It was therefore essential to examine the fundamental theological, psychological, philosophical, moral and ethical beliefs and principles on which traditional religion is based. Biblical teachings and the biblical worldview must be related to these traditional beliefs, attitudes, behaviours, and social and religious practices in a meaningful way.

The Bible as God's authoritative book has already defined the nature and status of traditional religion. However, if Christianity seems to fail to meet these needs and expectations, African converts to Christianity may well revert to their traditional religion in order to have their needs fulfilled and met.

Applying Biblical Knowledge and Understanding to Traditional Religious Beliefs and Practices in Order to Formulate a Christian Theology
This working knowledge and understanding helped us to move on to step three. We began to apply the teachings of the Bible to the religious foundations of traditional beliefs, expectations and aspirations. This prepared the ground for an effective presentation and application of the gospel of Christ.

So that we could relate the biblical and Christian theology effectively, we considered why Africans need a power religion. The purpose and meaning of each religious practice, ritual, ceremony or festival was outlined, and we saw how each religious practice relates to the "potential power source." We saw that, because traditional religion is a religion of power and spirituality, Christianity must be seen to be all the more powerful and spiritual. This led us to discuss the theology of power which is demonstrated in the nature, character and attributes of God.

We recognized that the gospel of Christ must be presented in such a way that this inner longing and inner searching for power is addressed and assuaged. Christ-power must be seen to allay anxieties and fears about spirit-powers.

This book developed an extensive biblical theology through which these issues of life can be addressed. We recognized that the sovereignty of God, his nature, character and attributes, and Christology were central in addressing many of these life issues, traditional religious beliefs and practices. Knowledge and understanding of the Bible and Christian theology are essential because these provide a clear definition of traditional beliefs and practices.

It is our sincere belief that the African cultural and religious background provides a medium through which one can express a deep knowledge and understanding of Christianity that is uniquely African and yet biblically sound and profound. Christians who have a deep knowledge and understanding of African Traditional Religion, beliefs, practices, behaviour and worldview will be enriched when they study the formulation of Christian theology. They will discover that it is possible to use neutral African cultural and religious values or practices to explain and express biblical and Christian concepts and ideas, something which cannot be done adequately using Western theological terms and concepts.

When they are informed by biblical and Christian values, the traditional values and institutions can address the problem of youth delinquency and youth culture. The problem of modern individualism can be addressed by using the traditional communal values and institutions creatively in conjunction with the biblical and Christian values of the messianic community. Enriched by Africa's traditional background, an African conception and interpretation of human rights and human autonomy is bound to be different from that of the West.

An African theologian does not have to change the meaning of biblical concepts, terms, or meanings of symbols in order to make them more African or relevant. Rather, one's primary task is one of faithful transmission and translation of concepts, terms, and symbols so that Africans can fully understand the message of the Bible and the gospel. The best medium for this is through the African traditional religious background, culture, worldview, and the mother tongue. When African theologians are not faithful in these regards, they fall into the trap of negative syncretism that changes the true faith into something else. Africa needs the checks and balances of the Holy Scriptures and the gospel of Christ to prevent syncretism and changes in the symbolic wisdom of biblical and Christian teachings. Furthermore, a theologian must be guided by the wisdom of God and the Holy Spirit so the truth of God is not changed, corrupted or compromised.

It is important to repeat that not every theology done by Africans is a correct biblical theology. Every product of theology is a reflection of one's faith, commitment and knowledge. Those ignorant of the teachings of the Bible will reflect this in a defective theology. Those that are not committed and serious Christians will develop a superficial theology. Those who have a shallow knowledge of traditional religious beliefs, practices and worldview are also likely to produce defective, shallow and syncretistic theologies for the African church. For this reason, the expressions of Christianity in Africa are bound to vary. It is the task of the Christian community to ascertain which expressions are biblically sound, which are christologically, ecclesiologically and missiologically profound, and which ones are not.

A Christian, however, does not have to jettison his biblical beliefs and worldview in order to relate to traditional religious beliefs and worldview. Philip Steyne offered this comment: "The biblical perspective must be embodied in the old if it is to replace the old weakness with a new strength. In other words, the Gospel must become incarnated in the frame of reference of the receptor, if it is to bring about change."[2]

Steyne went on to list the following as points of contact between Christianity and traditional religion. These are the bridges or stepping stones that Christianity can use in evangelism and in presenting the gospel.

Africans have a spiritual view of life: Christianity and traditional religion both believe in spirit beings and in supernatural powers, even though the content and the meanings of traditional beliefs and practices will have to be "evaluated and submitted to the judgment of the Bible."

Africans are *open to the message of the Bible*: There are "perceptions of the word of power" in both religious worldviews. Both acknowledge that God speaks and that God's word, which is spoken, is full of power. Furthermore, both religions acknowledge that God is the source of all power.

Africans are *providentially disposed for response to the gospel*: There are religious concepts that are common to both religions: salvation, reconciliation, retribution, punishment, sacrifices, offerings, religious rituals and ceremonies. All of these and many more "have parallels in the Bible which [can be used] to communicate the gospel."

Africans have *a concept of power encounter*: The idea of a "power encounter," especially with regard to supernatural powers and spirit beings, is common to both Christianity and traditional religion. Christ-power, the Holy Spirit and the biblical conception of spiritual powers and principalities can therefore be understood by the adherents of traditional religion.

---

2. Steyne, *Gods of Power*, 207.

Africans *desire contact with the spirit world*: The desire to have "contact with the spirit world" through prayers, rituals, sacrifices, worship, ceremonies, and other religious practices is common to both religious worldviews.

Africans long for *a personal relationship with a spirit being*: This desire is common to both Christianity and traditional religion and can lead to a personal relationship with and faith in God and Christ.

Conclusion

The objective of this study has been to develop a theological method, as well as a biblical and Christian theology in answer to traditional social and religious beliefs, attitudes, behaviour, and practices. This is a comprehensive biblical and Christian theological guide to the study of African Traditional Religion, worldview and culture. The target in this study is the traditional African mind and thought world that needs to be addressed by the gospel of Jesus Christ and the Bible. The focus is not on how Africans understand and interpret the Bible and Christianity from the perspective of their religion and culture, but how the Bible defines Africans in terms of their traditional religion, culture and worldview. The gospel of Jesus Christ and the Bible address the African, whether traditional, Christian or modern, at the root of his religious and social beliefs, attitudes, behaviours, and practices.

The gospel of Jesus Christ and the Bible can be used as powerful instruments to renew and transform African peoples, societies, and nation-states. Africans who have embraced the gospel of Jesus Christ and who believe in the inerrancy and authority of the Bible must be faithful to the Christian faith. It is hoped that this study will have served to strengthen the faith and commitment of African Christians to their Lord Jesus Christ, the Bible and the church.

Bibliography

This bibliography will also serve the needs of those who are interested in further studies on the interactions of Christianity and African Traditional Religion.

Adegbola, E. A. A., ed. *Traditional Religion in West Africa*. Nairobi: Uzima, 1983.
Adeyemo, T. ed. *Africa Bible Commentary*. Nairobi: WordAlive, 2006.
———, ed. *A Christian Mind in a Changing Africa*. Nairobi: AEAM, 1993.
———. *Is Africa Cursed?* Nairobi: Christian Learning Materials Center, 1997.
———, ed. *Making a Difference: Christian Leaders in Society*. Nairobi: AEA, 1997.
———, ed. *The Making of a Servant of God*. Nairobi: Christian Learning Materials Centre, 1993.
———. *Salvation in African Traditional Religion*. Nairobi: Evangel, 1979.
Adler, Margot. *Drawing Down the Moon: Witches, Druids, Goddess-Worshippers, and Other Pagans in America Today*. New York: Penguin Compass, 1979.
Adler, M. J. *A Guidebook to Learning: For a Lifelong Pursuit of Wisdom*. New York: Macmillan, 1986.
Africa Report 39, No. 5, 40th Anniversary Edition. September-October, 1994.
Albrecht, P. *The Churches and Rapid Social Change*. New York: Doubleday, 1961.
———, ed. *Faith and Science in an Unjust World: Report of the World Council of Churches' Conference on Faith, Science and the Future, Vol. 2, Reports and Recommendations*. Minneapolis, MN: Fortress Press, 1980.
———, ed. *Faith, Science and Future*. Minneapolis, MN: Fortress Press, 1978.
Allen, R. B. *The Majesty of Man: The Dignity of Being Human*. Portland: Multnomah Press, 1984.
Anderson, G., and T. Stransky, eds. *Christ's Lordship and Religious Pluralism*. Maryknoll, NY: Orbis, 1981.
———, eds. *Mission Trends No. 5: Faith Meets Faith*. Grand Rapids: Eerdmans, 1981.
Appiah-Kubi, K., and S. Torres, eds. *African Theology en Route*. Maryknoll, NY: Orbis, 1975.
Arias, M. "Contextual Evangelization in Latin America: Between Accommodation and Confrontation." *Occasional Bulletin of Missionary Research* 2, no. 1 (1978).
Arruda, M., ed. *Ecumenism and a New World Order: The Failure of the 1970s and the Challenges of the 1980s*. Geneva: WCC, 1980.
Augsburger, M. S. *The Christ-Shaped Conscience*. Wheaton: Victor Books, 1990.
Ayisi, E. O. *An Introduction to the Study of African Culture*. London: Heinemann Education, 1979.

Ayittey, G. B. *Africa Betrayed*. New York: St Martin's Press, 1992.
———. *Africa in Chaos*. New York: St Martin's Press, 1998.
Babbage, S. B. *Man in Nature and in Grace*. Grand Rapids: Eerdmans, 1957.
Barrett, A. *Dying and Death among the Turkana*, Parts I and II. Eldoret: Gaba Publications, 1987.
———. *Sacrifice and Prophecy in Turkana Cosmology*. Nairobi: Paulines Publications Africa, 1998.
Barrett, D. *Schism and Renewal in Modern Africa: An Analysis of Six Thousand Contemporary Religious Movements*. Nairobi: Oxford University Press, 1968.
Barth, K. *Christ and Adam: Man and Humanity in Romans 5*. London: Oliver & Boyd, 1956.
Bascom, W. *Ifa Divination: Communication between Gods and Men in West Africa*. Bloomington: Indiana University Press, 1969.
———. *Sixteen Cowries: Yoruba Divination from Africa to the New World*. Bloomington: Indiana University Press, 1980.
Bates, R. H. "Ethnic Competition and Modernization in Contemporary Africa." *Comparative Political Studies* 6, no. 4 (1974).
Baum, R. C. "Authority Codes: The Invariance Hypothesis." *Zeitschrift Für Soziologie* 6, no. 1 (1977).
Baxter, P. T. W., and U. Almagor, eds. *Age, Generation and Time: Some Features of East Africa Age Organizations*. New York: St Martins Press, 1978.
Bediako, K. "Biblical Christologies in the Context of African Traditional Religions." In *Sharing Christ in the Third World*, edited by V. Samuel & C. Sugden. Bangalore: Partnership in Mission-Asia, 1983.
———. *Christianity in Africa: The Renewal of a Non-Western Religion*. Edinburgh: Edinburgh University, 1995.
———. *Jesus in African Culture: A Ghanaian Perspective*. Accra: Asempa Publishers, 1990.
———. *Theology and Identity: The Impact of Culture upon Christian Thought in the Second Century and Modern Africa*. Oxford: Regnum, 1992.
———. "Understanding African Theology in the Twentieth Century." *Bulletin for Contextual Theology in Southern Africa and Africa* 3, no. 2 (1996): 1–11.
Bennett, J. C., ed. "Augusan's Disorder and God's Design: Preparatory Program for the First Assembly of the World Council of Churches." Geneva: WCC, 1948.
Berkouwer, B. C. *Man: The Image of God*. Grand Rapids: Eerdmans, 1962.
Bickersteth, J., and T. Pain. *The Four Faces of God*. Eastbourne: Kingsway, 1993.
Bidney, D. *Theoretical Anthropology*. New York: Schocken Books, 1970.
Birch, C., W. R. Eakin, and J. B. McDaniel, eds. *Liberating Life: Contemporary Approaches to Ecological Theology*. New York: Orbis, 1990.
Bitrus, D. *The Extended Family: An African Christian Perspective*. Nairobi, CLMC, 2000.
Bjerke, S. *Religion and Misfortune: The Bacwezi Complex and the Other Spirit Cults of the Zinza of Northwestern Tanzania*. Oslo: Universitetsforlaget, 1981.

Blum, W. *Forms of Marriage, Monogamy Reconsidered.* Eldoret: AMECEA Gaba, 1989.

Blyden, E. W. *Christianity, Islam and the Negro Race.* Edinburgh: Edinburgh University Press, 1887; reprint, 1998.

Bock, P. *In Search of a Responsible World Society.* Philadelphia: Westminster Press, 1974.

Bohannan, P., ed. *Law and Warfare: Studies in the Anthropology of Conflict.* Garden City, NY: Natural History Press, 1967.

Bolt, C. *Victorian Attitude to Race.* London: Routledge, 1971.

Bonhoeffer, D. *Ethics.* London: SCM, 1971.

Booth, N. S., ed. *African Religions: A Symposium.* New York: NoK Publishers, 1977.

Boulaga, E. *Christianity without Fetishes: An African Critique and Recapture of Christianity.* Trans. by R. R. Barr. New York: Orbis, 1984.

Bowers, P. "African Theology: Its History, Scope, Dynamics, and Future." *Africa Journal of Evangelical Theology* 21, no. 2 (2002): 109–125.

———. "Beyond Kato: Embracing Christian Intellectual Responsibilities in Africa." Byang Kato Memorial Lectures. Jos ECWA Theological Seminary, Jos, Nigeria, March 2008.

———. "Christian Intellectual Responsibilities in Modern Africa." In *Africa Journal of Evangelical Theology* 28, no. 2 (2009): 91–114.

———. "Evangelical Theology in Africa: Byang Kato's Legacy." *Themelios* 5, no. 3 (1980): 33–34.

———. "Notable Books for Christian Reflection in Africa: A Review Article." *African Journal of Evangelical Theology* 24, no. 2 (2005).

Brant, H. "Power Encounter: Toward an SIM Position." *International Journal of Frontier Missions* 10, no. 4 (1993): 185–192.

Breman, C. M. *The Association of Evangelicals in Africa: Its History, Organization, Members, Projects, External Relations and Message.* Zoetermeer: Uitgeverij Boekencentrum, 1996.

———. "Byang H. Kato: A Bibliography." Ndola, Zambia, 1997. https://www.acteaweb.org/downloads/tools/Tools%20and%20Studies%2016.pdf.

Bruce, F. F. *The Message of the New Testament.* Carlisle, UK: Paternoster, 1972.

Brunner, E. *The Christian Doctrine of Creation and Redemption.* Philadelphia: Westminster, 1952.

Buconyori, E. A., ed. *Tribalism and Ethnicity* [Tribalism et Ethnicity]. Nairobi: AEA, 1997.

Bujo, B. *African Theology in Its Social Context.* Nairobi: Paulines Publications Africa, 2003.

———. *Foundations of an African Ethic: Beyond the Universal Claims of Western Morality.* Nairobi: Paulines Publications Africa, 2003.

Bujo, B., and J. I. Muya, eds. *African Theology*, 2 volumes. Nairobi: Paulines Publications Africa, 2003.

Buswell, J. O. *A Systematic Theology of the Christian Religion.* 2 Vols. Grand Rapids: Zondervan, 1962.

Campolo, A. *A Reasonable Faith: The Case for Christianity in a Secular World*. Waco, TX: Word, 1983.

Carlson, K. S. *Social Theory and African Tribal Organization: The Development of Socio-Legal Theory*. Urbana: University of Illinois Press, 1987.

Catholic Documents. October 16, 1979. *The Church in Africa*, no. 58.

Chambers, O. *Studies in the Sermon in the Mount*. London: Oswald Chambers Publications Association; Marshall, Morgan & Scott, 1960.

Chapin, Jon, ed. *An Introduction to a Christian Worldview*. London: Open Christian College, 1986.

Christensen, T. G. *An African Tree of Life*. Maryknoll, NY: Orbis, 1990.

Clarke, T., ed. *Above Every Name: The Lordship of Christ and Social Systems*. Ramsey, NJ: Paulist, 1980.

Cohen, Y. A. *The Transition from Childhood to Adolescence: Cross-Cultural Studies of Initiation Ceremonies, Legal Systems, and Incest Taboo*. Chicago: Aldine Publishing, 1964.

Cole, V. B. "The Christian and African Traditional Religion and Culture: Some Basic Principles of Understanding and Approach." Unpublished, 1989.

Colson, C. W., and N. Pearcey. *How Now Shall We Live?* Wheaton, IL: Tyndale Audio, 1999.

Cox, R. "The Lord's Work: Perspectives of Early Leaders of the Evangelical Church of West Africa Regarding the Spread of Christianity." PhD Dissertation, Trinity Evangelical Divinity School, 2000.

Curtin, P. D. "Scientific Racism and British Theory of Empire." *Journal of the Historical Society of Nigeria* 2, no. 1 (1960): 40–51.

D'costa, G. *Christian Uniqueness Reconsidered*. New York: Orbis, 1990.

Dedji, V. *Reconstruction and Renewal in African Christian Theology*. Nairobi: Acton, 2003.

de Heusch, L. *Sacrifice in Africa: A Structuralist Approach*. Trans. by L. O'Brien and A. Morton. Bloomington: Indiana University Press, 1985.

de Rosny, E. *Healers in the Night*. Trans. by R. R. Barr. Maryknoll, NY: Orbis, 1985.

Dickson, K., and P. Ellinworth, eds. *Biblical Revelation and African Beliefs*. London: Lutterworth, 1969.

Diop, C. A. *The African Origin of Civilization: Myth or Reality*. Translated by M. Cook. New York: Lawrence Hill & Co., 1974.

Douglas, M. *Purity and Danger: An Analysis of the Concept of Pollution and Taboo*. London: Routledge, 1966.

Dovlo, E. "Ancestors and Soteriology in African and Japanese Religions." *Studies Interreligious Dialogue* 3, no. 1 (1993).

Duff, E. *The Social Thought of the World Council of Churches*. New York: Longmans & Co., 1956.

Durkheim, E. *The Elementary Forms of Religious Life*. Trans. by J. W. Swain. New York: Free Press, 1965.

Edwards, J. *Religious Affections: A Christian Character Before God*. Portland, OR: Multnomah Press, 1984.
Eerdmans Bible Dictionary. Grand Rapids, MI: Eerdmans, 1987.
Einwechter, W. O. *Ethics and God's Law: An Introduction to Theonomy*. Mill Hall, PA: Preston/Speed Publications, 1995.
Eitel, K. E. *Transforming Culture: Developing a Biblical Ethic in an African Context*. Nairobi: Evangel, 1986.
Ela, J.-M. *African Cry*. New York: Orbis, 1986.
———. *My Faith as an African*. New York: Orbis, 1988.
Ellis, E. E. *Pauline Theology: Ministry and Society*. Grand Rapids: Eerdmans, 1989.
Elwell, W. A. *The Concise Evangelical Dictionary of Theology*. Grand Rapids: Baker, 1991.
Etherington, N., ed. *Missions and Empire*. Oxford: Oxford University Press, 2005.
Evans-Pritchard, E. E. *Kinship and Marriage among the Nuer*. Oxford: Clarendon, 1951.
———, ed. *Man and Woman Among the Azande*. New York: Free Press, 1974.
———. *Nuer Religion*. Oxford: Clarendon, 1956.
———. *Theories of Primitive Religion*. Oxford: Clarendon, 1965.
———. *Witchcraft, Oracles, and Magic among the Azande*. Oxford: Clarendon, 1937.
Fashole-Luke, E. W. et al., eds. *Christianity in Independent Africa*. Bloomington: Indiana University Press, 1978.
Ferdinando, K. *The Triumph of Christ in African Perspective: A Study of Demonology and Redemption in the African Context*. Carlisle, UK: Paternoster, 1999.
Fiedler, K. *The Story of Faith Missions*. Oxford: Regnum, 1994.
Fitzmyer, J. A. *Pauline Theology: A Brief Sketch*. Englewood Cliffs, NJ: Prentice-Hall, 1967.
Fleming, D. *Bridge Bible Directory*. Brisbane: Bridgeway, 1990.
Fleming, H. C. *The Age-Grading Cultures of East Africa: An Historical Inquiry*. Ann Arbor, MI: University Microfilms, 1965.
Fortes, M., and G. Diertelen. *African Systems of Thought*. London: Oxford University Press, 1965.
Fry, P. *Spirits of Protest: Spirit-Mediums and the Articulation of Consensus among the Zezuru of Southern Rhodesia (Zimbabwe)*. Cambridge: Cambridge University Press, 1976.
Gaskiyane, I. *Polygamy: A Cultural and Biblical Perspective*. Carlisle, UK: Piquant, 2000.
Geertz, C. *The Interpretations of Cultures*. New York: Basic Books, 1973.
Gehman, R. J. *African Traditional Religion in Biblical Perspective*. Kijabe, Kenya: Kesho Publications, 1989.
———. *Doing African Theology: An Evangelical Perspective*. Nairobi: Evangel, 1987.
Getui, M. N., and M. M. Theuri. *Quests for Abundant Life in Africa*. Nairobi: Acton, 2002.
Gibellini, R. *Paths of African Theology*. London: SCM Press, 1994.
Gifford, P. *The Christian Churches and the Democratisation of Africa*. Leiden: Brill, 1995.
———, ed. *African Christianity: Its Public Role*. London: Hurst & Co., 1998.

Gilkey, L. *Maker of Heaven and Earth: The Christian Doctrine of Creation in the Light of Modern Knowledge*. Lanham, MD: Doubleday, 1959.

Glock, C. Y., and P. E. Hammond. *Beyond the Classic? Essays in the Scientific Study of Religion*. New York: Harper & Row, 1973.

Gluckman, M. *The Judicial Process among the Barotse of Northern Rhodesia*. Manchester: Manchester University Press, 1955.

———. *Politics, Law and Ritual in Tribal Society*. Chicago: Aldine Publishing, 1965.

Gnanakan, K. *Kingdom Concerns: A Biblical Exploration towards a Theology of Mission*. Bangalore: Theological Book Trust, 1989.

———. *The Pluralistic Predicament*. Bangalore: Theological Book Trust, 1992.

Goldsmith, M. *What about Other Faiths?* London: Hodder & Stoughton, 1989.

Gossett, T. F. *Race: The History of an Idea in America*. New York: Schoecken Books, 1965.

Gregorios, P. *The Human Presence: An Orthodox View of Nature*. Geneva: WCC, 1978.

Gremillion, J., ed. *The Gospel of Peace and Justice: Catholic Social Teaching Since Pope John*. Maryknoll, NY: Orbis, 1976.

Grudem, W. *Systematic Theology: An Introduction to Biblical Theology*. Grand Rapids, MI: Zondervan, 1994.

Guthrie, D. *New Testament Theology*. Downers Grove: InterVarsity Press, 1981.

Haack, Dennis. "The Neo-Pagan Resurgence." In *Critique* 4 (2005): 13. https://ransomfellowship.org/wp-content/uploads/2016/10/Critique_2005_04.pdf.

Harris, G. G. *Casting Out Anger: Religion among the Taita of Kenya*. Cambridge: Cambridge University Press, 1978.

Hastings, A. *A History of African Christianity 1950–1975*. Cambridge: Cambridge University Press, 1979.

Hatfield, C. R. "The Njumu in Tradition and Change: A Study of the Position of Religious Practitioners Among the Sukuma of Tanzania, East Africa." PhD Dissertation. Washington, DC: Catholic University of America, 1968.

Haule, C. "Bantu 'Witchcraft' and Christian Morality: The Encounter of Bantu Uchawi with Christian Morality – An Anthropological and Theological Study." Schoneck-Beckenried: Nouvelle Revue de Science Missionaire, 1969.

Hayakawa, S. I. *The Penguin Guide to Synonyms and Related Words*, 2nd ed. London: Penguin Books, 1994.

Haye, S. *Byang Kato: Ambassador for Christ*. Achimota, Ghana: African Christian Press, 1986.

Hedlund, R. E. *Roots of the Great Debate in Mission*. Madras: Evangelical Literature Service, 1981.

Heller. A. *The Power of Shame: A Rational Perspective*. London: Routledge, 1985.

Hiebert, P. G. *Anthropological Reflections on Missiological Issues*. Grand Rapids: Baker, 1994.

Hiebert, P. G., R. D. Shaw, and T. Tienou. *Understanding Folk Religion: A Christian Response to Popular Beliefs and Practices*. Grand Rapids: Baker Books, 1999.

Hillman, E. *Polygamy Reconsidered: African Plural Marriage and the Christian Churches.* New York: Orbis, 1975.

Hobsbawm, E., and T. Ranger, eds. *The Invention of Tradition.* Cambridge: Cambridge University Press, 1983.

Hoebel, E. A. *The Law of Primitive Man: A Study in Comparative Legal Dynamics.* Cambridge, MA: Harvard University Press, 1961.

Hofstede, G. *Cultures and Organizations: Software of the Mind.* New York: McGraw-Hill, 1991.

Hollenbach, D. "The Development of Catholic Rights Theory." Unpublished. 1978.

Horton, R. "Judeo-Christian Spectacles: Boon or Bane to the Study of African Religions?" *Cahiers d'Etudes Africaines* 24, no. 4/96 (1984): 392–436.

———. *Pattern of Thought in Africa and the West: Essays on Magic, Religion and Science.* Cambridge: Cambridge University Press, 1993.

Houtondji, P. *African Philosophy: Myth and Reality.* Translated by H. Evans in collaboration with J. Rée. London: Hutchinson University Library, 1983.

Howell, A. *Encouraging Language and Culture Learners.* Accra: SIM Ghana,1997.

Huntington, S. P. *The Clash of Civilizations and the Remaking of World Order.* New York: Simon & Schuster, 1996.

Idowu, E. B. *African Traditional Religion: A Definition.* London: SCM, 1973.

———. *Olodumare: God in Yoruba Belief.* London: Longman, 1962.

———. *Towards an Indigenous Church.* London: Oxford University Press, 1965.

Ikenga-Metuh, E. *Comparative Studies of African Traditional Religions.* Onitsha, Nigeria: IMICO Publishers, 1987.

———. *God and Man in African Religion: A Case Study of the Igbo of Nigeria.* London: Geoffrey Chapman, 1981.

———. *Towards an African Theology of Man.* Unpublished paper, 1981.

Imasogie, O. "The Church and the Theological Ferment in Africa." *Evangelical Review of Theology* 9, no. 4 (1985): 359–371.

———. *Guidelines for Christian Theology in Africa.* Achimota, Ghana: African Christian Press, 1983.

International Bulletin of Missionary Research. Overseas Ministries Study Centre Publication, 1989–1992.

The International Standard Bible Encyclopedia, Vol. 4. Grand Rapids, Eerdmans, 1955.

Irele, A. "The African Scholar: Is Black Africa Entering the Dark Ages of Scholarship?" *Transition* 51 (1991): 56–69.

Isizoh, C. D. *Christianity in Dialogue with African Traditional Religion and Culture.* Lagos: Ceedee Publications, 2001.

Iwuagwu, A. O. *The New Religious Movements: Their Dynamic and Psycho-Analysis.* Owerri, Nigeria, 1975.

Jacques, M. *The Guardian.* February 17, 2006.

Jenkins, P. *New Faces of Christianity: Believing the Bible in the Global South.* New York: Oxford University Press, 2006.

Kabongo, J. B., F. Kabasele, J. Doré, and R. Luneau, et al. *Chemins de la Christologie Africaine*. Paris: Desclée, 1986.

Kac, A. W. *The Messianic Hope: A Divine Solution or the Human Problem*. Grand Rapids: Baker, 1975.

Kalilombe, P. A. "The Salvific Value of African Religions." In *Mission Trends* 5, edited by H. G. Anderson and T. Y. Stransky. Grand Rapids: Eerdmans, 1981.

———. "Spirituality in the African Perspective." In *Paths of African Theology*, edited by R. Gibellini, 115–135. London: SCM Press, 1994.

Kalu, O. U., ed. *African Christianity: An African Story*. Perspectives on Christianity. Department of Church History: Pretoria University, 2005.

Ka Mana. *Foi Africaine, Crise Africaine et Reconstruction de L'Afrique*. Lome: HAHO/CETA, 1992.

Karp, I., and C. S. Bird, eds. *Explorations in African System of Thought*. Bloomington: Indiana University Press, 1980.

Kato, B. H. *African Cultural Revolution and the Christian Faith*. Jos, Nigeria: Challenge, 1975.

———. *Biblical Christianity in Africa*. Achimota, Ghana: African Christian Press, 1985.

———. "Christianity as an African Religion." *Perception* 16 (1979): 1–6.

———. "The Gospel, Cultural Context and Religious Syncretism." In *Let the Earth Hear His Voice*, edited by J. D. Douglas. Minneapolis: Worldwide Publications, 1975.

———. *Theological Pitfalls in Africa*. Nairobi: Evangel, 1975.

Katongole, E. M. *A Future for Africa: Critical Essays in Christian Social Imagination*. Scranton, PA: University of Scranton Press, 2005.

Kauuova, W. *Religious Pluralism: A Challenge to the Church in South Africa* (Series F2, no. 69). Potchefstroom: IRS, 1997.

Kenyatta, J. *Facing Mount Kenya: The Tribal Life of the Gikuyu*. New York: Vintage, 1962.

Kibicho, S. G. "The Continuity of the African Conception of God into and through Christianity: A Kikuyu Case Study." In *Christianity in Independent Africa*, edited by E. Fashole-Luke et al., 1978.

King, N. Q. *African Cosmos: An Introduction to Religion in Africa*. Belmont, CA: Wadsworth Press, 1986.

———. *Religion of Africa: Pilgrimage into Traditional Religions*. New York: Harper & Row, 1970.

Kingsley, M. H. *West African Studies*. London: Frank Cass & Co., 1964.

Kinoti, G. *Hope for Africa and What the Christian Can Do*. Nairobi: AISRED, 1994.

Kirwen, M. C. *The Missionary and the Diviner: Contending Theologies of Christian and African Religions*. New York: Orbis, 1987.

Kisembo, B., L. Magesa, and A. Shorter. *African Christian Marriage*. Nairobi: Paulines Publications Africa, 1998.

Kluckhohn, C. "Values and Values-Orientation in Theory of Action: An Explanation in Definition and Classification." In *Toward A General Theory of Action*, edited by T. Parsons and E. Shils. Cambridge, MA: Harvard University Press, 1951.
Knitter, P. F. *No Other Name?* London: SCM, 1985.
Knitter, P. F., and J. Hick. *The Myth of Christian Uniqueness: Towards a Pluralistic Theology of Religions*. Maryknoll, NY: Orbis, 1987.
Koech, K. "African Mythology: A Key to Understanding African Religion." In *African Religions: A Symposium*, edited by S. N. Booth, 117–139. New York: NOK Publisher, 1977.
Kraemer, H. *The Christian Message in a Non-Christian World*, London: n.p., 1938.
Kraft, C. H. *Christianity in Culture: A Study in Dynamic Biblical Theologizing in Cross-Cultural Perspective*. New York: Orbis, 1979.
Kung, H. *Global Responsibility: In Search of a New World Ethic*. New York: Continuum, 1993.
Kunhiyop, S. W. *African Christian Ethics*. Kaduna: Baraka Press, 2004.
Lausanne Committee for World Evangelization. *The Manila Manifesto: An Elaboration of the Lausanne Covenant, Fifteen Years Later*. Pasadena: Castle Press, 1989.
The Leadership Bible, New International Version. Grand Rapids: Zondervan, 1988.
Lee, F. N. *The Central Significance of Culture*. Philadelphia: P&R, 1976.
Levy-Bruhl, L. *Primitive Mentality*. New York: AM Press, 1978.
Lightner, R. P. *Evangelical Theology: A Survey and Review*. Grand Rapids: Baker, 1986.
Luzbetak, L. J. *The Church and Cultures: New Perspectives in Missiological Anthropology*. Maryknoll, NY: Orbis, 1989.
Magesa, L. *African Religion: The Moral Traditions of Abundant Life*. Nairobi: Paulines Publications Africa, 1998.
———. *Anatomy of Inculturation: Transforming the Church in Africa*. Nairobi: Paulines Publications Africa, 2004.
———. *Christian Ethics in Africa*. Nairobi: Acton, 2002.
Maigadi, B. S. *Divisive Ethnicity in the Church in Africa*. Kaduna: Baraka Press, 2006.
Mair, L. *Witchcraft*. New York: World University Library, 1969.
Maloney, C., ed. *The Evil Eye*. New York: Columbia University Press, 1976.
Maquet, J. *Africanity: The Cultural Unity of Black Africa*. Translated by J. R. Rayfield. New York: Oxford University Press, 1972.
———. *Civilizations of Black Africa*. Translated by J. R. Rayfield. New York: Oxford University Press, 1972.
Mazrui, A. A. *The African Condition: A Political Diagnosis*. London: Cambridge University Press, 1980.
———. *The Africans: A Triple Heritage*. Boston: Little, Brown & Co., 1987.
———. *Political Values and the Educated Class in Africa*. London: Heinemann, 1978.
Mbiti, J. S. *African Religions and Philosophy*. London: Heinemann Educational Books, 1969.

———. *Bible and Theology in African Christianity*. Nairobi: Oxford University Press, 1986.

———. *Concepts of God in Africa*. London: SPCK, 1970.

———. *Introduction to African Religion*. London: Heinemann, 1975.

———. *Prayer and Spirituality in African Religion*. Bedford Park: Australian Association for the Study of Religions, 1978.

———. *The Prayers of African Religion*. London: SPCK, 1975.

McVeigh, M. J. *God in Africa: Conceptions of God in African Traditional Religion and Christianity*. Cape Cod, MA: Claude Stark, 1974.

Meek, C. K. *The Northern Tribes of Nigeria: An Ethnographical Account of the Northern Provinces*. London: Oxford University Press, 1925.

Mendonsa, E. L. *The Politics of Divination: A Processual View of Reactions to Illness and Deviance among the Sisala of Northern Ghana*. Berkeley, CA: University of California Press, 1982.

Michael, M. "Foundational Biblical Principles for Doing African Theology: The Place of Bibliocentric and Christocentric Methodologies." Class Term Paper. Jos, Nigeria: ECWA Theological Seminary, 2006.

———. "An Introduction to Third World Theologies." Unpublished. 2006.

Middleton, J., ed. *Gods and Rituals: Readings in Religious Beliefs and Practices*. Garden City, NY: Natural History Press, 1967.

———, ed. *Magic, Witchcraft and Curing*. Garden City, NY: Natural History Press, 1967.

———, ed. *Myth and Cosmos: Readings in Mythology and Symbolism*. Garden City, NY: Natural History Press, 1967.

Middleton, J., and D. Tait, eds. *Tribes without Rulers: Studies in African Segmentary Systems*. London: Routledge, 1958.

Milne, B. *Know the Truth: A Handbook of Christian Belief*. Leicester, UK: Inter-Varsity Press, 1982.

Minogue, M., and J. Molloy, eds. *African Aims and Attitudes: Selected Documents*. London: Cambridge University Press, 1974.

Molyneux, K. G. *African Christian Theology: The Quest for Selfhood*. San Francisco: Mellen Research University Press, 1993.

Moore, B., ed. *Black Theology: The South African Voice*. London: Hurst, 1973.

———, ed. *The Challenge of Black Theology in South Africa*. Atlanta: John Knox Press, 1974.

Moreau, A. S. *The World of the Spirits: A Biblical Study in the African Context*. Nairobi: Evangel, 1990.

Morel, F. D. *Affairs of West Africa*. London: Frank Cass, 1968.

———. *Nigeria: Its People and Problems*. London: Frank Cass, 1968.

Morgan, J. "Religion and Culture as Meaning Systems: A Dialogue between Geertz and Tillich." *The Journal of Religion* 57, no. 4 (1977): 363–374.

Motlhabi, M. *Essays on Black Theology*. Johannesburg: University Christian Movement, 1972.

———. "The Theory and Practice of Black Resistance to Apartheid: A Social-Ethical Analysis of Internal Struggle for Political and Social Change in South Africa 1948–1978." PhD dissertation, Boston University, 1980.
Mott, S. C. *Biblical Ethics and Social Change*. Oxford: Oxford University, 1982.
Muelder, W. G. *Foundations of the Responsible Society*. New York: Abingdon, 1959.
———. "A Just, Participatory and Sustainable World Society." *Nexus* 59: *Social Ethics Tradition* 23, 1980.
———. *Moral Laws in Christian Social Ethics*. Richmond: John Knox Press, 1966.
Mugambi, J. N. K. *African Christian Theology*. Nairobi: Heinemann, 1989.
———. *Christian Theology and Social Reconstruction*. Nairobi: Acton Publishers, 2003.
———. *From Liberation to Reconstruction: African Christian Theology after the Cold War*. Nairobi: East African Educational Publishers, 1995.
Mugambi, J. N. K., and L. Magesa, eds. *The Church in African Christianity: Innovative Essays in Ecclesiology*. Nairobi: Acton Publishers, 1985.
———, eds. *Jesus in African Christianity: Experimentation and Diversity in Christology*. Nairobi: Acton Publishers, 1989.
Mugambi, J. N. K., and A. N. Wasike, eds. *Moral and Ethical Issues in African Christianity: Exploratory Essays in Moral Theology*. Nairobi: Acton Publishers, 1999.
Munby, D., ed. *World Development Challenge to the Churches*. Washington, DC: Corpus Books, 1969.
Murray, A. *The Power of the Blood of Jesus*. Grand Rapids: Zondervan, 1987.
Mutiso, G-C. M., and S. W. Rohio, eds. *Readings in African Political Thought*. London: Heinemann, 1975.
Mutungi, O. K. "The Legal Aspect of Witchcraft in East Africa with Particular Reference to Kenya." Nairobi: East African Literature Bureau, 1977.
Muzorewa, G. *The Origins and Development of African Theology*. Maryknoll: Orbis, 1985.
Nabofa, M. Y. "The Significance of Blood in African Traditional Religion." Unpublished Paper, 1980.
Nadel, S. F. *Nupe Religion: Traditional Beliefs and the Influence of Islam in a West African Chiefdom*. New York: Schocken Books, 1970.
Nassau, R. H. *Fetishism in Africa: Forty Years' Observation of Native Customs and Superstitions*. New York: Charles Scribner's Sons, 1904.
Ndiokwere, N. *Prophecy and Revolution*. London: SPCK, 1995.
Nee, W. *Questions on the Gospel*. Anaheim, CA: Living Stream Ministry, 1992.
———. *The Spiritual Man*. New York: Christian Fellowship, 1977.
Neill, S. *Christian Faith and Other Faiths*. London: Oxford University Press, 1970.
Nelson, J. R. "Class Notes TH 842 Medical Ethics." Boston: Boston University, 1978.
Newbigin, L. *Foolishness to the Greeks: The Gospel and Western Culture*. Grand Rapids: Eerdmans, 1986.
———. *The Gospel in a Pluralist Society*. Grand Rapids: Eerdmans, 1989.
New Concise Bible Dictionary. Downers Grove, IL: InterVarsity Press, 1989.

New International Encyclopedia of Bible Words. Grand Rapids: Zondervan, 1999.

Ngewa, S., M. Shaw, and T. Tienou. *Issues in African Christian Theology.* Nairobi: East African Educational Publishers, 1998.

Nicholls, B. J., ed. *The Unique Christ in Our Pluralistic World.* Carlisle, UK: Paternoster, 1994.

Nida, E. A. *Customs and Cultures: Anthropology for Christian Missions.* New York: Harper & Brothers, 1954.

NIV Compact Dictionary of the Bible. Grand Rapids, MI: Zondervan, 1989.

NIV Study Bible. Grand Rapids, MI: Zondervan, 1995.

Njenga, J. "Customary African Marriage." *AFER* 16, nos. 1–2 (1974).

Nkafu, M. N. *African Vitalogy.* Nairobi: Paulines Publications Africa, 1995.

Nkansah-Obrempong, J. "The Contemporary Theological Situation in Africa: An Overview." *Evangelical Review of Theology* 31, no. 2 (April 2007).

Nkrumah, K. "Consciencism: Philosophy and Ideology for Decolonisation." *Monthly Review.* New York, 1970.

Nthamburi, Z. *The African Church at the Crossroads.* Nairobi: East African Educational Publishers, 1991.

Nyamiti, C. *African Tradition and the Christian God.* Spearhead 49. Eldoret: Gaba Publications, 1989.

———. *Christ as Our Ancestor: Christology from an African Perspective.* Gweru: Mambo Press, 1984.

———. *Jesus Christ, the Ancestor of Humankind: An Essay on African Christology.* Studies in African Christian Theology 2. Nairobi: Catholic University East Africa Publications, 2006.

———. *Jesus Christ, the Ancestor of Humankind: Methodological and Trinitarian Foundations.* Studies in African Christian Theology 1. Nairobi: Catholic University East Africa Publications, 2005.

———. *The Scope of African Theology.* Kampala: Gaba Publications, 1973.

———. *Some Contemporary Models of African Ecclesiology: A Critical Assessment in the Light of Biblical and Church Teaching.* Studies in African Christian Theology 3. Nairobi: Catholic University East Africa Press, 2007.

———. *The Way to Christian Theology for Africa.* Eldoret: Gaba Publications, 1977.

Nyerere, J. *Ujamaa: Essays on Socialism.* London: Oxford University Press, 1968.

Nyirongo, L. *Dealing with Darkness: A Christian Novel on the Confrontation with African Witchcraft.* Potchefstroom, SA: Potchesfstroom Universiteit vir Christelike Hoër Onderwys, 1999.

———. *The Gods of Africa or the God of the Bible? The Snares of African Traditional Religion in Biblical Perspective.* Potchefstroom: IRS (series f2, no. 70), 1997.

O'Conohue, J. *Magic and Witchcraft in Southern Uganda.* Kampala, Uganda: Gaba Publications, n.d.

O'Donovan, W. *Biblical Christianity in African Perspective.* Carlisle, UK: Paternoster, 1997.

———. *Biblical Christianity in Modern Africa*. Carlisle, UK: Paternoster, 2000.
Oborji, F. A. "In Dialogue with African Traditional Religion: New Horizons." *Mission Studies* 19 (2002): 1–37.
———. "Revelation in African Traditional Religion: The Theological Debate since Vatican II." *Studies in Interreligious Dialogue* 12, no. 1 (2002): 5–22.
———. Towards a Christian Theology of African Religion: Issues of Interpretation and Mission. Eldoret, Kenya: AMECEA Gaba Publications, 2005.
Ochollo-Ayayo, A. B. C. *Traditional Ideology and Ethics among the Southern Luo*. Uppsala, Sweden: Scandinavian Institute of African Studies, 1976.
Oduyoye, M. A. *Beads and Strands: Reflections of an African Woman on Christianity in Africa*. Maryknoll, NY: Orbis, 2004.
———. *Hearing and Knowing: Theological Reflections on Christianity in Africa*. Maryknoll, NY: Orbis, 1986.
Oji, E. D. *Ikpu Alu (Atonement) in Igbo Traditional Religion*. BA Thesis: Jos ECWA Theological Seminary, 1988.
Okonjo, I. N. *British Administration in Nigeria: 1900–1950: A Nigerian View*. New York: NOK, 1974.
Olabimtan, A. "Symbolism in Yoruba Traditional Incantatory Poetry." *Nigeria Magazine* 114 (1994): 36–42.
Olaniyan, R., ed. *African History and Culture*. Lagos: Longman, 1996.
Olowola, C. *African Traditional Religion and the Christian Faith*. Achimota, Ghana: ACP, 1993.
Olupona, J. K., ed. *African Spirituality: Forms, Meaning and Expressions*. New York: Herder & Herder, 2000.
———, ed. *African Traditional Religions in Contemporary Society*. New York: Paragon House, 1991.
———, ed. *Beyond Primitivism: Indigenous Religious Traditions and Modernity*. New York: Routledge, 2004.
Omoni, O. "Colonial Policies and Independent Movements." In *African History and Culture*, edited by R. Olaniyan, 81–110. Lagos: Longman, 1996.
Onaiyekan, J. "Divine Mysteries and Secret Cults in the African Traditional Religions and in Christianity." Unpublished Paper, 1980.
Onwubiko, O. A. *The Church in Mission in the Light of Ecclesia in Africa*. Nairobi: Paulines Publications Africa, 2001.
The Open Bible: Expanded Edition, New King James Version. New York: Thomas Nelson, 1983.
Oruka, H. O. *Trends in Contemporary African Philosophy*. Nairobi: Shirikon, 1990.
Ottenberg, S., and P. Ottenberg. *Cultures and Societies in Africa*. New York: Random House, 1960.
Outka, G., and J. P. Reeder, eds. *Religion and Morality: A Collection of Essays*. Garden City, NY: Anchor Press/Doubleday, 1973.

Owen, J. *Sin and Temptation: The Challenge to Personal Holiness.* Portland, OR: Multnomah, 1983.

Page, S. *Powers of Evil: A Biblical Study of Satan and Demons.* Grand Rapids: Baker/Apollos, 1995.

Paris, P. J. *The Spirituality of African Peoples: The Search for a Common Moral Discourse.* Minneapolis: Fortress, 1994.

Parratt, J., ed. *A Reader in African Christian Theology.* London: SPCK, 1987.

———. *Reinventing Christianity: African Theology Today.* Grand Rapids: Eerdmans, 1995.

Parrinder, G. *African Traditional Religion.* London: Hutchinson, 1954.

———. *West African Psychology: A Comparative Study of Psychological and Religious Thought.* London: Lutterworth, 1951.

———. *West African Religion: A Study of the Beliefs and Practices of Akan, Ewe, Yoruba, Igbo, and Kindred Peoples.* London: Epworth, 1961.

Pascal, B. *The Mind on Fire.* Portland: Multnomah, 1989.

p'Bitek, O. *African Religions in Western Scholarship.* Nairobi: East African Literature Bureau, 1970.

Peek, P. M., ed. *African Divination Systems: Ways of Knowing.* Bloomington: Indiana University Press, 1991.

Peil, M. *Consensus and Conflict in African Societies.* London: Longman, 1977.

Pelton, R. D. *The Trickster in West Africa: A Study of Mythic Irony and Sacred Delight.* Berkeley: University of California Press, 1980.

Philips, D., and Y. Turaki. "An Evaluation of Nigeria's Ethical Structure." National Institute for Policy and Strategic Studies (NIPSS), 1984.

Phillips, A., ed. *Survey of African Marriage and Family Life.* London: Oxford University Press, 1953.

Plantinga, A. *God, Freedom, and Evil.* New York: Harper & Row, 1974.

Pobee, J. *Skenosis: Christian Faith in an African Context.* Gweru: Mambo, 1992.

———. *Towards an African Theology.* Nashville: Abingdon, 1979.

———. *West Africa: Christ Would Be an African Too.* Geneva: WCC, 1996.

Potts, M. *Ancestors in Christ.* Pastoral Papers 17. Kampala: Pastoral Institute of Eastern Africa, 1970.

Radcliffe-Browne, A. R., and D. Forde, eds. *African Systems of Kinship and Marriage.* London: Oxford University Press, 1950.

Rahner, K. *Theological Investigations 1–12.* New York: Seabury Press, 1972–1975.

Ray, B. C. *African Religions: Symbol, Ritual and Community.* Englewood Cliffs, NJ: Prentice-Hall, 1976.

Renn, S. D., ed. *Expository Dictionary of Bible Words.* Peabody, MA: Hendrickson, 2005.

Richards, L. O. *The Teacher's Commentary.* Wheaton, IL: Scripture Press Publications, 1987.

Rothchild, D. *Managing Ethnic Conflict in Africa: Pressures and Incentives for Cooperation.* Washington, DC: Brookings, 1997.

Samuel, V., and C. Sugden, eds. *Sharing Jesus in the Two-Thirds World*. Bangalore: Partnership in Mission-Asia, 1983.

Sanneh, L. "Christian Mission in the Pluralist Milieu: The African Experience." *Missiology: An International Review* 12, no. 4 (1984): 421–433.

———. *Encountering the West: Christianity and the Global Cultural Process*. Maryknoll, NY: Orbis, 1993.

———. "The Horizontal and the Vertical in Mission: An African Perspective." *International Bulletin of Missionary Research* (1983): 165–171.

———. *Translating the Message: The Missionary Impact on Culture*. Maryknoll, NY: Orbis, 1989.

———. *Whose Religion Is Christianity? The Gospel Beyond the West*. Grand Rapids, Eerdmans, 2003.

Sawyerr, H. *Creative Evangelism: Towards a New Christian Encounter with Africa*. London: Lutterworth Press, 1968.

———. *God: Ancestor or Creator? Aspects of Traditional Belief in Ghana, Nigeria and Sierra Leone*. London: Longman, 1970.

Schaaf, Y. *On Their Way Rejoicing: The History and Role of the Bible in Africa*. Translated by P. Ellingworth. Carlisle: Paternoster, 1994.

Schapera. I. *A Handbook of Tswana Law and Custom*. London: Oxford University Press, 1955.

———. *Married Life in an African Tribe*. Evanston: Northwestern University Press, 1966.

Schreiter, R. J. *Constructing Local Theologies*. Maryknoll, NY: Orbis, 1995.

Senghor, L. S. *Liberté, Negritude et Humanisme*. Paris: Editions du Seuil, 1964.

Shaw, M. *The Kingdom of God in Africa: A Short History of African Christianity*. Grand Rapids: Baker, 1996.

Shinn, R. L. *Faith and Science in an Unjust World: Report on the World Council of Churches' Conference on Faith, Science and the Future, Vol. 1, Plenary Presentations*. Philadelphia: Fortress Press, 1980.

Shorter, A. *African Christian Theology: Adaptation or Inculturation*. New York: Orbis, 1977.

———. *African Culture and the Christian Church: An Introduction to Social and Pastoral Anthropology*. New York: Orbis, 1974.

———, ed. *Dialogue with African Traditional Religions*. Kampala: Gaba Publications, 1975.

———. *Jesus and the Witchdoctor: An Approach to Healing and Wholeness*. Maryknoll, NY: Orbis Books, 1985.

———. *Prayer in the Religious Traditions of Africa*. Nairobi: Oxford University Press, 1975.

———. "Songs and Symbols of Initiation: A Study from Africa in the Social Control of Perception." Nairobi: Catholic Higher Institute of Eastern Africa, Monograph One, 1987.

———. *Towards a Theology of Inculturation.* New York: Orbis, 1988.

———. "The Word That Lives: An Anthology of African Prayers." New York: Mimeo, n.d.

Shorter, A., and J. N. Njiru. *New Religious Movements in Africa.* Nairobi: Paulines Publications Africa, 2001.

Simmons, L. W. *The Role of the Aged in Primitive Society.* New Haven: Yale University Press, 1945.

Skinner, E. P., ed. *Peoples and Cultures of Africa: An Anthropological Reader.* Garden City, NY: Doubleday/Natural History Press, 1973.

Smith, E. W., ed. *African Ideas of God.* London: Edinburgh House Press, 1950.

———. *The Christian Mission in Africa.* London: International Missionary Council, 1926.

Son, B. H. "Cultural Relativism and the Transformation of Culture." *Philosophia Reformata* 66, no. 1 (2001): 9–22.

Steiner, F. *Taboo.* London: Cohen & West, 1956.

Steyne, P. M. *Gods of Power: A Study of the Beliefs and Practices of Animists.* Houston: Touch, 1989.

———. *In Step with the God of the Nations: A Biblical Theology of Missions.* Houston: Touch, 1992.

Stinton, D. *Jesus of Africa: Voices of Contemporary African Christology.* Nairobi: Paulines Publications Africa, 2004.

Sundkler, B. *Bantu Prophets in South Africa.* London: SCM Press, 1961, 1970.

Sundkler, B., and C. Steed. *A History of the Church in Africa.* Cambridge: Cambridge University Press, 2000.

Swartz, M. J. et al. *Political Anthropology.* Chicago: Aldine Publishing, 1966.

Tanner, R. E. S. *Transition in African Beliefs: Traditional Religion and Christian Change: A Study in Sukumaland, Tanzania, East Africa.* Maryknoll, NY: Maryknoll Publications, 1967.

Taylor, J. V. *Christian Presence Amid African Religion.* Nairobi: Acton, 2001.

———. *Primal Vision.* London: SCM, 1963.

Tempels, P. *La Philosophie Bantoue [Bantu Philosophy].* Paris: Presence Africaine, 1948.

Thielicke, H. *Being Human . . . Becoming Human.* Garden City, NY: Doubleday, 1984.

———. *Theological Ethics: Foundations.* Grand Rapids: Eerdmans, 1984.

Thorpe, S. A. *African Traditional Religions: An Introduction.* Pretoria: University of South Africa, 1991.

Tienou, T. "Indigenous African Christian Theologies: The Uphill Road." *International Bulletin of Missionary Research* 14, no. 2 (1990): 73–77.

———. "The Right to Difference: The Common Roots of African Theology and Africa Philosophy." *African Journal of Evangelical Theology* 9, no. 1 (1990): 24–34.

———. "Threats and Dangers in the Theological Task in Africa." *Evangelical Review of Theology* 5, no. 1 (April 1981): 40–41.

———. *The Theological Task of the Church in Africa.* Achimota, Ghana: ACP, 1990.

———. "Which Way for African Christianity: Westernisation or Indigenous Authenticity?" *African Journal of Evangelical Theology* 10, no. 2 (1991): 3–12.

Turaki, Y. "African Christianity in Global Religious and Cultural Conflict." World Evangelical Alliance (WEA) Theological Commission. Nairobi Evangelical Graduate School of Theology, 2006.

———. "Biblical Principles of Good Leadership and Governance." Unpublished, 2007.

———. *The British Colonial Legacy in Northern Nigeria: A Social Ethical Analysis of the Colonial and Post-Colonial Society and Politics in Nigeria.* Jos, Nigeria: Challenge, 1993.

———. "Christian Worldview Foundations: A Methodological Approach." *Orientation* (1993): 67–70.

———. *Christianity and African Gods: A Method in Theology.* Potchefstroom: IRS, Potchefstroom University, 1999.

———. "Culture and Modernization in Africa." In *Cultural Diversity in Africa: Embarrassment or Opportunity?*, edited by B. J. Van der Walt, 123–144. Potchefstroom: IRS (series F3, no. 40), 1991.

———. *Ethical and Cultural Foundations of Good Governance and Leadership in Nigeria.* Kuru: National Institute for Policy and Strategic Studies, 2002.

———. *Foundations of African Traditional Religion and Worldview.* Nairobi: IBS Press/WordAlive, 2002, 2006.

———. *The Future of South Africa: An African Response to the Question of Apartheid.* Potchefstroom: Institute for Reformational Studies, Potchefstroom University, 1992.

———. "God's Universal Moral Laws." Unpublished, 2008.

———. "Human Dignity and Identity and Reconciliation." In *Visions of Man and Freedom in Africa*, edited by M. Waijaki et al., 9–29. Potchefstroom: IRS (series F1, no. 302), 1992.

———. "The Institutionalisation of the Inferior Status and Socio-Political Role of the Non-Muslim Groups in the Colonial Hierarchical Structure of the Northern Region of Nigeria: A Social-Ethical Analysis of the Colonial Legacy." PhD Dissertation, Boston University, 1982.

———. "Is Democracy the Ideal Universal Political System?" *Philosophia Reformata* 66, no. 1 (2001): 132–138.

———. "A Prospectus on Repentance and Forgiveness: A Part of New Testament Theology." Unpublished, 1977.

———. *The Techniques of African Pagan Spirituality: Christian Witness to a Pagan Planet.* Escondido, CA: New Life Presbyterian Church, 2008.

———. "The Theological Legacy of the Reverend Doctor Byang Henry Kato." *Africa Journal of Evangelical Theology* 20, no. 2 (2001): 133–155.

———. *Theory and Practice of Christian Missions in Africa: The History and Legacy of SIM/ECWA in Nigeria, 1893–1993.* Revised Edition. Potchefstroom: IBS, 2019.

———. *Tribal Gods of Africa: Ethnicity, Racism, Tribalism and the Gospel of Christ.* Jos, Nigeria: Cross Roads Communications, 1997.

———. *The Trinity of Sin.* Nairobi, Kenya: HippoBooks, 2011.

———. "Understanding Folk Elements in Christian Expressions of African Religion: A Methodological Approach." Unpublished, 1994.

———. "The Unique Christ for Peace and Justice." In *The Unique Christ in Our Pluralistic World*, edited by B. J. Nicholls. Carlisle, UK: Paternoster, 1994.

———. *The Unique Christ for Salvation: The Challenge of the Non-Christian World Religions and Cultures.* Nairobi: IBS Press, 2002.

———. *The Uniqueness of Jesus Christ.* Nairobi: WordAlive, 2006.

Turner, James E., ed. *The Next Decade: Theoretical and Research Issues in African Studies.* Ithaca, NY: Cornell University Press, 1984.

Turner, Victor. *The Drums of Affliction: A Study of Religious Processes among the Ndembu of Zambia.* Oxford: Clarendon Press, 1968.

———. *The Forests of Symbols: Aspects of Ndembu Ritual.* Ithaca, NY: Cornell University Press, 1967.

———. *Revelation and Divination in Ndembu Ritual.* Ithaca, NY: Cornell University Press, 1975.

———. *The Ritual Process: Structure and Anti-Structure.* Ithaca, NY: Cornell University Press, 1984.

Twesigye, E. K. *Common Ground: Christianity, African Religion and Philosophy.* New York: Peter Lang, 1987.

Tylor, E. B. *Religion in Primitive Culture.* New York: Harper Torchbooks, 1958.

Ukpong, J. S. *African Theologies Now: A Profile.* Eldoret, Kenya: Gaba Publications, 1984.

Ungar, S. J. *Africa: The People and Politics of an Emerging Continent.* 3rd ed. New York: Simon & Schuster, 1989.

Van der Walt, B. J. *Afrocentric or Eurocentric?: Our Task in a Multicultural South Africa.* Potchefstroom: IRS (series F2, no. 67), 1997.

———. *A Christian Worldview and Christian Higher Education for Africa.* Potchefstroom: IRS, 1991.

———, ed. *Cultural Diversity in Africa: Embarrassment or Opportunity.* Potchefstroom: IRS (series F3, no. 40), 1991.

———. *The Liberating Message: A Christian Worldview for Africa.* Potchefstroom: IRS (series F3, no. 44), 1994.

———. "Preface." In *Embracing Christian Intellectual Responsibilities in Africa*, edited by P. Bowers. Leicester, UK: Inter-Varsity Press, 1999.

———. *Responsibility, Conversion, Confession, Forgiveness, Restitution and Reconciliation: Six of God's Requirements for a New South Africa.* Potchefstroom: IRS (series F1, no. 337), 1996.

———. *Transformed by the Renewing of Your Mind: Shaping a Biblical Worldview and a Christian Perspective on Scholarship.* Potchefstroom University, 2001.

Van Gennep, A. *The Rites of Passage*. Translated by M. Vizedom. Chicago: University of Chicago Press, 1960.
Van Niekerk, Jr., A. S. "Western Culture, Africa and the Kingdom of God." *Theological Forum: The Reformed Ecumenical Synod* 16, no. 1 (1988): 1–17.
Vatican. John Paul II. *Apostolic Exhortation Catechesi Tradendae*. No. 53: AAS 71, 1319.
———. *John Paul II's Encyclical on Evangelization: Redemptoris Missio*. www.youtube.com/watch?v=snRYbpA2vM8.
Vatican Council II. *Gaudium es Spes*, 1965.
Vaughan, B. N. Y. *The Expectation of the Poor*. Valley Forge: Judson, 1972.
Vine, W. E. *Expository Dictionary of New Testament Words*. London: Oliphants, 1970.
Walls, A. F. *The Missionary Movement in Christian History: Studies in the Transmission of Faith*. New York: Orbis, 1996.
Walsch, B. J., and J. R. Middleton. *The Transformation Vision: Shaping a Christian Worldview*. Leicester, UK: Inter-Varsity Press, 1984.
Watkins, M. G., and L. J. Watkins. *The Complete Christian Dictionary for Home and School*. Ventura, CA: Gospel Light; Colorado Springs, CO: All Nations Literature, 1992.
Webber, R. E. *The Church in the World*. Grand Rapids: Zondervan, 1986.
Webster, H. *Taboo: A Sociological Study*. New York: Octagon Books, 1973.
Webster's New Collegiate Dictionary. Springfield, MA: G & C Merriam, 1977.
Weinrich, A. K. H. *African Marriage in Zimbabwe and the Impact of Christianity*. Gweru: Mambo Press, 1982.
West, G., and M. Dube. *The Bible in Africa: Transactions, Trajectories and Trends*. Leiden: Brill, 2000.
Westerlund, D. *African Religion in African Scholarship: A Preliminary Study of the Religious and Political Background*. Stockholm: Almqvist & Wiksell, 1985.
———. *Pluralism and Change: A Comparative Historical Approach to African Disease Etiologies*. Stockholm: Universitet Stockholm, 1989.
Wight, F. H. *Manners and Customs of Bible Lands*. Chicago: Moody, 1953.
Willard, D. "Being a Christian in a Pluralistic Society." Publishing in *The Student*, 1992. http://www.dwillard.org/articles/individual/being-a-christian-in-a-pluralistic-society.
———. *Renovation of the Heart: Putting on the Character of Christ*. Colorado Springs: NavPress, 2002.
Willmington, H. L. *Willmington's Guide to the Bible*. Wheaton, IL: Tyndale House, 1984.
Willoughby, W. C. *The Soul of the Bantu: A Sympathetic Study of the Magico-Religious Practices and Beliefs of the Bantu Tribes of Africa*. Garden City, NY: Doubleday, 1928.
Wilson, M. *Religion and the Transformation of Society: A Study in Social Change in Africa*. Cambridge: Cambridge University Press, 1971.
Wiredu, K. *Philosophy and an African Culture*. Cambridge: Cambridge University Press, 1980.

Wolters, A. M. *Creation Regained: Biblical Basics for a Reformational Worldview*. Grand Rapids: Eerdmans, 1985.

World Council of Churches. *Statements of the World Council of Churches on Social Questions*. Geneva: WCC Department on Church and Society, 1956.

Wright, C. J. H. *Living as the People of God: The Relevance of Old Testament Ethics*. Leicester, UK: Inter-Varsity Press, 1983.

Young, J. *African Theology: A Critical Analysis and Annotated Bibliography*. Westport, CN: Greenwood Press, 1993.

Youngblood, R. *The Heart of the Old Testament*. Grand Rapids: Baker, 1971.

Zahan, D. *The Religion, Spirituality, and Thought of Traditional Africa*. Translated by K. E. Martin and L. M. Martin. Chicago: University Press of Chicago, 1979.

———. "Some Reflections on African Spirituality." In *African Spirituality: Forms, Meanings and Expressions*, edited by J. K. Olupona. New York: Herder & Herder, 2000.

Zeusse, E. M. *Ritual Cosmos: The Sanctification of Life in African Religions*. Athens, OH: Ohio University Press, 1979.

Zondervan Bible Dictionary. Grand Rapids: Zondervan, 2008.